HUMAN INFORMATION PROCESSING: TUTORIALS IN PERFORMANCE AND COGNITION

THE EXPERIMENTAL PSYCHOLOGY SERIES

Arthur W. Melton · Consulting Editor

MELTON AND MARTIN · *Coding Processes in Human Memory, 1972*
MCGUIGAN AND LUMSDEN · *Contemporary Approaches to Conditioning and Learning, 1973*
ANDERSON AND BOWER · *Human Associative Memory, 1973*
GARNER · *The Processing of Information and Structure, 1974*
MURDOCK · *Human Memory: Theory and Data, 1974*
KINTSCH · *The Representation of Meaning in Memory, 1974*
KANTOWITZ · *Human Information Processing: Tutorials in Performance and Cognition, 1974*

HUMAN INFORMATION PROCESSING: TUTORIALS IN PERFORMANCE AND COGNITION

EDITED BY BARRY H. KANTOWITZ

PURDUE UNIVERSITY

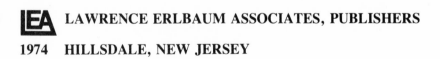 LAWRENCE ERLBAUM ASSOCIATES, PUBLISHERS

1974   HILLSDALE, NEW JERSEY

DISTRIBUTED BY THE HALSTED PRESS DIVISION OF

JOHN WILEY & SONS
New York   Toronto   London   Sydney

Copyright © 1974, by Lawrence Erlbaum Associates, Inc.

Lawrence Erlbaum Associates, Publishers
62 Maria Drive
Hillsdale, New Jersey 07642

Distributed solely by Halsted Press Division
John Wiley & Sons, Inc., New York

Library of Congress Cataloging in Publication Data

Kantowitz, Barry H.
   Human information processing: tutorials in performance and cognition.

   Includes bibliographies.
   1. Human information processing. I. Title.
BF455.K28   153   74–19028
ISBN 0–470–45674–4

Printed in the United States of America

CONTENTS

Preface   ix

1   HUMAN PERCEPTUAL-MOTOR PERFORMANCE, Richard W. Pew ..   1
    Prologue   1
    Inner Loop Control   3
    Higher-Order Control Mechanisms in Tracking   12
    Voluntary Movement   22
    General Issues and Summary   33
    References   36

2   THE INTERPRETATION OF REACTION TIME IN INFORMATION-
    PROCESSING RESEARCH, Robert G. Pachella   41
    Introduction   41
    Experimental Logic and Reaction Time Measures   45
    Reaction Time and Performance Accuracy   58
    Theoretical Conceptions of Reaction Time and Speed-
        Accuracy Relations   71
    Summary   79
    References   80

3   DOUBLE STIMULATION, Barry H. Kantowitz   83
    Paradigms   86

Models   90
Data, Models, and How They Interact   101
Attention and Double Stimulation   116
References   127

4   ISSUES AND MODELS CONCERNING THE PROCESSING OF A
FINITE NUMBER OF INPUTS, J. T. Townsend 133
Introduction   133
The Serial vs. Parallel Processing Issue   139
The Self-Terminating vs. Exhaustive Processing Issue   147
The Independence vs. Dependence Issue   152
The Limited vs. Unlimited Capacity Issue   158
An Experimental Application and Consideration of General
    Models of Short-Term Memory and Brief Visual Display
    Search   167
Summary   183
References   183

5   COGNITIVE REPRESENTATIONS OF SERIAL PATTERNS, Mari
Riess Jones 187
Introduction   187
Theories and Issues   193
General Characteristics of Pattern Processing   200
Reconsideration: A Representational System   220
References   226

6   THE PERCEPTION OF PRINTED ENGLISH: A THEORETICAL
PERSPECTIVE, Edward E. Smith and Kathryn T. Spoehr 231
Some Basic Considerations   232
Perception of Unrelated Letters   239
Perception of Words and Other Strings of Related
    Letters   247
Perception of Words with Context   267
Summary and Conclusions   270
References   271

7   THE MECHANICS OF THOUGHT, Earl B. Hunt and Steven
E. Poltrock 277
Introduction   277
Extending the Simulation Programming Idea to the
    Computer System Model   280

Data Types   285
A System Architecture for Cognition   294
Programming Concepts   302
Data Structures and Long-Term Memory   325
Conclusions   344
References   347

Author Index **353**

Subject Index **361**

PREFACE

This volume presents seven detailed views of human information processing. While no single volume can do justice to the breadth of the area, we hope that the present selections reflect both the content and methodological approaches currently used by experimental psychologists concerned with the issues and problems of human information proccessing.

Research on human information processing can often be placed on a continuum whose extremes represent "hardware" and "software" approaches to the discipline. There has been a tendency for advocates of the software approach to concentrate upon the more cognitive aspects of human information processing while those advocating hardware approaches concentrate upon human performance. This divergence in content has been accompanied by a corresponding divergence in methodologies, with software methodology seldom applied to human performance and hardware methodology seldom applied to human cognition. This schism is unfortunate since both approaches have much to offer. The present volume stresses the commonality between human performance and human cognition aspects of information processing, in the hope that readers primarily concerned with one approach will perhaps be able to find some utility at the other end of the continuum.

The tutorial style is aimed at two audiences. Graduate students who have yet to select an area of specialization should find the broad coverage an aid to this end. Sophisticated researchers who wish to learn more about a particular area of human information processing sufficiently removed from their own speciality so that obtaining this information from a literature search might prove tedious should also find this volume helpful. Both groups should benefit from the heavy emphasis upon methodology present throughout the volume. Thus, this book should protect the researcher who is new to an area or an approach from repeating some of the errors that have been noted by the authors.

The organization of the book is simple, proceeding from the human performance end of the continuum, an overview of which is given in the first chapter. Successive chapters are progressively more concerned with human cognition, and the last chapter gives an overview of human cognition. The intervening chapters are devoted to more specific topics and yield a detailed portrait of the models, findings, and methodology of human information processing.

While the graduate student would probably be best served by reading the chapters in the order in which they have been presented, the sophisticated researcher is invited to plunge in wherever his interest alights. Some topics are treated in more than one chapter so that a glance through the index may prove worthwhile. While each author has his own unique view of information processing, the chapters are not intended as a platform for an author's own models but instead offer balanced coverage of a topic. Thus, the book offers a broader picture of the entire human information-processing enterprise than does a text primarily concerned with a single approach. Each author has reviewed at least two other chapters so that the revision process has served as a check whereby any single author's enthusiasm for past theoretical positions has been tempered, resulting in a moderately unbiased text.

It is hoped that the present combination of tutorial style, in which minimal assumptions are made about the reader's prior knowledge, and broad coverage will fill a gap in the presently available literature. The information presented is comparable to that found in other volumes, in that it is sufficiently detailed to be of value to the professional researcher and the advanced student. However, the aim of each chapter has been to provide tutorial assistance rather than to further an author's own position. Finally, the emphasis upon methodology should prevent the material from becoming dated too quickly.

This books reflects the labors of many people. My first debt is to the authors who cheerfully tolerated many critical comments and with patience and fortitude revised their chapters quite substantially. The publisher provided every assistance, including holding the editor's hand in times of stress. The heaviest burden, however, has fallen upon my wife Susan, whom I thank and to whom I offer abject apologies for many meals delayed or missed entirely.

October, 1974   B.H.K.
West Lafayette, Indiana

HUMAN INFORMATION PROCESSING: TUTORIALS IN PERFORMANCE AND COGNITION

1
HUMAN PERCEPTUAL-MOTOR
PERFORMANCE[1]

Richard W. Pew
The University of Michigan

PROLOGUE

It is fitting for two reasons that the first chapter of this book about human information processing be concerned with perceptual motor performance. First, it is only in recent years that motor performance has begun again to be dealt with as process (Keele, 1973) in contrast with the task-oriented analyses that have dominated the post-World War II period (Poulton, 1966) or the learning theory approach that emerged in the 1930's and continues to have its vocal advocates (see, for example, Bilodeau, 1966). Motor performance has been the laggard in this respect. Process-oriented views of perception, memory, and decision are already well-advanced (Broadbent, 1971; Neisser, 1967). The difficulty is documented in Welford's ency-clopedic work on skills (Welford, 1968). A glance at Professor Welford's chapter headings clearly confirms his belief in an information-processing orientation to skills; however, the one chapter in which his retreat to a descriptive level is particularly noticeable is the chapter on movement.

Second, it is very difficult to discuss perceptual motor performance without embracing the entire domain of human information processing. Inferences about

[1]The writing of this chapter and some of the author's research reported herein were supported by the Advanced Research Projects Agency, United States Department of Defense, and monitored by the United States Air Force Office of Scientific Research, under Contract F44620-72-C-0019 with The University of Michigan's Human Performance Center. Other research reported herein was supported by NASA Contracts NASr-54-(06) and NSR-23-005-364 with the National Aeronautics and Space Administration. The author is grateful to R. G. Pachella and J. I. Laszlo, and to R. J. Jagacinski, A. Rose, C. D. Wickens, G. Rupp, and other students, for many helpful discussions and critiques from which this chapter emerged. Cogent reviews of the chapter draft were provided by S.W. Keele, R. A. Schmidt, B. H. Kantowitz, B. O'Neill, and E. Hunt.

processing acquired by examining time delays in following a target course are closely related to the inferences derived from measurement of discrete reaction times (Pachella, Chapter 2). Producing a movement pattern that varies in space and time presupposes the capability to organize other classes of events serially (Jones, Chapter 5), and a hierarchical structure appropriate to the synthesis of motor skills surely must draw on such structures as they are revealed in intellectual tasks (Hunt, Chapter 7). While this chapter will make contact with topics discussed in virtually all the other chapters in this book, the subject matter and perspective are necessarily different. In this sense it should at once introduce the diversity of information-processing activities while it also communicates the unique subject matter of motor performance: movement control, utilization of response-produced feedback, and the organization and patterning of behavior in time.

Overview of What Is to Come

There is no one theory that encompasses all we want to know about motor performance. A myriad of processes and mechanisms act in concert to make possible the exquisite control and organization, the sheer grace and beauty, that typify the performance of the skilled athlete, musician, or experienced industrial worker.

This chapter will deal with three levels at which this control and organization are manifest. At the lowest level an individual brings to bear on any skilled task a rudimentary servomechanism, a system that permits the generation of a stream of simple motor outputs that is responsive to perceived differences between a desired state and an actual state. At the simplest level, with an unpredictable environment, this system, which is representable in terms of elementary concepts drawn from the theory of feedback control, acts point by point in time, contingent on changes in the environment and on the results of immediately preceding movements. It provides the basis, both conceptually and practically, for all higher levels of organization and programming. When prediction and programming fail to produce the desired performance, the servo system takes up the slack and provides appropriate corrective signals. Successively higher levels of organization construct more integrated streams of motor commands, which are then executed and corrected by elements of the lower-level feedback control system. The chapter will begin with an introduction to the properties and performance of this rather mechanistic and ''simple-minded'' error-correction system.

If error correction were the limit of capability of the human motor system, as it is in lower organisms (e.g., the tropisms of single-celled animals), our performance would be crude and inadequate. At the next level to be explored in this chapter we must deal with an individual's capacity to act on the basis of the coherence and predictability of the environment with which he is interacting. At this level the performance is still highly stimulus bound, but the actor is capable of superseding the elementary control loop to generate more complex patterned outputs and to monitor the correspondence between the generated pattern and the desired pattern, by using more sophisticated error-detection mechanisms. In this section we must consider an individual's capacity to track predictable signals and to produce response sequences that take account of the dynamic responsiveness of the limb or external system being controlled. Even if the stimulus pattern to be followed is the same, the motor command stream appropriate to driving a sports car is not the same as that appropriate to a cross-country bus.

Finally, the full richness of human skilled performance depends on capacities not captured by strict stimulus-bound representations derived largely from the study of tracking tasks. Instead it is embodied in the ability to draw from the environment the appropriate initial conditions and to call up from memory integrated patterns of movement consonant with a desired goal. The third level of organization to be considered deals with the production of these self-initiated movements. It is at this level that our understanding and models are most incomplete.

It is clear that this division into three levels is at best a pedagogical convenience. The reader should think of motor control in terms of a hierarchically organized system in which the distinction among levels is diffuse and in which there is a rich interplay among the various processes that the individual calls upon to complete a given task. The relative importance of each depends on the environmental constraints, the criteria with respect to which performance is to be optimized, and the level of experience the performer brings to that activity.

INNER LOOP CONTROL

Minimizing Residual Motor Noise

Consider the task described by the block diagram of Fig. 1. The subject manipulates a rigidly-mounted control stick that produces an electrical output directly proportional to the force applied to it. He watches a display of his own output in comparison to a reference line that indicates the fixed magnitude of force he is requested to produce. The scale of the display is greatly magnified so that his most minute deviations from the desired force are presented to him. His task is to hold the prescribed force as accurately as he can. These conditions are designed to bring out the best a subject can do. He has only to correct for his own errors, and the display conditions make it easy for him to see them. In fact, in unpublished studies conducted by J. K. Thomas and myself, the average absolute error under these conditions (that is, the average deviation from the desired force when the sign of the error is disregarded) was of the order of 1.4 gm (.003 lb) when the commanded force was 454

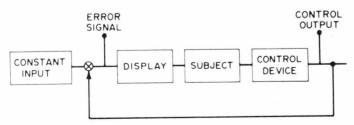

FIG. 1. Block diagram of the task of maintaining a constant force with visual feedback.

gm (1 lb). With a 1400 gm commanded force, the average absolute error increased to 4.2 gm. We interpret this residual noise level in the output as a fundamental limitation in human motor control. A signal to noise ratio of 50 dB is about as good as he can do; the magnitude of the error scales multiplicatively with the magnitude of the applied force.

It is also instructive to examine the temporal properties of this residual motor noise. Since the error signal fluctuates randomly as a function of time, the appropriate way to capture its character is to compute its power spectrum, the average power or energy in the signal at each frequency, just as one would perform a frequency analysis of the noise produced by a jet aircraft or a motorcycle.[2]

The results of such an analysis are shown in Fig. 5 on page 11. The spectrum shown for the "no delay" condition closely approximates the spectra obtained in the Thomas and Pew force-holding experiment, although in the case of the spectrum shown in Fig. 5, a sinusoidal input signal having a frequency of 0.1 Hz (one cycle every ten seconds) was actually used instead of a constant input. Virtually all the power in human motor output is concentrated at frequencies below 15 Hz. There is a relatively sharp peak in the spectrum at approximately 10 Hz, which may be identified with normal physiological tremor. Then there is a much broader peak that extends roughly from 0.5 Hz to 3.0 Hz that may be associated with the subject's attempts to correct for both his own minute errors and the inevitable drift in produced force that results from trying to sustain an output force level.

In order to grasp the meaning of this spectral peak, suppose that the subject made corrections discretely and that the smallest time between responses were 200 msec. If, for tutorial purposes, we also suppose that corrections were made alternately to the left and right at the maximum rate possible, the subject would generate a waveform that completed one cycle of left and right alternations in 400 msec. If we analyzed the frequency of this waveform we would find that one cycle every 400 msec corresponds to 2.5 cycles per second (Hz). Under the assumption of discrete corrections, the implication here is that 3 Hz corresponds to a minimal time between changes in applied force of approximately 160 msec, a figure that is not unreasonable in light of simple reaction-time data. Similarly, the peak extending down to roughly 0.5 Hz implies that sometimes intervals as long as one second elapse between corrections. The analogy between discrete correction intervals and frequency should not be taken too literally; however, the intuitions implied by it are an appropriate way to interpret the frequency variable.

[2]A signal that varies randomly as a function of time cannot be described in terms of its repeating patterns because in principle every finite-length sample is different from every other sample. It is instead necessary to specify two average statistics that may be computed from any sample. One of these is the signal's amplitude distribution: the probability distribution that describes the relative likelihood that the signal will be at various distances away from some reference value. The second one is the power spectrum or power spectral density. Any random signal can be reproduced exactly by adding together an infinite sum of pure sinusoidal signals each having the proper frequency, amplitude, and time relation to all the others. The power spectrum is an estimate of the average power (amplitude squared) at each frequency that would be required in principle to reproduce a particular random signal. The shape and extent of the spectrum tells us a great deal about the effects of a signal that cannot be deduced by direct inspection of the waveform itself.

The subject in this experiment is being asked to perform a task that could easily be undertaken by an automatic system. Maintaining a constant level of a signal in the face of disturbances is called technically the *regulator problem*, and systems that are nothing more than refined versions of a thermostatically-controlled home heating system can be designed to solve the regulator problem to virtually any level of accuracy desired.

A regulator is conceptually the simplest form of feedback control system. It consists of an error detector and a controller. The error detector senses the difference between the desired state and the actual state of the system, which, of course, implies that knowledge of the actual state is available through feedback from the output. The controller provides command signals to drive the device being controlled, whether it is a furnace or simply a control stick. The controller may vary widely in the complexities of its dynamic characteristics. If we were to use a regulator system as a model for our subject who is attempting to maintain a constant force output, it would have to incorporate nothing more than a *gain* or sensitivity factor appropriate to reproduce the signal to noise levels we observed and an effective time delay reflecting the subject's processing delays. In short, a model for the performance of a human subject in this simple task requires postulating nothing more complicated than a regulator and implies little in the way of cognitive control functions.

Tracking Random Signals

It is a conceptually simple step to generalize the task required of our subject by relaxing the constraint on the force level to be maintained and permitting it to vary over time in an unpredictable manner. Unpredictable signals are specified statistically, since their waveforms are never the same from trial to trial. The most important aspect of the signal that affects the accuracy with which a human subject can track is the signal's *bandwidth*. The technical definition of bandwidth refers to the range from lowest to highest frequency present in the signal. A hi-fi amplifier is said to transmit a band from 25 to 20,000 Hz. In the signals with which we deal, the low frequency is fixed and extends rather close to zero frequency, and we vary the high frequency cut-off. This has the effect of varying the rate of change or oscillation frequency of the signal from very slow (narrow bandwidth) to rather fast (wide bandwidth). As you will see from Fig. 2, an unpredictable signal having a bandwidth as wide as 1 Hz is very difficult for a human subject to follow. This figure presents the mean square error produced by a subject when he was attempting to track signals of different bandwidths (Elkind, 1956). The signals were random-appearing and had well-defined bandwidths. There was no power in the signal above the frequency F_{co}, but all frequencies below F_{co} were equally represented. The figure shows performance for both pursuit and compensatory displays. The compensatory display is of greatest interest at this point in the discussion. With such a display the subject sees only the error signal. He must move his control stick so as to return a cursor to the center of the display and thereby correct for any deviations introduced by the input signal. The output is literally subtracted from the input before it is presented to the subject, as is indicated by the circle with an X in it in Fig. 1. With a pursuit display, the subject is

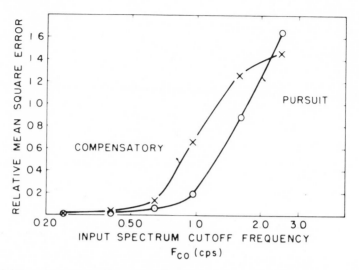

FIG. 2. Relative mean square tracking error as a function of the bandwidth of the random signal having an ideal rectangular spectrum with cutoff-frequency F_{co}. The error score is computed as the ratio of mean square error relative to mean square input amplitude. Both pursuit and compensatory performance are shown (data from Elkind, 1956).

presented with a moving target corresponding to the pattern of the input and a moving cursor responsive to his control motions. His task in this case is to keep the cursor superimposed on the target as well as he can. I will return to a discussion of the implications of pursuit displays in a later section.

As can be seen from the curve for compensatory tracking in Fig. 2, the amount of tracking error rises slowly up to a bandwidth of approximately 0.6 Hz and then begins rising rapidly, until above a bandwidth of 1.2 Hz the subject would be better off to leave the control stick at rest since he is creating more error than he is eliminating.

A Simple Model of Compensatory Tracking

Let us consider in detail the block diagram of a feedback model of a subject performing the task of compensatory tracking of a random signal as shown in Fig. 3. This description takes the model of Lemay and Westcott (1962) (see also Wilde & Westcott, 1963) as its referent because, conceptually, it is an easy model to understand and because it embodies the principle components needed to represent the subject's behavior.

The model assumes that the subject operates on a discrete time base, executing one movement every 200 msec. Beginning with the output end of the system, the Motor Command Generator and Muscle Mechanism act together to produce a "ballistic" movement every 200 msec. The input to this motor system is a desired change in the position of the limb. As shown in Fig. 4, the Motor Command Generator produces a pair of equal and opposite pulses of acceleration, each 100 msec in duration, the two together comprising the command for a simple movement. The amplitude of these

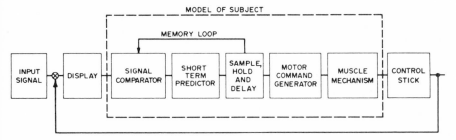

FIG. 3. Block diagram of feedback model for a subject performing a compensatory tracking task (based on the model of Lemay & Westcott, 1962).

pulses, and thereby the amplitude of the movement, is the only thing that is allowed to vary. These pulses are then transmitted to the Muscle Mechanism, which integrates them twice to produce a smooth change in position at its output, as shown also in the responses of Fig. 4. This representation of the muscle and limb system is a crude simplification that treats them together as a simple mass to which the accelerating forces are applied and neglects the physiological details of exactly how the muscles act to generate forces that move the limb. It is important to remember that all movements produced by this system take the same 200-msec to execute. Only the size of the movement may be changed on the basis of information received from earlier elements in the system.

How does the model decide what magnitude of correction to introduce? It is to this aspect that we turn our attention next. This process begins with the Signal Comparator. In general, the Comparator is the element of the system that examines the correspondence between the desired result and the actual output produced and generates a correction signal that represents the change in output that is needed to make them correspond. The general case will become important later, but in this instance of simple compensatory control the Signal Comparator has the trivial role of comparing the displayed error signal with the desired state of zero error and transmitting a signal corresponding to that difference, which is, in fact, the error signal itself.

Consider next the Short-Term Predictor. This element is simple in concept but important to the representation of the subject's behavior. It takes the error transmitted from the Signal Comparator and computes its instantaneous velocity or rate of change. The output of the Short-Term Predictor is a signal that comprises the weighted sum of position plus velocity of the error signal. The assumption embodied in the introduction of this element is that the subject does not execute error corrections on the basis of position errors alone, but rather takes account of trends and rates of change of the error signal in making his decision about what size correction to make. Poulton (1952) defined this kind of prediction as *perceptual anticipation*, and it is one way that the subject partially compensates for the intrinsic delays he introduces into the overall feedback system. The relative importance of position and rate information is specified by a weighting constant, a parameter of the model that is selected to produce good correspondence between the model and the subject's behavior.

Because the model operates on a discrete time base, executing one response every 200 msec, the Motor Command Generator needs information about what response to produce only once every 200 msec. This fact, together with the assumption that the subject has an effective time delay in executing responses on the basis of perceived error, results in the sample-and-hold elements in the model. Once every 200 msec the sampler takes a reading of the magnitude of the desired error correction at the output of the Short-Term Predictor. That value is held in store for one sample period (200 msec) and then released for execution in the form of a movement by the Motor Command Generator. Thus movements are always being executed 200 msec after the errors to which they are responsive have been sensed.

With the exception of the Memory Loop to be considered in a moment, all the machinery is at hand to begin following signals. To make its operation clear, consider the model's response to the series of step input commands shown in Fig. 4.

The sampler takes samples at t_0, t_1, t_2, etc. At t_0 no error is detected and no command programmed. At t_1 an error of amplitude A_1 is detected. Since the rate of change of error is zero at t_1, an error correction is set up and held for one sample period and the pair of acceleration pulses is executed as shown beginning at t_2 to produce the movement shown. This movement is completed at t_3. Meanwhile the sampling element takes a new sample at t_2 and senses the same error of magnitude A_1. This creates a logical difficulty, since a correction for this error has already been implemented and is about to be triggered off. The solution to this difficulty is provided by the Memory Feedback Loop. Its function is to feed back to the error detector the magnitude of corrections already accounted for, so that they may be subtracted from the detected error and not corrected again. Thus, the effective error detected at t_2 is zero and no new error is sensed. As a result, the output remains constant between t_3 and t_4, the time when corrections sensed at t_2 would be executed. It should be clear that the concept of such a memory feedback path is necessary in any system in which there are delays in response execution. In essence it implies that the subject must take account of his "intentions" to act in planning the next correction.

Continuing with the example of Fig. 4, a new sample is taken at t_3. An error of magnitude $A_2 - A_1$ is sensed, and a new correction is held and executed during the interval t_4 to t_5. The sample at t_4 detects no new error beyond that already accounted for at t_3, and no further corrections are needed.

When Lemay and Westcott (1962) compared the performance of this model with that of real subjects, it was found that the model accounted for approximately 90% of the operators' output. The model also produced time histories of tracking performance that were remarkably similar to the actual subjects' output point by point in time. Although it was not tested in this way, it seems likely that the model would also produce error scores as a function of input bandwidth not unlike those from Elkind's experiment shown in Fig. 2.

There are two main reasons for introducing this rather mechanistic description of simple tracking behavior. The most important one is to point out that at this level the process of tracking can be represented without placing much demand on human intellectual abilities. The ability to make simple positional corrections is always with

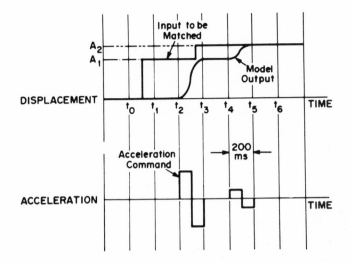

Fig. 4. Time history of the model output and the acceleration commands produced in response to the step input signal shown. This response is derived from the model of Lemay and Westcott (1962).

us, and this basic correction system produces outputs that confound the observation of more sophisticated levels of programming organization that we as experimenters would like to examine in isolation.

The other reason for introducing it is that the performance of this kind of task embodies many of the fundamental properties of motor control. As we will see in later developments of this chapter, these component processes, such as error detection and motor command execution, become the building blocks of higher levels of skilled performance.

It would be possible to analyze some of these processes in much greater detail and to consider their relationship to what is known about the motor physiology involved (see Houk & Henneman, 1967; McRuer, Magdaleno, & Moore, 1968). However, such detail is not really germane to the picture I want to present and would divert us from the present discussion.

On the Relation between Discrete and Continuous Models of Tracking Performance

All of the foregoing discussion has taken the view first put forward by Craik (1947) that the performance of skills is discontinuous. Craik argued that man behaves like an intermittent correction servo system. However, the student of skills should be aware that virtually all of the predictions derived thus far from discrete representations can be predicted equally well by a continuous linear transmission system represented by a differential equation that includes a time delay but makes no assumptions of discontinuity in the human motor system (McRuer & Jex, 1967).

The difference between a discrete and continuous representation can be likened to the difference in locomotion of a caterpillar and a snake. The caterpillar moves his head and waits for his tail to catch up before initiating a new movement, while a snake moves his whole body continuously. In either case there will be a finite time before the tail reaches the point the head just left. Thus both discrete and continuous representations imply a delay in the transmission of signals. The sampling system described in Fig. 3 produces the delay by assuming intermittent sampling and response execution, while a continuous system model implies continuous adjustments on the part of the subject with the output always delayed with respect to the input by a finite time interval.

It is beyond the scope of this chapter to present a detailed illustration of models based on continuous linear differential equations. They have much to recommend them for many practical applications (Frost, 1972, Weir & McRuer, 1970) and for some theoretical purposes (for example, see Pew & Rupp, 1971). Their success emphasizes the point that it is the processing delay rather than any intrinsic discontinuities imposed by the subjects that produces many of the qualities of human tracking performance. Just how important that role can be is illustrated by Pew, Duffendack, and Fensch (1967a). Subjects were instructed to minimize their tracking error while following a very low-frequency sine wave (0.01 Hz) as accurately as they could with a compensatory error display and a rigidly-mounted force stick similar to that described earlier. The output of the control stick was artificially delayed by recording the output on a tape recorder and immediately playing it back through the playback head of the recorder. By varying the speed of the tape drive it was possible to produce transport delays of 180, 360, 720, and 1440 msec, as well as the condition of no delay, in much the same way that delayed auditory feedback experiments are conducted. The subject saw the difference between the desired pattern and the delayed results of his own control actions on the display. Since the sine wave pattern was changing so slowly, the main component of the subject's response served to correct for the inaccuracies he had produced himself.

Figure 5 shows what a profound effect the tape-recorder delays had on the subject's performance as represented by the power spectrum of the error signal, that is, the average power at each frequency. These spectra have a well-defined periodic structure consisting of only odd harmonics. Consider the case of 360 msec delay. The lowest frequency peak occurs at 0.90 Hz. The subsequent peaks occur at approximately 2.70, 4.50, 6.30 Hz, etc.: the third, fifth, seventh, etc. multiple of 0.90 Hz. It is particularly interesting to note that the fundamental spectral peak shifted systematically to lower frequencies with increasing tape-recorder delay and that the case of no external delay appears to be an orderly extrapolation from the cases with delay added to the system.

These spectra are consistent with the behavior of the model of Fig. 3. Suppose that the subject perceives his error and produces a discrete correction that appears at the output after a time corresponding to the sum of his intrinsic delay together with the added tape-recorder delay. Such a strategy would produce periodicities in the output or error signal with a period of twice the total time delay or at a frequency corresponding to the reciprocal of that period. Taking these assumptions, it is possible to work backward from the observed spectra. For the case of 360-msec external delay, for

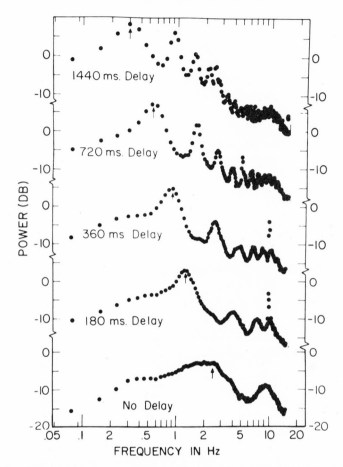

FIG. 5. The effect of introducing an external time delay into the tracking loop on the power spectral densities of the tracking error velocity. Velocities were analyzed instead of error directly in order to obtain a computer scaling advantage at high frequencies. These velocity spectra may be translated into error power spectra by subtracting $20\log_{10}2\pi f$ throughout the range of f, the measurement frequency in radians/sec. (Reproduced from Pew et al., 1967a.)

example, the fundamental peak occurs at a frequency of 0.90 Hz. The period of one half cycle at this frequency is 555 msec. Subtracting the external delay of 360 msec leaves us with an estimate of the subject's internal processing delay of 195 msec. For the three subjects and five time delays studied in this experiment, the range of these estimates of internal delay was between 179 to 212 msec, with a mean of 198 msec, a very reasonable estimate for a subject's delay in processing visual signals.

Second, and more importantly for the main thread of this discussion, it is possible to derive substantially equivalent predictions from a linear continuous model of the sort previously described. Although it is not particularly intuitive, it can be shown in general that if a broad-band noise of the sort produced by human-sensing and response-execution errors is recirculated through a system having a time delay but no discontinuous elements, the output will still exhibit the kind of periodic resonant peaks shown in Fig. 5. Further, fitting parameters to such a model in the manner I have just shown for the discontinuous model produces values for effective time delay that are just as plausible as those given above.

After working for several years to try to decide whether a discrete or a continuous representation was more appropriate, I have found no prediction that unambiguously distinguishes the two possibilities and have concluded that while the discrete representation is more intuitively compelling, both kinds of analyses are useful and provide different perspectives and insights into the nature of performance at the level of the simple corrective feedback system.

Summary

This section has described the performance of a subject in a simple tracking task in which the signal to be followed is essentially unpredictable. Under these conditions we know enough to formulate rather detailed models or specifications for what mechanisms or processes are needed to produce performance equivalent to that of our human subject, and these models involve very little "intelligence." Nevertheless, taken in a broader perspective, many properties of motor performance in general are manifestations of this simple feedback system. It is always with us and takes over a controlling position in behavior early in practice or when higher-level control mechanisms to be considered next fail to produce desired results.

HIGHER-ORDER CONTROL MECHANISMS IN TRACKING

If the elemental servomechanism that has been the focus of discussion thus far were our only means for dealing with changing environmental conditions, automobile speed limits would be severely restricted, many sports activities would be reduced to trivial interest, and penny arcade games of skill would never have been developed. The fact is, however, that we have a variety of mechanisms for taking advantage of the predictability in our environment, and it is to these aspects of performance that we turn next.

Sources of Signal Predictability

There are several lines of evidence supporting the role that predictability can play in enhancing tracking performance. Simply providing the subject with a pursuit display, instead of the compensatory one described previously, produces reliably better tracking performance for just about all conditions that have been studied (Poulton, 1966). Since the pursuit display provides input and output information separately as well as permitting inferences about the error signal, it is generally assumed that it permits the subject to formulate commands on the basis of the pattern and predictabilities of the input signal unconfounded by the output signal.

A further improvement in tracking performance results if the concept of viewing the input independently is extended to include a preview of the path to be followed in advance of the time when control actions must be taken, such as are provided to the automobile driver when he looks down the road (Crossman, 1960; Johnson, 1972; Poulton, 1954). The amount of preview that can be effectively utilized depends in part on the complexity or bandwidth of the input signal to be followed (Johnson, 1972). Johnson showed that the major reduction of error was contributed by the first 100 msec of preview and that it produced much smaller improvements out to a preview of 1.0 sec, but only when the bandwidth of the input was extended to 1.0 Hz, that is, when there was little significant power (or amplitude) in the input signal above a frequency of 1.0 Hz. With a bandwidth of 0.5 Hz, only 100 msec of preview was useful, and when the bandwidth was reduced to 0.25 Hz, preview appeared to be unnecessary for good performance.

Poulton (1952) used the term anticipation rather than prediction and has distinguished between receptor anticipation, that based on extra information provided by modifying the presentation mode, such as preview, and perceptual anticipation, that based on the subject's ability to learn the predictabilities of the input. While I recognize this distinction, it is not particularly important for this discussion, because the mechanisms with which I want to deal are more concerned with taking advantage of the fact of predictability than with the source of this predictability; it just happens that some modes of presentation make it easier to predict than others.

Poulton, in the same paper, also describes effector anticipation, a further source of advantage for pursuit and predictive displays, in which knowledge of the effects of motor commands is available in terms of the system responses they produce. This concept will be dealt with in detail in a later section.

The ultimate in predictability is achieved when the input signal to be followed is repetitive or periodic. A triangular, square, or sine wave is a limiting case in which the periodicity becomes obvious almost immediately, but repetitive signals having complex wave forms and arbitrarily long periods become more and more predictable with practice. In principle, after sufficient practice with such signals, they should produce tracking performance that approaches that produced from tracking sinusoidal signals having comparable frequencies.

Sine Wave Tracking as an Example

The tracking of sine waves provides an interesting illustrative case for the advantages of dealing with predictable signals. In a study by Pew, Duffendack, and Fensch (1967b), three subjects practiced tracking pure sine waves with frequencies ranging from 0.1 to 5.0 Hz with an arm control stick for 32 daily one-hour sessions. A variety of system variables were manipulated, but the main results are shown in the three-dimensional plot of Fig. 6. In the figure each block represents four one-hour daily sessions of practice. During each four-day block, performance was evaluated at each of the five input frequencies shown for both pursuit and compensatory displays. The vertical axis displays the average performance of three subjects as measured by their mean integrated-absolute-error score.

At the lowest frequency, 0.1 Hz, practice effects were rather small, a pursuit display was only slightly better than a compensatory one, and the subjects appeared to

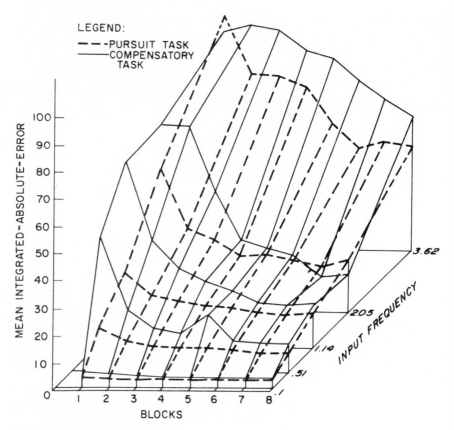

FIG. 6.   Integrated-absolute-tracking-errors as a joint function of blocks of practice and input frequency for pursuit and compensatory displays. (Reproduced from Pew et al., 1967b, Fig. 1.)

follow the signal point by point in time by using the kind of error-detection scheme previously discussed. The advantages of predictability were slight in this case where the period of the signal (10 sec) was long with respect to the intrinsic delays imposed by the subject. However, with the higher input frequencies, the differences in performance with the pursuit and compensatory displays were much larger for Block 1. As practice was extended, however, performance with the compensatory display still approached that of its pursuit counterpart. At 3.62 Hz, it did not make much difference what kind of display the subject had—even after 32 days of practice his performance was 2 or 3 times worse than it was at 2 Hz. The data provide an interesting precautionary note to experimenters who think tracking a sine wave of a frequency as low as 0.5 Hz is relatively easy. Even after 16 days (Block 4) compensatory display performance was still improving.

The role of signal predictability was clearly evident in this experiment. With a pursuit display and with frequencies above approximately 0.75 Hz, the subject could detect the sinusoidal pattern almost immediately. He made use of this information to generate his own approximation to a sine wave and attempted to synchronize his generated pattern with the desired input pattern. In the range of frequencies between 0.75 and about 1.5 Hz, it was relatively easy to produce this synchronization. As the input frequency was increased, it became harder and harder to produce synchronization, and more and more practice was required to do so. With a compensatory display, however, even at relatively low frequencies it took substantial practice to make use of the input pattern predictability, but as that was achieved, compensatory display performance began to look much like pursuit performance. The transition point between 0.5 and 1.0 Hz was critical. Below this frequency the subject appeared to operate on the signal moment by moment in time, making use of the regularity to obtain good predictions of the corrections that were needed. However, he was still operating in a discrete correction mode, and the frequency content of the error signal looked much like it does for very low frequency signals (see Pew, Duffendack, & Fensch, 1967b).

Above this critical frequency the mode of control changed. The subject shifted from an error correction mode to a pattern generation mode. Whereas at lower frequencies he was restricted to making corrections on the basis of short-term predictions of the error signal alone, now the error correction mechanism took on a new role, that of assessing the difference between the amplitude, frequency, and phase of the sine wave he was attempting to generate and the same parameters of the input sine wave. This kind of higher-level correction process was clearly evident in the time histories and spectra of the error signal when the task was to track frequencies of 1.0 Hz and higher.

It is interesting to note as an aside that the transition point between 0.5 and 1.0 Hz was also critical in the build-up of error in Elkind's experiment depicted in Fig. 2. In the case of Elkind's random signals, no mode switching was possible, and the error continued to build up rapidly. The pursuit display was able to sustain good performance out to somewhat higher frequencies, however, even with these random signals.

Magdaleno, Jex, and Johnson (1970) carried the analysis of modes used in tracking sine waves one step further in studies they conducted in support of their Successive Organization of Perception Model. They argued that the pattern prediction and generation mode began at approximately 0.5 Hz and that prediction and generation were used in combination with an error correction mode up to about 1.0 Hz. From 1.0 to approximately 1.7 Hz, the subject used a relatively pure form of prediction and generation, and above 1.7 Hz, it became increasingly difficult to achieve good synchronization. The subject just did his best to make the two match, but the parameter matching mode became relatively ineffective above approximately 2.0 Hz. They supported these assertions with quantitative measurements of performance together with the subjects' rather interesting introspections when tracking different frequencies. The latter are reproduced in Fig. 7.

The subjects' use of pattern generation is reflected in their comments about how they took advantage of the rhythm in the frequency range from 0.5 to 1.5 Hz. Magdaleno, Jex, and Johnson (1970) also put sine wave tracking in the context of input signal predictability more generally in a way that is entirely consonant with the perspective I am presenting here. They argue that it represents the most easily predictable end of a continuum that extends to very complex waveforms that repeat after arbitrarily long periods and that become subjectively predictable like sine waves only as a function of extended practice. The frequency content of these complex but highly over-learned waveforms will dictate the mode of control that will predominate after this level of predictability has been achieved.

An example of this complex end of the continuum is provided in a study I conducted with C. D. Wickens (see Pew, 1974). Subjects were required to track a one-minute signal, the first and last 20 sec of which changed randomly from trial to trial, but in which the middle 20 sec was repeated exactly on every trial. The amplitude distribution and frequency spectrum of the random pattern from which the middle segment was drawn were identical to that from which the changing first and last segments were drawn. Thus on the first trial the subject had no reason to believe, and was not told, that there was anything special about the middle segment. As a function of practice, performance on all three segments improved. However, the performance advantage of the middle segment gradually increased in comparison with performance on the first and last segments that served as controls. After 11 one-hour practice sessions, integrated absolute-error on the repeated segment was 15% lower than that on its random counterparts. The subjects had obviously learned to take advantage of the extra predictability of the repeated piece, although interestingly they had only a very diffuse idea of why they were doing better. After 16 sessions they were 28% better on the repeated piece and presumably would continue to improve to the level comparable to that of a completely predictable signal, such as a sine wave, given sufficient practice.

A Generalization of the Control Theory Model

These examples provide the ingredients and the motivation to examine how the elemental correction servo system can be generalized to account for a subject's abilities to deal with signal predictability. Some of the answers have already been suggested. In the simple model presented earlier the motor system was limited to producing simple responses by introducing two equal and opposite pulses of acceleration that the muscle system then converted into smooth parabolic movements lasting exactly 200 msec. The first generalization required is to admit the formulation of motor-command strings of longer duration than 200 msec that can be more complex than the simple parabolic form hypothesized there.

A second generalization that is required to take account of the advantages of pursuit displays and preview of the path to be followed is the ability to formulate these motor-command strings on the basis of information about the behavior of the environmental input signal directly, in addition to the previously discussed ability to act on perceived discrepancies between output and input. I need to introduce an additional signal path that includes a pattern detection and generation capability but that bypasses the signal comparator and the sampling system on its way to the motor-command generator.

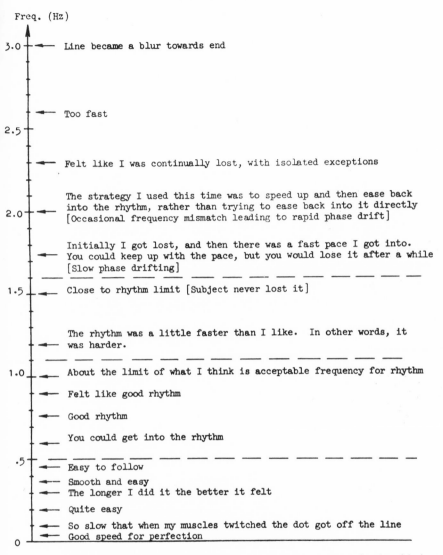

Freq. (Hz)

3.0 ← Line became a blur towards end

2.5 ← Too fast

← Felt like I was continually lost, with isolated exceptions

2.0 ← The strategy I used this time was to speed up and then ease back
into the rhythm, rather than trying to ease back into it directly
[Occasional frequency mismatch leading to rapid phase drift]

← Initially I got lost, and then there was a fast pace I got into.
You could keep up with the pace, but you would lose it after a while
[Slow phase drifting]

1.5 ← Close to rhythm limit [Subject never lost it]

← The rhythm was a little faster than I like. In other words, it
was harder.

1.0 ← About the limit of what I think is acceptable frequency for rhythm

← Felt like good rhythm

← Good rhythm

← You could get into the rhythm

.5 ← Easy to follow
← Smooth and easy
← The longer I did it the better it felt
← Quite easy
← So slow that when my muscles twitched the dot got off the line
← Good speed for perfection

0

FIG. 7. Subjective comments concerning the difficulty of tracking sine waves as a function of the input frequency. Experimenter's comments are in brackets. (After Magdaleno et al., 1970, Fig. 5.)

This generalization can be understood most easily by analogy with the eye-movement system. Our eyes are capable of two distinct modes of operation, the well-known saccadic jumps that correspond to the corrective movements described here and a pursuit movement. If a visual target is moving at a relatively constant rate the eye will follow that target with a continuous pursuit movement. The eye cannot generate such continuous movements except in response to a moving visual target and, as far as we know, is not able to generate more complex patterns of movement than simple fixed velocity tracks (Rashbass, 1961). In a model of the eye movement control, Young, Forster, and Van Houtte (1968) postulate a pursuit system that estimates the velocity of target movement directly and produces a smooth constant-velocity component of eye movement output. (See Pew, 1970, for a simplified description of their model.) If a mismatch between the target path and the eye-fixation path results, the saccadic correction system introduces a discrete correction, and the eye then either continues with the same velocity movement or takes up a new rate representing a better approximation to the target path.

By analogy, then, the way we take advantage of predictabilities manifest in the input either from a pursuit display, from preview of the course to be followed, or even from a compensatory display after sufficient practice, is by directly formulating motor commands that are responsive to our best estimates of the pattern of the input signal.

It is important to emphasize that this pattern detection and generation capability acts together with error correction to produce the behavior we observe. This is a concept that is important to the further development of the picture of motor performance I am trying to portray. A hierarchy of such mechanisms is always operating, complementing one another to produce the sometimes bewildering complexity of performance that characterizes skilled behavior.

One final generalization is required to complete the picture of how we deal with predictable signals. Whereas previously the error comparator dealt only with direct differences between input and output signal amplitude, that capability needs to be generalized to include comparison of estimates of higher-level parameters of the input and output signals. In the example of the pursuit eye movement system it was argued that velocity estimates of the input signal were made and smooth, constant speed movements of the eye were produced. Then a comparison was made between the produced output velocity and the input velocity estimates, and a revision of the generated velocity was introduced to bring these two into correspondence. A multilevel model of this sort has also been proposed by Gibbs (1970).

This capability for estimating discrepancies between input and output in terms of parameters of the input pattern is even more important in the case of repetitive signals such as a periodic step input or sine wave. The effects of predictability of various parameters of the pattern on step input tracking are nicely summarized in Noble and Trumbo (1967).

In the case of sine waves above 0.5 Hz, it is the capability to make this kind of comparison and adjustment that makes it possible to produce synchronization by subtle adjustments of the frequency of the pattern. Presumably such adjustment processes operate on the sine wave amplitude as well. Since at least one cycle of the signal is required to estimate frequency discrepancies, it seems likely that the time delay in executing adjustments to produced frequency or amplitude should depend on the frequency being generated, and this delay is over and above that due to intrinsic processing delays.

Figure 8 represents an attempt to incorporate these generalizations into the block diagram of Fig. 3. While Fig. 3 has been translated into a working simulation of the

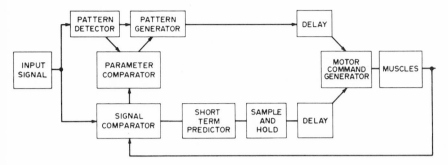

FIG. 8. Generalization of the block diagram of Fig. 3 to include the effects of signal predictability.

behavior of a subject performing a random signal tracking task, Fig. 8 should be regarded as nothing more than a conceptual summary of the generalizations to that model. At this point in the development of my thinking it represents a kind of logical flow chart of the operations that seem necessary, and while I believe that it can be reduced ultimately to the level of an operating computer program, I have not attempted to do so as yet. In the diagram the input signal is introduced into both the signal comparator and the pattern detector. Whereas before, with a compensatory display, only the error signal was available to the comparator, now both input and output are available separately. The role of the pattern detector is to identify the predictable aspects of the input signal that can be used to formulate motor commands over time spans longer than can be accomplished by the error sampling system. At the simplest extreme this may mean nothing more than estimating segments of the input that can be usefully approximated by a constant velocity component of the output. In a more complex task it may mean estimating the parameters of the amplitude, frequency, and phase characteristics of an input sinusoid. With these parameters available a pattern corresponding to them is generated and, after a processing time delay, translated into the appropriate set of motor commands. The Parameter Comparator may be regarded as a higher-level aspect of the Signal Comparator. It is this element that transmits corrective information to the pattern generator on the basis of discrepancies between the pattern actually generated and the desired pattern. Note that this corrective information takes the form of required changes in amplitude or frequency, not the kind of discrete corrections generated by the error sampling system. The role of this parameter comparator is best understood in the context of repetitive signals for which adjustments taking substantially more than 200 msec are important for improving tracking performance.

   The location of the processing time-delay element is not too important, but it is important to recognize that changes are not implemented until the processing delay has elapsed, and this is a delay in addition to any delays produced by the finite time it takes to detect changes in parameter values. Synchronization with repetitive signals is achieved through the comparators by noting that a phase difference between input and output exists due to the processing delay and introducing a parameter adjustment to compensate for this delay.

   One final note concerning the time span of pattern generation is in order. Many motor theorists have postulated the concept of a motor program, a pattern that is fired off "open-loop" without the benefit of feedback. The position taken here, especially in the context of a tracking task, is that no behavior is undertaken completely open-loop unless the stimulus conditions are so impoverished that there is no alternative. What happens instead is that patterns are generated, and they may be formulated for arbitrarily long periods into the future, but that the signal and parameter comparators are working all the time and serve to modify the generated patterns as needed. At the brief end of the scale, discrete positional commands cannot be modified oftener than once every 200 msec. Pattern commands can be expected to have a longer minimum time before they can be corrected, but given that the signal comparator is not detecting discrepancies, a periodic signal may continue to be generated without modification for arbitrarily long periods. Studies of sine wave tracking in which the input signal is turned off after synchronization has been achieved suggest that drift in the parameters occurs within 5 to 10 seconds (Magdaleno et al., 1970).

As early as 1960, Krendel and McRuer (1960) proposed a series of control modes to describe how a subject utilizes the coherence or predictability of the input signal. The most recent statement of this model is reported in Krendel and McRuer (1968). According to this theory, which they call "Successive Organization of Perception," early in practice with either a compensatory or pursuit display the subject behaves as if he had only error information in accordance with the low-level servo system described here. As the subject gains experience, especially with a pursuit display, but also with a compensatory display as a result of knowledge gained from observing the pattern of movements of his control stick, he begins to operate on the input signal directly to produce a component of the output and uses the error servo system as a "vernier adjustment" superimposed on this output. The ultimate stage of learning these authors call the "Precognitive Stage," in which pattern perception is brought into play to generate and produce an output open-loop on a preprogrammed basis for extended periods of time. Although I have not emphasized the learning aspects of tracking to the extent that they do, and my proposed mechanization deviates from theirs, I have been influenced by their development of this theory and am in agreement with many of their ideas.

Development of a Model of the Dynamic Systems Being Controlled

On the output side we need to be concerned with predictability of a different kind. A fiftieth percentile male adult arm weighs approximately 3.75 kg (8.33 lbs). Some years ago Richard Vanderkolk and I tried to set up an experiment in which a subject performed a tracking task with his arm supported in an apparatus connected to a computer-driven torque-motor that reduced the effective forces required to move the arm. To the subject it felt like we had reduced the mass of his arm. Although we had some reservations about the effectiveness of our manipulation, the pilot data confirmed that upon initial exposure to this condition of reduced mass the subject produced motor commands more appropriate to the normal arm mass, and with reduced mass this led to more overshooting of movement corrections and a more oscillatory response.

This example serves to emphasize the important role played by the dynamic responsiveness of our limbs, or any physical system we are attempting to control. As a result of previous learning we begin to predict or anticipate the set of motor commands that are appropriate to produce a desired output. This ability is related to what Poulton has called effector anticipation. We might say that we build up an internal model of our own limb dynamics, or of the automobile or aircraft dynamics we are controlling, and use this model to assist in formulating the appropriate control actions. The experienced race-driver knows in great detail the effects of steering wheel and accelerator movements on his car's response, and these vary over an incredible range as a function of speed, position on the track, and a myriad of other variables. The car almost becomes an extension of his own body.

There is another analogy that will illustrate this idea. Early in the space program the National Aeronautics and Space Administration was interested in studying the effects of very high intensity noise on the fatigue strength of the materials used to construct large boosters. To examine these effects they commissioned a study to expose these materials to pure sinusoidal vibrations at 160 dB, a very loud sound indeed. The engineering problem was how to produce pure sinusoidal wave forms at this intensity. Everyone knew that if they started with a sine wave signal, any sound transmission or loudspeaker system would severely distort it, and the actual sound produced would hardly be a high-fidelity pure tone. The solution was obtained by working backwards. The engineers asked, in effect, what kind of a wave shape must we put in such that the distortions introduced by the system will leave us with a pure sine wave at the output?

The analogy is direct. In formulating motor commands the subject must utilize knowledge about the transmission properties of the muscle system, the limbs and any external devices being controlled, so that the desired output will be produced. An important component of skill acquisition is the building up of this model for the particular skill task of concern, and its fidelity or accuracy is one key to successful motor performance. All of the literature on the effects of manipulating the dynamics being controlled, differences between position, rate, and acceleration control systems, etc., can be thought of as studies of the success at building up such an internal model (see Poulton, 1966). A more detailed account of prediction based on stored representations is presented in Kelley (1968).

It is relatively easy to represent this kind of predictive capacity in the general model I am building by providing a block representing a model of the system being controlled. This block receives information from motor output and provides information to the motor program generator. It is much more difficult to say anything profound about the structure of such a model or how it is acquired.

It is clear from vehicle simulation studies with naive subjects that it is possible for a subject to acquire some knowledge of the behavior of the vehicle on the basis of vision only, that is, with a visual feedback loop reporting the results of his control actions, but with no force feel in the control and no actual motion or acceleration cues. However, it can also be shown that when there is a correlation between proprioceptive feedback and visual feedback, so that the system response can be felt as well as seen, as in the case of light aircraft in which the resistance to motion of the stick reflects the actual forces on the elevator tabs, then learning to build this kind of internal model and to produce the appropriate string of motor commands is greatly speeded-up and improved (Herzog, 1968; Notterman & Page, 1962).

Summary

The elemental feedback control system described in the section on inner loop control, while an important building block, is inadequate to predict performance even in highly constrained tracking tasks when either the presentation mode or the properties of the input signal to be tracked provide structure that permits us to go beyond simple error correction. A pattern detection scheme must be postulated and utilized to formulate temporally-organized motor commands that are more complex in pattern and longer in duration than simple corrections. The parameters of these more complex patterns are monitored and adjusted along with the monitoring and correction of simple positional errors, forming a series of levels at which attention and control are required—compatible with the extent of structure and predictability in the input signal. Finally, a central representation of the dynamic properties of the effectors, together with any systems in the environment that form natural extensions of the effectors, such as baseball bats, pole-vaulting poles, or bicycles, must be postulated to account for the relationships between required motor commands and effective system response, when motor patterns of any significant level of complexity are produced.

VOLUNTARY MOVEMENT

While our knowledge of skilled performance has been advanced on many fronts through the study of tracking performance, and while there is much interest in tracking *per se* from the perspective of man-machine system design, the ultimate goal of much research on perceptual-motor skills concerns the understanding of the acquisition and performance of so-called voluntary movements. There are three properties that distinguish such movements: (1) the path of the movement is less important than the goal that is achieved, (2) the pattern of the movement is largely formulated internally on the basis of a backlog of experience with movements designed to achieve similar goals, and (3) the conduct of the movement is paced largely by the subject and not driven by an external forcing function.

Speed and Accuracy of Simple Positional Movements

I will begin the discussion of voluntary movements by considering the performance and theoretical analyses of simple positional movements in which both speed and accuracy are important. It is this class of voluntary movement that fits most closely the development of my analysis thus far.

The setting for this discussion starts with a subject seated before a table on which he may rest his hands. He grasps a stylus, usually in his preferred hand. On the table target circles or boundaries are indicated, and the subject is instructed to tap alternately in each of the circles, moving as rapidly and as accurately as he can between targets. In Fitts' version of this task, on different trials the targets were either of different sizes, different distances apart, or both (Fitts, 1954). The research focus has been on the time required to make movements of this sort as a function of the constraints imposed, but various investigators have examined a variety of measures of performance.

Recognition of the interrelations of movement distance, speed, and accuracy date back at least to Woodworth (1899), who also made the distinction that is still relevant today between what he called the "initial impulse" and "current control." A simple movement of the hand from one position to a well-defined target involves an initial acceleration phase, which .Woodworth called the "initial impulse" and which appears to be triggered off as a unit, and a deceleration phase, the accuracy of which Woodworth showed could be influenced by peripheral feedback, hence the term "current control."

Fitts (1954) was the first investigator to formulate a quantitative expression of the relationship among distance, accuracy, and movement time, in the form,

$$MT = a + b \log_2 \frac{2A}{W}.$$

This equation, which has come to be called Fitts' Law, implies that movement time (MT) is a linear function of an index of difficulty of the movement, defined by the logarithm of the ratio of movement amplitude (A) to target width (W), the latter representing a constraint on movement accuracy. Fitts derived this relationship from informational concepts, argued that there was a fixed informational capacity for producing accurate movements and that the trade-offs among movement amplitude, accuracy, and time embodied in Fitts' Law were a reflection of this limited "channel capacity." Although the fits to data of this equation are remarkably good, usually accounting for more than 90% of the variance in movement times, Welford (1968) has shown that some improvements in the empirical fit to the data sometimes can be made if one assumes a two-component representation, one component involving the contribution to accuracy of the initial adjustment phase and a second related to the accuracy of the current control phase, to use Woodworth's terms.

It has since been repeatedly shown that Fitts' Law can be derived from a variety of perspectives that make various assumptions about the role of feedback in control of skilled movement. Crossman and Goodeve (1963) showed that a first-order differential equation simply postulating that the velocity of movement was inversely proportional to the remaining distance away from the target led to the equation of Fitts' Law. Langolf (1973) showed that a second-order underdamped differential equation relating the acceleration and velocity of the movement to the distance away from the target also captures the temporal predictions of Fitts' Law and in addition reproduces some of the oscillatory properties of hand motion usually observed in movements of this type. The most intuitively appealing formulation was developed by Crossman and Goodeve (1963) and by Keele (1968), based on a first-order difference equation.

It is not necessary to go into the full derivation here. The importance of the model lies in the implications of its assumptions for understanding the mechanism of simple movements. Keele's derivation postulates that the subject makes an initial adjustment and as many discrete corrections to the initial impulse as are necessary to converge on the target area. He explicitly assumes that each correction takes exactly the same amount of time to complete and uses estimates of the time necessary to process visual feedback for the value of the time between successive corrections. An experiment of Keele and Posner (1968) estimated this time to be between 190–260 msec. The derivation of the model also assumes that the average accuracy of a correction is a constant proportion of the distance moved, and Keele takes the constant of proportionality to be between 0.04 (Woodworth, 1899) and 0.07 (Vince, 1948, Exp. IV). With the time equal to 260 msec and the accuracy constant equal to 0.07 Keele reports that he can fit the slope of the Fitts' Law function reported by Fitts and Peterson (1964) quite nicely. Although this model has great intuitive appeal, I never took it to be more than an analogy to real performance until Langolf (1973) performed a Fitts' Law experiment in which subjects manipulated a probe-mounted peg under a 10-power microscope, simulating the performance of microscopic assembly operations. He obtained time histories of the motion profile of the probe used to move the 1.1 mm diameter peg distances of 1.27 or 0.254 cm into holes of varying tolerances. He found the Fitts' Law prediction quite satisfactory for this performance under a microscope. Moreover, by performing ensemble averaging of the motion trajectories of several of these movements he found clear evidence for discontinuities in the path to the target and, amazingly, the times (200 msec per correction) and movement accuracies were not inconsistent with Keele's estimates.

Beggs and his colleagues, in a series of reports beginning with Beggs and Howarth (1970) and including Howarth, Beggs, and Bowden (1971), have formulated a different analysis of a similar aiming task that is particularly interesting because it utilizes some assumptions very similar to those of Keele. The task on which their analysis is based involves repetitive aiming at a vertical line target. Whereas virtually all the empirical studies of Fitts' Law have used a target of defined width and instructions to move as rapidly as possible consistent with achieving the required level of accuracy (see Fitts & Radford, 1966, for one exception), Beggs and Howarth chose to instruct their subjects to be as accurate as possible and to constrain movement speed by pacing them with a metronome. By measuring the duration and accuracy of various phases of the movement as a function of different movement speeds, and by manipulating the distance from the target at which they turn off target illumination, thus removing the opportunity for utilization of visual feedback, these authors arrived at some rather profound conclusions about the important variables relating the speed and accuracy of simple movements. Taking the same position as Keele (1968) and others, that a visually mediated intermittent correction mechanism is operating, they conclude that the primary determinant of movement accuracy is the distance remaining at the time the last correction is initiated. They conclude in Beggs and Howarth (1970) that the last correction is always initiated at a fixed *time* before the movement is terminated and take that time to be 290 msec, on the basis of analyses of aiming accuracy when the target is obscured at various times before the movement is completed. Thus they argue that the trade-off between speed and accuracy of movement is simply a result of the fact that when movements are made more rapidly, the critical 290 msec cut-off occurs at a greater distance away from the target and hence results in reduced accuracy. Their formulation of a prediction comparable to Fitts' Law results in a power function relation between speed and accuracy having the form

$$E^2 = E_0{}^2 + K^2\sigma_\theta (\frac{t_u}{T})^{2.8}$$

where E^2 is the mean square deviation of target hits from the target; $E_0{}^2$ is a residual noise component in motor output that might be attributed to tremor; K is a constant depending on the deceleration profile of the movement; σ_θ is the angular aiming accuracy of movements in the absence of visual feedback; t_u is the time remaining after the last correction (taken to be 290 msec); and T is the total duration of the movement. (See Howarth et al., 1971, for a detailed derivation of the formula.) They argue that their data are better fitted by this model than by Fitts' Law but point out the procedural differences between the two experimental paradigms.

Relation of Simple Movement Mechanisms to Tracking Mechanisms

These results and models are of interest in and of themselves for the student of skilled performance, but they also contribute some fundamentals to my growing picture of perceptual-motor skill. I find the similarities of Keele's and of Beggs and Howarth's conceptions more notable than their differences. Both postulate that visually guided movements are in fact modified during their execution, given that they are made slowly enough that at least one round of visual feedback processing is possible. When not otherwise instructed and when an accuracy constraint requires them, subjects will *choose* to move at a speed that will make such corrections possible. Both positions assume that the accuracy of blind positioning will be inversely proportional to the distance moved. The conception that emerges is one that fits closely with the analyses of tracking performance discussed earlier. Whereas in the case of tracking predictable signals, commands that would correspond to the initial impulse described here are initiated on the basis of predictive information obtained from the input signal itself, in this case the formulation of the initial impulse is based on information about the initial position of the hand, the perceived goal of the movement, and any other constraints imposed on the movement by the experimenter. Corrections are executed, in my opinion, not on the basis of deviations from a predetermined path but rather on the basis of revised estimates of where the target is with respect to where the subject's hand now is. Of course, one visual reaction time must be added in to determine where the hand will be when the correction is actually initiated.

Latency of Current Control Based on Proprioceptive Cues

Suppose the basis for corrections is proprioceptive rather than visual. For some time it has been maintained that proprioceptive reaction time may be somewhat shorter than latency to a visual stimulus. Chernikoff and Taylor (1952) produced some of the shortest estimates by measuring the onset of deceleration of the hand after it was allowed to begin free-falling at an unexpected time. Their estimates were between 112–129 msec. Recently Jordan (1972) conducted an experiment that confirmed the shorter latency of proprioceptive cues in a more practical context. He set a group of naive fencers on-guard against a mechanically mounted fencing foil and instructed them to respond as rapidly as possible to a movement of the mechanical blade under three conditions. In Condition I their own fencing blade was set 15 cm away from the mechanical blade, and the stimulus for a movement was a visual observation of the moving blade. In Condition II the subject's blade was resting against the mechanical foil, and the stimulus was both visual and the proprioceptive feel of the mechanical blade's movement. Condition III was the same as Condition II, except the subject was blindfolded and had only the feel of the blade to react to. The mean response time was measured from onset of blade movement to the first change in the action potential in the flexor muscles of the fingers. After some practice, for the three conditions the mean response times were respectively 129, 136, and 109 msec. The blindfolded condition was reliably faster than either of the other two, suggesting not only that proprioception produced faster times but also that vision was dominant over proprioception when both were available (Condition II).

These results are made even more plausible by some recent work of Evarts (1973). He used a monkey as the experimental subject and a simple plunger movement by its hand as the response. When the stimulus for a corrective response was a sudden change in force on the plunger, he found EMG activity in the arm attributable to cortical involvement, with a latency as short as 30 to 40 msec. Evarts emphasizes that these were not simple spinal-level reflexes. They did not occur prior to some experience with the stimulus situation, and they did not occur when the direction of the force cue was unexpectedly changed. We must conclude that when the stimulus situation provides proprioceptive cues, the time constants associated with corrective activity will be shorter, but we have at this point no reason to propose any different mechanisms for movement execution.

Properties of Motor Memory

When we shift from tracking performance to voluntary movement perhaps the biggest gap lies in the different roles played by memory in the two cases. In the first two sections of this chapter I had little occasion to refer to memory *per se*, except as it is implied in prediction and extrapolation from what is given. However, when we speak of movements produced to the subject's specifications, memory becomes paramount. One is led to ask almost immediately, ''What is it that is stored when we acquire the ability to perform an organized pattern of movement?''

One approach to this question has been to examine the short-term retention of the accuracy of simple movements over a specified distance or to a specified location. In the typical experiment the blindfolded subject's hand is first passively or actively moved to a stop. Then a period of rest or activity intervenes. Then the subject is asked to reproduce the movement to the same place with the stop removed. This task is frequently considered to be a movement analog of the verbal short-term memory experiment referred to as the Brown-Peterson Paradigm. It can be shown that repetition of the to-be-recalled movement improves accuracy, and it becomes necessary to distinguish the case with location cues available from the case in which only distance cues can be utilized. In general, location cues seem to be a more robust source of information on which to base storage. The greatest interest has focused on the question of whether it is possible to demonstrate interference effects by occupying the subject with various tasks during the retention interval and thereby to infer the kind of coding implied in memory. It seems clear that performance of other movements similar to the criterion movement interfere, but with the many other kinds of perceptual, verbal, or intellectual tasks that have been tried, no clear conclusion has been reached. The question of appropriate memory coding for simple positional responses remains an open and viable one. While it is interesting, I will not elaborate on this work further because it does not represent a central issue from the perspective of this chapter. The reader is referred to a review of the motor memory literature by Stelmach (1974) for a detailed discussion.

The properties of motor memory that seem particularly important to the understanding of the production of organized movement patterns are captured in the following simple exercise: Sign your name on the dotted line on your examination paper and then go to the blackboard and sign it again. The limb is used differently. Different muscles are involved. The size is different. Nevertheless, the movement pattern produced can still be clearly identified as your signature; it is unique to you. This homely example supports the interpretation that whatever it is that is stored, it is not simply a specific set of motor commands. In fact, no two repetitions of the same movement are ever exactly alike. Bernstein (1967) distinguishes between the topological properties (spatial patterns) of a movement and its metric properties (size and dimensions) and emphasizes the dominance of its topological properties. As he says (Bernstein, 1967), referring to a similar demonstration involving drawing circles,

> It is clear that each of the variations of a movement demands a quite different muscular formula and even more than this involves a completely different set of muscles in the action. The almost equal facility and accuracy with which all these variations can be performed is evidence for the fact that they are ultimately determined by one and the same higher directional engram in relation to which dimensions and position play a secondary role [p. 49].

The concept of schema learning introduced by Bartlett (1958) and defined experimentally by Posner and Keele (1968) seems an appropriate way to think about the generalized nature of what is stored for the production of movement patterns. Posner and Keele trained subjects to classify distortions of nonsense dot patterns without ever showing them the prototypes from which the patterns were distorted. The subjects were then tested for recognition of the distortions they had learned, of new distortions of the same set of prototypes, and of the prototypes themselves. Recognition performance was as good on the prototype they had never seen before as on the distortions of them that they had learned. Recognition for both these sets of patterns was significantly better than that for the new distorted patterns. This experiment together with a follow-up (Posner & Keele, 1970) argues effectively that during the process of classification learning a generalized schema related to the prototype itself was built up. Although this kind of study has not been performed for motor patterns, I believe it captures the essence of the kind of schema that must be stored for the production of motor patterns.

Of course, identification of a motor schema as a critical aspect of acquiring motor skill raises more questions than it answers. What properties of a movement sequence are encoded? What properties are intrinsic to a particular schema, and what properties are only dimensional parameters that are free to vary from one execution to another?

A possible direction to pursue to answer these questions is given by a transfer condition in the study by Pew and Wickens (Pew 1974) referred to earlier. After subjects had practiced the tracking task for 11 days, in which the middle 20 sec of each one-minute trial was repeated exactly on every trial, a block of 10 trials was run in which the repeated segment was exactly reversed—wherever it moved to the left before, the signal now moved to the right, and vice versa. Under this condition the subjects' performance was significantly better on the inverted segment ($p < .05$) than their performance on the beginning and ending segments averaged together, but significantly worse than on the preceding trials with the middle segment repeated. Thus there was some but not perfect positive transfer to the inverted segment, a result that would not be expected if they had been learning a very specific sequence of motor commands. This kind of transfer paradigm, in which simple metric transformations of highly practiced voluntary movement patterns are tested, should provide fruitful grounds for gaining further understanding of the nature of motor schema learning.

The Schema Instance and Its Perceptual Consequences

It is proposed, then, that a particular movement pattern, an instance, is selected from the generalized schema for movements of that particular class, such as signing one's name or drawing a circle, and it is the specific instance that actually gets translated into real movements. However, following the view put forth by Adams (1971), one further implication of the instance must be postulated. It is not enough that the instance is executed as a string of motor commands. A further consequence of the selection of an instance is that an image of the sensory consequences of actually producing that movement is also generated. Adams refers to this image as the "Perceptual Trace" and devotes substantial discussion to the way it is built up as a function of practice and to its importance as the basis for comparing expected sensory consequences with actual sensory consequences. Laszlo and Bairstow (1971) capture the same idea in their notion of a standard for comparison with actual feedback. It is the perceptual trace that makes possible the detection and, occasionally, the correction of errors in movement sequences prior to or in the absence of confirming knowledge of results about the success or failure of the pattern to achieve its goal.

Effects of Feedback Manipulation

Some implications of feedback were indicated in the description of models of tracking control and of models for the production of rapid, accurate simple movements, but these models represent a rather indirect approach to evaluation of the role of feedback in the conduct of a skill. More direct experimental approaches have been taken. Studies of delayed, distorted, and transformed feedback and attempts to eliminate all feedback are examples of these more direct approaches.

Experimental studies of the effect of delayed, distorted, and transformed feedback, many of which are summarized in Smith (1962), report the not surprising finding that the more degraded feedback is, the more degraded is the performance that results. For example, delayed speech (Yates, 1963), delayed handwriting (Van Bergeijk & David, 1959), and delayed tracking (Pew et al., 1967a) all produce a tendency toward repeated elements or stuttering and a stretching out or increased number of pauses in the motor sequence. These studies suffer from a difficulty of interpretation, however. While the authors are usually interested in the assessment of the effect of modifying one or another source of feedback, manipulation of that one not only degrades it, but also places it in conflict with the remaining undegraded sources. For example, studies of delayed auditory feedback from speech have not effectively eliminated the normal feedback from the speech musculature.

There are now a number of studies, many of which are reviewed in Taub and Berman (1968), that support the contention that in higher animals rudimentary movements can be performed in what appears to be the total absence of feedback from the periphery. The most recent and conclusive report is that of Taub, Perrella, and Barro (1973), who have shown that monkeys deafferented at birth and having their eyelids sewn closed are still able to locomote and can be trained in relatively precise hand to mouth coordination. Thus, acquisition of new responses was possible as well as sustained performance in the absence of peripheral feedback. There are at least two kinds of evidence that support the generalization of these results to man. First, there is Lashley's (1917) classic analysis of a patient with an unusual gunshot wound in the spine, which produced effective sensory anesthesia of the leg below the knee. He showed that the patient could produce movements of the limb with no peripheral feedback and could even make gross judgments of the relative sizes of the different movements that he produced.

Laszlo has used a blood-pressure cuff to eliminate sensory feedback by applying a compression block on the arm. She argues that the loss of blood circulation below the cuff for 20 minutes or so produces selective loss of the afferent feedback from the hand and reports that, at least for some subjects, tapping without visual feedback was possible "under the cuff" (Laszlo & Manning, 1970). These authors also argued that some improvement in tapping rate resulted from practice "under the cuff." Having served as a subject for this procedure, I must say the subjective effects are compelling, but I feel that Laszlo's evidence should be taken as supportive rather than definitive in light of the uncertainties of interpretation of exactly what musculature and receptors are affected and to what degree.

Feedback Levels for Goal-Oriented Movements

Feedback concerning the results of voluntary movements operate at many different levels of specificity. Verbal reports of the results of an activity are the most global and occupy the most peripheral position in the sense that their correspondence to neuromotor events is the least direct. Next most specific in the series and somewhat closer to neuromotor events are the exteroceptors, primarily vision and audition, followed by the proprioceptors, including labyrinthine sensation, as well as the information feedback from the muscles, joints, tendons, etc.

At the level above the proprioceptors I propose to consider some central representation of motor outflow—efferent signals that provide: an "Efferent Copy" (von Holst, 1954); the "Feeling of Innervation" (Lashley, 1917); a "Copy of the Command" (Anokhin, 1969); or James' "The Idea of an Action" (see Greenwald, 1970). Greenwald, following James, actually proposes that efferent signals representing the consequences of motor activity play an active role in movement production, going beyond their role as feedback.

Even taken simply as feedback, such a concept seems necessary to explain Lashley's finding of reportably different perceptions of active movement of the patient's deafferented lower leg, and Taub and Berman (1968) argue that something resembling efferent copy is needed to explain the deafferented monkey's acquisition of a new response. If he had no image of the movement he had just made, what is it he would compare with the expected consequences and modify on the next attempt?

Actually, these are largely default arguments: They postulate an explanation for results that are otherwise unexplainable, but there is also substantial direct empirical evidence in support of such a concept. At the physiological level Taub and Berman cite electrophysiological data of Chang (1955), Li (1958), and others for efferent collateral discharge flowing back to the cerebral cortex. At the behavioral level the converging operations that support the case for an efferent copy-like mechanism are summarized by Gyr (1972) in the context of his active theory of perception.

Returning now to the levels of feedback from which this digression began, it seems appropriate to consider efferent signals as the highest level of feedback that may be kept distinct in some way from the representation of a goal-oriented schema or plan of a movement. In the absence of all lower-level feedback it is sufficient for crude monitoring of the results of a motor act, but this is rather academic since movements are seldom produced under such deprived circumstances. The real importance of this efferent copy lies in its role in the communication of what string of motor commands was actually executed, even if further downstream, at a more peripheral level, the muscular results went awry. The experiment described in an earlier section in which the perceived inertia of the arm was manipulated could be thought of as a disturbance of the relationship between proprioceptive and efferent copy cues.

A Block-Diagram Summary of "Voluntary" Motor Control

With the introduction of the idea of multilevel feedback my discussion of the machinery out of which voluntary movements might be built is relatively complete. The processes involved might be summarized in the form of the very tentative block diagram of Fig. 9.[3] It captures ideas similar to Bernstein's (1967) scheme of "circular

---

[3]This representation was developed in discussion with J. I. Laszlo.

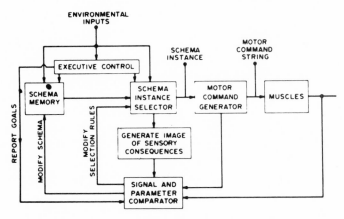

FIG. 9. Block diagram representing the essential components of a descriptive model of the performance of self-initiated movements.

control," of Anokhin's (1969) "afferent synthesis," and of Adams' (1971) closed-loop model.

The model postulates a Schema Memory as the generalized source of stored information about the organization of movements with respect to particular goals. When the stimulating conditions are such that a movement is motivated, then a specific instance is selected from the schema memory for execution. The particular instance selected depends intimately on the dynamic state of the subject and the environment at the time the selection is made. The magnitude or length of the instance depends on the predictability of the environment, and on the task demands of the movement.

A golf swing might be fully represented as an instance, whereas only the initial segments of a pole vaulter's trajectory might be formulated as an instance. The instance may be thought of as a stored representation of a path in space through which the members of the body will move. The schema instance exists in complete form at a single point in time. It is like a computer program waiting to be read.

The next stage in this hypothesized system is a translation of the stored program into a temporal string of motor commands. One can postulate that the timing scale factor of a planned movement is added at this point—the sequence can be speeded up or slowed down as a unit—and while we have some evidence that such scaling is possible (Armstrong, 1970), I certainly have no strong defense for placing the timing control at exactly this point in the sequence. Once a string of muscle commands has been formulated, all that remains is the activation of the muscles to produce a pattern of movement in space and time.

As Bernstein (1967), Anokhin (1969), and Adams (1971) emphasize, an essential component of the process is the Signal Comparator. It is here that Anokhin's afferent synthesis is focused. Whereas in the case of tracking, the source of signals to be compared was straightforward, now many highly interrelated signals come into play, and it is difficult to represent them all in a block diagram and even harder to differentiate them experimentally. First, there is information about the goal to be achieved, which comes from some higher-level executive program and can be considered one level of expected consequences. Depending on the nature of that goal, feedback from vision, audition, and proprioception may be relevant to evaluating whether the goal has been achieved. Then there is the perceptual trace, an image of the *expected* sensory consequences of the movement. This, in turn, may be compared with the actual sensory consequences. It is important to remember that the actual sensory consequences are represented at various levels of specificity, ranging from efferent copy to knowledge of results, and it must be postulated that the image of expected sensory consequences has a corresponding dimensionality, although Fig. 9 does not make this point explicit. It is equally difficult to delineate the results of this comparison operation. They fall into two main categories. First, given sufficient time, there are evaluative results that serve to modify the ongoing course of the movement pattern. Either lower-level corrective mechanisms may be brought into play, or modified schema instances might be initiated. Perhaps more important is the impact of the evaluation of the results of a movement on the course of generation of similar movements in the future.

At this time it appears to be impossible to delineate in any detail the nature of the changes brought about by experience, but they must include modifications to the generalized schema stored in memory (Adams' memory trace), modification to the interplay among environmental stimuli and the schema selection process, modification and increased specificity of the perceptual trace, and modification of the implementation of the motor command sequence so that the expected consequences and the actual consequences are brought into closer correspondence.

A practical example. It is illuminating to watch a mail clerk sorting packages for outgoing delivery. The clerk stands near a source of packages some 5–10 feet away from an array of perhaps 25 mailbags attached to a rectangular frame. The sorter examines each package, decides on its destination, and then makes a hefty toss to place it in the right mailbag. The novice has little initial success but the experienced sorter can hit the right bag virtually every time.

These clerks, I would argue, have built up a generalized schema for package tossing; however, they do not always stand in exactly the same place and no two packages are alike in weight, size, or shape. Thus the clerk selects an instance from the general schema in accordance with his location in relation to the bags, together with the initial conditions defined by the properties of the package. Note that both visual and proprioceptive properties are important in this case. He then initiates a temporal stream of commands that his muscles translate into a trajectory of his arm and the appropriate release point of the package. For some odd-shaped packages the orientation at the time of release is as important as the release velocity.

While it is certainly important, it is not sufficient to say that success or failure at hitting the right bag provides the knowledge of results required for improving the clerk's skill. According to the model proposed here information about the *expected* sensory consequences, and about the actual sensory consequences together with the success or failure of the movement pattern, all converge in the Comparator

Mechanism to produce the basis for modifications to the generalized schema, the instance selection rules, and the temporal implementation of the command sequence. In some cases the clerk, especially a highly practiced one, may be able to report a failure as the package leaves his hand. It seems likely that this kind of error detection depends on a lack of correspondence between the expected sensory consequences and the actual sensory consequences, even before the package trajectory is complete. It is based on acquiring a strong *a priori* association between successful patterns and their expected sensory consequences.

The viability of this distinction is supported by a study by Schmidt and White (1972) that was undertaken to test predictions of Adams' (1971) theory. Subjects were required to move a slider 24.1 cm in exactly 150 msec. The movements were initiated by the subject and follow-through beyond the 24.1-cm point was permitted. In addition to measuring the average absolute timing accuracy, the experimenter obtained the subject's *estimates* of movement duration as a measure of the accuracy of his perceptual trace.

Performance during the training phases measured by average absolute accuracy improved as a function of practice, but more importantly the correlation between a subject's estimate of his duration and the actual duration increased substantially, indicating the build-up of association between the successful movements and their expected sensory consequences. The fact that performance was maintained at about the same level even when knowledge of results was withdrawn, and that the level of correlation between estimated and actual error increased in this case, supports the idea that the relationship between expected and actual sensory consequences provides the error comparator with a useful source of information for the purpose of monitoring and adjusting the schema instance on subsequent trials. Schmidt and Wrisberg (1973), using a 66-cm, 200-msec slider movement, obtained similar results but failed to confirm the finding of sustained levels of timing accuracy under knowledge-of-results withdrawal. However, this failure could be attributed to providing insufficient practice prior to withdrawal on this more difficult task.

GENERAL ISSUES AND SUMMARY

The outline of this process-oriented view of skilled performance is now as complete as I can make it. If not wrong, the picture is surely incomplete. Especially with respect to voluntary movements, about all I have been able to do is organize our ignorance on the basis of logic, speculation, and some limited evidence. There are, however, general issues that I want to address from the perspectives presented here.

The question of what is a motor program and what do we mean by ''automating'' a movement are to me inseparable from a more global analysis of temporal and spatial organization. There is no level in the motor system at which I am willing to say, ''Here is where a motor program comes into play.'' As I see it, even the corrections initiated on a closed-loop basis by the error servomechanism discussed first constitute an elementary form of motor program. At that level all that is formulated is how far to move in the next instant in time. As the level of environmental predictability increases, so does the complexity and extent of movement sequences that are formulated as Gestalts or integral units. In the discussion of tracking periodic signals the concept of a parameter comparator was introduced. It can be thought of as one mediator of higher-level temporal organization. When following sinusoidal signals the subject focuses his attention on monitoring and controlling amplitude, frequency, and phase of the sine wave pattern, rather than on the position to be at the next instant in time. Thus we might say he has automated the process at a lower level and the sine wave pattern corresponds to another level of motor program, but the more important point is that the subject has shifted his perspective concerning the level of organization at which he is working. He is simply solving a different problem at a new level. Piano playing and typing are skilled activities that can carry this concept of parameter control to very high levels of organization indeed.

Similarly it would be easy to argue that a schema instance, as defined here, represents a genuine motor program, but again I see that as merely another locus of attention and organization in which the goal to be achieved takes precedence over the stimulus situation. Rather than requiring the subject to conform to a rigid input sequence he must instead formulate a motor act to accomplish a goal consistent with the stimulus conditions that exist at the time. As a function of practice the subject builds up more and more general schemata and higher-level goals on which to focus his attention and from which to evaluate success. One key to skill training is to provide knowledge of results consistent with the level of organization at which the subject is operating at each stage in the development of the skill.

The concept of a hierarchy of levels of organization in motor skills dates back to Bryan and Harter (1899) and their analysis of telegraphic signal transmission skills. It includes Book's (1908) work on typewriting and is captured effectively by Miller, Galanter, and Pribram (1960). These authors also emphasize the generality of the concept for virtually all kinds of behavior. The idea was further supported empirically in my doctoral thesis (Pew, 1966) in which subjects performed a task requiring rapid systematic alternation of key responses in order to control the movement of a target. Early in practice they responded point by point in time, waiting for the result from one response before initiating the next one. After several days of practice they began responding with much shorter interresponse times, and the pattern of their responses revealed the development among different subjects of two higher-level strategies, one of them a rather sophisticated temporal modulation strategy to promote more efficient performance. I infer from these subjects' performance, and I believe the result to be general, that they were not operating completely open-loop; they were not ignoring feedback in order to impose a structure on their skill but rather were using feedback to monitor and control their performance at a level removed from the representation of individual key strokes.

Proponents of the concept of a motor program appeal to the now popular evidence for triggered-off motor sequences in lower animals such as locusts (Wilson, 1972) or in the development of bird songs (Nottebohm, 1970). It is interesting that these results are consonant with the idea of a memory schema, a rather high level of sophistication in terms of the hierarchy of control levels I have described here, but at the same time they imply a nonadaptive rigid structure to the resultant program, which is only rarely observed in man. The human swallow reflex is the closest human equivalent. At the level of animal behavior, however, Tinbergen (1951) points out one example that is more consistent with the multilevel representation of skills:[4]

> The grey lag goose reacts to eggs that have rolled out of the nest by stretching the neck towards it, bringing the bill behind the egg and with careful balancing movements rolling it back into the nest. The innate releasing mechanism of this response reacts to relatively few sign stimuli; objects of very different shape and size, provided they have a rounded contour, release it. In spite of the balancing movements the bird sometimes loses control of the egg and then the egg slips sideways. In this case the egg-rolling movement does not always break off, but it may be completed, very much as if it were a vacuum activity. If this happens, the sideways balancing movements are absent. This indicates that the balancing movements are dependent on continuous stimulation from the egg, probably of a tactile nature, while the other component, a movement in the median plane, is not dependent on continuous stimulation but, once released, runs its full course [p. 84].

The stereotyped motion coaxing the egg back into the nest is representative of the nonadaptive program usually associated with lower animals. However, the lateral balancing movements are not. It appears that they were sensitive to tactile response-produced feedback and are representative of the servo-level corrective control I have described in the early pages of this chapter. Here, then, is a clear example of multilevel control typical of human skilled performance manifest in the grey lag goose.

One definition of a motor program or "automation" of a movement sequence implies that "automation" releases the requirement for attention to the execution of a skilled act. This definition is operationalized in the form of a time-sharing paradigm in which one attempts to assess the change in attention requirements of the skill in question as it is being practiced by measuring the improvement in performance on a subsidiary task performed concurrently (Bahrick & Shelley, 1958). While this may be realistic for certain kinds of tasks for which adequate performance can be produced at restricted levels of control, I do not believe it to be a general result. Rather it seems likely that practice shifts the level of organization at which attention is focused, but does not in principle reduce the task demands. The piano player who is focusing on the level of emotional communication via his music may not show performance differences as reflected in measures of keying accuracy, but an extra task would surely influence his ability to communicate an emotional interpretation of his piece, as reflected by subtle shifts in the temporal or intonational structure of his performance.

Even at the level of a tracking task, Pew and Wickens (Pew, 1974) found in the study of performance of repeated and nonrepeated sequences that the addition of a simple memory task produced an approximately equal increase in error score for the repeated and nonrepeated segments at three different points during a 16-hour period of practice, even though performance on the repeated segment was as much as 28% better than on its random counterpart.

[4]The author is indebted to R. J. Jagacinski for pointing out this example.

Underlying this discussion of attention to various levels of a hierarchy of control processes is the tacit assumption that a subject's attentional capacity is limited and cannot be focused on several levels of control at once. While the fundamental information-processing assumption of a limited-capacity channel has not been a central concept from which my discussion of skills has been derived, it should certainly be clear that the proposal of specific control loops leans heavily on the assumption that an individual cannot, or at least does not choose to, operate at all levels in parallel.

Many of the chapters that follow (see particularly Pachella, Chapter 2, Townsend, Chapter 4, and Kantowitz, Chapter 3) raise the question of whether in fact a model that assumes limited capacity is viable and, if so, in which information-processing stages that capacity limit imposes its constraint. An analysis of the attentional demands of the kinds of processes and control modes described here could prove to be a fruitful direction, leading to insights about the processes themselves, as it has been in understanding more standard information-processing stages such as stimulus encoding or response selection (Posner & Boies, 1971). Thus far, however, there is little to say about attention demands of movement control processes beyond Ells' (1969) analysis showing somewhat decreasing attention demand as a movement progresses and the possibility of a further involvement of attention in monitoring the result of a movement.

A Tempting Synthesis

The block diagrams of Figs. 8 and 9 have been presented separately because they are complicated enough as they are. While a great deal of detail remains to be worked out, the main thrust of this chapter is that there is nothing incompatible among the representations of inner-loop control, higher-order tracking control, and the formulation and execution of so-called voluntary movements. Rather, as was noted at the beginning, we should think of a continuum of levels of control and feedback, that the signal comparator operates at different levels at different times, and can even operate at different levels at the same time. What we observe in human skilled behavior is the rich intermingling of these various levels of control as a function of the task demands, the state of learning of the subject, and the constraints imposed on the task and the subject by the environment. The job of the researcher is different, depending on the level of analysis in which he is interested, but a general theory of skill acquisition will only result from consideration of all the ramifications of this kind of multilevel process-oriented description of skilled performance.

REFERENCES

Adams, J. A. A closed-loop theory of motor learning. *Journal of Motor Behavior*, 1971, **3**, 111–150.
Anokhin, P. K. Cybernetics and the integrative activity of the brain. In M. Cole & I. Maltzman (Eds.), *A handbook of contemporary Soviet psychology.* New York: Basic Books, 1969.
Armstrong, T. R. Training for the production of memorized movement patterns. (Tech. Rep. No. 26) Ann Arbor: University of Michigan, Human Performance Center, 1970.

Bahrick, H. P., & Shelly, C. Time-sharing as an index of automatization. *Journal of Experimental Psychology*, 1958, **56**, 288–293.

Bartlett, F. C. *Thinking: An experimental and social study.* London: Allen & Unwin, 1958.

Beggs, W. D. A., & Howarth, C. I. Movement control in a repetitive motor task. *Nature*, 1970, **225**, 752–753.

Bernstein, N. *The co-ordination and regulation of movements.* Oxford: Pergamon Press, 1967.

Bilodeau, E. A. (Ed.), *Acquisition of skill.* New York: Academic Press, 1966.

Book, W. F. *The psychology of skill.* Missoula: Montana Press, 1908.

Broadbent, D. E. *Decision and stress.* New York: Academic Press, 1971.

Bryan, W. L., & Harter, N. Studies on the telegraphic language: The acquisition of a hierarchy of habits. *Psychological Review*, 1899, **6**, 345–375.

Chang, H. T. Activation of internuncial neurons through collaterals of pyramidal fibers at cortical level. *Journal of Neurophysiology*, 1955, **18**, 452–471.

Chernikoff, R., & Taylor, F. V. Reaction time to kinesthetic stimulation resulting from sudden arm displacement. *Journal of Experimental Psychology*, 1952, **43**, 1–8.

Craik, K. J. W. Theory of the human operator in control systems. I. The operator as an engineering system. *British Journal of Psychology*, 1947, **38**, 56–61.

Crossman, E. R. F. W. The information capacity of the human motor system in pursuit tracking. *Quarterly Journal of Experimental Psychology*, 1960, **12**, 1–16.

Crossman, E. R. F. W., & Goodeve, P. J. Feedback control of hand-movement and Fitts' Law. Paper presented at the Experimental Psychology Society, July, 1963.

Elkind, J. I. Characteristics of simple manual control systems. (Report III) Lexington, Mass.: MIT Lincoln Laboratories, 1956.

Ells, J. G. Attentional requirements of movement control. Unpublished doctoral dissertation, The University of Oregon, 1969.

Evarts, E. V. Motor cortex reflexes associated with learned movement. *Science*, 1973, **179**, 501–503.

Fitts, P. M. The information capacity of the human motor system in controlling the amplitude of movement. *Journal of Experimental Psychology*, 1954, **47**, 381–391.

Fitts, P. M., & Peterson, J. R. Information capacity of discrete motor responses. *Journal of Experimental Psychology*, 1964, **67**, 103–112.

Fitts, P. M., & Radford, B. K. Information capacity of discrete motor responses under different cognitive sets. *Journal of Experimental Psychology*, 1966, **71**, 475–482.

Frost, G. Man-machine dynamics. In H. P. van Cott & R. G. Kinkade (Eds.), *Human engineering guide to equipment design.* (Rev. ed.) Washington, D.C.: U.S. Government Printing Office, 1972.

Gibbs, C. B. Servo-control systems in organisms and the transfer of skill. In D. Legge (Ed.), *Skills.* Middlesex, England: Penguin Books, 1970.

Greenwald, A. G. Sensory feedback mechanisms in performance control: With special reference to the ideo-motor mechanism. *Psychological Review*, 1970, **77**, 73–99.

Gyr, J. W. Is a theory of direct visual perception adequate? *Psychological Bulletin*, 1972, **77**, 246–261.

Herzog, J. H. Manual control using the matched manipulator control technique. *IEEE Transactions on Man-Machine Systems*, 1968, **MMS-9**, 56–60.

Houk, J., & Henneman, F. Feedback control of skeletal muscles. *Brain Research*, 1967, **5**, 433–451.

Howarth, C. I., Beggs, W. D. A., & Bowden, J. The accuracy of aiming at a target: Some further evidence for intermittent control. *Acta Psychologica*, 1971, **36**, 171–177.

Johnson, G. C. Human operator performance in preview tracking. Unpublished doctoral dissertation, University of California, Berkeley, 1972.

Jordan, T. C. Characteristics of visual and proprioceptive response times in the learning of a motor skill. *Quarterly Journal of Experimental Psychology*, 1972, **24**, 536–543.

Keele, S. W. Movement control in skilled motor performance. *Psychological Bulletin*, 1968, **70**, 387–403.

Keele, S. W. *Attention and human performance.* Pacific Palisades, Cal.: Goodyear, 1973.

Keele, S. W., & Posner, M. I. Processing visual feedback in rapid movements. *Journal of Experimental Psychology*, 1968, **77**, 155–158.

Kelley, C. R. *Manual and automatic control*. New York: Wiley, 1968.

Krendel, E. S., & McRuer, D. T. A servomechanisms approach to skill development. *Journal of the Franklin Institute*, 1960, **269**, 24–42.

Krendel, E. S., & McRuer, D.T. Psychological and physiological skill development—a control engineering model. In, *Proceedings of the Fourth Annual NASA-University Conference on Manual Control*. (NASA SP-192) Ann Arbor, Michigan, 1968.

Langolf, G. D. Human motor performance in precise microscopic work—development of standard data for microscopic assembly work. Unpublished doctoral dissertation, University of Michigan, 1973.

Lashley, K. S. The accuracy of movement in the absence of excitation from the moving organ. *American Journal of Physiology*, 1917, **43**, 169– 194.

Laszlo. J. I., & Bairstow, P. J. Accuracy of movement, peripheral feedback and efference copy. *Journal of Motor Behavior*, 1971, **3**, 241–252.

Laszlo, J. I., & Manning, L. C. The role of motor programming, command and standard in the central control of skilled movement. *Journal of Motor Behavior*, 1970, **2**, 111–124.

Lemay, L. P., & Westcott, J. H. The simulation of human operator tracking using an intermittent model. Paper presented at the International Congress on Human Factors in Electronics, Long Beach, California, May, 1962.

Li, C. L. Activity of interneurons in the motor cortex. In H. H. Jasper, L. D. Proctor, R. S. Knighton, W. C. Norsbay, & R. T. Costello (Eds.), *Reticular formation of the brain*. Boston: Little, Brown, 1958.

Magdaleno, R. E., Jex, H. R., & Johnson, W. A. Tracking quasi-predictable displays: Subjective predictability gradations, pilot models for periodic and narrow band inputs. In *Proceedings of the Fifth Annual NASA-University Conference on Manual Control*. (NASA SP-215), 391–428, 1970.

McRuer, D. T., & Jex, H. R. A review of quasi-linear pilot models. *IEEE Transactions of Human Factors in Electronics*, 1967, HFE-8, 231–249.

McRuer, D. T., Magdaleno, R. E., & Moore, G. P. Neuromuscular actuation system models. *IEEE Transactions on Man-Machine Systems*, 1968, MMS-9, 61–71.

Miller, G. A., Galanter, E., & Pribram, K. H. *Plans and the structure of behavior*. New York: Holt, Rinehart & Winston, 1960.

Neisser, U. *Cognitive psychology*. New York: Appleton-Century-Crofts, 1967.

Noble, M., & Trumbo, D. The organization of skilled response. *Organizational Behavior and Human Performance*, 1967, **2**, 1–25.

Nottebohm, F. Ontogeny of bird song. *Science*, 1970, **167**, 950– 956.

Notterman, J. M., & Page, D. E. Evaluation of mathematically equivalent tracking systems. *Perceptual and Motor Skills*, 1962, **15**, 683–716.

Pew, R. W. Acquisition of hierarchical control over the temporal organization of a skill. *Journal of Experimental Psychology*, 1966, **71**, 764–771.

Pew, R. W. Toward a process-oriented theory of human skilled performance. *Journal of Motor Behavior*, 1970, **11**, 8–24.

Pew, R. W. Levels of analysis in motor control. *Brain Research*, 1974, **71**, 393–400.

Pew, R. W., Duffendack, J. C., & Fensch, L. K. Temporal limitations in human motor control. Paper presented at the Eighth Annual Meeting of the Psychonomic Society, Chicago, October, 1967. (a)

Pew, R. W., Duffendack, J. C., & Fensch, L. K. Sine-wave tracking revisited. *IEEE Transactions on Human Factors in Electronics*, 1967, HFE-8, 130–134. (b)

Pew, R. W., & Rupp, G. L. Two quantitative measures of skill development. *Journal of Experimental Psychology*, 1971, **90**, 1–7.

Posner, M. I., & Boies, S. J. Components of attention. *Psychological Review*, 1971, **78**, 391–408.

Posner, M. I., & Keele, S. W. On the genesis of abstract ideas. *Journal of Experimental Psychology*, 1968, **77**, 353–363.

Posner, M. I., & Keele, S. W. Retention of abstract ideas. *Journal of Experimental Psychology*, 1970, **83**, 304–308.

Poulton, E. C. Perceptual anticipation in tracking with one-pointer and two-pointer displays. *British Journal of Psychology*, 1952, **43**, 222–229.

Poulton, E. C. Eye-hand span in simple serial tasks. *Journal of Experimental Psychology*, 1954, **47**, 403–410.

Poulton, E. C. Tracking behavior. In E. A. Bilodeau (Ed.), *Acquisition of skill*. New York: Academic Press, 1966.

Rashbass, C. The relationship between saccadic and smooth tracking eye movements. *Journal of Physiology*, 1961, **159**, 326–338.

Schmidt, R. A., & White, J. L. Evidence for an error detection mechanism in motor skills: A test of Adams' closed-loop theory. *Journal of Motor Behavior*, 1972, **4**, 143–154.

Schmidt, R. A., & Wrisberg, C. A. Further tests of Adams' closed-loop theory: Response-produced feedback and the error detection mechanism. *Journal of Motor Behavior*, 1973, **5**, 155–164.

Smith, K. U. *Delayed sensory feedback and behavior*. Philadelphia: Saunders, 1962.

Stelmach, G. E. Retention of motor skills. In J. H. Wilmore (Ed.), *Reviews of exercise and sports sciences*. Vol. II. New York: Academic Press, 1974.

Taub, E., & Berman, A. J. Movement and learning in the absence of sensory feedback. In S. J. Freedman (Ed.), *The neuropsychology of spatially oriented behavior*. Homewood, Ill.: Dorsey, 1968.

Taub, E., Perrella, P., & Barro, G. Behavioral development after forelimb deafferentation with and without blinding. *Science*, 1973, **181**, 959–960.

Tinbergen, N. *The study of instinct*. London: Oxford University Press, 1951.

Van Bergeijk, W. A., & David, E. E. Delayed handwriting. *Perceptual Motor Skills*, 1959, **9**, 347–357.

Vince, M. A. Corrective movements in a pursuit task. *Quarterly Journal of Experimental Psychology*, 1948, **1**, 85–103.

von Holst, E. Relations between the central nervous system and the peripheral organs. *British Journal of Animal Behavior*, 1954, **2**, 89–94.

Weir, D. H., & McRuer, D. T. Dynamics of driver/vehicle steering control. *Automatica*, 1970, **6**, 87–98.

Welford, A. T. *Fundamentals of skill*. London: Methuen, 1968.

Wilde, R. W., & Westcott, J. H. The characteristics of the human operator engaged in a tracking task. *Automatica*, 1963, **1**, 5–19.

Wilson, D. M. Genetic and sensory mechanisms for locomotion and orientation in animals. *American Scientist*, 1961, **60**, 358–365.

Woodworth, R. S. The accuracy of voluntary movement. *Psychological Review*, 1899, **3** (2, Whole No. 13).

Yates, A. J. Delayed auditory feedback. *Psychological Bulletin*, 1963, **60**, 213–232.

Young, L. R., Forster, J. D., & Van Houtte, N. A revised stochastic sampled-data model for eye tracking movements. In *Proceedings of the Fourth Annual NASA-University Conference on Manual Control*. (NASA SP-192), 489–502, 1968.

2
THE INTERPRETATION OF REACTION TIME IN INFORMATION-PROCESSING RESEARCH[1]

Robert G. Pachella
The University of Michigan

INTRODUCTION

Reaction time measures have become increasingly prevalent in human information-processing research. This increased use over the past few years has taken two distinct forms. First, a large number of experiments utilizing reaction time as the major dependent variable have appeared in the literature on substantive psychological problems. Included among these problems are such topics as sensory coding and selective attention, the retrieval of information from long- and short-term memory, psychological refractoriness, parallel and serial information processing, the psychological representation of semantic and logical relations, and the selection and execution of responses. Indeed, reaction time has become about as common a dependent variable as there is in human experimental psychology.

The goal of this substantive research has been to understand basic psychological processes. In this endeavor, reaction time measures have sometimes been used as much for convenience as for any particular theoretical purpose. Deriving predictions about the duration of psychological processes from the theoretical models describing such processes has become a common practice. These derivations seemingly involve only a few straightforward assumptions that link the duration of a process to what it accomplishes. However, as intuitive as these assumptions seem, the *implicit* acceptance of them on the part of many researchers has limited the potential contribution of their work. Without the explicit statement of how reaction time is related to the

[1]The preparation of this chapter was supported by the Advanced Research Projects Agency, United States Department of Defense and monitored by the United States Air Force Office of Scientific Research, under Contract F44620-72-C-0019 with The University of Michigan's Human Performance Center. The author would like to acknowledge the helpful conversations and correspondence with J. Lappin, R. W. Pew, S. Sternberg, R. G. Swensson, and E. A. C. Thomas.

ongoing process, it is often difficult to relate the observed variation in the obtained reaction times to the informational transformations and manipulations that are supposed to be going on in the hypothesized processing network. In other words, it is not always obvious how information about process durations is psychologically meaningful. Deese (1969), for example, expressing some doubts about contemporary cognitive psychology, has observed that, "We have insisted upon the measurement of behavior to the extent that most of the things we observe in experiments have no relevance for the process of thinking, other than the empty observation that thinking, like most processes, takes a measurable amount of time [p. 518]." Thus, there is a need to examine explicitly the assumptions upon which the use of reaction time measures in substantive research is founded.

A second area of research, also making use of reaction time measures, has concerned itself more directly with the study of reaction time *per se*. This kind of research has generally been concerned with discovering the conditions and parameters that produce and account for variation in reaction time without regard for specific experimental paradigms and substantive problems. Such factors as the distribution of stimuli (e.g., the number, frequency, and presentation order of specific stimuli), the distribution of responses, the intertrial intervals, and the relative emphasis of speed vs. accuracy have all been shown to have systematic effects on reaction time in various different experimental paradigms.

This class of research has been seen by some investigators to be of limited value to the class of research on substantive issues. To some extent, work such as this has been considered methodological in nature. It has attempted to discover the conditions and procedures under which reaction time measures can be collected most reliably and interpreted most reasonably. Until recently, parameters that were known to affect reaction time *per se* were thought to be artifacts to be removed from experiments on problems of substance in which reaction time was simply being used as a dependent variable. Some psychologists have actually found it disquieting that there exist researchers who seem to have actively taken up the study of a dependent variable *per se* and its associated experimental artifacts. In fact, one psychologist, who was studying problems of human memory, was once asked by a reaction time researcher to describe his own work; he claimed sarcastically that he was engaged in the study of "percent correct." The point, of course, is that reaction time, like percent correct, is simply a measure. It is neither a process nor a mechanism, and thus some people feel it should not be an object of direct attention. Nevertheless, given the prevalence of reaction time measures in contemporary experimental work, it is clear that what is known about reaction time *per se* should be related to reaction time as it is used as a dependent variable.

The purpose, then, of this chapter will be to examine some reaction time research. It is not intended as a review of literature about particular substantive issues, but rather it is an attempt to extract from that literature the manner in which reaction time measures have been used to draw inferences about psychological processes. Furthermore, an attempt will be made to examine some of the assumptions and principles upon which the interpretation of reaction time measurement is based. It is hoped that the juxtaposition of these sets of issues will lead to the more careful use and interpretation of reaction time measures in the understanding of human information processing.

The Use of Reaction Time as a Dependent Variable

To some extent the prevalence of reaction time measures over the past few years can be traced to the concurrent resurgence of interest in cognitive psychology. In contrast to earlier, more behavioristic approaches, modern cognitive psychology can be characterized as the study of events that *cannot* be directly observed. The events of interest to a cognitive psychologist usually take place when the subject is not engaged in any overt activity. They are events that often do not have any overt behavioral component. Thus, reaction time is often chosen as a dependent variable by default: There simply isn't much else that can be measured.

It is true, of course, that one can make inferences about unobservable mental events by studying subsequent behavior that results from or is dependent upon this cognitive activity. Much cognitive research is done in this manner. However, these indirect procedures are not always useful in situations where a subject is not making a lot of errors or where experimental conditions have not drastically degraded performance. The only property of mental events that can be studied directly, in the intact organism, *while* the events are taking place, is their duration.

A second and perhaps more important consideration accounting for the popularity of reaction time measures is the indisputable nature of time as a meaningful quantity. It is often the case that dependent variables in psychology are only arbitrarily related to the underlying construct for which they are a measure. For example, an investigator interested in the amount of learning that can be produced by some experimental manipulation might choose the percentage of correct items on a posttest as his dependent variable. Percent correct in this case is only a surrogate for the real variable of interest, ''amount of learning.'' Any monotonic transformation of percent correct would likely do as well. By contrast, one would not arbitrarily transform the time scale, because time itself is directly meaningful. The events being studied are considered to be filling real time, and thus real time *is* the variable of interest.

This point takes on particular significance if the independent variables in an experiment interact in a statistical sense, that is, if the effect of one independent variable is fundamentally changed, as a function of the level of some other independent variable. For the purposes of constructing theories, multifactor experiments that test for the existence of such interactions have more efficacy than experiments testing the simple effects of individual variables. However, the interpretation of data from multifactor experiments is contingent upon the scalability of the dependent variable. Many statistical interactions can be either produced or eliminated by a suitable monotonic transformation of the dependent variable. Thus, given the inviolable character of reaction time against such arbitrary rescaling, the interpretation of such interactions or lack thereof, when obtained, is that much more secure.

Reaction Time as Commonly Defined

What is it that is measured when the dependent variable in an experiment is reaction time? This question should be kept distinct, for the moment, from the related question of how reaction times are interpreted once they are obtained. The question here concerns simply how reaction times are obtained, what they mean in an operational sense.

Reaction time most typically is defined as the interval between the presentation of a stimulus to a subject and the subject's response. More operationally stated, this interval is usually measured from the *onset* of the stimulus presentation to the *initiation* of the subject's response. Certain definitional problems must be solved in order to measure reaction time in this way. To begin with, the constitution of a stimulus presentation and, thus, the definition of its onset, is not always psychologically obvious. For example, auditory and visual stimuli have fundamentally different temporal characteristics in the way in which they can be presented; auditory stimuli must necessarily be spread out in time, while visual stimuli can, in principle, be presented instantaneously. Further, occasionally a stimulus presentation will consist of a discrete, temporal sequence of items. In this case reaction time is measured, operationally, from the onset of the last item. In a more functional sense, however, defining "stimulus presentation" in this manner may be somewhat dubious, especially when such a sequential presentation is compared to one in which all of the items are presented simultaneously.

Similar problems exist at the response end of the reaction time interval. Occasionally, the initiation of a response is also not well defined. Variability in reaction time can be obtained strictly as a function of a response's susceptibility to physical measurement. For example, different initial phonemes in a vocal response will take differential amounts of time to activate a voice key. Furthermore, the amount of time it takes to *initiate* a response is not always free of the effects of response characteristics, such as response length or complexity, which temporally follow the initiation of the response. Thus, the operational definition of reaction time as the interval between the onset of the stimulus and the initiation of a response is not always a simple matter: It is intimately linked to whatever operational definitions are supplied to the terms "stimulus" and "response." To the extent that these operational procedures become confounded with experimental conditions, the further interpretation of the obtained reaction times is limited.

There is another more subtle procedural question involved in defining the reaction time interval. It is more subtle because it involves the intentions of the experimental subject. Reaction times are generally assumed, on the basis of either explicit or implicit instructions, to be generated under conditions where the subject is trying to minimize his response time. It is generally assumed that the subject in a reaction time experiment waits for the stimulus to be presented, does whatever he has to do in his usual manner in order to respond correctly, and then responds immediately. In other words, the subject is not rushing his response, nor is he wasting any time: Reaction time is taken to be the minimum amount of time needed by the subject in order to produce a correct response.

Since instructions to the subject are not the type of procedure that always produce the desired result, the obtained reaction times sometimes require *post hoc* editing. These procedures consist of eliminating from the data those responses that for one reason or another seem out of the ordinary, and while it is likely that such editing procedures are often carried out for superstitious reasons, they nevertheless tend to have a definitional effect. That is, the data that are most typically *reported* in experiments utilizing reaction time as the dependent variable are from the responses that seem most likely to represent the minimum intervals needed by subjects to produce correct responses. For example, very fast responses are occasionally eliminated on the grounds that they represent "anticipation" responses that seem to have been initiated without the subject strictly waiting for the stimulus to appear. Sometimes extremely slow responses are eliminated. This can be accomplished by simply removing responses that are longer than some predetermined criterion, or by reporting the *median* reaction time for a condition. This will tend to eliminate the effect of the generally positively-skewed tail of a reaction time distribution.

While the practice of removing responses from data on the basis of their being "too fast" or "too slow" is perhaps arbitrary, a more common practice, the removal of error responses, has seemed somewhat more justifiable. This is because these trials are well-defined and are clearly in violation of the basic definition of reaction time. A trial on which an error is made is apparently the result of activity that is not related to the process under investigation; clearly, if the subject has made an error he has done something out of the ordinary on that trial. Thus, investigators generally examine and report only the reaction times resulting from correct responses.

Whether such editing of experimental data can actually be justified will be the focus of later discussion. Nevertheless, in practice, the reaction times that are reported in experimental literature generally conform to the above requirements and thus serve as the basis for any further theoretical interpretations that may be called for in an experiment.

EXPERIMENTAL LOGIC AND REACTION TIME MEASURES

Aside from questions about the conditions under which reaction time measures are obtained, the further interpretation of reaction time is dependent upon the experimental logic involved in specific situations. For example, experimenters often desire to interpret the reaction times obtained in an experiment as "the time to recognize," "the time to deduce," "decision time," or "the time to search memory." In order to allow any of these specific interpretations, an experiment must employ a design that is suitable to the conclusion that the obtained variation in reaction time is related to the variation in the duration of the particular mental process under study. Since most of these processes are unobserved and mediational, it is almost always necessary to employ the kind of experimental designs classified by Garner, Hake, and Eriksen (1956) as converging operations: They must include several conditions, none of which uniquely identify the effect of the process under study, but which taken together define such an effect.

Of course, all of the general principles of experimental design and deductive logic are applicable when reaction time is a dependent variable. However, at present two commonly used types of converging operations have particular significance for information-processing research. These are the Subtraction Method and the Additive Factor Method, which will be discussed in some detail below. Each of these methods can be contrasted with a more molar approach to experimentation in which obtained reaction times are of interest essentially without further interpretation. That is, whereas the methods to be described below have as their purpose the subdividing of the time interval between stimulus and response into mediational effects, the molar approach takes the entire interval as its unit of interest. It is, for example, a suitable approach in situations where the immediate function of an experiment is to discover how long it takes to perform some relatively well-defined perceptual-motor task. In such cases converging operations are hardly necessary. Thus, while such an approach is of great value to some areas of research (e.g., applied problems), it is of only marginal significance to information-processing research that attempts to investigate the mental processes intervening between a stimulus and a response.

The Subtraction Method

One of the problems confronting an information-processing researcher regarding the interpretation of reaction time measures is the attribution of the effect of some experimental manipulation to a particular mediating process. This is a problem because a reaction time interval always involves other processes besides the one of interest. The Subtraction Method is a set of converging operations that is commonly used, often without being labeled as such, to eliminate this problem. When applicable, it allows for the isolation of a mediating process and the measurement of its duration. The method is applicable when the performance of an experimental task involves the sequential action of a series of discrete mental events. In order to measure the duration of one of these mental events, the reaction time for an experimental task containing the event as a subprocess is compared to that for a comparison task that differs from the experimental task only by the deletion of the process of interest. In other words, the comparison task must involve all of the processes contained in the experimental task, except for the process that is to be isolated. The difference in reaction time for these two conditions will then be equal to the duration of the isolated process. Thus, if an experimenter is interested in the effect of an independent variable on the duration of a particular mental process, he needs only to compare the difference obtained between an experimental and comparison condition of the type indicated above as a function of the independent variable.

A recent experiment by Eriksen, Pollack, and Montague (1970) illustrates the application of this reasoning particularly well. These investigators were interested in studying the processes involved in the encoding of visually presented words. The experimental task involved having subjects simply name stimulus words that were presented one at a time. Reaction time was measured from the onset of a stimulus word to the *initiation* of the vocal response naming the word. That is, the first sound emitted in making the response triggered a voice key that terminated the reaction time interval. The independent variable of interest was the length, in syllables, of the stimulus word. The results showed that one-syllable words could be named faster than three-syllable words.

This seemingly straightforward result might have been taken at face value to indicate that it takes more time to *encode* longer words. The problem with this interpretation is that it equates "reaction time" with "encoding time," and this is not strictly correct. The naming task described above must involve several distinct operations. For one, the stimulus word must be encoded. This is the process in which Eriksen, Pollack, and Montague were interested. Additionally, the response, vocalizing the stimulus word's name, must be performed. Variability in reaction time, due to the effect of the length of the stimulus word on the process of executing the response, is irrelevant to the question of the effect of word length on encoding time. Note that it makes no difference that reaction time was measured to the *initiation* of the response. This is because it may simply take longer to *initiate* a longer word than a shorter one. In other words, it is possible that it may take no longer to encode perceptually a three-syllable word than a one-syllable word; it may only take longer to initiate a three-syllable response than a one-syllable response.

In order to assess this possibility, Eriksen et al. (1970) applied the Subtraction Method. A comparison task was constructed in which the subject was presented with a stimulus word. He did not respond to the stimulus word directly, however; he merely encoded it. Following a short time interval, a light was presented to the subject. The subject responded to this stimulus light by emitting the name of the encoded word. Reaction time in this condition was measured from the onset of the stimulus light to the initiation of the vocalized response. Thus, this reaction time interval involved everything the interval in the experimental task involved except for the encoding of the stimulus word. In this comparison condition there was no difference in reaction time for one- vs. three-syllable responses. Therefore, the authors concluded that the entire difference obtained in the experimental condition could be attributed to the perceptual encoding of the stimulus.

Criticism of the Subtraction Method

The conclusions drawn by Eriksen et al. are dependent upon the applicability of the Subtraction Method. To the extent that general criticisms can be levied against this method their conclusions must suffer. At least two general criticisms have been levied.

First, the Subtraction Method begs one of the most fundamental questions underlying information-processing research, namely, the description of the mental events involved in an experimental task. The starting point for the application of the method is a relatively sophisticated one: In order to construct a comparison task, one must already know the sequence of events that transpire between stimulus and response. Such sophisticated knowledge is rarely available. Rather, it is more often the case that the structure of the mental events is presented with only logical or intuitive (as opposed to empirical) justification. Obviously, the conclusions reached on the basis of the application of the method can then be no stronger than the substantiation of the initial conceptualization of the experimental task. Thus the experiment by Eriksen et al. purports to show the effect of word length on stimulus encoding, but it has presupposed with only the meagerest of justifications the existence of such a process and its independence from response execution. This general class of criticism will be discussed in greater detail below in connection with the Additive Factor Method.

A second general criticism of the Subtraction Method concerns the comparability of the experimental and comparison tasks, or as Sternberg (1969b) has called it, the assumption of pure insertion. This refers to the assumption that it is possible to delete (or insert) completely mental events from an information-processing task without changing the nature of the other constituent mental operations. In order for the difference in reaction time between the experimental and comparison task to represent meaningfully the duration of an isolated process, all of the other processes common to both tasks have to be strictly comparable. For example, in order to accept the conclusion of Eriksen et al., that the effects of word length are localized in the encoding process, it must be assumed that the response execution processes for the two tasks in their experiment are identical. There is nothing in the application of the method itself, or in the data collected therefrom, that can justify this assumption.

A recent series of experiments by Egeth and his colleagues (Egeth, Atkinson, Gilmore, & Marcus, 1973; Egeth & Blecker, 1971; Egeth, Jonides, & Wall, 1972; Egeth, Marcus, & Bevan, 1972) have demonstrated the importance of this issue. These experiments have utilized subtractive logic for ostensibly methodological purposes. They have employed what are known as ''C-reactions'' in order to simplify their experimental tasks from the subject's point of view, thereby reducing extraneous variability and thus requiring less data per subject in order to produce stable results.

A C-reaction calls on a subject to respond as quickly as he can when a stimulus from a particular class is presented, and not to respond if any other stimulus is presented. This can be contrasted to the more common practice of having the subject execute a unique, overt response for each potential class of stimuli used in an experiment. For example, in a commonly used experimental task subjects are presented with pairs of letters. They are to judge whether the letters are the same or different. Common practice, utilizing manual responses, would assign ''same'' responses to the index finger of one hand and ''different'' responses to the index finger of the other hand. The utilization of a C-reaction makes response type (i.e., same vs. different) a ''between subjects'' variable. That is, each subject makes only one response. Some subjects respond only on same trials, not responding at all on different trials, and other subjects respond in the opposite manner.

Egeth's argument runs as follows[2]: In the above example, for instance, subjects must decide whether the presented letters are the same or different. It is this decision process that is of interest to most cognitive psychologists. However, in the usual experimental setup, after noting whether the letters are the same or different, the subject must remember which response to make for same stimuli and which response to make for different stimuli. Since this assignment is arbitrary, it must be learned, and this learning is reflected in the amount of practice necessary in order for a subject to produce stable data. Furthermore, variability in the produced reaction times due to

---

[2]Egeth has made this argument only by way of very informal personal communication with the author. It is reconstructed here for pedagogical purposes and should not be taken as a formal position on Egeth's part.

deciding what response to make is not relevant to the process of interest — deciding whether the letters are the same or different. On top of all this, subjects undoubtedly make errors in this task, not because they have misclassified the stimulus letters, but because once they have classified the letters they have executed the wrong response. With the C-reaction, once the stimulus pair is classified as the same or different, the subject needs only remember whether he is a "same responder" or a "different responder." Certainly this condition also involves memory, but it is much simpler and requires less practice and learning than remembering which overt response goes with each class of stimuli. Thus, by eliminating the response decision process from the experimental task, response decision time has been removed (i.e., subtracted) from the obtained reaction time, thereby reducing subsequent variability.

In order for this argument to be truly persuasive one would need to be assured that this methodological innovation did not fundamentally modify the processes of interest underlying the experimental task. That is, in order for data collected with C-reactions to be comparable to data collected in the usual way with choice reactions, it must be assumed that the rest of the cognitive processes involved are not affected by the presence or absence of the response decision stage.[3] It is possible, however, to construct an alternative argument that encoding *changes* as a function of the inclusion of the response decision stage, and in this situation the alternative seems introspectively reasonable. For example, "same responders" (i.e., subjects who respond only on same trials) might be conceived of as subjects who are "looking for" sameness. Their decision processes, as compared to those for subjects who have to respond to both sameness and difference, might be biased in favor of sameness, and the duration of the decision process on same trials might be affected by this bias.

Egeth and Blecker (1971) investigated this possibility. In an experiment designed to study the effects of orientation (rightside up vs. upside down) on the type of letter classification described above, both C-reaction conditions and choice reaction conditions were utilized. The patterns of results for both sets of conditions were remarkably similar. The only major difference was the fact that the reaction times for the C-reaction conditions were considerably faster than those for the choice reaction conditions, presumably because of the deletion of the response decision stage. Thus, in this situation the logic of the Subtraction Method seemed tenable.

On the other hand, Egeth, Marcus, and Bevan (1972) have shown that such good fortune cannot always be expected. In a somewhat different type of letter classification task they again utilized both C-reactions and choice reactions. This time, however, the two sets of conditions produced remarkably different patterns of results. It appeared that in this situation the deletion of the response decision stage drastically affected the nature of the processing, thus illustrating the lack of comparability that was noted above.

Since, *a priori*, it is impossible to know when the deletion of a stage will drastically affect processing, this question of comparability can always be put forward in

[3]The importance of the comparison of C-reactions and choice reactions is relevant only with regard to the argument constructed earlier about the application of subtractive logic to the methodological advantages of C-reactions. The nature and value of Egeth's research is not directly dependent upon this comparison.

criticism of the Subtraction Method: The method involves the comparison of similar but nevertheless different tasks. It can always be asserted that the information processing for the two tasks, aside from the simple deletion or addition of a particular mental event, is fundamentally different.

Another way of looking at the above criticism is to say that the data collected by using the Subtraction Method generally yield no evidence about the adequacy of the assumptions underlying its use. If one accepts the assumption that the converging tasks are comparable, then one can interpret the data collected. But the data themselves give no indication about the comparability of the converging tasks.

This does not always have to be the case, however. In some situations the data obtained using the Subtraction Method can provide a built-in indication of the reasonableness of the assumption of comparability. The experiments of Egeth discussed above are one such case. In doing his experiments both ways (with C-reactions and choice reactions), he can check the comparability of his tasks. However, it should be noted that the alleged methodological advantages of C-reactions are then lost. Another situation of this kind has been developed and used extensively by Sternberg in the study of short-term character recognition (Sternberg, 1969a, 1969b). The experimental task utilized in the study of this problem starts with the subject memorizing a short list of characters (usually letters or digits) before each trial. The subject is then presented with a probe character and he is to decide whether or not the probe is contained in the memorized list. Reaction time measured from the onset of the probe character is taken as the dependent variable.

The processing model developed by Sternberg to account for the performance of this task hypothesizes that the internalized or encoded probe character is compared sequentially with each item on the memorized list. Each comparison, then, comprises one mental operation in the processing sequence. Thus, if two conditions that differ from each other in list length by only one item are compared, the difference in their reaction times can be interpreted as the duration of a mental comparison. This is an elementary application of subtractive logic and it is limited, just as the other examples mentioned above were limited, by the assumption of comparability—the assumption that the deletion of one mental comparison leaves the others intact. However, in this case, successive list lengths can be compared. List length 2 can be compared with list length 3; list length 3 can be compared with list length 4; and so on. If strict comparability holds, that is, if the deletion of one mental operation doesn't affect the others, then the successive differences in reaction time should all be identical. The data relating list length to reaction time should be linear. In other words, an obtained linearity of the data can be used to check the applicability of the subtractive logic.

In general, in order to get away from this pervasive criticism of the Subtraction Method (i.e., the comparability of tasks) the critical difference of interest must be embedded in a more complex set of converging operations. In the above instance several conditions were compared, varying the number of identical operations contained from condition to condition. Thus, these repeated applications of the Subtraction Method allow for the detection of any drastic changes in processing as a result of the number of stages — provided, of course, that such drastic changes result in changes in the duration of the affected mental operations. Looking at only one difference in reaction time between one experimental condition and one comparison is tantamount to accepting all of the assumptions underlying the method.

One last point should be mentioned with regard to this criticism about the comparability of tasks in the Subtraction Method. The criticism is not unique to this situation, but rather, it is a criticism that can be applied to the use of converging operations in general. Converging operations, by definition, involve several tasks or conditions that differ from each other in certain systematic ways. They must do this; otherwise they wouldn't converge on some theoretical construct. The argument can thus be made that the converging tasks may involve fundamentally different mediational components. In situations of this type, perhaps conservatism is not the best policy, since converging operations of one form or another would seem always to be necessary in the study of mental events. Thus, data collected and interpreted with the use of subtractive logic should not necessarily be dismissed on these grounds alone. Such criticism deserves attention only when it is accompanied by other persuasive evidence or argumentation indicating that the tasks used to converge are not comparable. In other words, since it is impossible to *prove* that comparability holds, and since it is, in principle, always possible to demonstrate that it doesn't hold, when in fact it doesn't, an hypothesis garnered via subtractive logic might be maintained, at least in a tentative way, until it is disproven. Thus, any particular application of converging operations, such as the Subtraction Method, will leave open an obvious direction for further experimentation: the search for data demonstrating that the common components of the converging operations are not comparable.

The Additive Factor Method

The Additive Factor Method, developed by Sternberg (1969a), has as its principal concern the first of the problems discussed above in conjunction with the limitations on the use of the Subtraction Method. In particular, it concerns procedures for deriving an initial conceptualization of the sequence of cognitive processes that happen between the presentation of a stimulus and the subject's response to that stimulus. It thus represents a level of inquiry that is somewhat more basic than that of the Subtraction Method, whose starting point is an already well-developed theory about the nature of the processing sequence.

Like the Subtraction Method, the Additive Factor Method is a set of converging operations. Therefore, the processing schema derived by it can be identified by unique conjunctions of its operational procedures and assumptions. That is, each process identified by the Additive Factor Method receives its definition from a *pattern* of data which is the result of a *set* of operations.

The basic logic underlying this method involves the following conceptions. First, it is assumed that the reaction time interval is filled with a sequence of independent stages or processes. It is the purpose of each of these stages to receive an input from the preceding stage and to perform a particular translation of it or transformation on it. The output is then passed along to the next stage or process. Each stage produces a particular transformational effect in the sequence of information processing. That is, while the input to each stage will vary in form from trial to trial, it will nevertheless have had the same transformations applied to it as any other input at that point in the sequence. The output of a stage will likewise have achieved some particular level of information processing. Thus, the purpose of a stage is to produce a constant informational transformation.

The nature of the informational transformation produced by a stage is taken to be independent of the *durations* of the stages that have preceded it. Furthermore, the output of a stage represents a constant informational translation, regardless of its own duration. Thus, the nature of the input and output of each stage is independent of factors that influence its duration. It is the durations of these stages and the factors affecting their durations that are the primary concern of the Additive Factor Method.

For example, consider an information-processing stage that finds the name of a stimulus, that is, a stage that receives an essentially spatial representation of a stimulus (i.e., a representation with properties isomorphic to the spatial properties of a stimulus) and translates it into an acoustic representation (i.e., a representation with properties isomorphic to the stimulus name). This spatial representation is the result of the preceding stages of processing. It may, of course, vary from trial to trial in its particular form, depending on what the actual stimulus is, but it will have been processed on each trial to the same degree (e.g., it will be *spatial* and it will have similar resolution and detail). Further, the nature of this input is not dependent on how long it took to get through the preceding stages, but only on the fact that it has gotten through them. The input is now processed by the stage in question. The result is an acoustic representation that will go on to the next stage. Again, the nature of this output representation is not dependent upon the duration of this particular translation process, but only on the fact that the process has been completed. Thus, the input and output of a stage are independent of the duration of the stage in question and of those of the preceding stages.

This conception of stage leads to several implications regarding the relationship between the durations of stages and experimental manipulations. First, total reaction time is simply the sum of the stage durations. When an experimental manipulation affects the reaction time for a particular information-processing task, it does so by changing the durations of one or more of the constituent stages of processing. Second, if two different experimental manipulations affect two different stages, they will produce independent effects on total reaction time. The effect of one manipulation will be the same, regardless of the level of the other variable. In other words, the effects of the two experimental factors should be additive; they should not interact in a statistical sense. This fact follows quite directly from the relationships described above, between the durations of stages and their inputs and outputs. Third, if two experimental factors mutually modify each other's effect, that is, if they interact in a statistical sense, they must affect some stage in common. Figure 1 illustrates the nature of the additivity in a situation where two experimental factors (F and G) affect two different stages of processing (*b* and *c*). Figure 2 shows the resultant additivity in graphical form.

In using the Additive Factor Method to interpret reaction time measures the above implications are applied to data from multifactor experiments. In order to apply the

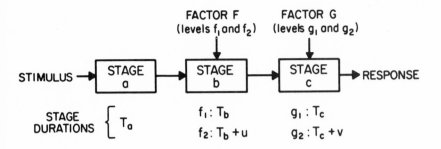

FACTOR F
(levels f_1 and f_2)

FACTOR G
(levels g_1 and g_2)

STIMULUS → STAGE a → STAGE b → STAGE c → RESPONSE

STAGE DURATIONS { T_a

$f_1 : T_b$
$f_2 : T_b + u$

$g_1 : T_c$
$g_2 : T_c + v$

TOTAL REACTION TIME

$$RT = T_a + T_b + T_c + \begin{cases} - & \text{for } f_1, g_1 \\ u & \text{for } f_2, g_1 \\ v & \text{for } f_1, g_2 \\ u+v & \text{for } f_2, g_2 \end{cases}$$

FIG. 1. Stage durations and the additive effects of independent factors on reaction time (after Sternberg, 1971).

method, a well-defined information-processing task (where reaction time is being measured as the dependent variable) must be embedded in a multifactor experimental design. The larger the number of experimental factors that are manipulated, the finer will be the analysis of the constituent stages of the experimental task and/or the better will be the definition of each constituent stage. Basically, the data from such an experiment are simply analyzed in order to find pairs of factors that have additive effects on reaction time. Each time such a pair is discovered it is concluded that each factor affects a different stage. Further, from the patterns of interactions it is possible to give definition to the processing that is accomplished by various stages. Thus, if factors A and B are found to interact, then it can be asserted that there is some stage

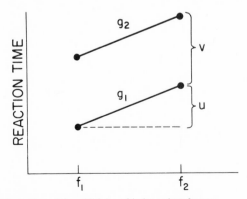

FIG. 2. Graphical illustration of the additivity of independent factors.

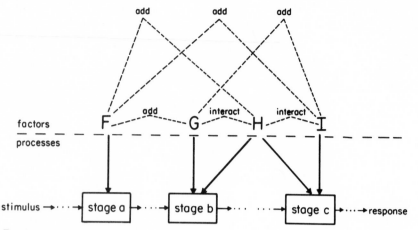

FIG. 3. The effect of factors F, G, H and I on stages a, b and c and the pattern of additivity and interaction among the factors (after Sternberg, 1969a).

whose process is such that it can be affected by both Factor A and Factor B. Figure 3 illustrates how the pattern of additivity and interactions among four experimental manipulations (F, G, H, and I) can be used to define a processing schema. The concrete examples given below will also illustrate the methodology.

Prior to looking at these examples, however, three additional methodological points should be noted. First, the analysis of an information-processing task into component stages by looking at the pattern of additive factors is contingent upon the previously discussed inherent scalability of reaction time measures. Additivity and interaction have meaning only in the context of a dependent variable that is immune to arbitrary monotonic rescaling. In the present context, the obtained reaction time measures are directly of interest because the additivity is a property of the real time durations of the stages. Consequently, not only are transformations of the time scale inappropriate, but so are measures of reaction time, such as medians, which are themselves not in principle additive.

Second, care must be taken that the manipulation of experimental factors does not redefine the experimental task or its component stages. The experimental factors should be reasonable within the context of the experimental task. For example, in a certain sense, the construction of a comparison task in the Subtraction Method might be considered as a limiting case of a factor manipulation. Of course, in such a case the limitations of comparability that were discussed earlier would then apply to the present method. More will be said about this below; for the moment it will suffice to note that one of the motivations behind the development of the Additive Factor Method was the notion that changing the levels of a factor is a somewhat weaker manipulation of information processing than the deletion of entire processes.

Finally, the Additive Factor Method represents a clear conjunction of the interest in substantive issues with that of the study of reaction time *per se*. Clearly, the Additive Factor Method supplies at least one context in which the direct discussion of the effects of experimental manipulations on reaction time are not simply the study of artifacts. The more factors that can be found that systematically affect reaction time in general, the greater the likelihood that the underlying process structure of any information-processing task will be elucidated.

An additive factor case study. The usefulness of the Additive Factor analysis was originally demonstrated by Sternberg (1969a, 1969b) in connection with the study of short-term character recognition. The typical experimental task used to study this problem requires a subject to make a positive response, if the stimulus is one of a previously memorized positive set of stimuli, and a negative response otherwise. This simple information-processing task was embedded in a series of multifactor experiments that investigated the effects of the following factors: the quality of the stimulus (either clear or degraded), the size of the previously memorized set (from one to six digits), response type (whether the trial required a positive or a negative response), and relative frequency of a response type (a positive response was required 25, 50, or 75% of the time in various conditions). A typical trial from an experimental condition, for example, might have been embedded in a series of trials where the positive response was required 25% of the time. The set of digits memorized prior to the trial might have had four members. The stimulus may have been degraded, and the correct response might have been negative. Each trial could thus be represented by a configuration of particular factor levels, and each possible configuration of factor levels occurred in the series of experiments.

The results of these experiments showed that all four factors had significant effects on reaction time. Furthermore, five of the six possible pairings of the four factors had clearly additive effects on reaction time. That is, their interactions were found to be zero. One of the six two-way interactions, that of stimulus quality and relative frequency of the positive response was not explicitly tested in these experiments. Sternberg, however, presented supplementary considerations that argued for the independence of these two factors (see Sternberg, 1969a, page 295). Thus, Sternberg's tentative description of the information processing involved in this task had four stages, one stage defined by each of the factors tested: an initial stimulus encoding stage, in which the visual image of the stimulus is converted into a representation that can be held in short-term memory; a comparison stage, in which the stimulus representation is compared with each memorized positive set stimulus; a response choice stage, in which the output of the comparison stage is tested to see whether or not the stimulus matched a positive set item; and a response execution stage, in which the motor commands for the appropriate response are carried out.

It should be noted that the Additive Factor Method itself does not supply either the description of each stage, as given above, or the order in which the stages are effective. Those conjectures arise from a consideration of the nature of each factor and a logical argument concerning the dependency of each subsequent transformation on the processes preceding it. For example, it seems reasonable to hypothesize that the stage affected by stimulus quality would be a stimulus encoding stage, and it also seems reasonable to believe that stimulus encoding would precede any of the other stages. Only the study of additional factors and the pattern of interaction obtained with them can supply additional evidence about the adequacy of such a conceptualization.

An example of this type of theoretical substantiation has recently taken place within the problem area of short-term recognition memory. Sternberg (1966) originally hypothesized that the memory comparison stage consists of a serial exhaustive search of the items of the memorized positive set. That is, the comparison stage involves the sequential comparison of the probe with *each* item from the positive set, regardless of whether or not a match is found along the way. The basis for this conjecture involved, first, the linear form of the function relating reaction time to size of the positive set. This linear relation, taken in conjunction with subtractive logic, implicates the serial nature of the comparisons (see page 50). Second, the additivity of the factors of size of the positive set and response type implicates the exhaustive nature of the search. If the comparison stage were not exhaustive, that is, if the stage terminated itself upon finding a match, then differential effects of size of the positive set would be expected for positive and negative responses. Response type and positive set size would interact. This follows from the fact that in such a self-terminating search all of the items in memory have to be searched on negative trials, whereas on positive trials only about half of the items, on the average, need to be searched in order to find a match. Thus, since set size has the same effect on both positive and negative responses, it was concluded that all of the memorized items are checked on both positive and negative trials.

An extensive analysis of an additional factor, the probability of particular probe stimuli occurring, led Theios, Smith, Haviland, Traupmann, and Moy (1973) to challenge this position. They found that reaction time in a short-term recognition experiment decreased as a function of stimulus probability, and this fact seemed inconsistent with the hypothesis that the memorized list is searched exhaustively. How could stimuli, because of their particular probability of occurrence, have different reaction times if the probe stimulus had to be compared with *all* of the stimuli in memory? They concluded that the memory comparison stage must be serial and *self-terminating* with the order of comparisons determined, at least to some extent, by stimulus probability. Unfortunately, the experimental design of Theios et al. did not allow for the clear demonstration of the interaction of stimulus probability and memory set size as the Additive Factor Method would predict if the effect of stimulus probability was localized in the memory comparison stage.

Recently, however, two independent Additive Factor experiments have clarified this issue to some extent. In one, Klatzky and Smith (1972) varied stimulus probability and size of the positive set and found no evidence for an interaction. This would indicate that these two factors have their effects on different stages. In the other experiment, Miller and Pachella (1973) varied stimulus probability and stimulus quality and found that these factors strongly interact. Therefore, it seems reasonable that the stimulus probability effect found by Theios et al. (1973) is localized, not in the comparison stage, but in the encoding stage. Thus, Sternberg's original conjecture about the nature of the comparison process still seems momentarily plausible. Furthermore, the interaction of stimulus probability and stimulus degradation adds still further definition to the transformation that takes place in stimulus encoding: Whatever its nature, it must involve a process such that the effect of stimulus probability can be modified by the clarity of the stimulus.

Criticism of the Additive Factor Method

The above examples are intended as a demonstration of the usefulness of the Additive Factor Method. It is a useful method because it is unambiguous enough to allow investigators to examine independently findings arising out of its application and either to agree on their interpretation or to express their disagreements in a meaningful empirical discourse. On the other hand, because of certain limitations underlying the method, it would be more than naive to hold with any tenacity a model having the Additive Factor analysis as its sole justification.

One of these limitations has been alluded to above. It is simply the argument that the manipulation of factor levels may cause a fundamental change in the processing sequence as may happen with the deletion of an entire stage within the Subtraction Method. From a procedural point of view, the difference between the Subtraction Method and the Additive Factor Method can be quite subtle. Thus, "number of overt responses" in a short-term recognition experiment (e.g., one vs. two responses as in Egeth, Marcus, & Bevan, 1972) is taken to modify fundamentally the processing sequence, whereas "stimulus quality" (e.g., the presence vs. the absence of a checkerboard noise pattern as in Sternberg, 1967) is taken to modify simply the duration of the encoding stage.

Second, the demonstration of additivity in multifactor experiments often amounts to the acceptance of a null hypothesis concerning the interaction between two variables. Great caution needs to be exercised in such instances. The data needed in order to demonstrate true additivity require a precision that few reaction time experiments obtain. Furthermore, as Sternberg (1969a) has pointed out, experimental artifacts are more likely to obscure *true* additivity than *true* interaction. Thus, two factor interactions are best believed when they are obtained in experiments that also contain convincing demonstrations of additivity.

Finally, any particular conception of "information-processing stage" and its properties may be more problematic than determinate. On the one hand, the Additive Factor analysis can be taken as definitional, as it has been in the present paper. The concept of "stage" can be simply *defined* by the pattern of additivity and interaction that is achieved from sets of multifactor experiments. In such a case a "stage" is operationally defined, albeit from a set of converging operations, and its properties will be those inherent in the assumptions underlying the methodology. This is then a functionally based approach to theorizing. It represents a shorthand for conceptualizing the effects of experimental variables.

On the other hand, there can be independent conceptions of processing stages which have external justification. These may be derivable from other forms of data outside of the context of reaction time and/or information-processing based theory (e.g., from psychobiology, psycholinguistics, or psychophysics). In such cases, it becomes an empirical question as to whether or not these "stages" have the properties that satisfy the definition of stage derivable by the Additive Factor Method.[4] In situations where stages have some independent definition, it is perfectly conceivable that two factors might affect a single stage in an additive manner or that they might affect different stages and interact. This latter possibility would be the result, for example, when a given factor modified not only the duration of a stage, but also the nature of the output from that stage. In this situation the pattern of data obtained from multifactor experiments would serve not so much for the discovery of the stages themselves, but rather for the determination of their specific properties. Thus, a model of processing in which the stages are defined by an Additive Factor analysis may not be identifiably different from an alternative model *based on a different definition of stage* in which the properties of the stages do not lead to the simple patterns described above. They may be just two different conceptualizations of the structure underlying some body of data.

REACTION TIME AND PERFORMANCE ACCURACY

The interpretation of reaction time measures necessarily depends upon the precision of their measurement. With regard to experimental data, this precision is usually discussed in the context of the inter- and intrasubject reliability that is necessary to draw certain statistical conclusions. For example, the last section presented the partitioning of the reaction time interval into stages on the basis of the additivity and interaction among independent variables. The ability to detect such relations depends upon the amount of extraneous variability that is inherent in the obtained reaction time measures. The present section further discusses the precision of reaction time measures. The limitations on interpretability to be presented here, however, concern the variability that can be attributed to a covariate measure, performance accuracy.

The Definition of Reaction Time as an Empirical Question

It was stated earlier that reaction time is commonly defined as the minimum amount of time needed for a subject to produce a correct response. For the purposes of theorizing, it is this property that makes reaction time useful. Unfortunately, this definition is not an operational or procedural definition; rather, it simply represents an assumption on the part of the experimenter or theorist. Other than the instructions given to the subject, there is generally no evidence within a typical reaction time experiment that the times produced by the subject are really the minimum possible while the subject is maintaining accurate performance.

Whether or not subjects actually produce latencies that conform to the above requirements is, in fact, an empirical question. Consider, for example, an information-processing experiment in which the subjects are instructed to work at various different rates of speed. That is, in addition to a condition in which the

[4]It should be noted that the original explication of the Additive Factor Method by Sternberg (1969a) was made in this broader context. The rather narrow description presented in the present chapter is done for tutorial purposes, although it accurately reflects the manner in which the method has been applied by many investigators.

subjects are given the usual instructions to respond as fast as possible without making errors, there are other conditions in which the subjects are induced to work at various speeds that are either faster or slower than this normal reaction time. Thus, on some blocks of trials, speed of responding is greatly emphasized; on other blocks, speed is only moderately emphasized; and on still other blocks, great accuracy and caution are emphasized.

Figure 4 represents the outcome of such an experiment in idealized form. Pew (1969) has called this type of function a *speed-accuracy operating characteristic*. Such a curve plots the average latency of response (e.g., mean reaction time) against the average accuracy of responses (e.g., the percentage of correct responses) for each of the various speed emphasis conditions for a particular experimental task. Virtually all of the speed-accuracy operating characteristics that have been reported in the literature share the basic properties of the hypothetical data of Fig. 4. They are monotonically increasing functions and, when accuracy is measured in percentage of correct responses, they are typically negatively accelerated.

The open circle on Fig. 4 is the point at which subjects are assumed to be operating according to the common definition of reaction time. It represents the fastest reaction time at which maximum accuracy is maintained. It is extremely doubtful that experimental subjects ever adopt this speed-accuracy criterion. Errorless performance is a rare occurrence when the usual reaction time instructions are given to subjects. Even experienced subjects whose data are exemplary in all other respects (e.g., consistent, low variability) will generally make 2–3% errors in most reaction time tasks, and much higher rates are often reported in published experiments. Thus,

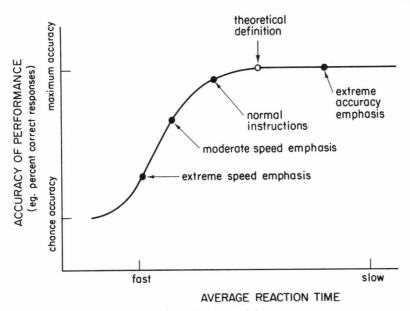

FIG. 4. An idealized speed-accuracy operating characteristic.

experimental subjects almost always operate at a point that is *below* maximum accuracy.

Several things should be noted about these errors with regard to their limiting effects on the interpretability of reaction time. First, low error rates are generally dismissed by experimenters as inconsequential. They are assumed to be a part of the inherent variability of performance that one can expect of experimental subjects. Such an assumption is undoubtedly wrong and can lead to serious errors of interpretation.

Reaction time measures are usually derived from extremely simple information-processing tasks. Subjects would probably never make an error in them if they were not being timed, and if they were not trying to minimize their response time. Consider, for example, the vocal naming task that is often used in information-processing research. This task simply requires a subject to say aloud the name of a familiar stimulus, often a letter or number, when it is presented visually on a screen. In situations where time is not a factor, it is indeed doubtful that a literate adult would ever misname a letter or a number. Note that the occasional, "real-life" instances of mistaking the identity of a letter or number usually occur as a result of not taking *enough* time in responding. However, the general interpretation of reaction time assumes that subjects are not rushing their response; they are supposed to be taking the amount of time *necessary* for the successful completion of their task.

Thus, it seems unlikely that even low error rates are a result of inherent subject variability. More likely they result from subjects responding just a little faster than they should, because they are trying to minimize their response time. Furthermore, it is not unreasonable that subjects should do this. The problem confronting a subject when faced with the usual reaction time instructions is to find the optimal speed at which to work. If he never made an error, a subject would not know if he could still go a little faster without making errors. Undoubtedly, the subject chooses a speed-accuracy criterion at which he will, in fact, rush his response—at least to the extent that he will make an occasional error, and within a range such that his error rate will seem acceptable to him and/or to the experimenter.

Second, it is not, in itself, a matter of great concern that subjects do not operate at the point assumed by the general definition of reaction time. Of much greater importance is the possibility that differences in the speed-accuracy criterion may be correlated with experimental conditions. That is, it is possible that subjects may vary from condition to condition the extent to which they tend to rush their responses. Thus obtained differences in reaction time may not be due entirely to underlying processing differences. This possibility takes on added significance when the error rates in an experiment are ignored or go unreported, since the differences in reaction time that are obtained, while artifactual in some sense, may be statistically significant.

Third, the limitations on the interpretability of reaction time as a result of variability in error rates is further accentuated by the general form of the speed-accuracy operating characteristic. The practical significance of the negative acceleration of such curves, given error rate as the accuracy measure, lies in the fact that small differences in error rate can lead to large differences in reaction time. This is particularly true for the range of high, overall accuracy (90 to 100%) typically found in reaction time experiments. This means, of course, that what may look like relatively meaningless error differences might contaminate reaction time values extensively.

An Example of the Speed-Accuracy Problem

A recent experiment by Theios (1972a) illustrates the problems that can result from the above considerations. Subjects were visually presented with single digits. Their task was simply to name the digits under the constraints usually applicable in reaction time experiments and to be as fast as possible while maintaining maximum accuracy. The particular parameter of interest in the experiment was the effect of stimulus probability. Thus, in various conditions the probability of particular stimuli was varied from .2 to .8. The results of the experiment are shown in Table 1. As a result of the essentially invariant reaction times that were obtained, Theios concluded that stimulus probability had no effect on the information processing involved in this simple naming task.

However, before such a conclusion can be believed several things about the pattern of the error data must be noted. First, across all conditions the subjects averaged about 3% errors. As noted above, this is not unusual for reaction time experiments. But, again, consider the simplicity of this experimental task. These subjects made on the average 3% (and in one condition as many as 6%) errors in a task that simply required them to name a visually presented digit. Outside of the context of a reaction time experiment such an error rate in such a task would be quite unacceptable.

Second, the variability of the error rates was quite small. This again is typical. However, the error rates were systematically related to the probability conditions. Thus, the subjects in the .2 probability condition made 6% errors when they averaged 356 msec per response. The relevant question to ask is: What would their average reaction time be if they were only making 1–2% errors as they did in the .7 and .8 probability conditions? In other words, if the subjects had been able to adopt a uniform accuracy criterion for all of the probability conditions, would reaction time have been found to be invariant? From a more practical point of view, the question might be put this way: How much difference in reaction time could possibly result from such small error differences?

A second experiment by Theios from the same series of experiments as the one described above will perhaps shed some light on these questions. This experiment

TABLE 1

Mean Reaction Time and Proportion of Errors as a Function of Stimulus Probability
(from Theios, 1972a)

Stimulus probability	.2	.3	.4	.5	.6	.7	.8
Mean naming time (msec)	356	356	351	357	348	347	346
Mean proportion errors	.06	.04	.03	.02	.02	.01	.02

contained one condition that was methodologically identical to one of the conditions whose results are presented in Table 1. In particular, it duplicated almost exactly the .5 probability condition from the experiment described above. However, in this experiment the subjects performed more accurately than the subjects in the first experiment, making fewer than 1% errors, while their reaction times were considerably slower, by about 100 msec.

Theios (1972b) has attributed this performance difference to a difference in the speed-accuracy criterion of the subjects in the two experiments. If this is the case, then it is certainly conceivable that such a speed-accuracy trade-off might produce at least as large a difference in going from the .2 to the .8 probability conditions of the first experiment. That is, in order for the subjects to have reduced their error rate by 4% in the .2 probability condition, they might have had to lengthen their reaction time by as much as 100 msec. Thus, it is doubtful that the data in Table 1 can be used to substantiate the claim that stimulus probability does not affect naming reaction time. It is alternatively possible that, for some reason, the subjects produced roughly equal reaction times in each of the probability conditions, thereby causing the effect of stimulus probability to appear as error differences.

Some Attempted Solutions to the Problem of Variable Error Rates

The above example was selected because it illustrates particularly well the potential problems associated with variable error rates in reaction time research. This ubiquitous problem has received little systematic attention. Nevertheless, when errors occur in reaction time experiments investigators must do something about them. Thus, several procedures have evolved and are in current use even though there exists a paucity of justification for their application.

The first and by far most common procedure for handling errors is to simply ignore them. As noted earlier, the data most often reported in published reaction time experiments are the reaction times from the correct responses only. The data from the trials on which errors are made are simply not included in the analysis of the experimental results. Furthermore, summary statistics about errors (e.g., error rate for each condition) are also sometimes missing. Such a procedure implies obvious assumptions about the relationship between correct and incorrect trials, particularly if such a procedure is believed to "solve" the error problem. In particular, the ignoration of errors assumes that the reaction time for correct responses is not affected by the overall error rate for an experimental condition.

Such an assumption, in most instances, could not be more false. In the type of experiment described earlier, which leads to the kind of speed-accuracy characteristic pictured in Fig. 4, reaction time for correct responses follows a speed-accuracy characteristic which is similar to that for total reaction time. That is, when subjects adjust their speed-accuracy criterion from block to block (or condition to condition), average correct reaction time decreases as error rate increases. In fact, one thing that each of the general classes of models to be discussed in the next section assert is this fact: *Average correct reaction time is inversely related to error rate.* Thus, this procedure does not represent a solution to the error problem. Furthermore, justification for its use in the context of experimental reports is universally absent.

A second procedure, which would be most convenient, would be to make subjects produce the same error rate in all the conditions of an experiment. This, unfortunately, is usually impossible. However, experimenters often attempt to have subjects produce small differences in error rate by inducing them to be extremely conservative and having them emphasize accuracy to a great degree. This procedure also has its difficulties. Great caution on the part of the subjects is associated with the flattest portion of the speed-accuracy operating characteristic. Small error differences close to the maximum accuracy level can be associated with large differences in reaction time. In the extreme, if subjects actually produced zero errors in all conditions (as the general reaction time instructions ask of them), the reaction times would be essentially uninterpretable. This is because an infinite number of average reaction times can result in zero errors (i.e., all points to the right of the open circle in Fig 4). Thus, very low error rates, while often the mark of a careful experiment, may also result in artifactual differences in reaction time.

Two statistical approaches to the error problem have occasionally been attempted. The first is the application of the analysis of covariance to experimental data. Such an analysis consists of a standard analysis of variance of *adjusted* reaction time measures. The adjustment of the reaction time measures is brought about on the basis of a linear regression of reaction time against errors suitable to the particular experimental design. In other words, the scores that get analyzed are the reaction times predicted by a regression equation for some constant level of error rate (e.g., the mean value).

There are a number of technical statistical considerations that dictate great caution in the application of this covariance technique to the error problem in reaction time studies (see particularly, Evans & Anastasio, 1968). Furthermore, one less subtle difficulty is the assumption on the part of this analysis of a *linear* relation between accuracy and reaction time measures. As noted above, when the error measure is percentage of error, this relation is not linear; therefore, the model underlying this statistical procedure is not suitable. However, it is possible (although not always feasible) to base the predicted reaction time measures on nonlinear functions or to apply a suitable transformation to the experimental data in order to make the relevant speed-error relation linear. The latter possibility is often accomplished by using the logarithm of the accuracy odds, i.e., $\log \left[p(\text{correct})/p(\text{error}) \right]$, or the information transmitted (in bits) by the subject's responses. Each of these transformations has the effect of producing an essentially linear speed-accuracy characteristic. Thus, under certain highly favorable conditions, covariance analysis might be an aid in handling the problem of variable error rates.

A second statistical procedure that has occasionally been suggested as a solution to the error problem involves the application of the multivariate analysis of variance (MANOVA). In short, this analysis treats the reaction time and accuracy measures as a bivariate dependent variable. The variance-covariance matrix for this vector variable can be partitioned into independent component effects in a manner analogous to the partitioning of total variance in the standard analysis of variance. These effects are then tested statistically against the null hypothesis that they simply represent samples from the same bivariate normal population. As illustrated by the Theios experiment discussed in the last section, such a procedure would seem ideal for handling the error problem in reaction time research. However, it should be noted that the constraint of a linear relation between reaction time and accuracy measures is again present. That is, the dependent vector variable is assumed to be sampled from a bivariate normal population which has the linear correlation coefficient, ρ, as a parameter. Furthermore, in situations where the application of MANOVA techniques seems reasonable the statistical-computer software necessary for complex experimental designs may still need development. Nevertheless, such a technique seems promising, even if it only awakens the realization of the multivariate nature of reaction time-accuracy data.

An Experimental Approach to the Speed-Accuracy Problem

A somewhat more drastic approach to the problems cited above is to draw conclusions about human information processing from data other than the usual reaction time measures. As pointed out earlier, reaction time measures, as commonly defined, have much intuitive and theoretical appeal; however, as also noted, it may not be possible to obtain empirical measures that coincide exactly with these intuitive and theoretical notions. The examples to be presented below utilize as their data base, not ordinary reaction time measures, but rather the speed-accuracy characteristic itself. That is, the conclusions to be drawn are based on the *relationship* between reaction time and error measures over a wide range of speed-accuracy criteria.

The general experimental paradigm involves inducing subjects to work at various different rates of speed in each of the conditions in an experiment. Functions of the type shown in Fig. 4 are then derived for each condition. Conclusions about the relevant information processing are based on the changes from condition to condition of the function that relates reaction time to the accuracy measures.

Inducing subjects to work at different rates of speed has been accomplished in several different ways. Hick (1952) and Howell and Kreidler (1963, 1964) verbally instructed subjects to work at different rates of speed on different blocks of trials or in different conditions. Fitts (1966) and Swensson (1972) utilized explicit payoff matricies providing monetary incentives favoring speed vs. accuracy to produce the same kind of shift in speed-accuracy criterion. Recently, Pachella, Fisher, and Karsh (1968) and Yellott (1971) have described a procedure that involves defining for the subject a response time limit and asking that the subject attempt to produce his responses faster than this deadline. Subjects are provided with feedback on each trial as to whether or not they have successfully beaten the deadline, and from one block of trials to the next the deadline is manipulated in order to produce shifts in the speed of responding. Each of the above techniques is quite effective in producing trade-offs that are highly consistent across subjects. The latter deadline technique, however, is most efficient methodologically and is the procedure that is utilized in the examples described below.

At the outset of this presentation, however, one point should be made perfectly clear. While an attempt will be made to show that the data in these examples are consistent with other knowledge obtained by use of reaction time measures, the techniques illustrated here should not be considered as simply a correction procedure for reaction time experiments. An experiment that derives a speed-accuracy characteristic is potentially a different kind of an experiment than the usual reaction time procedure. Thus, there is no reason to believe that subjects performing under the kind of speed stress present in these experiments are necessarily processing information in the same manner that they might in the corresponding conditions of the more typical reaction time situation. In general, data obtained in this manner must be first evaluated in their own right and then, if consistent with other procedures, generalized accordingly.

Speed-Accuracy Relations and Stimulus Discriminability

Pachella and Fisher (1969) obtained speed-accuracy operating characteristics for a task involving simple absolute judgments of spatial position. On each trial a bar marker assumed one of ten horizontal positions across a uniform visual field. The subject indicated which of the positions he judged the marker to be in by pressing one of ten keys on which his fingers rested. In addition to an unspeeded condition, three deadline conditions were used in the experiment. On some blocks of trials subjects attempted to make each of their judgments in less than 1.0 sec. On other blocks of trials the deadline was 0.7 sec, and on still other blocks the deadline was 0.4 sec. The subjects were explicitly instructed to try to beat the deadline on each trial and within this constraint to be as accurate as possible. Stimulus discriminability was varied in two different ways: by varying the spacing of the possible stimulus positions (wide vs. narrow spacing) and by varying the contrast of the stimulus against the background (bright vs. dim background).

The speed-accuracy operating characteristics for the three stimulus conditions that were run are presented in Fig. 5. Note that the accuracy measure displayed on the ordinate is information transmission, which in this situation, where stimulus information is held constant across conditions, becomes a measure of performance accuracy. The results show that varying discriminability by reducing stimulus contrast has a different effect than changing discriminability by increasing stimulus similarity. While both manipulations produce decrements in performance, decreasing similarity changes the *rate* at which speed is traded for accuracy, and reducing stimulus contrast does not.

These data are thus consistent with the stage analysis of choice reaction time tasks arrived at by Sternberg (1969a, Exp. V). This analysis distinguishes between an early stimulus encoding stage, which is affected by stimulus degradation (in the present case, stimulus contrast), which adds only a constant to the time needed to attain a given level of accuracy and higher-level processes that analyze this encoded representation in greater detail. These processes are affected by stimulus similarity, which thus affects the rate at which performance accuracy is acquired.

These data are also consistent with the distinction made recently by Garner (1970) between *state* and *process* limitations on performance and are similar to data collected by Flowers and Garner (1971) concerning this distinction. State limitations, exemplified by stimulus contrast, affect the opportunities for central information processing but not the nature of the processing itself. Thus, the rate of accuracy acquisition should not be affected by such variables. On the other hand, process

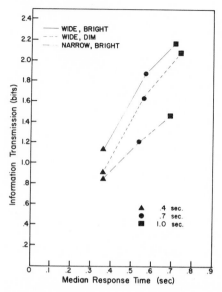

FIG. 5. The relationship between information transmission and response time as a function of discriminability and speed constraint conditions (from Pachella & Fisher, 1969).

limitation concerns the limits on the processing as defined by the experimental task. Thus, stimulus spacing in the present experiment defines the dimension along which the information processing must be carried out, and therefore changes in spacing affect the rate at which accuracy can be obtained.

In any event, the speed-accuracy operating characteristic is diagnostic of differences in stimulus discriminability and permits distinctions between types of discriminability. Further, the data of Fig. 5 are not limited in their interpretability in the way that regular reaction time measures are.

Speed-Accuracy Relations and Memory Scanning

The short-term character recognition paradigm discussed earlier (see pp. 50–51 and 55–56) provides a second context in which to illustrate the direct use of speed-accuracy relations.[5] In this experimental task the subject is presented with a short list of letters on each trial. This list is followed by a probe letter and the subject indicates, by pressing buttons, whether or not the probe letter is contained in the list. In the present experiment subjects performed this task under normal reaction time instructions and under instructions to respond faster than response time deadlines. In a typical session the subject started out on a block of trials with normal reaction time instructions. On a second block of the session a relatively lenient response time deadline was imposed, and on each subsequent block the deadline was made more stringent.

[5]This experiment was originally presented at the Forty-fourth Annual Meeting of the Midwestern Psychological Association, May, 1972.

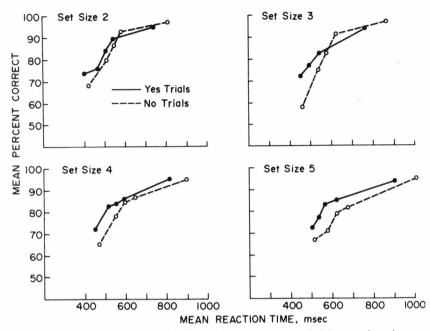

FIG. 6. The speed-accuracy operating characteristic as a function of trial type and set size.

Twenty practiced subjects participated in four experimental sessions. Each session contained five blocks of 44 trials (reaction time instructions, plus four deadline conditions). The length of the list presented on each trial was varied from session to session. Thus, within one session a subject saw only one list length. Subjects, days, and list lengths were counterbalanced in order to eliminate specific practice effects.

The speed-accuracy operating characteristics obtained for each set size (i.e., list length) are presented in Fig. 6. The functions for "yes" and "no" *trials* (not responses) are plotted separately in each panel. Note that the curves share the general features of the hypothetical curve in Fig. 4. Also note that the functions for "yes" and "no" trials for each set size are quite similar—at least for set sizes 2, 4, and 5 (set size 3 seems to be a little noisy). Further, the curves for "yes" and "no" trials tend to separate as a function of set size: For set size 2 the functions are right on top of one another, while for set size 5 they are quite separate. In fact, for the set size 5 condition there is a difference of over 100 msec between the "yes" and "no" functions for some levels of accuracy.

The import of these features (and others) can be seen somewhat more easily in Figs. 7 and 8. Here iso-accuracy contours have been constructed from Fig. 6. These functions represent the predicted reaction time (based on linear interpolation) for specific accuracy levels as a function of set size.

In Fig. 7 four accuracy levels, 95, 90, 85, and 80% correct are plotted on the same axes, averaged across trial type. The first thing to note about this figure is that in going from 95% to 90% correct, there is a large effect on the intercept of the function

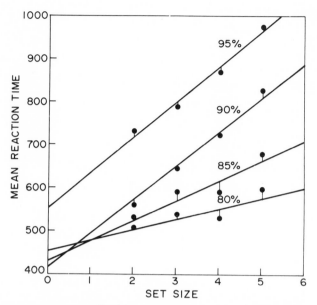

FIG. 7. Iso-accuracy contours predicted for reaction time as a function of set size.

relating reaction time to set size. In other words, the initial effect of stressing speed appears to be located in what was described earlier as the encoding and/or the responding stages of processing. This result agrees well with a previous finding of Swanson and Briggs (1969). They placed subjects under speed stress in a task similar to the present one and, for error rates down to about 10%, found only intercept effects. The present data show, on the other hand, that if subjects are further pressed for speed, no further intercept effects are obtained, but instead the slope of the function decreases. Thus, more extreme speed emphasis seems to affect the memory searching stages of processing.

Figure 8 shows the same four accuracy contours as Fig. 7, only here the "yes" and "no" trials have been separated out. In each panel the equation of the best fitting straight line for each function is also presented. First, note that the data are quite noisy when analyzed this finely. Thus, considerable caution should be taken in believing them. Nevertheless, for each accuracy level the slopes of these functions are considerably steeper for the "no" trials than for the "yes" trials. Such a result, if real, would support strongly the possibility of a self-terminating scan of memory. It should be noted, however, that besides being noisy, the present data are also somewhat contradictory. If the data from the normal reaction time conditions (i.e., the rightmost point for each function in Fig. 6) are plotted by themselves, they present evidence which is typical of an exhaustive scanning process. That is, these points, as shown in Fig. 9, are quite parallel.

One might be tempted to construct a rather elaborate hypothesis for this situation: Under normal reaction time conditions, subjects utilize an exhaustive scan of mem-

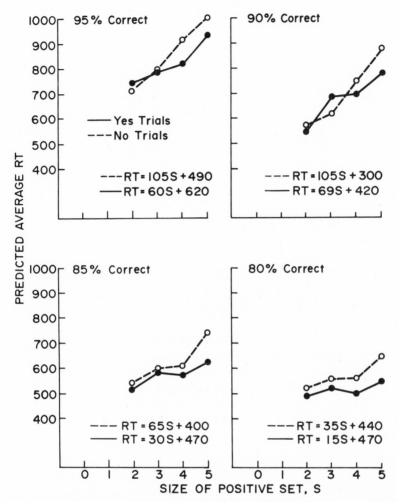

FIG. 8. Iso-accuracy contours predicted for reaction time as a function of set size and trial type.

ory. However, when pressured to emphasize speed they go to a self-terminating procedure. That is, speed stress leads to a basic change in processing strategy.

Before letting this kind of speculation get too far out of hand, though, a less dramatic possibility should be explored. This notion has to do with the general problem of interpreting reaction time data in the presence of variable error rates. Note the small differences in accuracy for the various list length conditions of Fig. 9. The numbers above each point indicate the appropriate percent correct. These small accuracy differences are slightly correlated with set size (particularly for the "no" trials). Correlations of this type are not only typical, in many memory scanning experiments they are even stronger. By contrast, the data of Fig. 8 represent an attempt (albeit somewhat of an approximation) to control for error differences. The

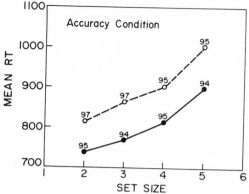

Fig. 9. Reaction time as a function of set size and response type for the normal reaction time conditions. The numbers above each point indicate percentage of correct responses.

functions plotted there are *equal-accuracy contours*. Thus, the differences in slope values in Figs. 8 and 9 may be the result of subtle differences in speed-accuracy operating criteria. Reaction time data in general may not be precise enough to make the distinction necessitated by the above hypotheses.

Figure 10 has been constructed to further illustrate this point. This figure has been constructed in the following way: Reaction times were selected from Fig. 6 that would exactly fit the predictions of either an exhaustive or a self-terminating scanning process. The corresponding accuracy levels for each of these reaction times were also noted. These have been indicated above each point in Fig. 10. The result shows that either hypothesis can be fit exactly with the data from Fig. 6, and a range of only about 7% errors is necessary to bring this about. The point is to show that either hypothesis might have been supported with data, had this been real data, whose error

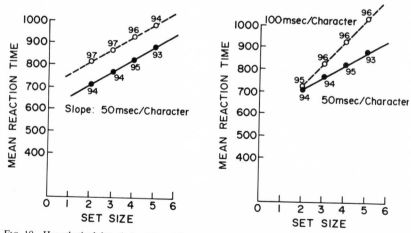

Fig. 10. Hypothetical data derived from Fig. 6 for two alternative memory scanning hypotheses. The numbers associated with each point indicate the predicted percentage of correct responses.

differences might have been dismissed as insignificant. And while the present data are not really good enough to justify seriously the strong manipulation that went into creating Fig. 10, they illustrate the fact that reasonable attention must be paid to even small error rates. Thus, great caution must be exercised in evaluating this kind of data.

THEORETICAL CONCEPTIONS OF REACTION TIME AND SPEED-ACCURACY RELATIONS

The last section discussed the difficulty of interpreting reaction time data in the presence of variable error rates. Attempted solutions to this problem depend, either explicitly or implicitly, upon theoretical conceptions of the nature of speed-accuracy relations and these relations, in turn, depend upon conceptions of reaction time in general. The present section will outline a few of these formulations in their simplest form and will emphasize particularly how each conceives the relationship between speed and accuracy. More complex versions of each of these models are available and the reader is urged to turn to the original sources for detailed analyses. The purpose of the present section is basically pedagogical: to place in some theoretical perspective the notions whose importance were noted in the last section. To be sure, as each model is made more complex it is more capable of accounting for more phenomena, but it is then more difficult to distinguish each from the others. And for the present purposes, it is the *distinctions* between the models that will be emphasized.

The Fast-Guess Model

One of the simplest conceptions of speed-accuracy relations in reaction time has been presented by Yellott (1971). This model states that the decrement in accuracy produced by emphasizing speed is due to a failure of stimulus processing on some proportion of the trials. In a series of trials under speed stress there will be two kinds of responses. One class of responses will be the same as those produced under normal reaction time instructions. That is, they will be produced in their usual manner by the subject taking the amount of time necessary for an accurate response. These responses are called *stimulus controlled responses*. The other class of responses, called *fast-guess responses,* are initiated without the usual stimulus processing. These responses will be much faster than stimulus controlled responses, but they will have only a chance probability of being correct. The greater the emphasis on speed, the larger will be the percentage of these fast-guess responses. Thus, speed emphasis will increase error rates and decrease average reaction time.

Some of the more subtle implications of this conception become apparent if the basic speed-accuracy relation described earlier is replotted in a somewhat different form. For the moment consider a simple two-choice experiment with various speed-emphasis conditions like those which led to the creation of Fig. 4. Instead of plotting average *total* reaction time for each speed-emphasis condition, however, in this case the difference between average *correct* reaction time and average error reaction time, each weighted by its respective proportion of trials, will be used. Thus, the quantity

$(p_c M_c - p_e M_e)$ will appear on the ordinate, where p_c and p_e are the probabilities of correct and error responses and M_c and M_e are mean correct and mean error reaction times, respectively. Further, instead of simply using percent correct as a measure of accuracy, the difference between percent correct and percent error $(p_c - p_e)$ will be plotted on the abscissa.

In situations where the model described above is correct, a function such as that shown in Fig. 11 will result. The important features of such a graph (and hence, also the reasons for creating it) are as follows: First, a condition consisting of nothing but stimulus controlled responses will yield the highest and rightmost point on the function. In such a condition (for such a simple task) perfect accuracy would obtain and $(p_c - p_e) = 1.0$. Furthermore, the value of $(p_c M_c - p_e M_e)$ will equal the average duration of stimulus controlled responses (shown in Fig. 11 as μ_s) since there are neither fast-guess responses nor errors in this condition. Second, a condition consisting of nothing but fast-guess responses will yield the origin of the graph [i.e., the point $(0,0)$]. In such a case, $p_c = p_e$ and $M_c = M_e$, since all responses are fast-guess responses. Third, Yellott (1971) has derived the fact that the form of the function for the two quantities in question, as shown in Fig. 11, is linear. This fact can be seen in an intuitive manner from the realization that the intermediate points on the function result from simple linear mixtures of the conditions at the extremes of the function. Finally, given the ranges of the ordinate (from 0.0 to μ_s) and the abscissa (from 0.0 to 1.0), it can be seen that the slope of the function is equal to μ_s, the average duration of stimulus controlled responses. This fact is particularly valuable in situations where

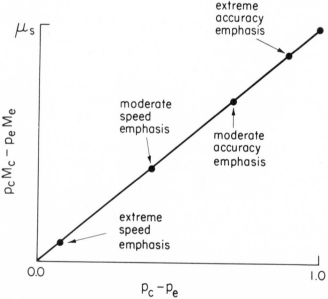

FIG. 11. The form of speed-accuracy operating characteristic utilized by the Fast-Guess Model; μ_s is the average duration of stimulus controlled responses.

one wants to estimate the duration of stimulus controlled responses but where perfect accuracy conditions are not available.

On the basis of the presentation made in the last section, the fast-guess model represents a mixed blessing. On the one hand, the basic notion of a speed-accuracy operating characteristic becomes essentially an elaborate artifact if fast-guessing in this simple form were the only mechanism underlying such relations. That is, the mechanism accounting for speed-accuracy trade-offs is not a processing mechanism, but rather it is a gross, relatively peripheral strategy on the part of subjects in order to handle speed stress. Thus, the idea of using speed-accuracy relations directly in the study of information processing as illustrated earlier loses some of its force.

On the other hand, if fast-guessing is the only mechanism underlying the production of errors in reaction time experimentation, then the precise formulation given by Yellott (1971) represents a powerful solution to the problem of variable error rates. The average duration of stimulus controlled responses, μ_s, which is easily derivable from experiments in which speed-accuracy criteria are manipulated, is exactly the parameter about which information-processing researchers wish to theorize. In other words, the fast-guess model represents a theoretically well-founded correction for variable error rates.

Is Fast-Guessing Enough?

The question must be faced as to whether or not subjects are capable of producing speed-accuracy trade-offs in some way other than the simple strategy outlined above. To begin with, it should be noted that no experimental demonstration can rule out fast-guessing as a potential strategy on the part of subjects. Subjects can always choose to make fast-guess responses if they want to. Thus, what follows below is simply an attempt to show that subjects are able to produce speed-accuracy trade-offs with some strategy or mechanism *other than* simple fast-guessing.

This illustration[6] utilizes as its experimental task a simple letter classification of the type that has been studied extensively by Posner. On each trial the subject is presented with a pair of letters. He must decide whether the two letters are both vowels or both consonants, that is, if they belong to the same CLASS, in which case he is to make a same response. If one of the letters is a vowel and the other a consonant, that is, if they don't belong to the same CLASS, he is to make a different response. A same response is to be made, of course, if the two letters differ from each other only in case (e.g., A a), that is, if they have the same NAME, since they will then both be vowels, or consonants. Trials of this type where the letters match in NAME as well as CLASS are typically classified on the order of 70 msec faster than pairs of letters that match in CLASS only (see Posner & Mitchell, 1967). Likewise, a same response is appropriate if the letters are physically identical (e.g., A A). These PHYSICAL matches are typically 70 msec faster than NAME matches. The stimulus sequences used in the present experiment had equal proportions of each of these three kinds of same trials, as well as equal proportions of same and different

---

[6]This experiment was originally presented at the Thirteenth Annual Meeting of the Psychonomic Society, November, 1972.

trials. Under the fast-guess strategy described above, errors produced by speed stress should be just as likely for all kinds of same and different trials, since the stimulus is not processed on error trials. In other words, if the decision to produce a fast-guess is made prior to stimulus processing, then the random presentation of trial types should yield a rectangular distribution of errors. Six subjects were run in the experiment for five sessions, each session consisting of 440 trials. The first two sessions were for practice during which subjects simply performed the letter classification task under typical reaction time instruction. The data from the last half of the second session were analyzed, and the mean reaction times for the CLASS matches and the NAME matches were computed.

The last three sessions of the experiment were each divided into three blocks. On one of these blocks the subject performed the classification task just as he did during the practice sessions. On each of the other two blocks the subject attempted to produce all of his responses faster than a response time deadline. For one of these blocks the deadline was equal to the mean reaction time of the CLASS matches from the second practice session, and for the other block the deadline was equal to the mean reaction time of the NAME matches from the second practice session. Note that these deadlines were individually computed for each subject on the basis of his own data from session two. The order of the blocks was counterbalanced across subjects and sessions. Subjects were given immediate feedback on each trial as to the speed and the accuracy of their responses.

The results are presented in Table 2. The rows present the various types of trials that could occur in each block. Across the columns are the mean percent error and mean reaction time for each block (accuracy, slow deadline and fast deadline) for the experimental days.

TABLE 2

Mean Reaction Time and Error Rate for each Trial Type and Deadline Condition

Trial type	Accuracy (no deadline)		Slow deadline (equal to mean of CLASS matches)		Fast deadline (equal to mean of NAME matches)	
	% error	RT (msec)	% error	RT (msec)	% error	RT (msec)
Physical same AA	1.0	510	1.8	471	2.7	463
Name same Aa	2.8	577	3.8	531	10.5	504
Class same AE	3.9	661	16.0	593	23.7	546
Different Ab	3.2	624	5.8	569	11.5	533

The basic result is quite clear. The error distributions are not rectangular. Speed stress affects CLASS matches more than it affects NAME matches, and it affects NAME matches more than it affects PHYSICAL matches. The pattern of results produced here clearly eliminates the simple version of the fast-guess model from being the only source of errors in this situation.

Cumulative Speed-Accuracy Models

The above experiment would seem to indicate that, at least for this task, subjects accumulate information over time and that they respond, when time pressure requires, on the basis of whatever information is available at that moment. According to this idea, speed stress should first affect those stimuli that require the most processing and affect lastly those stimuli that require the least processing. Thus, as the present data indicate, CLASS matches, involving a high level of information extraction, should be affected most by speed stress, while PHYSICAL matches should be affected the least.

Numerous cumulative processing models exist as alternatives to simple fast-guessing. A number of these have been summarized by Broadbent (1971) and Audley (1973). Two will be briefly presented here because of the particular way in which they characterize speed-accuracy relations. They will be labeled the Accumulator Model and the Random Walk Model. Again, only very simple versions of these models will be presented.

Both of these models assume that responses are contingent upon central decision processes. These decisions are based on evidence about the stimulus situation that is acquired over time. Both models assume that the accumulated evidence is inherently probabilistic, that it is imperfect or fallible. The models differ from each other in the way in which the evidence is used in making decisions.

The Accumulator Model assumes that evidence regarding each possible (or expected) stimulus alternative is simply aggregated. As evidence pertinent to any particular stimulus is received, it is added in or totaled with all other evidence about that stimulus which has been received up to that moment. A decision to respond is made when the evidence favoring any particular stimulus reaches some critical value. The higher this critical value, the greater is the amount of evidence needed in order to respond. Since it takes time to accumulate evidence, high critical values will lead to long reaction times. However, decisions that result from high critical values will be based on more evidence than those that result from low critical values; thus, they will have a higher probability of being correct. Cognitive adjustments to speed stress involve adjusting these critical values to which stimulus evidence must be accumulated. Speed stress will lead to low critical values, which in turn will lead to fast reaction times and high error rates.

In the Random Walk Model evidence about the various stimulus alternatives is also aggregated. However, the decision to respond is based on a relative criterion rather than an absolute one. When the evidence favoring one alternative exceeds the evidence in favor of any of the other alternatives by some critical amount, a response is initiated. The model is called a Random Walk Model because the state of the evidence from moment to moment can be conceived of as a random walk among the various alternatives. Over time the accumulated evidence will tend toward favoring one of the possible alternatives, but the state of the evidence at any moment will vacillate as a result of the probabilistic nature of the datum that is acquired.

Reaction time will be a function of the size of the critical value by which the evidence for a particular alternative must exceed any of the others. If this critical value is high, that is, if the evidence favoring one alternative must exceed that of the other alternatives by a large amount, then reaction times will be long. Again, however, in this situation the decision will have been based on a large amount of aggregated evidence, and thus the probability of error will be small. By contrast, small critical values will lead to fast reaction times and high error rates. Cognitive adjustments to speed stress are made by adjusting the size of the critical value. The more speed is emphasized, the lower the critical value.

The important difference between these two models is this: In the Accumulator Model evidence is aggregated separately for each alternative. A single datum favoring one alternative does not affect the state of evidence favoring other alternatives. In the Random Walk Model, a single datum affects the state of evidence for all alternatives, increasing the chances of one response and decreasing the chances for the others.

The following simple analogy derived from Edwards (1965) may serve to make these models more concrete. Imagine two bags full of poker chips. One bag, which will be called the "red" bag, contains 60 red poker chips and 40 blue poker chips. The other bag, called the "blue" bag, contains 60 blue and 40 red chips. One of these bags is presented to a subject and he is to determine whether it is the "red" or the "blue" bag. The subject makes this determination by sequentially drawing single poker chips from the bag. In the analogy the bags correspond to stimuli. The sequential sampling corresponds to the process whereby evidence is aggregated. Reaction time is represented by the number of poker chips drawn before the subject reaches his decision. The mixture of red and blue chips in each bag causes the data on which a decision is based to be inherently probabilistic.

If the subject behaves in a manner analogous to the Accumulator Model he will draw chips until he has some particular number of red or blue chips, in which case he will respond accordingly. For example, he may continue to draw until he has drawn either five red or five blue chips in the sequence, in which case he will respond "red" bag or "blue" bag, respectively. If he is pressed for time he may decide to respond after drawing either three red or three blue chips. In this case, however, his chances of being in error are increased. If accuracy is emphasized, the subject may decide to sample until he has drawn a total of ten or twelve chips of one color. Given the composition of the two bags, it is quite improbable (though not impossible) that this decision will be wrong.

A subject behaving in a manner analogous to the Random Walk Model will continue to sample until the number of chips of one color exceeds the number of chips of the other color by some particular amount. The larger the excess needed for a response, the more time it takes to reach a decision, but the higher the probability that the decision will be correct. Thus, the margin of difference between the accumulated totals determines the operating point on the speed-accuracy characteristic. Under this strategy, after some particular number of draws, if the same number of red and blue chips have been accumulated, the subject is no closer to a decision than when he started sampling. By contrast, with the Accumulator strategy each datum (or chip) contributed to reaching a decision.

Macro- vs. Micro- Speed-Accuracy Relations

Thus far three very simple models have been presented. While these models may be unrealistic in their simplicity, their variety allows for the consideration of relationships that are useful in understanding both the performance of subjects and the research strategies employed by experimenters in the study of speed-accuracy tradeoffs.

One of these relationships concerns the average speed of responses and the error rate for those responses for various speed-emphasis conditions. Up to this point the present paper has dealt exclusively with this relationship, which for the present purposes will be termed the macro-tradeoff. The three models discussed above make similar statements about this relation: Speed emphasis leads to a reduction in average reaction time and an increase in error rate. Furthermore, the experimental work presented earlier has shown that this relationship can be useful in the study of information processing.

A second relationship, which can be distinguished on the basis of these models, also involves a consideration of the speed and the accuracy of responses. In this case, however, the concern is with the speed of error responses relative to the speed of correct responses *within a particular speed-emphasis condition*. This relation, which will be termed the micro-tradeoff, will be shown to be independent of the macro-tradeoff, at least with regard to the present models, since each of these models makes a different prediction about the reaction time for errors relative to the reaction time for correct responses. In fact, every possible ordering of the speed of errors relative to the speed of correct responses will be represented among these predictions. Thus, the models agree about the general form of the macro-tradeoff but disagree about the form of the micro-tradeoff.[7]

The Fast-Guess Strategy predicts that error responses will, on the average, be faster than correct responses. This follows simply from the fact that errors occur only as a result of fast-guess responses, which are assumed to be faster than stimulus controlled responses. Correct responses represent a mixture of the fast-guess responses that happen to be correct by chance and stimulus controlled responses. This mixture will have a longer average duration than the average for error responses. However, average correct reaction time will, nevertheless, be a function of speed stress, since the proportion of correct-by-chance fast-guess responses in the mixture will increase with speed emphasis.

The Random Walk Model predicts that, within any speed-emphasis condition,

[7]The terms macro- and micro-tradeoff and this particular manner of discussing this distinction derives largely from many conversations between the present author and E. A. C. Thomas.

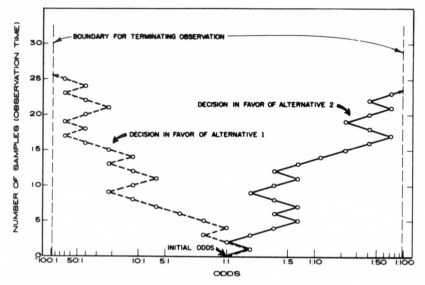

FIG. 12. The Bayesian, odds-revision Randon Walk Model.

errors and correct responses will have the same reaction time. A reconsideration of the poker chip analogy will make this prediction clear. Imagine that after each draw of a poker chip the subject evaluates the aggregated evidence by using Bayes Theorem. That is, after each draw he uses Bayes Theorem to revise the odds in favor of each alternative. Such an odds-revision process can be represented as a random walk between the two alternatives, as illustrated in Fig. 12. When the odds favoring one alternative over the other alternative reach some critical value or boundary a response is initiated. The important thing to note with regard to the micro-tradeoff is that any random walk terminating on one of the boundaries, regardless of how long it takes to get there, will have the same probability of being correct as any other walk terminating on that boundary. This follows from the basic definition of probability or "odds." Thus, the probability of being correct is independent of the duration of a particular random walk, and correct and error responses will have the same average reaction time.[8]

Finally, the Accumulator Model predicts that, within a particular speed-emphasis condition, errors will have longer reaction times than correct responses. Again, consider the poker chip analogy. In the Accumulator Model the subject samples poker chips until he has sampled some critical number of red or blue chips; for example, imagine the critical number to be five. A short reaction time will occur when the subject happens to sample only five chips and they all turn out to be either red or blue. Given the composition of the two bags, it would be relatively improbable

[8]It should be noted that this Bayesian odds criterion version of the Random Walk Model represents a monotonic transformation of the simple difference criterion version presented earlier. This elegant demonstration of the form of the micro-tradeoff was originally made by Wilfred Kincaid of The University of Michigan's Mathematics Department.

to sample such a sequence from the wrong bag. By contrast, a sampling sequence consisting of five chips of one color and four chips of the other color will represent the longest possible sequence, and it will have a relatively high probability of being in error. Thus, on the average, for a given criterion, errors will be associated with long sequences (by analogy, long reaction times) and correct responses with short sequences.

Quantification of the micro-tradeoff can be carried out in a more continuous manner than the simple relations described above between the means of error and correct responses. In particular, Rabbitt and Vyas (1970) and Lappin and Disch (1972a) have utilized a procedure for acquiring a function relating accuracy to reaction time for the micro-tradeoff in a form similar to that which has been described for the macro-tradeoff (e.g., as in Fig. 4). Under this procedure the reaction times for a particular speed-emphasis condition are ranked from fastest to slowest. These reaction times are then grouped within this rank-ordering. Thus, for example, the fastest 100 responses might be grouped together, the second fastest 100 responses grouped together, and so on, down to the slowest 100 responses. For each of these groups the error rate and average reaction time can then be computed and plotted against each other. Each of the above predictions about the micro-tradeoff can be generalized to data of this form: the Fast-Guess Model predicts a monotonically increasing relationship of accuracy as a function of reaction time; the Random Walk Model predicts the relation to be flat; and the Accumulator Model predicts a monotonically decreasing function.

Lappin (Lappin & Disch, 1972a, 1972b, 1973) has extensively studied these micro-tradeoff functions and has found them particularly valuable in the investigation of extremely fast processes, such as highly compatible, two-alternative reaction time situations. It has been generally found that such tasks are extremely difficult to study with macro-tradeoffs since subjects seem incapable of cognitively varying speed emphasis for such fast reactions (see, for example, Swensson, 1972). Nevertheless, Lappin has been able to identify a number of experimental variables that seem systematically to affect the micro-tradeoff.

It should be emphasized in this last regard that little is yet known about the relationship between these micro- and macro-tradeoffs. While the simple models presented here make the distinction quite clear, any reasonable complication of these models produces a confounding of the relations. For example, if in the Random Walk and Accumulator Models subjects vary their critical value for responding *within* a particular speed-emphasis condition, the micro-tradeoffs predicted for these models will show a positive correlation between accuracy and reaction time. Since it seems reasonable that such variation takes place, the precise untangling of these relations awaits further experimental and theoretical development.

SUMMARY

Reaction time measures have been used, and will continue to be used, extensively by researchers interested in substantive issues in experimental psychology. The value of this experimental work is naturally dependent upon the inherent strengths and weaknesses of the experimental logic used in the study of these issues. This logic, in turn, is dependent upon the precision with which reaction time measures themselves can be meaningfully interpreted.

Many of these substantive issues involve questions about processes that are mediational and unobservable. Hence, they require an experimental logic that has come to be known as "converging operations." Conclusions drawn from experimental designs of this type necessitate multifactor or multiple-task comparisons. In such situations it is always possible that the relevant processing on the part of the subject may become task or condition dependent. That is, the subject's processing strategy may change drastically from condition to condition; thus, the comparisons needed in order to converge on some theoretical concept may be invalidated. Obviously caution is needed in interpreting any particular set of experiments which involve such a sophisticated mode of investigation. In other words, it may be naive in such situations to allow theories and research strategies to become too dependent upon some limited set of observations. The idea of the single "critical" experiment for deciding between potential hypotheses may not be practicable for this kind of research.

Furthermore, the particular methods of converging upon information-processing constructs that have been discussed in the present chapter involve powerful assumptions about the precision of reaction time measures. In particular, they involve the use of interval properties of the reaction time measures that are obtained as data from experiments. The Subtraction Method leads to conclusions based directly upon the magnitude of a difference obtained for pairs of experimental conditions, and the Additive Factor Method utilizes differences between differences (i.e., interactions) in order to structure mental events. Given the variable error rates that are obtained in reaction time experiments, and the subtleties of speed-accuracy relations as discussed earlier, it is not clear that such interval properties should be ascribed to reaction time measures as they are obtained from current experiments. Indeed, for the purposes of theorizing, experimentally obtained reaction times may have only ordinal properties and even these can be negated by a large, positively correlated association between reaction time and accuracy.

Of great importance, then, to the development of methodologies involving reaction time measures in the investigation of substantive issues, is the careful study of reaction time as a measure, *per se*. Much more must become known about the general strategies used by subjects in the generation of reaction times before a high degree of confidence can be had about incorporating these measures in subtle substantive controversies. Until then, great patience and care must be taken in order to limit the possibility of serious error in their interpretation.

REFERENCES

Audley, R. J. Some observations on theories of choice reaction time: Tutorial review. In S. Kornblum (Ed.), *Attention and Performance IV*. New York: Academic Press, 1973.

Broadbent, D. E. *Decision and stress*. London: Academic Press, 1971.

Deese, J. Behavior and fact. *American Psychologist,* 1969, **24**, 515–522.

Edwards, W. Optimal strategies for seeking information: Models for statistics, choice reaction times, and human information processing. *Journal of Mathematical Psychology,* 1965, **2**, 312–329.

Egeth, H., Atkinson, J., Gilmore, G., & Marcus, N. Factors affecting processing mode in visual search. *Perception & Psychophysics,* 1973, **13**, 394–402.

Egeth, H., & Blecker, D. Differential effects of familiarity on judgments of sameness and difference. *Perception & Psychophysics,* 1971, **9**, 321–326.

Egeth, H., Jonides, J., & Wall, S. Parallel processing of multielement displays. *Cognitive Psychology,* 1972, **3**, 674–698.

Egeth, H., Marcus, N., & Bevan, W. Target-set and response-set interaction: Implications for models of human information processing. *Science,* 1972, **176**, 1447–1448.

Eriksen, C. W., Pollack, M. D., & Montague, W. Implicit speech: Mechanism in perceptual encoding? *Journal of Experimental Psychology,* 1970, **84**, 502–507.

Evans, S. H., & Anastasio, E. J. Misuse of analysis of covariance when treatment effect and covariate are confounded. *Psychological Bulletin,* 1968, **69**, 225–234.

Fitts, P. M. Cognitive aspects of information processing: III. Set for speed versus accuracy. *Journal of Experimental Psychology,* 1966, **71**, 849–857.

Flowers, J. H., & Garner, W. R. The effect of stimulus redundancy on speed of discrimination as a function of state and process limitation. *Perception & Psychophysics,* 1971, **9**, 158–160.

Garner, W. R. The stimulus in information processing. *American Psychologist,* 1970, **25**, 350–358.

Garner, W. R., Hake, H. W., & Eriksen, C. W. Operationism and the concept of perception. *Psychological Review,* 1956, **63**, 149–159.

Hick, W. E. On the rate of gain of information. *Quarterly Journal of Experimental Psychology,* 1952, **4**, 11–26.

Howell, W. C., & Kreidler, D. L. Information processing under contradictory instructional sets. *Journal of Experimental Psychology,* 1963, **65**, 39–46.

Howell, W. C., & Kreidler, D. L. Instructional sets and subjective criterion levels in a complex information processing task. *Journal of Experimental Psychology,* 1964, **68**, 612–614.

Klatzky, R. L., & Smith, E. E. Stimulus expectancy and retrieval from short-term memory. *Journal of Experimental Psychology,* 1972, **94**, 101–107.

Lappin, J. S., & Disch, K. The latency operating characteristic: I. Effects of stimulus probability on choice reaction time. *Journal of Experimental Psychology,* 1972, **92**, 419–427. (a)

Lappin, J. S., & Disch, K. The latency operating characteristic: II. Effects of visual stimulus intensity on choice reaction time. *Journal of Experimental Psychology:* 1972, **93**, 367–372. (b)

Lappin, J. S., & Disch, K. The latency operating characteristic: III. Temporal uncertainty effects. *Journal of Experimental Psychology,* 1973, **98**, 279–285.

Miller, J. O., & Pachella, R. G. On the locus of the stimulus probability effect. *Journal of Experimental Psychology,* 1973, **101**, 227–231.

Pachella, R. G., & Fisher, D. F. Effect of stimulus degradation and similarity on the trade-off between speed and accuracy in absolute judgments. *Journal of Experimental Psychology,* 1969, **81**, 7–9.

Pachella, R. G., Fisher, D. F., & Karsh, R. Absolute judgments in speeded tasks: Quantification of the trade-off between speed and accuracy. *Psychonomic Science,* 1968, **12**, 225–226.

Pew, R. W. The speed-accuracy operating characteristic. *Attention and Performance II. Acta Psychologica,* 1969, **30**, 16–26.

Posner, M. I., & Mitchell, R. F. Chronometric analysis of classification. *Psychological Review,* 1967, **74**, 392–409.

Rabbitt, P. M. A., & Vyas, S. M. An elementary preliminary taxonomy for some errors in choice RT tasks. *Attention and Performance III. Acta Psychologica,* 1970, **33**, 56–76.

Sternberg, S. High-speed scanning in human memory. *Science,* 1966, **153**, 652–654.

Sternberg, S. Two operations in character recognition: Some evidence from reaction time measurements. *Perception & Psychophysics,* 1967, **2**, 45–53.

Sternberg, S. The discovery of processing stages: Extensions of Donder's method. *(Attention and Performance II.) Acta Psychologica,* 1969, **30**, 276–315. (a)

Sternberg, S. Memory scanning: Mental processes revealed by reaction time experiments. *American Scientist*, 1969, **57**, 421–457. (b)

Sternberg, S. Decomposing mental processes with reaction time data. Invited Address presented at the meeting of the Midwestern Psychological Association, 1971.

Swanson, J. M., & Briggs, G. E. Information processing as a function of speed versus accuracy. *Journal of Experimental Psychology*, 1969, **81**, 223–239.

Swensson, R. G. The elusive tradeoff: speed versus accuracy in visual discrimination tasks. *Perception & Psychophysics*, 1972, **12**, 16–32.

Theios, J. The locus of cognition. Paper presented at Thirteenth Annual Meeting of the Psychonomic Society, November, 1972. (a)

Theios, J. Reaction time measurements in the study of memory processes: Theory and data. Wisconsin Mathematical Psychology Program, Report 72–2, December, 1972. (b)

Theios, J., Smith, P. G., Haviland, S. E., Traupmann, J., & Moy, M. C. Memory scanning as a serial self-terminating process. *Journal of Experimental Psychology*, 1973, **97**, 323–336.

Yellott, J. I. Correction for fast guessing and the speed-accuracy tradeoff in choice reaction time. *Journal of Mathematical Psychology*, 1971, **8**, 159–199.

3
DOUBLE STIMULATION[1]

Barry H. Kantowitz
Purdue University

Interest in double stimulation centers on the duration of psychological processes inferred from measurement of reaction time. Such questions as "When can you do two things at the same time" are answered by comparing the time required to perform one task alone with the time required to perform the same task in concert with some additional task. The outcomes of such experiments are varied, depending upon the constituent tasks themselves. We find not only the intuitively expected outcome, namely an interference effect with a second task increasing the time required to perform a primary task, but also instances of no increase in reaction time and even instances where dual-task performance becomes relatively more efficient as task complexity increases. These different outcomes enable us to make inferences about the cognitive processes required to perform the constituent tasks as well as inferences about internal relationships between these cognitive processes which would be difficult to establish if only one task was studied in isolation.

The bulk of this chapter will address instances where double-task performance is inferior to single-task performance, insofar as performance is measured by reaction time (RT). This means that we will be primarily concerned with the amount of time required to perform a task, although as the preceding chapter has amply demonstrated, our concern for the speed of performance must be tempered by a coincident

[1] This chapter was written at the University of Oregon while I was supported by Special Fellowship MH 54754 from the National Institute of Mental Health. My own research and conceptions of double stimulation, some of which appear in the chapter, were supported by grant MH 21169 from NIMH. I acknowledge with gratitude the helpful comments of Anthony Greenwald, Louis Herman, Steven Keele, Beth Kerr, Ray Klein, Jim Knight, Richard Pew, Michael Posner, Roger Schvaneveldt, and Ed Smith. Their constructive criticism greatly improved the chapter. Nevertheless, I claim full responsibility for any misinterpretations of some of their data and models described in the chapter.

regard for the accuracy of performance. In our examination of double stimulation we shall encounter models that try to specify a bottleneck where dual-task performance suffers, other models that try to specify conditions under which the bottleneck disappears, and even one model that tries to explain the difficulties encountered in dual-task performance while denying the very existence of any bottleneck. We shall find models that stress the role of short-term memory and others that minimize memory requirements, general models and quite specific ones, models that have antecedents in learning theory and models that spring from communication theory. In short we will treat a veritable cornucopia of models bolstered by an impressive data base. We will find no model that explains everything and no model that fails to grasp some portion of the cognitive processes demanded in double stimulation. But our search, while necessarily nonterminating, will illuminate the use of RT measures and methodology in a substantive area of human information processing.

The double-stimulation paradigm exploits a basic limitation in the human's ability to process information. People, like other systems (see Buckley, 1968), can handle only a finite amount of information in a specified time; indeed the human's capacity is small relative to simpler biological systems (Miller, 1964). When this limitation is exceeded, systematic deficits in performance are observed. These deficits offer important clues about more typical human information processing in situations characterized by a more reasonable processing load.

Subjecting a system to stresses beyond its capacity has proved to be a useful methodological tool in engineering (e.g., destructive testing). However, a more restrained implementation of overload is mandated in the study of human behavior. This has been accomplished by either *(a)* increasing the rate at which a series of stimuli impinge upon the human, or *(b)* requiring the simultaneous performance of two independent tasks. Both kinds of operation fall within the rubric of double stimulation. The most common implementations of the first type of overload limit the series to only two stimuli. The fine-grained analysis permitted by a double-stimulation task is lost when the double-stimulation task is immersed in a rapid series of required reactions (Triggs, 1968, p. 33). When pairs of responses, separated by substantial intertrial intervals, are required, it is relatively easy to examine the role of such factors as feedback associated with the first response and its effect upon the second response and vice versa. But when a chain of rapid responses is required, strong sequential effects are merged with postresponse processes, and it is more difficult to state that a given response was affected primarily by the immediately preceding response and not by a series of preceding responses (e.g., Hart & Huff, 1973; Remington, 1969; Schvaneveldt & Chase, 1969). Using a serial task to study double stimulation is like the mating of elephants: ponderous and followed by a long gestation period. The second type of overload, while having historical antecedents as old as Jastrow's (1891) combination of reading and mental arithmetic with a motor tapping task, has only in the last two decades enjoyed a renaissance following a long period of disuse; see Kerr (1973) for a review of this research. An optimal explanation of double-stimulation effects should embrace both kinds of overload.

Double stimulation is usually defined (e.g., Herman & Kantowitz, 1970) as the presentation of two stimuli in rapid temporal succession. The time intervening between the two stimuli, called the interstimulus interval or ISI, is typically well below 1 sec and use of intervals under 200 msec is quite common; when the ISI is zero secs, simultaneous task performance is required. This definition of double stimulation is theoretically neutral and covers a large class of behavior including such primarily sensory events as masking and phi phenomenon. In this chapter I will take a more restricted view of double stimulation by concentrating upon attentional aspects of information processing. We shall focus upon the human's ability to process one stimulus or response while another stimulus or response clamors for attention.

This chapter will examine data and models as they bear upon the double-stimulation task. While this focus upon a single paradigm may at first appear overly restricted, I shall try to present implications of these findings for broader areas of information processing, especially the subject of attention. This approach is more inductive than deductive, since expansion of the models will be attempted only after models are applied to double stimulation. Such a strategy is quite deliberate, since I feel it is preferable to first explain a restricted set of findings in some detail before expanding models to handle a greater scope of behavior. The generalist strategy of a unified model of information processing often fails at the level of some specific application, or else the model must be bolstered by stratagems peculiar to the particular application at hand. Since the goals of these two approaches are similar, the decision between them is more a matter of tactics than epistemology. Errors can be made by pursuing either tactic. A model may be so general and contain so many parameters as to be almost useless in guiding research within a particular paradigm. Similarly, a paradigm can be so narrow (e.g., paired-associate learning with one-digit numbers and consonant trigrams) as to defy expansion to issues of more general interest. The view to be presented here is that the double-stimulation paradigm represents a comfortable compromise between the perils of Scylla and Charybdis. The paradigm is broad enough to be a useful vehicle for testing different classes of models and yet sufficiently restricted so that models do not become vacuous.

The chapter will begin by first discussing paradigms that are traditional examples of double stimulation. The reasons why researchers have turned to these paradigmatic variations will be given along with some of the methodological considerations that are necessary to guarantee that data so obtained will be useful. We shall then turn to a review of the rather formidable array of models purporting to explain findings in the double-stimulation paradigm. Some of these models have been primarily limited to the double-stimulation paradigm, while others are more general models for which the area of double stimulation is but one test. This review leads naturally into a discussion of data with which the models can be evaluated. However, the major focus is not upon determining the "true" model of double stimulation, but instead emphasizes the delicate interrelationship between data and model and how data not only influence models but models influence data collection. This emphasis will be made salient by organizing the discussion around important, and formerly important, independent variables used in double stimulation. The point of view thus developed will be then extended to the more general area of attention.

PARADIGMS

The basic double-stimulation paradigms are listed in Table 1. All necessarily involve the presentation of two stimuli; however, response requirements differ among the three paradigms. The "grandfather" paradigm, S_1-R_1, S_2-R_2, requires responses to both stimuli. The interesting result in this paradigm is an increase in RT to the second stimulus (S_2), relative to a control condition in which only one stimulus is presented. This delay becomes more pronounced as the interstimulus interval (ISI) separating the first and second stimuli decreases, although grouping effects at very short ISIs may result in exceptions to this general outcome. Psychologists have called this delay the psychological refractory period (PRP) effect following a suggestion of Telford (1931) who believed that the human's central information-processing mechanism became refractory (i.e., turned off) for a brief period after the first stimulus, in much the same manner as a single neuron becomes refractory after excitation. This analogy is less than perfect since the absolute refractory period of a nerve fibre is relatively constant, lasting about .5 msec, and is then followed by a relative refractory phase in which increased stimulus intensity can overcome the elevated threshold; this relative phase is itself followed by supernormal and subnormal phases in which the threshold is lowered and then increased (Gardner, 1963). While Telford's analogy is no longer widely accepted, the term psychological refractory period (PRP) remains as a descriptive title. Since the focus of interest in this S_1-R_1, S_2-R_2 paradigm has been the latency of the second response, RT_2, many of the earlier PRP studies did not report RT_1 data.

More recently, investigators have become concerned with the effects upon the second response of omitting the first response. This led to a more extensive use of the second PRP paradigm of Table 1: S_1, S_2-R_2, where the first stimulus is presented but no overt response is required to it. Most studies have found greater RT_2 delay in the double-response paradigm (e.g., Davis, 1959; Kantowitz, 1974; Kay & Weiss, 1961; Nickerson, 1967; Smith, 1967b) although a few studies have obtained similar RT increments, especially at long ISIs (Davis, 1962; Koster & Bekker, 1967). It is important to realize that the PRP effect is still obtained in the S_1, S_2-R_2 paradigm, so that it cannot be attributed only to the requirement of executing two responses in close temporal contingency.

If the S_1-R_1, S_2-R_2 paradigm is considered the grandfather of the double-stimulation family, it is appropriate to call the S_1-R_1, S_2 paradigm the toddler of double stimulation. This paradigm does not require any response to S_2. A naive reader might wonder about the purpose of presenting a second stimulus, for which no response is demanded, after the first stimulus; why should this later stimulus have any effect whatsoever? Indeed, RT_1 effects in the S_1-R_1, S_2 paradigm are not so robust as the traditional PRP effect, with delay often limited to short ISIs less than RT_1 itself. However, small RT_1 effects have been found for greater ISIs (see Herman & Kantowitz, 1970). The earlier investigators of this paradigm (e.g., Fehrer & Raab, 1962; Helson & Steger, 1962) were interested in perceptual masking effects and did not see any contact between their research and the larger body of PRP research. The

TABLE 1

Stimulus and Response Requirements of Standard Double-Stimulation Paradigms

Paradigms	S_1	R_1	S_2	R_2
Full PRP (S_1–R_1, S_2–R_2)	Yes	Yes	Yes	Yes
PRP (S_1, S_2–R_2)	Yes	No	Yes	Yes
S_1–R_1, S_2	Yes	Yes	Yes	No
Single ⎱	Yes	Yes	No	No
Stimulation ⎰	No	No	Yes	Yes

Note.—A fourth double-stimulation paradigm, Yes No Yes No, has not been seriously investigated and will not be considered.

masking tradition has been maintained, especially in intersensory double stimulation, and the term used in more recent studies is stimulus onset asynchrony (SOA) instead of the term ISI used in refractory studies. The two terms, SOA and ISI, are often operationally identical and serve mainly to illustrate an author's identification with a conceptual framework regarding double stimulation, although there is some tendency for studies that manipulate SOA to have short ranges of ISI (about 100 msec). Other investigators (e.g., Gottsdanker, Broadbent, & Van Sant, 1963; Herman, 1969; Kantowitz, 1973) departed from this masking viewpoint and considered the S_1–R_1, S_2 paradigm in relation to findings concerning the PRP effect. These studies raised the question of whether the PRP effect might be only half the double-stimulation story and suggested that RT_1 and RT_2 effects in double stimulation were opposite sides of the same coin (Herman & Kantowitz, 1970).

Two special cases of the S_1, S_2–R_2 PRP paradigm are obtained when S_1 conveys information that is either useful or necessary for the determination of a particular S_2–R_2 combination. In the partial advance information (PAI) paradigm, the PAI conveyed by S_1 has most often been used to reduce response information by one bit, dividing the response set in half. The PAI technique was first developed by Leonard (1958) who used a row of six lights as his stimulus set. Leonard's PAI specified which set of three lights (left or right) would contain the final stimulus (S_2) and thus could reduce a six-choice RT task to a three-choice RT task. Leonard used the PAI paradigm to test the binary classification model proposd by Hick (1952). This test was based upon a comparison of two estimates of the time needed to process one bit of information. The first estimate was obtained by simply taking the difference between six- and three-choice (single stimulation) RTs. The second estimate was derived from the double-stimulation condition. For very long ISIs the task is essentially a three-choice task and RT should equal three-choice RT. For very brief ISIs it is essentially a six-choice task since insufficient time has been allowed for S_1 processing. At some intermediate ISI, just enough time will have elapsed since S_1 presentation to make the six-choice task into a three-choice task; let us term this the critical ISI, at which RT suddenly drops from the six- to the three-choice value. While RT did decline from the six- to the three-choice RT values as ISI increased, the decline was not sudden and the critical ISI was considerably greater than that obtained as the difference between six- and three-choice single-stimulation RT. This finding, however, does not invalidate Hick's model. As Leonard himself noted, his estimate of the critical ISI was inflated by the PRP effect since some elevation of RT_2 would be expected in an S_1, S_2–R_2 paradigm. Furthermore, Leonard's procedure used an external signal (S_1) to simulate an internal binary classification; hence, extra time was needed for perceptual processing of S_1 which also would inflate the estimate of the critical ISI. More recent investigations have replicated Leonard's findings (Remington, 1971) and have expanded his procedure as a method of evaluating models of the PRP effect (Kantowitz & Sanders, 1972; Sanders, 1971).

A closely related paradigm forces processing of S_1 information. As was noted by Kantowitz and Sanders (1972) the PAI used by Leonard was not necessary since the correct response could be made without any S_1 processing. By using a bidimensional S_2 with S_1 specifying the relevant dimension, PAI becomes necessary since a correct response cannot be made without processing S_1. This paradigm has been termed contingent information processing (Bernstein, Pederson, & Schurman, 1972; Biederman, 1972) and has been used in several studies (Bernstein & Segal, 1968; Davis, 1964; Davis & Taylor, 1967; Kamlet, 1969; Kantowitz & Sanders, 1972; Posner & Mitchell, 1967; Shaffer, 1965, 1966, 1967). Again, RT is a monotonically decreasing function of ISI.

The bottom lines of Table 1 represent a single-stimulation control condition used to provide a baseline for evaluation of double-stimulation effects. The need for this baseline is illustrated in Fig. 1. How might the decreasing RT function in Fig. 1 be described? If the single-stimulation control falls at point A, we can speak of an increasing facilitation of double-stimulation RT relative to the control condition. If the control falls at point C, we refer to decreasing delay or inhibition of double-stimulation RT. If the control falls at point B, there is both facilitation and inhibition, according to the ISI with which we are concerned. Thus, the monotonically decreasing function is not itself sufficient to specify the outcome of an experiment. While earlier authors sometimes assumed that a control condition, if included, would have fallen at point C, such an assumption is neither logically, nor necessarily empirically, correct.

While the need for some control condition is indisputable, the particular control condition to be used has been debated. The best single-stimulation control condition is a series of juxtaposed (blocked) single-stimulation trials. This was termed an informed control condition by Herman and Kantowitz (1970) since subjects always knew that only one stimulus would be presented. A catch-trial control, where some S_1-only trials are randomly inserted within a series of double-stimulation trials, should be avoided unless one is specifically interested in such variables as the proportion of catch trials, etc. Ditzian (1972) parametrically varied S_2 probablity in

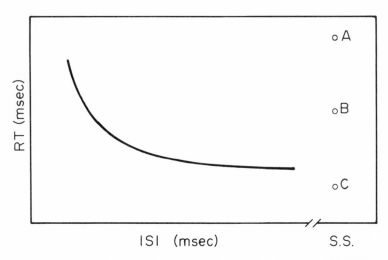

ISI (msec)   S.S.

FIG. 1. Typical outcome of a double-stimulation experiment. S.S. indicates a single-stimulation control condition. See text for explanation of points A, B, and C.

an $S_1 - R_1$, S_2 paradigm and in two experiments found no effect of S_2 probability for probabilities greater than zero. However, double-stimulation RT was elevated with respect to a between-S single-stimulation control group.

Some authors (e.g., Nickerson, 1970) have argued that a double-stimulation control condition is preferable to a single-stimulation control since the presentation of two stimuli is qualitatively different from the presentation of a single stimulus when no second stimulus is expected. Hence one preferred control condition would involve two stimuli separated by a relatively long ISI (Way & Gottsdanker, 1968). Presumably, this ISI should be sufficiently long to allow for dissipation of "normal" double-stimulation effects, i.e., the ISI should result in asymptotic RT although this is more likely for blocked rather than randomized ISI presentation. While the incorporation of a wide range of ISI is certainly desirable, asymptotic RT is most meaningful when the single-stimulation control falls at point C of Fig. 1. It is sometimes inappropriate to anticipate this outcome without actually incorporating a single-stimulation control. The safest procedure would be to use a single-stimulation control condition in addition to a double-stimulation condition with a large ISI.

The double-stimulation control condition proposed by Nickerson (1970) involved responding to a particular stimulus (a light instead of a tone) rather than to S_1 or S_2, i.e., the order of light and tone was random so that for any trial either light or tone could be S_1. Nickerson found RT to a light, when the tone followed the light by 400 or 800 msec, to exceed RT for a blocked single-stimulation control condition, and this outcome was interpreted as support for the utility of a double-stimulation control condition. Thus, while either control condition revealed RT facilitation for short ISIs, the amount of facilitation was greater when the double-stimulation control was used as a baseline. Use of this type of double-stimulation baseline blurs the distinction between $S_1 - R_1$, S_2 and S_1, $S_2 - R_2$ paradigms, i.e., Nickerson used the former as a control baseline for the latter. Unless the equivalence of these two single-response double-stimulation paradigms is firmly established empirically, discretion would indicate continued use of a single-stimulation control condition. Furthermore, a response to the light that preceded tone onset resulted in omission of the tone for that trial, so that very few tones were actually presented when the light preceded the tone by 400 or 800 msec. This complicates Nickerson's experiment even more since such trials are effectively catch trials. In this regard, Nickerson's finding of greater RT for catch trials relative to single-stimulation trials is in agreement with many similar findings (e.g., Bertelson, 1967; Smith, 1967b).

The final point in our discussion of paradigms concerns the treatment of error data. Most double-stimulation studies have regarded errors (incorrect responses) more as a nuisance than as a source of useful data, although there have been some notable exceptions (e.g., Rabbitt, 1969) which will be discussed in a later section concerning speed-accuracy tradeoff in double stimulation. Error trials have either been discarded and replaced with little or no reporting of the frequency and latencies of these discarded trials, or have been pooled with correct trials since error trials occurred with a low frequency (usually less than 10%). As has been amply demonstrated in the preceding chapter (Pachella, this volume) such a procedure is far too casual. However, before discussing implications of error data, we shall first turn to a review of the more important models of double stimulation.

MODELS

Limited Capacity Channel

The dominant model of double stimulation has been the limited-channel model originally proposed by Welford (1952) and Broadbent (1958) and later more (Broadbent, 1971), or less (Welford, 1967, 1968), modified in the fullness of time. Welford's single channel model explained RT_2 delay via a central decision mechanism that could deal with but one signal at a time. Data from S_2 was excluded until S_1 processing had been completed. This model predicts that for ISIs shorter than RT_1, RT_2 when plotted as a function of ISI would be a straight line with a slope of minus one.[2] When ISI exceeded RT_1, no delay in RT_2 would be expected, yielding a slope of zero. Since RT_1 varies from trial to trial, the sharp knee predicted by the determinist (fixed RT_1) model is replaced by the dotted function shown in Fig. 2. While this simple model does well in accounting for data, it can be improved by requiring feedback information, indicating that R_1 has been initiated, to trigger the gate allowing S_2 data to enter the decision mechanism (Welford, 1967). However, this improvement still does not allow the model to handle RT_2 delay at ISIs exceeding RT_1. Therefore, Welford added a feedback monitoring requirement so that the decision mechanism need be apprised not only of the initiation of R_1 but also of how well R_1 was doing. This monitoring requirement decreased with practice.

[2]This determinist prediction is strictly true only when RT_2 is plotted against response-stimulus interval rather than against ISI. This point will be expanded in a later section devoted to response-stimulus interval.

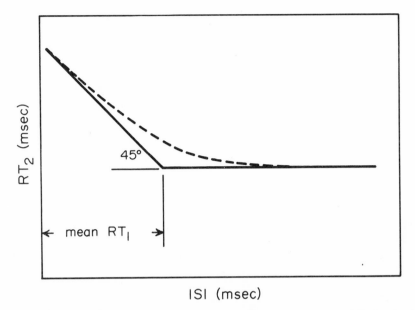

ISI (msec)

FIG. 2. Predicted RT_2 function for the single-channel model. (After Welford, 1967. Reprinted by permission of North-Holland Publishing Company, Amsterdam.)

In formulating his model, Welford was influenced by Craik (1947, 1948) and Welford's use of the term single channel refers to the inability of the decision mechanism to cope with more than one signal (or one group of signals occurring in very close succession) regardless of the processing load imposed by that signal. While this limitation did not originally depend upon the complexity of the data associated with a signal, Welford (1967) has allowed the possibility that high S_1-R_1 uncertainty might permit S_2 data to sneak into the decision mechanism between successive subdecisions (e.g., Hick, 1952) about S_1. This notion of an interruptable decision mechanism that can partially process incoming information, somehow store the intermediate outcome of such partial processing, and then later retrieve and complete processing is quite interesting but difficult to evaluate without a more detailed statement of the relationship between the successive subdecisions and interrupt mechanism. As has been noted by Ditzian (1972) and Tolkmitt (1973) a stimulus-interruption model might allow the single-channel model to deal with RT_1 delay. Even in its most recent formulation (Welford, 1968) single-channel theory does not seriously consider RT_1 effects. Although Welford (1968, p. 119) was aware of such data, he tends to dismiss these findings as "a change of strategy on the subject's part." More recent work has emphasized the importance of RT_1 data in understanding double-stimulation effects (Herman & Kantowitz, 1970). Without such an interrupt mechanism, the single-channel model is left only with the gate to the decision mechanism attenuating, rather than blocking, interfering signals (Welford, 1968, p. 119) but it is not at all clear how this attenuation hypothesis would predict RT_1 functions without substantial emendation.

While Welford's single channel can process but one signal at a time, Broadbent's (1958) limited-capacity channel is modeled after Shannon's (1949) work, and its limitation is on rate of information, e.g., bits/sec, transmitted through the channel. Broadbent's contribution was to replace the traditional stimulus-response framework of Welford with an informational analysis, although as Broadbent notes, Hick and Welford (1956) proposed that central processing time was shorter for higher probability stimuli; ordering events by their probability is tantamount to an informational analysis. Nevertheless, Broadbent is rightfully credited with developing the information-rate limited channel, since this concept was never stressed in Welford's later discussions of his single-channel model. Hence the limited channel may be viewed as a more generalized version of the single channel, and its explanation of double stimulation is essentially similar to that offered by the single channel.

The Welford (1968) and Broadbent (1958) model has been the benchmark against which newer models are tested. One important reason for this favored position has been the testability of the single-limited-channel model. The model's predictions for the PRP paradigm are clear and even quantitative (slope of minus one), although the model does not purport to be a mathematical model; indeed, a more specific mathematical statement of the model (Ollman, 1968) does not fare well. This outcome is related to the specificity of the predictions generated by the model. A model that is simple enough, and clearly articulated, will eventually be modified or perhaps even disproved to the extent that it cannot account for a large body of contradictory data. That such has been the fate of the limited-channel model (e.g., Herman & Kantowitz, 1970; Smith, 1967a) in no way diminishes its importance.

Broadbent's (1971) revision of his earlier model is considerably more complex than its precursor. This complexity follows directly from Broadbent's inductive method whereby the model is a summary of a tremendous corpus of research. The very success of the 1958 model in stimulating research poses the greatest hazard for the 1971 model. While this is not the place to review the 1971 model in all its scope (see Pew, 1971; Posner, 1972), it is appropriate to look at the current explanation of PRP. Posner (1972) has noted that the signal-detection framework adopted by Broadbent (1971) is not well-suited for a discussion of the speed of decisions. It is difficult to locate a change, other than in terminology, that distinguishes the 1971 model from the position in 1958 insofar as our concern is focused upon double stimulation. Broadbent (1971) attributes the PRP effect not to stimulus, response, or translation mechanisms but instead to the selection of a category state:

> The selection of the category state is an operation which loads the capacity of the system, and which therefore cannot be carried out as fast for two simultaneous processes as for one. This, as Welford suggested more than fifteen years ago, is undoubtedly the explanation of the delay to the second of closely successive reactions [p. 318].

The 1971 text also fails to consider RT_1 effects at all. Since this section of Broadbent's text does not cite any articles that occurred after 1967, it seems best to continue our discussion by emphasizing more recent models, put forth in the light of these later findings, as alternatives to the limited-capacity channel.

Variable-Allocation-Capacity Models

While a limited-capacity channel has a bottleneck (locus of limitation), no such locus is specified in a variable allocation model. Indeed this class of model emphatically denies the very existence of a bottleneck. According to variable allocation capacity models proposed by Moray (1967) and Kahneman (1973), effort or attention flows to meet task demands. The apparent bottleneck results from the nonlinear supply of effort as more capacity is demanded. While total capacity increases as a function of demand, this increase is at a slower rate than the increase in capacity flowing to the main or primary task, so that the net outcome is a decrease in excess or spare capacity with increasing capacity demanded. These relationships are illustrated in Fig. 3. However, in the limit as capacity demanded increases to some large value, no spare capacity is available and the variable allocation model asymptotically becomes a limited capacity model, with the locus of limitation being unspecified. A key assumption of Kahneman's (1973) model is that "the mobilization of effort in a task is controlled by the demands of the task, rather than by the performer's intentions [p. 17]." The variable allocation model is intended to be a rather general model of attention which can be applied to many situations. Thus, it is not surprising that the model, when restricted to the double-stimulation paradigm, offers few, if any, detailed predictions. Indeed Kahneman's chapter dealing with psychological refractoriness is devoted more to disproving other models than to asserting the predictions of the variable allocation model. One major difficulty in generating specific predictions for the model is the lack of an *a priori* standard that can allow distinction

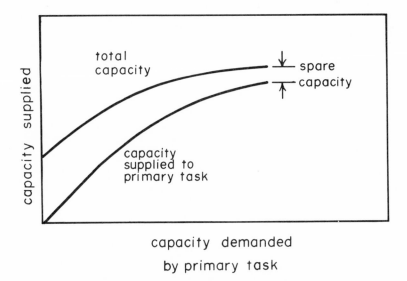

capacity demanded
by primary task

Fig. 3. Basic mechanism of Kahneman's variable-capacity model. Note that other variable-capacity configurations are possible, e.g., capacity supplied to primary task could continue to increase with a slope of one until the total capacity line is reached. (From Kahneman, 1973. Reprinted by permission of Prentice-Hall, Inc., Englewood Cliffs, New Jersey.)

between the task demands and the performer's intentions. This point can be illustrated by the $S_1 - R_1$, S_2 paradigm, findings from which are considered to be consistent with a shared-capacity model (Kahneman, 1973, p. 175). Since no response is ever demanded to S_2, one might assume that task demands direct the flow of effort to only $S_1 - R_1$ so that no RT_1 delay should be predicted. However, since Kahneman takes this finding as support for the model, presumably something else is intended as the demands of the task. If S_2 demands effort, then results are consistent with the model; however, there is no converging operation to help explain why S_2 does demand effort. Furthermore, it is not clear how the variable allocation model can explain Ditzian's (1972) finding that RT_1 delay did not vary as a function of S_2 probability.

Kahneman attributes the "survival of single-channel theory" to a tradition of plotting results as illustrated in Fig. 1, where RT varies as a function of ISI. He proposes that the interresponse interval (IRI) be substituted for RT_2 as a preferred dependent variable so that IRI would be plotted as a function of ISI. This has the advantage of transforming the prediction of single-channel theory from a slope of minus one to a slope of zero; Kahneman then argues that it is much easier to detect functions that are not horizontal rather than functions that deviate from a slope of minus one. However, most experimental psychologists are capable of drawing a 45° line and, if pressed, can even rotate the entire plot 45° to make the line appear horizontal. The single-channel model has considerably greater virtues, including its testability (e.g., Welford, 1967) which account for its longevity. Furthermore, using IRI as a dependent variable has two major disadvantages. First, it cannot be used in single-response double-stimulation paradigms or for first responses in the double-response paradigm so that we are forced to return to the traditional plot to compare results. Second IRI varies in part with ISI (IRI = ISI + $RT_2 - RT_1$), so that plotting IRI as a function of ISI may confound an independent variable (ISI) with a dependent variable (RT).

One recurrent problem with the models so far discussed is localization of the bottleneck in information processing. The single channel of Welford has a central decision mechanism as the bottleneck; however, since the Welford model has but three stages (perceptual mechanism, translator mechanism, and central effector mechanism), any one stage neccessarily covers a great deal. The limited channel of Broadbent is even less specific about the locus of limited-channel effects, and this ambiguity has increased in the latest version of the model. The variable allocation model attempts to make a virtue of this difficulty by categorically refusing to acknowledge any bottleneck, and this leads to the greatest ambiguity and most amorphous model.

The next class of models to be considered makes more specific predictions about the probable locus (or loci) of double-stimulation effects. The price for this ability to generate more detailed predictions is perhaps a loss of generality, although only very few of these models were formulated with explanation or description of psychological refractoriness as a final end.

Response Conflict Model

The response conflict model, originally proposed for single-stimulation data by Berlyne (1957), and extended to psychological refractoriness by Reynolds (1964) and to all double-stimulation paradigms by Herman and Kantowitz (1970), postulates response processing as the primary, but not necessarily the only, locus of double-stimulation effects. Two main themes can be discerned in the development of the response conflict model. The basic motif is the attribution of delay (or facilitation) to the interaction of competing (or summating) response *tendencies*. Every overt response has its corresponding response tendency. These tendencies are aroused directly by the stimuli which are mapped to the overt responses (Berlyne, 1957), by stimulus mediation when stimuli mapped to responses are repeatedly juxtaposed (Herman & Kantowitz, 1970), and by response generalization for similar response orientations (Kantowitz, 1973). Predictions of the response conflict model are derived in part from the relationship among response tendencies. Herman and Kantowitz (1970) distinguished three types of relationships. If S_1 and S_2 are mapped to the same response, the relationship was termed reinforcing, and either RT facilitation or, at least no RT delay, was predicted. If the stimuli serve a dual role, functioning as S_1 on some trials and S_2 on other trials (e.g., two lights either of which is randomly selected as S_1 with the other then S_2), the relationship was termed opposing and RT delay was predicted, provided of course that each stimulus is mapped to a unique response. The case where stimuli serve a unitary role, functioning always as either S_1 or S_2 (e.g., two pairs of lights with the left set always containing S_2) was not explicitly considered by Herman and Kantowitz (1970), but it also should be termed opposing, provided again that each stimulus is mapped to a unique response; however, the predicted delay would not be as great as for the opposing relationship with dual-role stimuli. Finally, if no response is mapped to either S_1 or S_2 the relationship was termed neutral and no delay was predicted (Herman, 1969). For the neutral mapping it is likely that factors that do not influence response selection (e.g., stimulus discriminability) would increase their relative importance.

Within the opposing relationship, responses and response tendencies can be more or less antagonistic. Thus, predicted RT delay is greater when S_1 signals a response that is UP, while S_2 signals a response that is DOWN, than if both responses were UP. This effect, supported by data (e.g., Kantowitz, 1973; Way & Gottsdanker, 1968), can be attributed to response generalization gradients which in turn might be related to similarity in motor programs governing execution and control of such related responses. Since a response tendency precedes response execution, the bottleneck for the response conflict model is the selection stage rather than the response execution stage. The difficulty in *selecting* from among a set of competing similar motor programs could be related to the organization of such programs residing in storage. In addition to the difficulties associated with indexing an array of similar programs in long-term storage, there may also be confusions in working memory which maintains the mappings between motor programs residing in long-term storage and specific motor effector units. The patterns of motor control mentioned earlier in the first chapter (e.g., Pew, 1966) could be related to more efficient interfacing between memory and controlling routines arising with practice. Hence, in double-stimulation response generalization effects would be greatest for naive subjects and would be decreased for practiced subjects.

A possible difficulty for the conflict model is *a priori* specification of degree of response antagonism. These problems are similar to those arising in attempts to specify stimulus-response compatibility. One solution would be the use of population stereotypes or ratings to determine response antagonism, as is the usual case with S–R compatibility. A better solution would be to search for indices of response generalization from converging operations derived perhaps from single-stimulation measures (confusions, etc.).

The second main theme of the response conflict model, composed by Herman and Kantowitz (1970), states that both RT_1 and RT_2 effects are opposite sides of the same coin; this theme is also common to the variable-allocation model previously discussed. This principle explains the great concern with RT_1 evinced by advocates of this model. Since all double-stimulation models postdict the PRP effect, models can be more easily rejected with RT_1 rather than RT_2 findings. Of course, this strategy assumes that a parsimonious model for all double stimulation is preferable to two separate models for RT_1 and RT_2 effects and that such a single model will explain RT_2 effects at least as well as a model devoted solely to the PRP effect. Note, however, that this second theme does not lead to the prediction of identical RT_1 and RT_2 effects in double stimulation. The model assumes that *prepotent* responses are less subject to delay (Reynolds, 1964). Response tendencies become prepotent either by having a temporal lead over other response tendencies (e.g., R_1 in the double-response paradigm) or by pay-off matrix manipulations or instructions. Thus RT_2 delay would exceed RT_1 delay if instructions gave equal weight to R_1 and R_2 and all other things were equal.

Berlyne (1957) first applied the concept of response conflict to RT and gave a formula for calculating the amount of conflict. He assumed the existence of a set of response tendencies $(r_1, \ldots, r_n)$ with some strength vector $(E_1, \ldots, E_n)$ mapped one-to-one to provide a measure for the response tendency set. The degree-of-conflict function $C(E_1, \ldots, E_n)$ was to satisfy six conditions (p. 332):

1. C is continuous and symmetric in the E;
2. $C \geqslant 0$;
3. if $n=1$, $C=0$;
4. with $\sum E_i$ held constant, C reaches an absolute maximum when $E_1 = E_2 = E_n$;
5. If $E_1 = E_n$, and a response R_{n+1} with strength E_{n+1} is added to the set, C increases:
6. if every E_i is multiplied by $k > 1$, C increases.

By transforming the measure function into a weight function, Berlyne translates the E set to a p set with each p_i representing a measure of probability on each R_i. One conflict function which satisfies the six conditions is $C = -\bar{E} \sum p_i \log_2 p_i$, which is the Shannon information metric multiplied by the mean E (strength) value. Thus, the conflict function provides an explanation of the well-known finding of a linear increase in single-stimulation RT with uncertainty; it is response uncertainty and not stimulus uncertainty that mediates Hick's Law. The relationship among response strength, response latency, and response probability poses a problem that has never been satisfactorily resolved. Luce (1960) applied his choice axiom to develop a very general model relating response latencies and probabilities. However, the very elegance and generality of his approach leads to complex mathematical issues that must be resolved prior to extending this approach to double stimulation where two overlapping response sets interact. However, the response conflict model does make one simple prediction for double stimulation. With zero response uncertainty, there is zero conflict; thus the simplest form of the response conflict model states that no RT delay should be encountered under conditions of response certainty. This prediction was confirmed by Herman (1969).

Ideomotor Mechanism

The basic concept of an ideomotor mechanism was first proposed by James (1890) and more recently revived by Greenwald (1970). The key concept in this model is an anticipatory image that governs response selection. The model shares certain features of the response conflict model previously discussed in that both models specify response selection as the locus of the bottleneck in information processing and both models have benefited from precepts of earlier learning theories. The anticipatory ideomotor image is similar to the fractional anticipatory goal response of Hull (1931) with one crucial distinction: For ideomotor theory it is not the ultimate goal response that is anticipated but instead the sensory feedback arising from the on-going response. The image, while arising from the sensory feedback (reafference) from responses, is not the same as the feedback itself but rather is a central representation of the feedback. Thus a response image is an abstraction of feedback information about a class of responses rather than a representation of some particular response within such a class. Here the ideomotor model differs from the response conflict model which deals directly with specific response tendencies and concerns classes of responses only when more general features such as response antagonism are invoked. A task has high ideomotor compatibility when a stimulus corresponds to the sensory feedback produced by its associated responses (Greenwald, 1972); thus, repeating an auditorally presented word is a task with high ideomotor compatibility. Response selection is bypassed for tasks with high ideomotor compatibility (Greenwald, 1972) since the stimulus automatically selects (addresses) the appropriate response code. According to the ideomotor model, the bottleneck in response selection varies with ideomotor incompatibility. Thus, with a highly ideomotor compatible task as one component of a double-stimulation task set, refractory delays should be entirely eliminated since the response selection mechanism is utilized by only one (the less ideomotor compatible) of the two responses.

Buffer Model

The model described in this section is included mainly for propaedeutic reasons since it has not yet exerted any influence upon double-stimulation research, i.e., the reader should not consider it as important as, say, the limited-channel model.

However, the buffer model does offer one unique advantage relative to the more established models. While the preceding models contain tacit provisions for memory mechanisms, the role of memory has not been stressed. No adaptive system can operate without some memory capability, and the human ranks as a superb adaptive control system which engineers and computer scientists strive to duplicate. We shall now consider a model in which the memory component is very explicit. This model, which specifically locates a response selection bottleneck in short-term memory, has been proposed by Smith (1972). Smith uses a two-stage model similar to that proposed by Atkinson and Juola (1973) to describe memory retrieval. In order for a response to be executed, the motor program residing in long-term memory needs to be accessed. If the stimulus can match some feature of the response representation, as might be expected for highly ideomotor-compatible tasks, long-term memory is contacted directly. Otherwise a short-term response buffer is required. Each entry in this buffer contains the starting location of a motor program in long-term memory and a marker indicating which stimulus is paired with that response program. This buffer is searched either sequentially or by a limited-capacity parallel process. (The following chapter by Townsend explains these concepts in some detail.) Response selection is achieved when an item is retrieved from the buffer or contacted directly in long-term memory for conditions with high ideomotor compatibility. This model has the great virtue of relating double-stimulation research to memory research by placing the bottleneck in short-term memory. Let us examine the behavior of the model in more detail.

Delay in the S_1-R_1, S_2-R_2 paradigm relative to the S_1-R_1 control condition is explained by the extra time needed to search the response buffer: There are more responses in the buffer in the S_1-R_1, S_2-R_2 paradigm than in the S_1-R_1 control. However, with sufficiently long ISIs, buffer entries pertaining to R_1 are replaced by R_2 items so that search time is decreased since search always starts from the top of the buffer. This yields decreasing RT_2 delays. There is at least one serious flaw in this argument. Let us take one of the simplest double-stimulation tasks with two stimulus lights mapped to two response buttons. In the double-stimulation S_1-R_1, S_2-R_2 condition the response buffer must contain two items even for the S_2-R_2 component items: These correspond to left and right buttons. However, in the S_1-R_1 control condition the buffer still must contain these same two items since both responses are possible with one bit of response uncertainty. Hence, the buffer model incorrectly predicts no RT difference between single- and double-stimulation conditions. This difficulty can be avoided by restricting the model to situations where R_1 and R_2 sets are independent. Even so, the model needs emendation to make differential predictions for single- and double-response double-stimulation conditions. In all fairness, it should be noted that this model was not proposed as a detailed model of double stimulation, but rather was constructed largely to stress possible commonalities between short-term memory and response selection. This basic idea may be correct although some of the details of Smith's formulation require reworking.

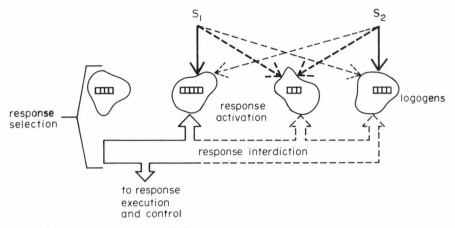

FIG. 4. Two stages of response selection.

Response Initiation Model

A rather different view of memory processes in double stimulation has been taken by Keele (1973). With evidence drawn from the Stroop effect[3] and an important experiment by Karlin and Kestenbaum (1968) (to be discussed in the next section), Keele concluded that memory retrieval was *not* implicated as the bottleneck in double stimulation. Instead, a response initiation stage (defined as that operation subsequent to retrieval) was specified as the locus of delay. Thus Keele, contrary to Smith, rejects response selection as the locus of refractory effects. Since Keele's model is in many ways quite similar to the response conflict model previously discussed, this rejection of response selection may at first appear surprising. This apparent difficulty arises from differences in terminology and confusion among concepts such as response selection, response competition, response initiation, and stimulus-response translation. It will therefore prove instructive to turn to a brief aside and examine similarities of the two models: the response conflict model of Kantowitz and the logogen[4] model of Keele.

A simplified schematic rendering of the response conflict-logogen model is portrayed in Fig. 4. Neither model emphasizes the role of stimulus identification/preprocessing in double stimulation, although Keele has been more emphatic in denying the relative importance of this stage of information processing. Both models agree that all stimulus information makes contact with memory, depicted as the row of blobs in Fig. 4. The blob, or logogen, is the stage at which memory information becomes activated.[4] The dotted lines leading to logogens

---

[3]The Stroop effect is an increased RT obtained when a color name (e.g., red) is printed in a different color ink (e.g., green). It takes longer to respond when the name and the ink are conflicting than when the colors are printed as non-letter forms (see Keele, 1973).

[4]A description of the logogen model can be found in Smith (this volume).

indicate that more than one stimulus may activate particular logogens via stimulus generalization (cf., Herman & Kantowitz, 1970). When a logogen is sufficiently activated, as determined by some decision rule, its output leads to the next stage of information processing. This process of selecting the output of *one* logogen from the set of possible logogen outputs is termed response activation. Since the logogen is conceived of as a stochastic mechanism rather than a deterministic mechanism (Knight & Kantowitz, 1974) on any trial the correct logogen output is activated only with a high probability rather than with certainty. In particular, the logogen is regarded as an *accumulator* of information (Audley & Pike, 1965); this class of model has been discussed in the preceding chapter by Pachella and will be again discussed by Smith (this volume). Furthermore, the time required to reach a sufficient level of activation also varies stochastically. A large set of decision rules can be used to determine a sufficient level of activation. Whether the decision rule is simple (e.g., select the logogen with the highest count) or complex (select the logogen based upon likelihood ratios[5]), effects of ISI and stimulus similarity will be reflected in speed/accuracy measures. However, activation of a response tendency at the level of logogen output reduces, but does not necessarily eliminate, response competition. As was noted by Kantowitz and Sanders (1972), competition can still exist between two *sets* of response tendencies even though competition within each set has been reduced. The second type of response selection necessary to remove this later source of response competition will be termed response interdiction[6] to distinguish it from response activation at the logogen level. This stage of information processing is represented in Fig. 4 as the heavy solid and dotted arrows aimed at the bottom of the logogens. The solid arrow represents the first response to be initiated (i.e., released from interdiction) while the dotted extension corresponds to the second response. Only one response can be initiated at a time, or equivalently, if responses can be initiated in parallel this can occur only within a limited-capacity parallel processor. (This equivalence is demonstrated in the following chapter by Townsend.) The response interdiction stage is always invoked in double stimulation when more than one logogen is activated, even if only one overt response is required (Kantowitz, 1973) so that even in single-response double-stimulation conditions two response initiation arrows (solid and dotted) need be drawn as in Fig. 4. The details of response interdiction depend upon whether the decision rule changes or is invariant after the first response has been selected. While response activation is primarily an excitatory process, response interdiction is primarily an inhibitory process.

Other Models

The preceding review of double-stimulation models has been illustrative rather than exhaustive; indeed, emphasis has been placed upon the more recent models.

[5]Pachella (this volume) terms this a random walk model.

[6]This is similar to Keele's (1973) response initiation. Interdiction and initiation are complementary terms since a response tendency that is not interdicted will be initiated. The term interdiction is used since this component of the response selection process is nonexcitatory. However, the term initiation permits simpler description.

Discussions of older models can be found in Bertelson (1966), Smith (1967a), and Herman and Kantowitz (1970). However, two older models should be mentioned. The *central-refractory* model of Telford (1931) has already been cited as the source of the term psychological refractory period. Its major premise is that a central mechanism becomes temporarily insensitive to additional input once some preceding input has been processed. While most reviewers have rejected this model, some interesting data (Koster & Peacock, 1969) based upon variations of stimulus intensity with simple (Donders *a*) reactions, suggest that a modified refractory model in which sensitivity is reduced, rather than eliminated completely, may be tractable. It has yet to be determined if such a model can deal with choice reactions and constant, rather than random, blocks of ISI.

The *expectancy* model (Adams, 1962) tries to explain refractoriness as resulting from temporal uncertainty associated with S_2. This model has proved lacking since RT delay has often been obtained with constant blocks of ISI, i.e., temporal certainty. The epitaph for this model was written by Nickerson (1965) who demonstrated that Adams' (1962) results were compatible with a single-channel model.

DATA, MODELS, AND HOW THEY INTERACT

While models are of great importance in guiding data collection and organizing the corpus of data, models are more transient than data since each new model must explain old data. This point is made rather dramatically by comparing the models summarized in the previous section with those summarized by Broadbent, either earlier (1958) or more recently (1971). It perhaps only borders on hyperbole to state that while models are evanescent, good (i.e., replicable) data are eternal. The focus of interest in this section is neither data, nor models exclusively, but rather the interaction between data and models. The model, of course, is used both to guide data collection and to provide a framework to help us to remember the data. The data are used to modify the model. This section highlights this interplay by showing how the choice of model limits the kind of data collected, and how experimental outcomes refine, or perhaps even reject, the model that engendered the data collection. Thus, this section will be organized around the crux of any experiment: the independent and dependent variables selected to control and measure behavior in the double-stimulation task. Independent and dependent variables are the vehicles through which models gain access to data. This progression could be extended an additional step by recalling the slogan of a major computer company: "not just data—reality." Unfortunately, reality, as obtained by experiments, comes in tiny pieces. Attempts at assembling the pieces of the puzzle take us away from the data base and back to the models.

Background

The major issue in the study of double stimulation has been psychological refractoriness. Investigators have concentrated their efforts, by definition, to relating RT_2 to ISI. Thus, the most salient independent variable (ISI) and the appropriate dependent variable (RT_2) have been dictated by the invisible hand of tradition. These strictures have been taken quite literally by many authors, and it is easy to find studies that demanded R_1 but did not present RT_1 data, or studies that reported RT_2 as a function of ISI but failed to report R_2 accuracy as a function of ISI, or even at all; both omissions testify to the sanctity of RT_2 as the only proper dependent variable. Investigators have been more inventive as to independent variables, since once ISI has been presented in blocked versus randomized trials, there is little else to vary and other independent variables then need be sought. Nevertheless, considerable effort has gone into various manners of permuting the ISI variable, as will be noted under temporal uncertainty. While these oversights may appear almost foolish in the pitiless spotlight of hindsight, it is important to realize that such deficits become more visible when the basic issue is redefined from the very specific problem of psychological refractoriness to the more general problem of double stimulation.

Sample Experiment

Karlin & Kestenbaum (1968). This experiment is, in many ways, typical of PRP research in the previous decade. It will be discussed in some detail, not only as an exemplar of a class of experiments, but also because of the importance of the manipulations of the major independent variable. We shall see how the experiment was derived as a test of the limited-capacity channel and how its results compel rejection of that model. Finally, and perhaps of greatest importance, we shall see how the data from this experiment have been used to support models that were not envisioned or discussed by the authors.

A trial in this experiment had the following attributes. First, a 1 KHz warning tone sounded for 40 msec. S_1 followed after a mean foreperiod delay of 2 sec; four equiprobable foreperiods ranging from 1.7 to 2.3 sec were used. The first stimulus was a digit exposed for 35 msec. Twelve ISIs ranging from 90 to 1150 msec were randomly presented so that both temporal uncertainty and event uncertainty were characteristic of all trials. The left hand controlled five buttons which corresponded to the digits 1–5 while the right hand controlled two buttons which corresponded to the two S_2 tones. In a later portion of the experiment, only one tone was presented so that S_2–R_2 was a simple, rather than a choice, reaction. The major independent variable was the number of choices associated with S_1–R_1: These conditions were denoted as 1-2, 2-2, and 5-2, where the first number indicates the size of the set of possible digits and the second number the set of two tones. Two additional conditions, 1-1 and 2-1, were also used to provide S_2–R_2 certainty. No single-stimulation control conditions were used in the experiment.

The major results of this experiment, based upon means of four subjects, are shown in Figs. 5 and 6. First, we shall examine the interpretation of these data given by Karlin and Kestenbaum. The basic equation of the single-channel model is $RT_2 = RT_1 -$ ISI $+ RT_N$, where RT_N is defined as the "normal" processing time for S_2, had S_1 not been presented. As RT_1 varies (due to variation in the number of choices associated with S_1–R_1) a family of parallel functions should be generated which differ as to knee, which occurs at ISI $= RT_1$. All the functions should reach the same asymptote

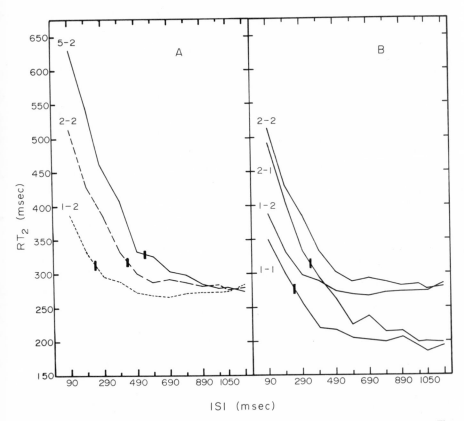

FIG. 5. Mean RT_2 as a function of ISI. (From Karlin & Kestenbaum, 1968. Copyrighted by The Experimental Psychology Society. Reprinted with permission.)

at long ISIs. The data of Fig. 5A generally support this prediction since the curves appear parallel at short ISIs. However, none of the functions asymptote (RT_N) at the vertical bars that give the predicted ISI at which RT_2 should asymptote; further analyses performed by Karlin and Kestenbaum indicate that this additional delay cannot be attributed to effects of averaging over subjects or to RT_1 variability.

A more important analysis is contained in Fig. 5B in which changes in both S_1-R_1 and S_2-R_2 load can be compared. As RT_N varies (due to variation in the number of choices associated with S_2-R_2), another parallel family of curves should be obtained for short ISIs if the single-channel model is correct. An illustration based upon the single-channel equation can be found in Table 2. This prediction is not supported in the data of Fig. 5B. When either conditions 2-1 and 2-2 or 1-1 and 1-2 are compared, the difference in RT_2 decreases as ISI decreases, whereas the single-channel model predicts a constant difference.

Figure 6 shows RT_1 as a function of ISI. Increasing the number of R_2 choices from 1 to 2 causes a consistent RT_1 increment of all ISIs. Although no single-stimulation

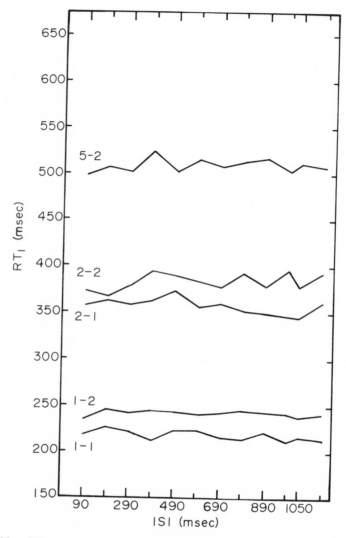

FIG. 6. Mean RT_1 as a function of ISI. (From Karlin & Kestenbaum, 1968. Copyrighted by The Experimental Psychology Society. Reprinted with permission.)

control condition was employed, comparison of these RT_1 data with asymptotic RT_2 data (1150 msec) reveals an RT_1 elevation of from 20 to 30 msec in all conditions. Thus, while RT_1 does not vary as a function of ISI it is elevated at all ISIs. This elevation was not noted by Karlin and Kestenbaum who evinced more concern over the flat shape of the RT_1 function. However, in the absence of error data at each ISI it is difficult to reach firm conclusions based solely upon the shape of RT_1 (or to a lesser extent, RT_2) data. Knight and Kantowitz (1974) obtained flat RT_1 functions under speed stress but found error frequencies to increase at shorter ISIs. Since it is

TABLE 2

Predicted RT_2 for the Single-Channel Model as a Function of Number of Choices (N)
Associated with $S_2 - R_2$

$$RT_2 = RT_1 - ISI + RT_N$$

ISI	Predicted[a] RT_2 (Smaller N)	Predicted[a] RT_2 (Larger N)
50	450	500
100	400	450
200	300	350
300	200	250

[a] RT_1 is assumed to be 300 msec in all cases. Asymptotic RT_N is assumed equal to 250 msec for larger N and 200 msec for smaller N.

well-known that accuracy can be traded-off for speed and vice-versa (see preceding chapter by Pachella) predictions generated from the single-channel model and indeed most other models of double stimulation tacitly assume a negligible error rate and/or no speed-accuracy trade-off.

Karlin and Kestenbaum have noted difficulties, as discussed above, with the single-channel model but did not offer an alternative model. This is, of course, an entirely reasonable approach, since difficulties with present models must be noted before there is either incentive or need to formulate additional models. The manipulations used in the Karlin-Kestenbaum experiment guarantee that their data will continue to remain useful both for established and nascent explanations of double stimulation. But it is also important to realize how preoccupation with only one model caused the experimenters to deemphasize other important features of their results. One such feature, the elevation of RT_1, has already been noted and is consistent with both response conflict and variable allocation models.

Another important feature has been stressed by Keele (1973). Examining data at the longest (1150 msec) ISI, Keele noted an 81 msec increase in RT_2 when two alternatives are compared with one alternative. When condition 2-2 is compared with condition 2-1 the RT_2 increase is only 27 msec at the shortest (90 msec) ISI. Similar findings were obtained when conditions 1-2 and 1-1 are compared with a 90 msec difference at the longest ISI and a 39 msec difference at the shortest. Keele used the difference at the longest ISI as an estimate of the difference between simple and choice RT; no better estimate was available since no single-stimulation control conditions were incorporated in the Karlin and Kestenbaum study. The 9 msec discrepancy between these two estimates is not appreciable unless the difference of differences $[(1-2$ minus $1-1)$ minus $(2-2$ minus $2-1)]$ is the object of scrutiny. Keele interpreted the increase in RT, when simple and two-choice single-stimulation tasks are compared, as increased time to obtain the appropriate response from memory for the two-choice task. If this assumption is granted, then the double-stimulation results of Karlin and Kestenbaum cannot be attributed to the inability of two signals to contact memory simultaneously. If such were the case, S_2 would be delayed by a constant amount (81 or 90 msec) at all ISIs while memory was occupied with S_1 processing. The obtained difference at brief ISIs, while less than 81 msec, was still greater than zero msec, which Keele might predict on the basis of a parallel memory system. Nevertheless, the 27 (or 39) msec difference is explained by Keele as due to the brief RT_1 so that memory retrieval for S_2 is not yet completed before RT_1. Hence, the refractory delay in RT_2 is due to a stage of information processing subsequent to memory retrieval; Keele has termed this later stage response initiation. Lest this theoretical aside obscure the important empirical finding noticed by Keele in the results of Karlin and Kestenbaum, it will be repeated: As the double-stimulation task is made more difficult (as viewed by most models) by decreasing the ISI, the amount of overlap between $S_1 - R_1$ and $S_2 - R_2$ increases, as evidenced by decreasing differences between simple and two-choice RT_2. We shall return to this important issue of overlap or timesharing in a following section on attention and double stimulation.

Event Uncertainty

After ISI, event uncertainty is one of the most salient variables in double stimula-tion since it allows us to control the processing time associated with R_1 and/or R_2. The Karlin and Kestenbaum experiment is a good example of the potency of this variable. The most recent review of double stimulation (Herman & Kantowitz, 1970) was organized around a taxonomy of event uncertainty. Herman and Kantowitz showed that the crucial dichotomy is between event-certain and event-uncertain arrangements. Many of the earlier double-stimulation studies utilized two lights mapped to two responses. If one light (e.g., the left light) always serves as S_1 then both $S_1 - R_1$ and $S_2 - R_2$ are simple reactions characterized by event certainty. While RT delays have been obtained in this condition (Koster & Peacock, 1969, among others) there are special considerations associated with event certainty. First, most investigators using simple reactions in double stimulation have felt impelled to randomize ISI within blocks of trials. This precaution can be attributed to the obvious difficulty in evaluating RT_2 had ISI been fixed. With event certainty and fixed ISI, S_1 functions as an additional warning signal so that R_2 can be emitted without any perceptual operations being performed upon S_2. Indeed, under such circumstances, RT_2 can be reliably faster than a single-stimulation simple RT (Knight & Kantowitz, 1974). It is difficult to distinguish effects of temporal uncertainty from other double-stimulation effects when randomized ISIs are used with simple reactions. Some investigators attempted to circumvent part of the difficulty with simple reactions by allowing the first of two lights to appear on either left or right spatial positions, thus ensuring event uncertainty for $S_1 - R_1$. The difficulty with this procedure is not that it is a partial advance information paradigm, but lies instead with the simple reaction still required for $S_2 - R_2$, so that temporal certainty would again lead to grouped responses. Of course, if only R_1 is required then event certainty for S_2 is not a problem (e.g., Kantowitz, 1969, 1972). In general, simple reactions minimize or eliminate RT delay (e.g., Brebner, 1971; Gottsdanker, 1969; Herman, 1969) so that tests of double-stimulation models are more appropriately conducted with choice reactions.

In virtually all double-stimulation experiments concerned with event uncertainty, use of a one-to-one mapping (i.e., each stimulus is assigned to only one response) of stimuli onto responses confounds stimulus and response information. It is impossible to establish how much of the uncertainty effect is due to stimulus uncertainty and how much to response uncertainty under this mapping. Such a comparison would aid in distinguishing between models that emphasize perceptual aspects of double stimulation and those that elevate response processes. An experiment that varied stimulus and response uncertainties (by manipulating number of alternatives) independently by using many-to-one mappings (i.e., more than one stimulus assigned to a response) in addition to one-to-one mappings has been conducted by Ditzian (1972). Ditzian used an $S_1 - R_1$, S_2 paradigm with two and three bits of stimulus uncertainty combined with one and two bits of response uncertainty. Constant blocks of ISI ranging from 25 to 400 msec were used. His results are shown in Fig. 7. A one bit increment in stimulus information resulted in a 14 msec RT_1 increment, while a one bit increment in response information resulted in a 116 msec RT_1 increment. Point estimates of variance showed that the treatment variance due to response information was 75 times that due to stimulus information. Finally, while the interaction between stimulus information and ISI was reliable, $F(4,192) = 2.53, p < .05$, the interaction between response information and ISI was considerably stronger, $F(4,192) = 6.92, p < .001$. Hence, while both stimulus and response effects are present in double stimulation, manipulation of event uncertainty indicates response processes as the more important locus.

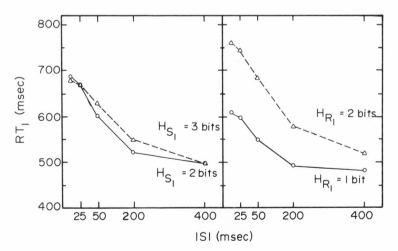

FIG. 7. Stimulus and response effects in the S_1-R_1, S_2 double-stimulation paradigm. (After Ditzian, 1972 with permission.)

Stimulus–Response Compatibility

Another method for increasing processing time of either S_1-R_1 or S_2-R_2 is utilization of unfamiliar S–R mappings. Such an experiment was conducted by Broadbent and Gregory (1967) using two pairs of neon stimulus lamps mapped to corresponding pairs of response keys. In the compatible conditions subjects responded by pressing the key directly beneath the neon lamp. In the incompatible condition the S–R mapping required the subject to press the key beneath the lamp that was not illuminated. The experiment included appropriate single-stimulation control conditions and ISI (0 to 550 msec) was constant for each block of trials. In the incompatible condition, RT_2 delay relative to an incompatible single-stimulation control was much greater at all ISIs. These results were taken as supporting the single-channel model of Welford.

A similar finding was obtained by Triggs (1968). While Broadbent and Gregory manipulated only S_1-R_1 and S_2-R_2 compatibility together, Triggs manipulated them independently for a total of four compatibility conditions: both compatible, both incompatible, and either S_1-R_1 or S_2-R_2 incompatible but not both. The compatibility manipulation was similar to that of Broadbent and Gregory with each pair of lights being mapped to a two-position toggle switch; incompatible mappings required an upward movement to the lower light and vice versa. Triggs' subjects were instructed to stress the speed of S_1-R_1 processing, and ISI (100 to 800 msec) was presented in a randomized series. The small number of subjects used by Triggs ($N=4$/condition versus 12/condition for Broadbent and Gregory) resulted in high variability which may have obscured some of his findings. Comparing RT_2 to a compatible S_2-R_2 when preceded by either compatible or incompatible S_1-R_1, slightly greater RT_2 was found for the incompatible S_1-R_1; however, this effect vanished for ISIs ≥ 500 msec. However, before concluding that this finding supports the limited-channel model, we should first examine another pair of conditions used by Triggs. When S_2-R_2 is incompatible what are the effects of compatible and incompatible mappings for S_1-R_1? According to the limited-channel model, RT_2 should again be greater for the incompatible S_1-R_1 mapping since it will follow a greater RT_1. Triggs obtained the opposite outcome: RT_2 was much greater when preceded by a compatible S_1-R_1. Although Triggs does not use this finding to reject the single-channel model, as it indeed should be faulted, he does offer an important explanation of this set of outcomes. Performance is always better when the rule controlling S_1-R_1 mapping is also the rule controlling S_2-R_2 mapping; in other terminology, a common rule decreases the degree of response antagonism. It is appropriate to note here a methodological shortcoming in studies, such as those just discussed, that attempt to vary either S_1-R_1 or S_2-R_2 processing time by manipulating the compatibility of only one set of mappings. Such studies, by forcing a rule change between sets of reactions, confound effects of response antagonism, especially when both sets of reactions are based upon spatial relationships.

Response-Stimulus Interval

In the typical double-stimulation experiment, mean[7] scores are reported. In the S_1–R_1, S_2–R_2 paradigm, such averaging can obscure the relationship between RT_1 and RT_2 for individual trials so that it is often desirable to concentrate upon pairs of RTs bereft of descriptive statistics (e.g., Kerr, Mingay, & Elithorn, 1965). It is well-known that RT_2 delays can and do occur at ISIs that exceed mean RT_1; indeed Welford (1952, 1967) proposed that such findings might be explained by a feedback monitoring process. Broadbent and Gregory (1967), in the experiment discussed in the preceding section, looked at individual RTs at ISIs near mean RT_1. In their compatible condition, when only pairs of RTs for which RT_1 was less than ISI are considered, no significant RT_2 delay was found. However, in their incompatible condition, RT_2 delay was obtained even when ISI exceeded RT_1. These findings were explained by a slight modification of Welford's feedback monitoring: It was assumed that the amount of time required to process feedback was proportional to RT_1 rather than being fixed for any given level of practice.

An obvious difficulty, when the focus of interest is bifurcating RT_1s into cases that either are greater or less than the ISI, is our dependence upon the distribution or variance of RT_1 to provide a sufficiency of both cases. Using a response-stimulus interval (RSI) in place of an ISI solves half this difficulty by guaranteeing that all RT_1s are bounded from above by the ISI. In an RSI procedure the time elapsing before S_2 onset is measured not from S_1 onset but instead from R_1 onset. Thus, S_2 is never presented before R_1 is completed. With the more common ISI procedure, RSI is uncontrolled so that the experimenter concerned with RSI is at the mercy of his subjects. With the RSI procedure, ISI is uncontrolled so that the experimenter concerned with RSI is less aware of his dependence upon his subjects.

Herman and Kantowitz (1969) used an S_1–R_1, S_2 paradigm with RSIs of 50, 100, and 150 msec. Although a matched earlier study (Herman & Israel, 1967) using ISI had obtained RT_1 delay, no such delay was found relative to a single-stimulation control group in the RSI design. This outcome was attributed to the insertion of S_2 after response selection had been completed.

Using an S_1–R_1, S_2–R_2 paradigm with variable RSI both Baumeister and Kellas (1967) and Koster and Bekker (1967) obtained a small RT_2 delay only when RSI was 200 msec or less; however, both studies required a simple R_2. Triggs (1968) improved upon these studies by using pairs of choice reactions and both fixed and variable RSI and ISI. For the ISI conditions, with RSI calculated as ISI-RT_1, RT_2 is flat for positive values of RSI (0–500 msec). Since no single-stimulation control conditions were included, it is difficult to establish whether RT_2 was delayed at these RSIs. However, if RT_2 at the greatest (calculated) RSI is used to estimate single-stimulation RT, then no RT_2 delay was obtained when S_2 followed R_1. If asymptotic

---

[7]Median scores, while frequently used, are less desirable since a median is a poorer estimator of a population value than a mean.

RT_2 at an 800 msec ISI is used as a baseline, then RT_2 is either undelayed or slightly facilitated for positive calculated RSIs. These results are in accord with those of the compatible condition of Broadbent and Gregory (1967). When Triggs manipulated RSI, a decreasing RT_2 function was obtained only for the condition stressing R_1 speed; in two other speed conditions flat RT_2 functions resulted. Note that decreasing ISI functions were obtained for all speed conditions, however. Again, the omission of appropriate single-stimulation control conditions, especially necessary when speed emphasis is manipulated, precludes any conclusions about possible RT_2 delay, particularly for the two speed emphases that produced flat RT_2 functions.

The most important finding obtained by Triggs concerns the slope of the RT_2 function when plotted against RSI. The single-channel model makes a clear prediction that this slope should be minus one, since S_1-R_1 and S_2 processing cannot overlap. Indeed, this prediction is stronger when RSI, rather than ISI, is manipulated. For negative RSIs, (i.e., RSI is calculated not manipulated) the RT_1 distribution cannot alter the slope as is the case when a curvilinear relationship (i.e., the dotted line in Fig. 2) is predicted between RT_2 and ISI since the *exact* amount of S_1-R_1 and S_2 overlap is given by the (negative) RSI. Thus a more powerful test of the limited-channel model is obtained when RSI is manipulated. Triggs found slopes that were flatter than the slope of minus one predicted by the limited-channel model.

Data on the effects of RSI in double stimulation are equivocal. The studies discussed do not provide firm estimates for amount of RT inhibition, if any, as a function of RSI in double stimulation. While it seems both reasonable and likely that refractory delays should occur when S_2 follows R_1 by a short interval, this impression is derived from a montage of several experiments. Detailed examination reveals either no effect or some shortcoming in the experiment which prohibits precise calibration of the effect. A careful demonstration of RSI effects in double stimulation is much needed. If RSI effects are small and limited to short RSIs (say, 150 msec or less) they might be accommodated within existing double-stimulation models; however, if RSI effects are large and persistent, then substantial alterations of most models would be in order.

Temporal Uncertainty

As has been previously noted, many earlier studies used simple, rather than choice, reactions so that temporal uncertainty was considered preferable to fixed blocks of constant ISI. Temporal uncertainty for S_2 in a double-stimulation experiment is obtained when the set of ISIs used in an experiment are combined randomly within a block of trials so that the subject cannot predict the time of S_2 onset. Temporal uncertainty for S_1 is provided by a variable foreperiod (warning signal to S_1 onset). In this chapter, the term temporal uncertainty used with no other referent connotes S_2 uncertainty. Thus, it is possible for an experiment to provide temporal uncertainty for S_1 and temporal certainty for S_2. The distinction between S_1 and S_2 temporal uncertainty is easily blurred, and occasionally ignored (Ollman, 1968), since the operations that create temporal uncertainty are identical for both S_1 and S_2. However, the foreperiod usually is an order of magnitude greater than the ISI; typical foreperiods in double-stimulation experiments range from .5 to several secs while ISIs greater than 500 msec are seldom of interest. Thus, even in the S_1, S_2–R_2 paradigm where S_1 conveys no event information (e.g., Nickerson, 1967) the formal distinction between S_1 (which acts as a "warning") and the warning signal preceding S_1 still needs to be maintained. Should the warning signal be omitted entirely, the paradigm approaches a vigilance paradigm (i.e., the warning interval becomes the intertrial interval) and RT increases.

Temporal uncertainty is an unwieldy independent variable at best. First, two components of temporal uncertainty, one associated with the subject's inability to estimate accurately temporal intervals, and the other associated with the distribution of ISIs, need to be separated (Klemmer, 1956). Second, it is difficult to compare experiments that used different ISI distributions, i.e., two experiments may have the same mean ISI but different ranges of ISI. Third, the subject's subjective uncertainty may not mirror the distribution presented by the experimenter, especially when nonaging foreperiods[8] are used (Nickerson & Burnham, 1969).

The use of temporal uncertainty in double-stimulation experiments, in great part attributable to the use of simple reactions instead of choice reactions (see event uncertainty section), has been largely responsible for various forms of expectancy models of double stimulation. As has already been noted, such models have not been well-supported, and only one experiment concerned with temporal uncertainty will be discussed. This excellent experiment of Bertelson (1967) lays to rest (again) the "curiously resistent" expectancy explanation. Bertelson used pairs of two-choice reactions for S_1 and S_2 with responses required to both. Nine ISIs ranging from 0–500 msec were presented in either fixed or randomized 12-trial blocks. Appropriate control conditions were included and error data were reported as a function of ISI. While several interesting results were reported in this study, the finding of immediate interest was the similarity for both RT_1 and RT_2 of fixed and varied ISI conditions. Since the same outcomes were observed for fixed ISI, expectancy explanations are unnecessary, although a die-hard expectancy theorist might wish to argue that the 12-trial blocks were too short to establish appropriate expectancies.

The expectancy story has implications for data collection. It is a rather interesting example of a model, which although inappropriate both in absolute and relative senses, exhibited an amazing persistence. This persistence may be due, as noted by Bertelson (1967), to expectancy being a reductionist explanation, or perhaps to the common intuitive feeling among experimenters that expectancies do exist. However, the existence of expectancies does not necessarily imply that expectancies play a major role in double-stimulation results unless the situation is "rigged" by using event certainty. It is fair to conclude that various parametric manipulations of temporal uncertainty did little to increase our understanding of double stimulation. But old models die hard and, like the phoenix, arise from their own ashes. The expectancy model may yet be revived.

[8]In a nonaging stochastic process the probability of an event is constant within successive small bands of time (epochs).

Speed-Accuracy Trade-off

As the preceding chapter by Pachella has demonstrated, instructions (payoffs) that favor speed or accuracy are important determinants of RT in single stimulation. Yet this potent variable has barely been investigated in double stimulation. Annett (1969) was one of the first authors even to address the payoff issue in double stimulation. Annett noted that under conditions of temporal uncertainty, an optimal strategy that would minimize anticipations but still provide for a reasonable number of fast RTs would have the subject waiting, rather than trying to respond immediately, so that shorter ISIs would lead to greater RT_2. The force of this criticism of many models of refractoriness, i.e., refractoriness is attributed to payoff (instructions) rather than, say, a single channel, is considerably weakened when we recall that temporal uncertainty is not a necessary condition for RT_2 delay. Nevertheless, Annett deserves credit for promoting the realization that payoff was and still remains a neglected factor in double stimulation.

Triggs (1968) manipulated speed-accuracy set via instruction. Three groups of 8 subjects were told either to stress speed of R_1, speed of R_2, or to give equal speed emphasis to both R_1 and R_2. It is regrettable that this study has never been published and thus is relatively inaccessible; however, its results can be briefly summarized as follows. With ISI fixed, under R_1 speed stress, RT_1 decreased slightly as ISI increased. Under equal speed stress a more pronounced RT_1 decrease was observed. For R_2 speed stress, a nonmonotonic but generally decreasing RT_1 function was also obtained. However, no significant effect of instruction was obtained for RT_2. Comparisons of absolute RT levels indicated that subjects generally followed instructions, although no difference was obtained between RT_2 for equal and stress-R_2 groups; indeed, a nonsignificant reversal occurred here. The absence of single-stimulation control conditions precludes more detailed analysis of these data. Furthermore, error data were not reported.

Knight and Kantowitz (1974) used an explicit payoff matrix to manipulate more precisely the speed-accuracy tradeoff. They were concerned with R_1 effects and thus used a two-light stimulus set which provided event certainty for S_2 given S_1, a procedure that does not illuminate R_2 effects, especially since trials were characterized by temporal certainty.

In addition to the S_1–R_1, S_2–R_2 paradigm, they also investigated the S_1–R_1, S_2 paradigm. For both paradigms, RT_1 decreased as a function of ISI under accuracy payoff. However, under speed payoff RT_1 was a fairly flat function of ISI. Indeed, under speed payoff the 23 msec difference between the single-stimulation group and S_1–R_1, S_2–R_2 groups was not statistically reliable, although significant elevations with respect to independent single-stimulation control conditions were found for all other such comparisons. At first blush, this finding of no RT_1 delay and a flat RT_1 function might be taken as evidence against models, such as response conflict, that argue that R_1 and R_2 effects are intimately related. However, such a conclusion would be premature until error data are considered. Knight and Kantowitz present one of the few studies in which errors were reported as a function of ISI. Under accuracy payoff, there is a decrease in accuracy only at the shortest (33 msec) ISI, but for greater ISIs, accuracy is high and equivalent to that of the single-stimulation control condition. For the speed payoff, however, a rather different picture emerges: Accuracy gradually increases with increasing ISI from roughly 60% correct at the 33-msec ISI to 93% correct at the 528-msec ISI and single-stimulation control condition. Thus, the RT_1 findings under speed stress cannot be evaluated without considering error data. Some form of decrement is associated with short ISIs, but this decrement can be reflected in either speed or accuracy, depending upon instructions or payoff. The failure to report error data as a function of ISI in the many studies that obtained either no RT_1 decrement or flat RT_1 functions precludes any firm conclusions about R_1 processes. Indeed, it is reasonable to suggest that reports of different RT_1 effects for different subjects (e.g., Helson & Steger, 1962; Nickerson, 1967) may merely reflect different interpretations of instructions by different subjects.

Speed-accuracy tradeoff is a powerful determinant of behavior in double-stimulation experiments. Perhaps future researchers will report their findings in sufficient detail so that speed-accuracy effects can be evaluated. A statement that "error rates were low" is grossly insufficient. Small, but systematic differences in error rates, e.g., more errors at shorter ISIs, can have large implications (Pachella, this volume).

Response Force

Until now we have been concerned only with RT and errors as dependent variables. Response force exerted on manipulanda, while hardly a new variable in psychology, may offer interesting insights in double-stimulation research. While response force is most highly associated with response typography in animal behavior (Notterman & Mintz, 1965), its application in studies of human RT, and even in an approximation of current double-stimulation tasks, can be traced to the nineteenth century. Delabarre, Logan, and Reed (1897) describe an ingenious device to record both RT (to .01 sec!) and pressure. The response "switch" was a hinged jaw whose lower end is joined, via a flexible leather surround, to a well and glass tube containing mercury. The pressure of reaction forced the mercury up the tube and a felt float atop the mercury column remained lodged within the tube to mark the pressure. A revolving drum was used to record RT. The most interesting finding obtained by Delabarre et al. was that for both simple and association RT, the quotient, pressure/RT, remained fairly constant for each subject.

Somewhat more recently, Kantowitz (1973) investigated force effects in an $S_1 - R_1$, S_2 paradigm. The mercury well and column of Delabarre et al. were replaced by strain-gauge force transducers, and the kymograph drum was replaced by a minicomputer. Kantowitz, who favors a response conflict model of double-stimulation, was particularly concerned with the response force observed on the S_2 transducer to which no overt response was demanded; in such a situation force can be observed while RT cannot. In a parallel orientation condition, both transducers moved in a vertical plane; in a perpendicular orientation condition, one transducer

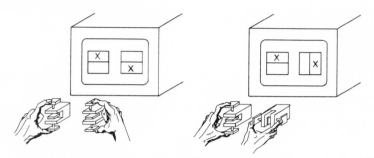

FIG. 8. Response manipulanda and display used by Kantowitz (1973). The parallel orientation is shown in the left panel and the perpendicular orientation in the right panel.

was aligned vertically and the other horizontally. These manipulanda are illustrated in Fig. 8. A significant three-way interaction among ISI, orientation, and R_1 direction (e.g., up-down) showed force effects only for the parallel orientation; furthermore, these effects were progressively greater at shorter ISIs (Fig. 9). While Kantowitz expected large effects of S_2 direction in the parallel orientation, R_1 direction was a more important determinant of direction of force, although S_2 direction also had an effect. Indeed, some response generalization effects were found

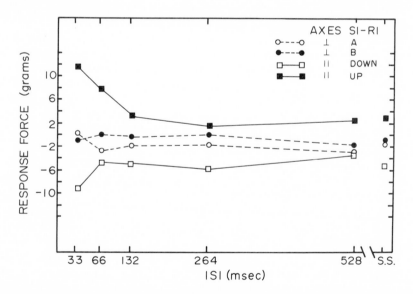

FIG. 9. Mean response force as a function of ISI for parallel and perpendicular axis orientations. The R_1 direction is either *up* or *down* for the parallel orientation; for the perpendicular orientation A and B represent arbitrary combinations of *up* and *down* with *right* and *left*. S.S. indicates the single-stimulation control condition. (From Kantowitz, 1973. Copyright 1973 by the American Psychological Association. Reprinted by permission.)

in single stimulation. These findings led Kantowitz to stress direct response-mediated arousal and response-response compatibility as important components of response selection. Of course, any one study does not establish the utility of a dependent variable. But it does seem likely that response force may lead to useful insights about double stimulation.

Reaction Time Facilitation

The data and models so far discussed have been concerned with RT inhibition in double stimulation. There is, however, an appreciable corpus of data documenting double-stimulation RTs that are faster than single-stimulation control RT; this outcome is termed facilitation and is most prevalent in studies of intersensory double stimulation when no response is mapped to one stimulus, called the accessory stimulus. If the accessory stimulus precedes the primary stimulus the paradigm is S_1, $S_2 - R_2$; if the accessory follows, it is $S_1 - R_1$, S_2.

A vigorous program of research in this area has been summarized by Bernstein (1972). Bernstein favors a two-component model in which facilitation is attributed to energy integration and to changes in preparatory state induced by the accessory stimulus. Bernstein, Rose, and Ashe (1970) report two experiments supporting summation of stimulus intensity. In their first experiment a visual event (10, 1, or .1 ftc) was followed by an auditory event (10-msec, 75, 95, or 120 db SPL) after variable ISIs of 0 to 45 msec. Subjects were instructed to respond to the visual event, but not to the auditory accessory, which served as a catch-trial when presented alone. While facilitation was obtained, results are difficult to interpret without more detailed false-alarm rate data. Only one subject exhibited increasing false-alarms (response to auditory catch trials) as auditory intensity increased. The second experiment had auditory events preceding as well as following the visual event. The amount of facilitation was roughly described by a symmetrical inverted U-shaped function about the 0 ISI, as predicted by an integration model. A greater facilitation obtained when the auditory event preceded the visual event was attributed to the preparatory state component of the model. It is interesting to compare this experiment with a similar study reported by Nickerson (1970, Exp. II). Nickerson's results were clearly asymmetrical, with RT facilitation occurring (relative to a light only condition—see previous discussion of this experiment) only when the tone followed the light. While Nickerson also favored an energy summation model, this discrepancy between the two experiments needs to be resolved. Perhaps the greater ISI range used by Nickerson (0 to 800 msec) is the salient difference, although given the findings of Bernstein et al. (1970) one might expect RT facilitation when the tone preceded the visual event at Nickerson's two shortest ISIs (25 and 50 msec).

Bernstein, Chu, Briggs, and Schurman (1973) contrasted effects of energy integration and preparatory state by varying not only light and tone intensity but also foreperiod duration (0.5 or 5.5 sec). The preparatory state hypothesis implies greater facilitation at the larger foreperiod since temporal uncertainty would be greater and therefore more reduced by the accessory tone. Predicted effects of foreperiod and intensity were obtained and these effects were additive. In this experiment false-alarm rates were reported in detail and were related to intensity of the auditory accessory. False-alarm rates were higher at the shorter foreperiod. Bernstein et al. used the term "triggering" to describe the mechanism of energy integration as a bias toward responding introduced by the accessory stimulus; this bias was made observable by an increase in false-alarm rates. Triggering was carefully distinguished from a "true" facilitatory effect of preparatory state in which RT decrements are not associated with increased false-alarm rates. Although Bernstein et al. concluded that they obtained facilitation rather than triggering, their false-alarm rates suggest triggering at the shorter foreperiod. This triggering view of preparatory state agrees with that of Posner, Klein, Summers, and Buggie (1973) who found RT decrements to be associated with increased error rate as foreperiod varied between 0 and 800 msec.

Perhaps this difference in interpretation, with Bernstein et al. claiming facilitation and Posner et al. claiming triggering, can be in part attributed to the use of choice (Donders' b) reactions by Posner et al. versus the go/no-go (Donders' c-reaction) used by Bernstein et al. The wide range of false-alarm rates obtained by Bernstein et al. may cause difficulty in comparing RTs from conditions that have quite different "goings" for no-go trials. Intersensory facilitation studies using b-reactions and reporting error data are badly needed.

Bernstein, Amundson, Lowrey, and Schurman (1972) have obtained evidence that conflicts with a pure energy integration model. Reaction times to a loud tone and a bright flash were equated. According to the energy integration model when either of these is preceded by the same dim flash, RT to either combination should be equal. However, RT to the dim-flash–bright-flash combination was slower than single-stimulation RT, while RT to the dim-flash–loud-tone combination was faster. While this may at first suggest that the crucial difference is intra- versus intersensory combinations, Bernstein (personal communication) has obtained the same findings when a soft tone is substituted for the dim flash. Bernstein interprets these findings as due to characteristics of a brief loud tone so that some additional process other than energy summation is operative for stimuli of brief duration. It is possible that this other process may be related to stimulus offset and also to response contingent termination of stimuli. Further research along these lines may clarify the relation between energy integration and more general models of double stimulation.

It appears that RT facilitation occurs in intersensory double-stimulation studies using neutral S–R mappings (see p. 95). The more typical RT decrement is obtained in studies using opposing mappings and both inter- and intrasensory stimulation.

ATTENTION AND DOUBLE STIMULATION

Several taxonomies have been proposed for the term attention (e.g., Kahneman, 1973; Posner & Boies, 1971; Treisman, 1969). Since the term attention has multiple meanings, it will be necessary first to specify the sense of the term in the present context. Physiological concomitants of attention and arousing or alerting functions of attention will be ignored in this discussion. Instead, emphasis will be placed upon what Treisman (1969) termed divided attention: man's ability to process two tasks simultaneously or near-simultaneously. In the double-stimulation task, division of attention would appear to impose maximal difficulties when ISI = 0 msec, and decreasing difficulties as ISI increased. While this statement is true when only the main effect of ISI is considered, our previous discussion of the Karlin and Kestenbaum experiment revealed that when interactions with ISI are considered, processing overlap is more efficient at shorter ISIs so that, in some sense, division of attention is easier. It is important to be aware of this distinction between task difficulty as established *a priori* by the methodology of the experimenter (i.e., setting ISI = 0), and the effects of that methodology as revealed by data and model. This section will deal with divided attention tasks characterized by either zero ISI, or ISI sufficiently short so that S_2 occurs before S_1 processing is completed. Some tasks, in addition to the double-stimulation tasks already discussed, that fall under this rubric include studies of dichotic stimulation, simultaneous performance of primary and secondary tasks, and probe RT tasks.

Grouping

The original limited-channel model assumed that signals were processed sequentially, i.e., in terms of Treisman's (1969) distinction between divided and focused attention, attention was first focused on S_1 processing and then refocused to S_2 processing. However, experimenters soon noticed that at short ISIs, subjects appeared able to defer S_1 processing until S_2 occurrence and then jointly process both S_1 and S_2. Welford (1952) put forth the idea of grouping to explain this exception to the limited-channel model. Grouping was considered a perceptual operation, somewhat akin to energy integration, in that attention was focused upon a joint event S_1–S_2 rather than being divided between S_1 and S_2. Later Sanders (1967) carefully distinguished between perceptual and response processes in grouping. Borger (1963) had previously suggested that subjects could store not S_1 but the response R_1 associated with S_1 and later execute a joint reponse R_1–R_2. Sanders (1967) partially unconfounded perceptual and response effects by using a factorial combination of two levels of stimulus-stimulus compatibility[9] and two levels of stimulus-response compatibility. Unhappily his grouping instructions ("carry out the reactions simultaneously") reconfounded stimulus and response effects, since it is impossible to determine if subjects are storing S_1, R_1, or both. Time from S_1 onset to R_2 (sequential handling) or to the grouped response was the major dependent variable; this can also be expressed as RT_2 + ISI or RT_1 + IRI. For both sequential handling and grouping instructions, effects of stimulus-stimulus (S–S) compatibility were found only for the compatible stimulus-response (S–R) mapping, as can be seen in Fig. 10, which is a different form of data presentation than used by Sanders. When statistically reanalyzed, these data revealed significant interactions only between S–S and S–R compatibility, $F(1,8) = 19.2$, $p < .005$, and S–R compatibility and handling

---

[9]Stimulus-stimulus compatibility was operationally defined by spatial grouping of stimulus lights. While this definition may be questioned, the present argument reveals that Sanders' conclusion need be modified, even if his initial premises are accepted.

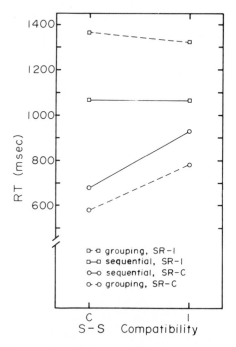

FIG. 10. Replotting of data from Sanders (1967). I indicates incompatible S-S or S-R combinations while C indicates compatible combinations.

strategy (grouping vs. sequential), $F(1, 8) = 14.78$, $p < .005$; no interaction between S–S compatibility and handling strategy was obtained, $F(1,8) < 1.0$. The failure to obtain this latter interaction suggests that Sanders' conclusion—that processing time depends upon the perceptual organization of the stimulus display—while correct (in terms of main effects with high S–S compatibility), may be misleading since both handling strategies are similarly effected by S–S compatibility. Attention does not narrow until after the perceptual processing of stimulus "organization." Such grouping as was obtained by Sanders, represents response, not perceptual processes; how strongly this can be attributed to grouping instructions requiring simultaneous emission of responses remains to be assessed. In terms of Treisman's dichotomy, attention is neither exclusively focused nor divided for all processing components of a task. Rather, attention is initially divided and later becomes focused. However, in terms of a logogen model, attention is not initially divided since it is not required for initial processing.

The importance of grouping is illustrated in a study of Greenwald and Shulman (1973) in which the term grouping never appears. Subjects were instructed that, most often, S_1 and S_2 would be simultaneous, although in actuality ISIs of 0, 100, 200, and 1000 msec were presented in constant blocks of trials. While this kind of "deception" instruction is common in social psychology, it is rather unusual in studies of double stimulation. It is difficult to imagine how a subject can experience a block of

1000 or even 200 msec trials and still believe that S_1 and S_2 appeared simultaneously. It is more likely that this instruction caused subjects to defer S_1-R_1 processing on some trials. This grouping strategy would explain the rise in RT_1 obtained by Greenwald and Shulman (Exp. II) as ISI increased from 0 to 200 msec.[10]

Dichotic Stimulation

In a dichotic stimulation task, two separate messages are simultaneously presented, one to each ear. Dichotic listening has been a dominant task in the study of attention and any review of such studies is well beyond the scope of this chapter. Instead, a sample study will be selected to illustrate the task.

Broadbent and Gregory (1963) presented a signal-detection task in one ear and a string of six digits in the other. In the divided attention condition, subjects first recalled the digits and then judged the presence or absence of a tone in the other ear. In the concentrated attention control condition, subjects only judged the tone and were instructed to ignore the digits. Broadbent and Gregory were concerned with the effects on the two parameters, d' and *beta,* of signal detection. They reasoned that a change in sensitivity or d' would support Treisman's attenuation model, while a change in *beta* would support Broadbent's (1958) filter model. (Broadbent, 1971, later realized that his model might also predict a d' change.) Results were quite clear, showing a greater d' for the control condition.

Egeth (1967) has noted a difficulty that applies to the Broadbent and Gregory study as well as to other studies using dichotic stimulation. In the divided-attention condition, tone report was delayed until after digit recall. Thus, the change in d' may reflect a memory process rather than an attentional process. A replication of the Broadbent and Gregory study conducted in my laboratory at Purdue used digit lists of lengths 2, 6, and 10 with tone report preceding digit recall. In the 6-digit condition, Broadbent and Gregory's results were replicated since d' was higher for the control

---

[10]Greenwald and Shulman attempted to circumvent this (and other) difficulties in their results by presenting the mean of RT_1 and RT_2 as the statistic best suited for discussion. Methodological objections against this average RT can be raised. First, on purely definitional grounds it is unreasonable to claim that the PRP effect was eliminated with a dependent variable other than RT_2. Indeed RT_2 data presented by Greenwald and Shulman (Exp. I) show a strong PRP effect although no effect of ISI on average RT was obtained. However, the RT_2 data of Exp. II did not show a PRP effect. Thus their RT_2 data offers more support for their conclusions than does the average RT data. Second, the simple mean of RT_1 and RT_2 neglects possible overlap in S_1-R_1 and S_2-R_2 processing. A better measure taking into account both RT_1 and RT_2 might be the S_1-R_2 latency (e.g., Sanders, 1967). Finally, and of greatest importance, averaging RT_1 and RT_2 has strong implications regarding the similarity of speed-accuracy operating characteristics (see Pachella, this volume) for R_1 and R_2. Finding errors to be more frequent in conditions yielding greatest RT does *not* imply an absence of speed-accuracy tradeoff effects (e.g., Knight & Kantowitz, 1974).

Greenwald (personal communication, Jan. 1974) has argued that no deception was involved in Exp. II since with the intervals used, subjective simultaneity was more frequent than not, even at 200 msec. Greenwald suggests that at 1000 msec certainly no subjects could have believed that they were being told that the stimuli were simultaneous. If RT is a more sensitive indicant than is an untimed report of simultaneity, these counter-arguments against deception are less compelling. Greenwald also noted that although the instructions of Exp. II may have enhanced the rise in RT_1, a similar rise was also obtained in Exp. I for which no simultaneity instructions were given.

condition. Indeed, the area under the receiver operating characteristic (a nonparametric measure similar to d') decreased from .93 in the 2-digit condition to .92 in the 6-digit condition to .73 in the 10-digit condition. Thus, memory loss during digit recall was not an important factor in the Broadbent and Gregory experiment. However, the possibility of memory loss after tone presentation but before completion of the digit string, especially for lists of 6 and 10 items, is not ruled out. It is very difficult to separate effects of attention from effects of memory in dichotic tasks, i.e., obtaining interference does not necessarily specify the locus of interference. In the Purdue experiment, an additional analysis of digit recall was performed for trials on which a tone had been presented versus trials on which no tone was presented; signal probability was .50. For both free and serial recall measures, an interaction between digit—list length and tone presence—absence was significant due to decreased digit recall in the 10-digit list when a tone had been presented. Did tone presentation interfere with the perception of the digit list or with retention?

In many studies of dichotic listening verbal material is presented to both ears. In order to ensure that attention is paid to one ear, subjects have often been instructed to repeat aloud (shadow) words presented in one ear. Such overt vocalization adds another source of interference to the dichotic paradigm (Norman, 1969; Underwood & Moray, 1972) and further complicates interpretation of data. Finally, the discriminability of the ears as two separate channels may depend upon the poor techniques generally used for production of dichotic stimulus material.[11] Onset asynchrony of word pairs is typically ten or more msec. When we realize that a single ear can resolve temporal differences of one or two msec (Green, 1971) and that both ears can detect microsec differences in laterality judgments (Howard & Templeton, 1966), it seems possible that uncontrolled differences in onset asynchrony of dichotic word pairs may play a part in the dichotic listening task. Computer generated stimulus material with controlled asynchrony in the order of microsecs (e.g., Knight & Kantowitz, 1973) may, in a curiously inverted fashion, lead to a decrease in popularity of the dichotic task. These several methodological difficulties in the dichotic stimulation paradigm suggest caution in interpreting such data, unless memory demands are minimal (e.g., Treisman & Fearnley, 1971).

Timesharing

Another common method used in the study of attention has required subjects to perform two independent tasks simultaneously so that dual-task performance may be compared with the performance of each task alone. Kerr (1973) has reviewed various

[11]Savin (1967) has obtained typical shadowing effects when pairs of messages are presented over a single loudspeaker. He therefore concluded that even when the two channels cannot be physically distinguished, the auditory system groups successive, rather than simultaneous, inputs. However, the technique he used to synchronize word pairs is, by present standards, crude. When computer-generated pairs are used, there is some evidence for grouping of simultaneous input. Day (1973) presented dichotic pairs of nonwords such as banket-lanket and was able to identify a class of individuals who consistently fused the two channels, incorrectly reporting "blanket."

dual-task combinations in order to evaluate processing demands; therefore, the present discussion will be illustrative rather than exhaustive. A typical timesharing experiment is one reported by Kantowitz and Knight (1974). The primary task to which attention was to be directed was a Fitts' Law tapping task (see Pew, this volume) paced at a rate of two taps/sec. Two levels of tapping difficulty were used so that if performance were without error, subjects would transmit 3.9 bits/sec (Low) or 10 bits/sec (High). The secondary task was a digit-naming task with four levels of complexity: name a visually presented digit, respond with the digit minus one, respond with the digit plus three, respond with nine minus the digit. Performance on the digit-naming task was best when no tapping was required. A more important finding, however, was an additional decrement in digit-naming performance as tapping difficulty increased. While digit-naming performance varied with complexity, the joint effects of complexity and tapping difficulty were additive. This finding is rather difficult to reconcile with variable-capacity models of attention (Kahneman, 1973) since more effort was demanded as task difficulty increased for single-task performance. Thus, a decrement which became more pronounced as the component task difficulties increased (i.e., an interaction) is predicted for dual-task performance.

In a similar experiment, Schvaneveldt (1969) did obtain an interaction in dual-task performance but the direction of his interaction was opposite to that predicted by both variable- and limited-capacity models of attention. Schvaneveldt required subjects simultaneously to respond to the position of an illuminated display (manual response) and to name the digit displayed in that position (verbal response). Component task difficulty was varied by increasing the information in each task and also by varying task complexity (e.g., name the digit plus one or push the button on the opposite side). As task difficulty increased, dual-task performance decrement decreased, indicating increased processing overlap. Kahneman (1973) has offered a most ingenious re-explanation of this finding in order to reconcile it with his variable allocation model. Kahneman argued that instead of performing two unrelated tasks, the subjects recoded the dual-task into one fat molar response. In support of this response-grouping hypothesis, Kahneman notes that RT for the manual response always occurred first and varied equally as a function of information in both verbal and manual tasks, rather than being dependent mainly upon manual task difficulty. Kahneman (1973, p. 161) then reinterprets the data as an increase in verbal RT as total (manual + verbal tasks) information increases, so that *less*, not more, overlap is encountered as task difficulty increases. This analysis would be more impressive had Kahneman dealt with both of Schvaneveldt's (1969) experiments and refuted Schvaneveldt's (1969, p. 293) analysis which ruled out response grouping. When either verbal or manual tasks were simple reactions, RT delay was still found. Such delay did not depend upon which response was first, but instead upon the response associated with uncertainty. Indeed, it is only a rather elastic notion about "looseness or tightness" of a response grouping that allows Kahneman to postulate response grouping in the face of variations in IRI. If a pair of responses were a functional unit, we would expect a considerable consistency in the temporal organization of the joint response. It is difficult to interpret Schvaneveldt's IRI variations as supporting this consistency.[12]

To recapitulate, we have discussed one experiment in which effects of dual-task complexity were additive (Kantowitz & Knight, 1974) and one in which an interaction revealed more overlap as complexity increased (Schvaneveldt, 1969). To complete our picture, Keele (1967) obtained a dual-task interaction that satisfied the predictions of a limited-capacity model: decreased overlap with increased dual-task complexity. It is difficult to reconcile these three disparate findings in similar experiments. Keele and Kantowitz used unpracticed subjects while Schvaneveldt used more practiced subjects; while degree of practice is an important factor in double stimulation, it probably is an insufficient explanation of these differences. Keele used two self-paced tasks (counting backwards and serial RT), Kantowitz used one self-paced task (digit naming) combined with an experimenter-paced task, and Schvaneveldt used two experimenter-paced tasks. Again, while the distinction between self-paced and experimenter-paced tasks, e.g., RSI versus ISI designs, is important, it also is probably insufficient to explain the set of three findings. Perhaps the answer lies in our inability to specify absolute values of task difficulty on a ratio scale. The most common measure of difficulty, transmitted information, requires only weak nominal measurement. Our models are not sufficiently refined to tell us in what sense Schvaneveldt's tasks are simpler than those of either Kantowitz or Keele.

However, Greenwald's conception of ideomotor compatibility may be a first step in this direction. Greenwald (1972) suggests that the different outcomes of the Keele and Schvaneveldt studies might be due to differences in the ideomotor compatibilities of their tasks. Greenwald presented auditory stimuli (the words left and right) and visual stimuli (arrows pointing left or right) simultaneously and required simultaneous responses to them. In the low-ideomotor-compatible task a manual response (moving a lever left or right) was required to the auditory stimuli and a vocal response was required to the visual stimuli. A reverse assignment was made for high-ideomotor-compatible conditions. Stimulus-response uncertainty could be either 0 bits (simple RT) or 1 bit for both tasks. Response conflict was present when a vocal response was the word "right" and a lever response was left, or vice versa.

Greenwald's results are impressive support for the ideomotor model. Let us consider the difference between 0 and 1 bit manual RT as the verbal task increases in difficulty from 0 to 1 bit. For the low-ideomotor-compatibility condition differences (1 bit minus 0 bit) of 185 and 215 msecs are obtained for no conflict combinations, and differences of 198 and 319 msecs for conflict combinations. These findings support a limited-channel model, as did Keele's (1967) findings, since processing is less efficient as information in the verbal task increases from 0 to 1 bit. Furthermore,

---

[12]The advantages of a discrete model of skill behavior have been discussed by Fitts (1964). Kahneman's suggestion of global integrated responses seems to be a retreat from this position. If discrete units are to be abandoned, there is a real danger that their replacement may be so amorphous as to resist *a priori* specification and definition. If response grouping is to be like the hipster's definition of jazz, "Jazz is when you dig it," cognitive psychology is being humanized too quickly.

this effect is more pronounced in the conflict combinations as would be predicted by a response conflict model of double stimulation. However, in the high-ideomotor-compatibility condition a dramatic reversal is obtained, similar to findings of Schvaneveldt. For the no-conflict combination, differences of 57 and 8 msecs were found, with differences of 52 and 16 msecs for the conflict combinations. Processing efficiency has increased along with task complexity. Furthermore, effects of conflict, while not entirely eliminated, are substantially reduced. High ideomotor compatibility minimizes processing requirements of response selection and/or initiation.

Nevertheless, these findings may not account for the greater processing overlap obtained by Schvaneveldt, whose verbal task required an auditory response to a visual stimulus, a combination classified by Greenwald as having low ideomotor-compatibility in Greenwald's experiment. Let us return briefly to Schvaneveldt's data to examine the difference in manual RT (incompatible minus compatible, or indirect minus direct in Schvaneveldt's terms), as the verbal task complexity is increased from naming the digit to naming the digit plus one; certainly this latter task is less ideomotor compatible than simple digit naming.[13] Thus, although both tasks have low ideomotor compatibility, according to the ideomotor model, the simple naming task should interfere less with the manual task. Schvaneveldt's results revealed a difference of 16 msec for the verbal naming (direct) condition and a difference of 17 msec for the more complex (indirect) task. Thus, the ideomotor prediction is not fulfilled. The distinction between high- and low-ideomotor-compatible conditions may be of quite limited generality. Nevertheless, in those situations where it is appropriate, the distinction is compelling.

Probe RT

A related double-stimulation task that is becoming more common in the study of attention (see Kerr, 1973) uses a simple or choice single-stimulation RT task, hereafter called the probe task, inserted at various points relative to some primary task. The attention demanded by the primary task controls processing capacity available for the probe task, so that probe RT can map attention demands during the time course of the primary task. If the probe occurs at some predetermined time relative to the primary task (e.g., Posner & Boies, 1971) the procedure resembles a standard double-stimulation task with ISI controlled by the experimenter. If probe presentation is contingent upon some portion of the subject's response (e.g., Ells, 1973) the procedure is akin to an RSI design. When S_2 in the standard double-stimulation task is viewed as a probe, it is easy to see that the decline in RT_2 as a function of ISI maps out the decreasing attentional demands of R_1 and/or S_1 process-

---

[13]Greenwald (personal communication, Oct. 1973) has argued that neither of the tasks remotely resembles an ideomotor compatible one. Therefore, this statement, while correct for stimulus-response compatibility, is incorrect for ideomotor compatibility. The difficulty with this view is that unless ideomotor compatibility is high, it is completely irrelevant. Until degrees of ideomotor compatibility can be established, the concept serves to discriminate only one special situation from all other situations. Indeed Greenwald and Shulman (1973) have discussed problems in the operational definition of ideomotor compatibility.

ing, as the probe is moved away from the primary stimulus. Of course, as has been amply documented earlier in the chapter, this is not sufficient information to determine the utility of any one model, especially if the S_2 probe requires only a simple reaction.

Despite the formal and operational equivalence of probe and other double-stimulation tasks, Posner (personal communication) has noted an important difference in the most common implementations of the two paradigms. In the probe RT task, the order of probe and primary responses usually cannot be predicted by the subject since a wide range of both positive and negative (probe stimulus precedes primary stimulus) ISIs is used. This prevents the subject from adopting some invariant strategy based upon the order of responses, e.g., left hand followed by right hand. Of course, this criticism of standard double-stimulation tasks does not apply to those in which the S_1 set contains the S_2 set so that stimuli serve a dual role (see p. 95) preventing fixed response orders (e.g., Kantowitz, 1972, 1973; Knight & Kantowitz, 1974).

There is one serious methodological problem with a probe RT task. The logic of the probe task demands that while the primary task limits attention available for probe processing, the probe must not limit processing of the primary task. A good probe, like a singer's piano accompanist, must remain unobtrusively in the background, demanding nothing from the primary task. Thus, a single-stimulation no-probe condition is required. If comparison of primary task performance under probe and no-probe conditions is equivalent, and this equivalence must, of course, be reflected in all relevant dependent measures, e.g., speed, accuracy, variance, etc., probe RT may be safely taken as an index of primary processing requirements.

Using a probe task, Posner and Boies (1971) concluded that encoding did not require processing capacity. However, limitations of capacity were linked with response selection. Posner and Boies (1971, Fig. 9) found a reliable increase in primary task RT when the probe occurred immediately after the first letter of the primary letter-matching task. Since first and second letters were separated by only 500 msec in this experiment, it is likely that interference occurred between response processes associated with probe and letter-matching RT. When Posner and Boies (1971, Fig. 11) increased the time between letters to 1 sec, letter-match RT was no longer elevated with respect to the no-probe condition. It is interesting to note that a slight facilitation of letter-match RT occurred when the auditory probe followed the second letter. While this effect resembles energy integration as postulated by Bernstein and others (see p. 115), speed-accuracy tradeoff cannot be ruled out without an examination of error data that were not presented.

The probe RT task will become an increasingly more useful tool for the study of attention. When it is considered within the double-stimulation framework, methodological suggestions come to mind. A more frequent use of choice, rather than simple, probe reactions is desirable (see p. 106). This would also permit reporting of probe error data as well as reporting of primary task error data which, alas, often goes unremarked. Finally, consideration should be given to the use of blocked no-probe trials, in addition to mixed trials with a probe probability usually equal to .5 (see p. 88).

TABLE 3

Cost-Benefit Analysis of Matching Task with Probabilistic Advance Information

	(1)	(2)	(3)	(1 – 2) Benefit	(3 – 1) Cost
S_1	+	A	B	—	—
S_2	AA	AA	AA	—	—
High Probability S_1 useful	450	380	520	70	70
Low Probability S_1 useful	450	420	450	30	ϕ

Note.—+ indicates a neutral S_1, A a useful S_1, and B an incorrect S_1. The two rows indicate different probabilities that S_1 will be useful.

Partial Advance Information

In the partial advance information (PAI) paradigm, S_1 conveys information that is useful but not necessary for the determination of $S_2 - R_2$ (see p. 87). Until quite recently research using this paradigm has focused upon the benefits of PAI and has been aimed at determining how long it takes for these benefits to be realized. At short ISIs PAI is not helpful, while at long ISIs it does reduce RT; however, as has already been noted, the search for some critical ISI is illusory.

While Leonard (1958) used PAI that always was useful, later investigators (LaBerge, Van Gelder, & Yellott, 1970; Posner & Snyder, 1973; Posner, Synder, & McKlveen, 1973; Sanders, 1971) have used unreliable or probabilistic advance information. Posner and Snyder have stressed the importance of trials for which S_1 provides occasional incorrect advance information instead of useful advance information. Such trials permit evaluation of the inhibitory effects of S_1 and when combined with trials for which S_1 provides correct advance information allow a "cost-benefit analysis" of attention. Costs or RT inhibition are calculated by subtracting RT for correct responses preceded by a neutral S_1, conveying only temporal information, from RT for correct responses preceded by an incorrect S_1. Benefit or facilitation is calculated by subtracting RT on useful S_1 trials from RT on neutral trials. Facilitation could be obtained at no cost. This is illustrated in Table 3.

Their results also showed facilitation and inhibition to be asymmetric over ISI. When inhibition occurred its time course lagged behind that of facilitation. Although these findings need to be expanded beyond the matching paradigm, which has its own peculiarities, they argue against both limited-channel models (Broadbent, 1971), which predict early inhibition, and variable allocation models (Kahneman, 1973), which predict symmetric effects of inhibition and facilitation. The most important aspect of cost-benefit analysis is its emphasis upon the relationship between facilitation and inhibition.

An example of undue preoccupation with facilitation is an experiment using probabilistic advance information (Sanders, 1971). In this experiment data for trials on which S_1 was incorrect were not even reported. Posner, Snyder, and McKlveen (1973) replicated this experiment using cost-benefit analysis. When S_1 was reliable as ISI increased from 0 to 1000 msec, RT and error rate decreased at a faster rate than when S_1 was neutral. When S_1 was unreliable, RT and error rate increased as ISI increased from 0 to 175 msec, after which both dependent variables decreased.

Contingent Information Processing

In the contingent information processing (CIP) paradigm, S_1 must be processed before a correct response can be made to S_2. A direct comparison of PAI and contingent processing paradigms was made by Kantowitz and Sanders (1972). Although S_1 was identical in both paradigms, different outcomes were obtained in the two conditions. In the PAI paradigm, a unidimensional S_2 could be either a form (circle or triangle) or a color (red or green), and S_1 indicated whether a form or color would occur as S_2. In the CIP paradigm, S_2 was a bidimensional stimulus (e.g., red square) and S_1 indicated the dimension to be attended. Bidimensional RT was considerably greater than unidimensional RT and this difference was greater at shorter ISIs. Comparisons with appropriate single-stimulation control conditions revealed that only a small portion of this difference could be attributed to the difficulty of filtering out an irrelevant stimulus dimension in the CIP paradigm. These results were discussed in terms of a response conflict model similar to that previously described (see Fig. 4). Conflict was attributed to the two *sets* of response tendencies associated with S_1 (e.g., green vs. red) and S_2 (e.g., red vs. circle) in the CIP paradigm.

A similar conclusion was reached by Bernstein, Pederson, and Schurman (1972), who compared visual-visual and auditory-visual stimulus pairs in CIP. According to channel-switching models of attention (e.g., Broadbent, 1958; Kristofferson, 1967) the intersensory contingent task should be more difficult than a comparable intrasensory task which does not require a switch between modalities. But for a noncontingent task in which S_1 was irrelevant, switching should not present a problem. Thus channel-switching models predict an interaction between these factors. Bernstein et al. found no evidence for channel switching and therefore concluded that RT delay occurred as an output rather than an input limitation. They supported a logogen model similar to that of Fig. 4 in which response interdiction (which, however, they termed response selection) was buffered by the logogen from direct contact with sensory information.

Summary

We have discussed several independent lines of investigation aimed at understanding attentional processes. The studies reviewed, although conceived within different frameworks, all satisfy the paradigmatic conditions of double-stimulation tasks. When viewed within this unifying framework, it is not surprising that there is considerable agreement concerning the locus of attentional limitations. These studies provide converging operations implicating response processes as the primary bottleneck in information processing. Since there is considerable agreement about the importance of response stages, the next step should be a more precise differentiation of the components of response selection. Figure 4 is a first step in this direction. The relationship between excitatory components of response processing, herein called response activation, and inhibitory components, herein termed response interdiction, is of considerable interest and will be a fruitful viewpoint from which to continue exploration of attention and processing capacity.

REFERENCES

Adams, J. A. Test of the hypothesis of psychological refractory period. *Journal of Experimental Psychology,* 1962, **64,** 280–287.

Annett, J. Payoff and the refractory period. *Acta Psychologica,* 1969, **30,** 65–74.

Atkinson, R.C., & Juola, J.F. Factors influencing speed and accuracy of word recognition. In S. Kornblum (Ed.), *Attention and performance IV.* New York: Academic Press, 1973.

Audley, R.J., & Pike, A.R. Some alternative stochastic models of choice. *British Journal of Mathematical and Statistical Psychology,* 1965, **18,** 207–225.

Baumeister, A.A., & Kellas, G.A. Refractoriness in the reaction time of normals and retardates as a function of response-stimulus interval. *Journal of Experimental Psychology,* 1967, **75,** 122–125.

Berlyne, D.E. Uncertainty and conflict: A point of contact between information-theory and behavior-theory concepts. *Psychological Review,* 1957, **64,** 329–339.

Bernstein, I.H. Double stimulation and intersensory information processing. Paper presented at the meeting of the American Psychological Association, Honolulu, September, 1972.

Bernstein, I. H., Amundson, V. E., Lowry, Y., & Schurman, D. L. Temporal integration effects in simple reaction time. Paper presented at the meeting of the Psychonomic Society, St. Louis, November, 1972.

Bernstein, I.H., Chu, P.K., Briggs, P., & Schurman, D.L. Stimulus intensity and foreperiod effects in intersensory facilitation.*Quarterly Journal of Experimental Psychology,* 1973, **25,** 171–181.

Bernstein, I.H., Pederson, N.N., & Schurman, D.L. Intersensory versus intrasensory contingent information processing. *Journal of Experimental Psychology,* 1972, **94,** 156–161.

Bernstein, I.H., Rose, R., & Ashe, V.M. Energy integration in intersensory facilitation. *Journal of Experimental Psychology,* 1970, **86,** 196–203.

Bernstein, I.H., & Segal, E.M. Set and temporal integration, *Perception & Psychophysics,* 1968, **4,** 233–236.

Bertelson, P. Central intermittency twenty years later. *Quarterly Journal of Experimental Psychology,* 1966, **18,** 153–163.

Bertelson, P. The refractory period of choice reactions with regular and irregular interstimuli intervals. *Acta Psychologica,* 1967, **27,** 45–56.

Biederman, I. Human performance in contingent information-processing tasks. *Journal of Experimental Psychology,* 1972, **93,** 219–238.

Borger, R. The refractory period and serial choice-reactions. *Quarterly Journal of Experimental Psychology,* 1963, **15,** 1–12.

Brebner, J. The refractoriness of regular responses. *Australian Journal of Psychology,* 1971, **23,** 3–7.

Broadbent, D. E. *Perception and communication.* London: Pergamon Press, 1958.

Broadbent, D. E. *Decision and stress.* London: Academic Press, 1971.

Broadbent, D. E., & Gregory, M. Division of attention and the decision theory of signal detection. *Proceedings of the Royal Society, Series B,* 1963, **158,** 222–231.

Broadbent, D. E., & Gregory M. Psychological refractory period and the length of time required to make a decision. *Proceedings of the Royal Society Series B,* 1967, **168,** 181–193.

Buckley, W.F. (Ed.) *Modern systems research for the behavioral scientist.* Chicago: Aldine, 1968.

128   BARRY H. KANTOWITZ

Craik, K.J.W. Theory of the human operator in control systems: I. The operator as an engineering system. *British Journal of Psychology*, 1947, **38**, 56–61.

Craik, K.J.W. Theory of the human operator in control systems: II. Man as an element in a control system. *British Journal of Psychology*, 1948, **38**, 142–148.

Davis, R. The role of "attention" in the psychological refractory period. *Quarterly Journal of Experimental Psychology*, 1959, **11**, 211–220.

Davis, R. Choice reaction times and the theory of intermittency in human performance. *Quarterly Journal of Experimental Psychology*, 1962, **14**, 157–166.

Davis, R. The combination of information from different sources. *Quarterly Journal of Experimental Psychology*, 1964, **16**, 332–339.

Davis, R., & Taylor, D.H. Classification on the basis of conditional cues. *Quarterly Journal of Experimental Psychology*, 1967, **19**, 30–36.

Day, R.S. Individual differences in cognition. Paper presented at the meeting of the Psychonomic Society, St. Louis, November, 1973.

Delabarre, E.B., Logan, R.R., & Reed, A.Z. The force and rapidity of reaction movements. *Psychological Review*, 1897, **4**, 615–631.

Ditzian, J.L. Reaction time to first signals in double stimulation under different probabilities of second signal occurrence. Unpublished doctoral dissertation, Purdue University, 1972.

Egeth, H. Selective attention. *Psychological Bulletin*, 1967, **67**, 41–57.

Ells, J.G. Analysis of temporal and attentional aspects of movement control. *Journal of Experimental Psychology*, 1973, **99**, 10–21.

Fehrer, E., & Raab, D. Reaction time to stimuli masked by metacontrast. *Journal of Experimental Psychology*, 1962, **63**, 143–147.

Fitts, P.M. Perceptual-motor skill learning. In A.W. Melton (Ed.), *Categories of human learning*. New York: Academic Press, 1964.

Gardner, E. D. *Fundamentals of Neurology*. Philadelphia: Saunders, 1963.

Gottsdanker, R. Interacting responses to crowded signals. In W. G. Koster, (Ed.), *Attention and performance II*. Amsterdam: North Holland, 1969.

Gottsdanker, R., Broadbent, L., & Van Sant, C. Reaction time to single and to first signals. *Journal of Experimental Psychology*, 1963, **66**, 163–167.

Green, D.M. Temporal auditory acuity. *Psychological Review*, 1971, **78**, 540–551.

Greenwald, A.G. Sensory feedback mechanisms in performance control: With special reference to the ideo-motor mechanism. *Psychological Review*, 1970, **77**, 73–99.

Greenwald, A.G. On doing two things at once: Time sharing as a function of ideomotor compatibility. *Journal of Experimental Psychology*, 1972, **94**, 52–57.

Greenwald, A.G., & Shulman, H.G. On doing two things at once: II. Elimination of the psychological refractory period effect. *Journal of Experimental Psychology*, 1973, **101**, 70–76.

Hart, S.G., & Huff, E.M. A test of the information, repetition, and recurrence pattern hypotheses in multistimulus choice reaction time tasks. Paper presented at the meeting of the Western Psychological Association, Anaheim, 1973.

Helson, H., & Steger, J.A. On the inhibitory effects of a second stimulus following the primary stimulus to react. *Journal of Experimental Psychology*, 1962, **64**, 201–205.

Herman, L.M. Effects of second signals on response to first signals under certainty and uncertainty. *Journal of Experimental Psychology*, 1969, **80**, 106–112.

Herman, L.M., & Israel, A. Decremental and facilitatory effects of second signals on response time to first signals under different levels of uncertainty. *Proceedings of the American Psychological Association*, 1967, **2**, 27–28.

Herman, L. M., & Kantowitz, B. H. Effects of second signals occurring after response selection on responses to first signals. *Journal of Experimental Psychology*, 1969, **80**, 570–572.

Herman, L.M., & Kantowitz, B.H. The psychological refractory period: Only half the double-stimulation story? *Psychological Bulletin*, 1970, **73**, 74–88.

Hick, W.E. On the rate of gain of information. *Quarterly Journal of Experimental Psychology*, 1952, **4**, 11–26.

Hick, W.E., & Welford, A.T. Comments on "Central inhibition: Some refractory observations. *Quarterly Journal of Experimental Psychology,* 1956, **8,** 39–41.

Howard, I.P., & Templeton, W.B. *Human spatial orientation.* New York: Wiley, 1966.

Hull, C.L. Goal attraction and directing ideas conceived as habit phenomena. *Psychological Review,* 1931, **38,** 487–506.

James, W. *Principles of psychology.* New York: Holt, 1890.

Jastrow, O. The interference of mental processes. *American Journal of Psychology,* 1891, **4,** 219–223.

Kahneman, D. *Attention and effort.* Englewood Cliffs, N.J.: Prentice Hall, 1973.

Kamlet, A.S. Processing of sequentially presented signals in information-combining tasks. Unpublished doctoral dissertation, University of Michigan, 1969.

Kantowitz, B.H. Double stimulation with varying response information. *Journal of Experimental Psychology,* 1969, **82,** 347–352.

Kantowitz, B.H. Response mechanisms in double stimulation. Paper presented at the meeting of the American Psychological Association, Honolulu, September, 1972.

Kantowitz, B.H. Response force as an indicant of conflict in double stimulation. *Journal of Experimental Psychology,* 1973, **100,** 302–309.

Kantowitz, B. H. Double stimulation with varying response requirements. *Journal of Experimental Psychology,* 1974, in press.

Kantowitz, B.H., & Knight, J.L. Testing tapping timesharing. *Journal of Experimental Psychology,* 1974, in press.

Kantowitz, B.H., & Sanders, M.S. Partial advance information and stimulus dimensionality. *Journal of Experimental Psychology,* 1972, **92,** 412–218.

Karlin, L., & Kestenbaum, R. Effects of number of alternatives on the psychological refractory period. *Quarterly Journal of Experimental Psychology,* 1968, **20,** 167–178.

Kay, H., & Weiss, A.D. Relationship between single and serial reaction time. *Nature,* 1961, **191,** 790–791.

Keele, S.W. Compatibility and time-sharing in serial reaction time. *Journal of Experimental Psychology,* 1967, **75,** 529–539.

Keele, S.W. *Attention and human performance.* Pacific Palisades: Goodyear, 1973.

Kerr, B. Processing demands during mental operations. *Memory & Cognition,* 1973, **1,** 401–412.

Kerr, M., Mingay, R., & Elithorn, A. Patterns of reaction time responses. *British Journal of Psychology,* 1965, **56,** 53–59.

Klemmer, E.T. Simple reaction time as a function of time uncertainty. *Journal of Experimental Psychology,* 1957, **54,** 195–200.

Knight, J.L., & Kantowitz, B.H. A minicomputer method for generating dichotic word pairs. *Behavior Research Methods & Instrumentation,* 1973, **5,** 231–234.

Knight, J.L., & Kantowitz, B.H. Speed-accuracy tradeoff in double stimulation: Effects on the first response. *Memory and Cognition,* 1974, in press.

Koster, W. G., & Bekker, J. A. M. Some experiments on refractoriness. *Acta Psychologica* 1967, **27,** 64–70.

Koster, W. G., & Peacock, J. B. The influence of intensity of visual stimuli on the psychological refractory phase. In W. G. Koster, (Ed.), *Attention and performance II.* Amsterdam: North Holland, 1969.

Kristofferson, A. B. Attention and psychological time. *Acta Psychologica,* 1967, **27,** 93–100.

LaBerge, D., Van Gelder, P., & Yellott, J. A cueing technique in choice reaction time. *Perception & Psychophysics,* 1970, **7,** 57–62.

Leonard, J. A. Partial advance information in a choice reaction task. *British Journal of Psychology,* 1958, **49,** 89–96.

Luce, R. D. Response latencies and probabilities. In K. J. Arrow, S. Karlin, & P. Suppes (Eds.), *Mathematical models in the social sciences.* Stanford: Stanford University Press, 1960.

Miller, J. G. Adjusting to overloads of information. In D. McK. Rioch, & E. A. Weinstein (Eds.), *Disorders of communication,* New York: Association for Research in Nervous and Mental Disorders, 1964.

Moray, N. Where is capacity limited? A survey and a model. *Acta Psychologica*, 1967, **27**, 84–92.

Nickerson, R. S. Adams' bisensory discrete tracking task and the psychological refractory period: A comment. *Psychonomic Science*, 1965, **3**, 87–88.

Nickerson, R. S. Psychological refractory phase and the functional significance of signals. *Journal of Experimental Psychology*, 1967, **73**, 303–312.

Nickerson, R. S. The effect of preceding and following auditory stimuli on response times to visual stimuli. In A. F. Sanders (Ed.), *Attention and performance III*. Amsterdam: North Holland, 1970.

Nickerson, R.S., & Burnham, D.W. Response times with nonaging foreperiods. *Journal of Experimental Psychology*, 1969, **79**, 452–457.

Notterman, J.M., & Mintz, D.E. *Dynamics of response*. New York: Wiley, 1965.

Norman, D.A. Memory while shadowing. *Quarterly Journal of Experimental Psychology*, 1969, **21**, 85–93.

Ollman, R.T. Central refractoriness in simple reaction time: The deferred processing model. *Journal of Mathematical Psychology*, 1968, **5**, 49–60.

Pew, R.W. Acquisition of hierarchical control over the temporal organization of a skill. *Journal of Experimental Psychology*, 1966, **71**, 764–771.

Pew, R.W. Review of D. E. Broadbent, *Decision and stress*. *Science*, 1971, **174**, 683–684.

Posner, M. I. After the revolution . . . What? (Review of D. E. Broadbent, *Decision and Stress*.) *Contemporary Psychology*, 1972, **17**, 185–187.

Posner, M.I., & Boies, S.J. Components of attention. *Psychological Review*, 1971, **78**, 391–408.

Posner, M.I., Klein, R., Summers, J., & Buggie, S. On the selection of signals. *Memory & Cognition*, 1973, **1**, 2–12.

Posner, M.I., & Mitchell, R.F. Chronometric analysis of classification. *Psychological Review*, 1967, **74**, 392–409.

Posner, M.I., & Snyder, C.R.R. Facilitation and inhibition in the processing of signals. In S. Kornblum (Ed.), *Attention and Performance V*, in press.

Posner, M.I., Snyder, C.R.R., & McKlveen, M.J. Stimulus and response set: A cost benefit analysis. Paper presented at the meeting of the Psychonomic Society, St. Louis, November, 1973.

Rabbitt, P. Psychological refractory delay and response-stimulus interval duration in serial, choice-response tasks. In W.G. Koster (Ed.), *Attention and performance II*. Amsterdam: North Holland, 1969.

Remington, R.J. Analysis of sequential effects in choice reaction times. *Journal of Experimental Psychology*, 1969, **82**, 250–257.

Remington, R.J. The effects of advance information on human information processing in a choice reaction task. *Psychonomic Science*, 1971, **24**, 171–173.

Reynolds, D. Effects of double stimulation: Temporary inhibition of response. *Psychological Bulletin*, 1964, **62**, 333–347.

Sanders, A.F. The effect of compatibility on grouping successively presented signals. *Acta Psychologica*, 1967, **26**, 373–382.

Sanders, A.F. Probabilistic advance information and the psychological refractory period. *Acta Psychologica*. 1971, **35**, 128–137.

Savin, H.B. On the successive perception of simultaneous stimuli. *Perception & Psychophysics*, 1967, **2**, 479–482.

Schvaneveldt, R.W. Effects of complexity in simultaneous reaction time tasks. *Journal of Experimental Psychology*, 1969, **81**, 289–296.

Schvaneveldt, R.W., & Chase, W.G. Sequential effects in choice reaction time. *Journal of Experimental Psychology*, 1969, **80**, 1–8.

Shaffer, L.H. Choice reaction with variable S-R mapping. *Journal of Experimental Psychology*, 1965, **70**, 284–288.

Shaffer, L.H. Some effects of partial advance information on choice reaction with fixed or variable S-R mapping. *Journal of Experimental Psychology*, 1966, **72**, 541–545.

Schaffer, L.H. Transition effects in three-choice reaction with variable S-R mapping. *Journal of Experimental Psychology*, 1967, **73**, 101–108.

Shannon, C.E. The mathematical theory of communication. In C.E. Shannon & W. Weaver, *The mathematical theory of communication*. Urbana: University of Illinois Press, 1949.

Smith, E.E. Where is the bottleneck in information processing? Paper presented at the meeting of the American Psychological Association, Honolulu, September, 1972.

Smith, M.C. Theories of the psychological refractory period. *Psychological Bulletin*, 1967, **67**, 202–213. (a)

Smith, M.C. The psychological refractory period as a function of performance of a first response. *Quarterly Journal of Experimental Psychology*, 1967, **19**, 350–352. (b)

Telford, C.W. The refractory phase of voluntary and associative responses. *Journal of Experimental Psychology*, 1931, **14**, 1–36.

Tolkmitt, F.J. A revision of the psychological refractory period. *Acta Psychologica*, 1973, **37**, 139–154.

Treisman, A.M. Strategies and models of selective attention. *Psychological Review*, 1969, **76**, 282–299.

Treisman, A.M., & Fearnley, S. Can simultaneous speech stimuli be classified in parallel? *Perception & Psychophysics*, 1971, **10**, 1–7.

Triggs, T.J. Capacity sharing and speeded reactions to successive signals. Unpublished doctoral dissertation, University of Michigan, 1968.

Underwood, G., & Moray N. Shadowing and monitoring for selective attention. *Quarterly Journal of Experimental Psychology*, 1972, **23**, 284–295.

Way, T.C., & Gottsdanker, R. Psychological refractoriness with varying differences between tasks. *Journal of Experimental Psychology*, 1968, **78**, 38–45.

Welford, A.T. The "psychological refractory period" and the timing of high-speed performance—A review and a theory. *British Journal of Psychology*, 1952, **43**, 2–19.

Welford, A.T. Single-channel operation in the brain. In A.F. Sanders (Ed.), *Attention and performance I*. Amsterdam: North Holland, 1967.

Welford, A.T. *Fundamentals of skill*. London: Methuen, 1968.

4
ISSUES AND MODELS
CONCERNING THE PROCESSING
OF A FINITE NUMBER OF INPUTS[1]

J. T. Townsend
Rockefeller University

INTRODUCTION

Eighty years ago or so the title would probably have been something like "An Attempt at Clarification of Proposed and Counter-Proposed Properties of Consciousness." The revolution in information, computer, and communication sciences (à la Shannon, Von Neumann, and Wiener) and the growing vapidity of behaviorism led in the 1950's and 1960's to a resurgent interest in centralism, that is, a renewed interest in the study of properties of the mind, as opposed to the exclusive peripheralistic study of stimulus-response correspondences. The terminology of the "new" psychology has been almost completely drawn from the above disciplines, but very recently investigators have become less self-conscious about employing mentalistic terms and concepts that would have brought applause from the structuralists and phenomenologists of yesteryear (see, e.g., Boring, 1950). Although skirting the interesting questions involving possible fruits and pitfalls of this trend, I might simply note that this chapter continues, after the introduction, in the recent tradition of use of information-processing argot.

In the present approach, we go inside the human *qua* information processor to as shallow or deep a level as we care to, and seize upon an abstract black box residing there in the processing chain. We shall think of our black box as engaging in the processing of some finite number of inputs (or elements). Words like "processing"

[1] I am grateful to W. K. Estes for the opportunity to spend the year 1972–1973 at Rockefeller University under Grant GM16735 from the National Institute for General Medical Sciences. During that time, much of the writing of this chapter was completed. I am indebted to W. K. Estes, B. Kantowitz, D. A. Taylor, D. Snuttjer, and L. Paul, as well as several helpful anonymous reviewers, for their comments on an earlier version of this manuscript. I benefited from conversations with W. K. Estes, R. N. Roos, D. A. Taylor, Joan G. Snodgrass, and D. Vorberg and from discussions with H. Schultz, J. Wandmacher, and D. Albert concerning the issues investigated herein.

and "elements" are purposely kept abstract to enhance the generality of our discussion. And the view we take is that we should endeavor to comprehend the possible workings and characteristics of fairly atomistic levels of processing, not necessarily before consideration of more complex levels (e.g., interaction of several black boxes), but at least concomitantly with the latter. The name we shall use for our black box is "system" albeit it may be a very small (sub) system relative to the total information-processing system in which it operates; the important matter is that we may conceive of it as a unit in its operations on the inputs. Our system could be as large as consciousness or as small as a set of hypothetical neural nets in the retina, depending on our level of analysis and the type of inputs under scrutiny.

Our concentration in this chapter will be on four dimensions or aspects of the system, posed, as they have been implicitly or explicitly in the literature, as dichotomies. It is convenient to introduce the issues in a different order than they will appear in the subsequent sections.

Independent vs Dependent Processing

The first of these is less molar than the others, but likely to be of interest as knowledge of processing in various kinds of experimental settings improves. It is the question of whether processing of the separate elements is statistically independent or not. To be more precise, assume that two elements are to be processed, and that the total time from when the processing system begins to work on the elements to the completion of each element is recorded. Then, if there is no interaction or dependence between the two total completion times, these times are said to be independent. If knowing that one of the elements took a long time to be completed makes it more likely that the other took a long time as well, a positive dependency exists. If the same knowledge increases the chances of a short total completion time by the other element, a negative dependency is said to occur.

Now, consider a situation where the processing system is allowed some fixed time t, through limiting the stimulus exposure duration for example. It may then be asked whether the knowledge that one element was completed during that time affects the likelihood that the other was completed. The answer to this question follows directly from the dependency relations, as discussed in the foregoing paragraph, between the unconstrained total completion times. Independence or dependence of the former implies independence or dependence of the latter. For example, assume that long unconstrained completion times of one of two elements are associated with long completion times of the other and that short times of the one are associated with short times of the other, that is, a positive dependency exists. Then, in the limited duration case, if it is known that one of the elements is completed the chances are increased that the other was also finished. Conversely, if it is known one of them did not complete processing, it is also likely the other did not. Recent examples of an experimental context wherein dependence has been investigated are found in Estes and Taylor (1966) and Wolford, Wessel, and Estes (1968). These studies used the detection paradigm, (Estes & Taylor, 1964) wherein the subject attempted to detect which of two target letters was embedded in a random array of noise letters on each trial. The exposure duration was limited, and it may be supposed the processor involved in comparing display with target letters also had only a limited time to perform its task. The variable of interest here was the manipulation of the number of repetitions of the target letter presented on a given trial. This technique permits a test of the independence assumption.

Self-terminating vs Exhaustive Processing

Another issue, pertinent to experimental trials where some proper subset of the inputs (that is, fewer elements than are input to the processor) or elements contain information sufficient to enable the subject to make the required response, is whether the system is capable of cessation of processing when that subset is completed (self-termination) rather than having to nevertheless do all the elements (exhaustiveness). One of the first mathematical processing models where self-termination was assumed is found in Estes and Taylor (1964), and attention has since been brought to bear on it in other recent papers (e.g., Atkinson, Holmgren, & Juola, 1969; Sternberg, 1966; Townsend & Roos, 1973). In the first of a series of papers employing the detection paradigm by Estes and his colleagues, the Estes and Taylor (1964) "serial processing model" was based on the assumptions of geometrically distributed durations of stimulus availability (e.g., an icon), serial (one-at-a-time) comparisons of target and display letters, and termination of processing when (and if) the target letter was located. Although this specific model has since met with severe difficulties, it contributed to elucidation of these and similar data at the time (see, e.g., Townsend, 1968).

Serial vs Parallel and Limited vs Unlimited Capacity Processing

The remaining two issues are probably the most important of the four and are considered together in our introduction; they are rather closely linked historically and have generated some mutual confusion even quite recently. The first is concerned with the question of capacity of a system—whether processing efficiency, in terms of speed or accuracy, is degraded or is unaffected when increased numbers of elements are input to the system.[2] This issue currently goes under the rubric "limited versus unlimited capacity." The second is whether the capacity of the system is applied to the inputs one at a time, or whether it is deployed simultaneously to all the inputs. For a large variety of contemporary experimental paradigms, the latter becomes the serial versus parallel processing issue.

The broadest and most critical arena of investigation and contention with regard to these two matters has always been consciousness itself. That is, can consciousness act on more than one element (thought, image, sensory impression, etc.) at a time (the serial-parallel issue), and when it has to deal with an increased amount of material, is it less effective (the capacity question)? The question of whether the mind (via

[2]The problem of effectiveness or efficiency immediately ramifies into questions as to what level of processing is under observation. For instance, are we concerned with effectiveness per unit of material or with total processing time for all the material, or some other level? These issues will be addressed in the section on capacity.

consciousness) is capable of engaging in more than one cognitive activity at a time can be traced back at least as far as Plato and Aristotle. But probably the first directly relevant experimental evidence came from the personal equation difficulties met by puzzled astronomers and later by the budding experimental psychology of the nineteenth century. The situation was simply this: A method of measuring positions and relative velocities of stellar bodies consisted of determining the amount of time necessary for a body to cross a reticle in an optical instrument. The time was calculated from (1) the number of complete tick-intervals from a nearby clock heard by the astronomer during the transit time plus (2) the perceived position of the body relative to the reticle, between the two final clicks. That is, the proportion of the interval between two marks corresponding to the body's position at the two clicks, that was in front of the reticle (e.g., if the movement was left-to-right, the proportion of the final interval to the left of the reticle was the required measurement), was the final proportion of the time interval added to the "whole" time intervals.

The dilemma was that different astronomers obtained different estimates of the times, and we are most of us acquainted with the famous story of an unfortunate assistant immortalized by being fired (his name was Kinnebrook) for producing transit times larger than his employer (who shall here remain nameless in retribution for this ignominious action). The difference between two observers subsequently came to be called the personal equation. Without getting involved in all the technicalities and subtleties of the matter, we may note that these astronomical observations involved the processing of information from two inputs, namely, the eyes and the ears. Computation of the "exact" transit time required knowledge of the temporal point between two ticks of the clock at which the stellar body crossed the reticle. If two observers differ in when they think the body crossed the reticle, we may infer that they differ in the time necessary to compare their visual with their auditory impressions. This suggests that in neither case are the comparisons simultaneous, and that the delay is simply greater for one observer than the other.

If it turned out that all the delay and differences in delay could be placed in the sensory channels themselves, then perhaps the delay and allied factors would not be of much psychological interest. However, it was found that predisposition and expectation affected the results, especially in the famous complication clock experiments of von Tchisch around 1885. When decision processes can asymmetrically influence tasks where it would be to the subject's advantage always to utilize information from the auditory and visual channels simultaneously, this suggests the possibility that in fact the cognitive processing of the information may not be able to proceed simultaneously (i.e., in parallel), or that if it does that there may occur a degradation in performance (the capacity question) as compared to only one channel being monitored cognitively at any given moment. Although an entirely satisfactory theory, from a modern point of view, has never been set down for these phenomena, we might note the recent reawakened interest in such topics (e.g., Sternberg & Knoll, 1972).

Another empirical problem, related in at least its systemic properties to the preceding, was illustrated by the philosopher Hamilton (1859), who convinced himself by tossing variable numbers of dice that consciousness is capable of simultaneously apprehending a maximum of 4 to 6 objects. Thus, 6 came to be thought of as the range of capacity of visual apprehension (or attention as we would probably say now). Hamiton himself believed that when attention was focused on fewer objects, the apprehension was superior to when it was focused on more objects. This is an example of a parallel, limited capacity system, since it can work on more than one object, but resolution suffers to some extent when this is done.

In his later work at least, the prodigious Wundt appears to have accepted this alleged limited capacity of parallelism, as well as the ability of the mind to "focus up or down" on larger or smaller numbers of objects, respectively. On the other hand, certain other investigators, such as Hylan, (1903), offered evidence for the proposition that attention was limited in capacity not because of a parallel spreading of attention over the set of objects to be apperceived, but because there occurs an all-or-none fluctuation of attention from one object to another. The latter was, of course, a serial type of mechanism. The fact that two early experimental psychologists argued, one for a serial type of limited capacity system and the other for a parallel limited capacity type, already suggests the logical independence of the serial-parallel and the capacity issues. In fact, the gist of our argument on all the issues in the sections to follow is that since a processing system can be made up by selecting a stance on each of the issues independently, that these *are* logically separate and independent. For instance, we could build a system that is serial, unlimited capacity (in one of the precise senses to be developed below), self-terminating, and is characterized by independent processing of the separate inputs. We could then change any or all of the stances on each of the issues (e.g., change serial to parallel) without logical or mathematical violation. An entirely distinct question is whether the system we build (or the model of this system) is realistic, that is, whether we expect to encounter such systems in nature. The problem of "intuitiveness" and "reasonableness" has, it seems, caused confusion as to the logical distinctions involved.

To proceed with our brief longitudinal view of parallel and serial hypotheses about apprehension, chinks in our knowledge continued to be filled in over the years, especially in the counting of objects in brief visual displays (see, e.g., Hunter & Sigler, 1940). However, the actual possible processing mechanisms and their properties appear to have been largely neglected. In any case, the whole story was reopened by Sperling's (1960) memory-apprehension study, in which an important dissection of processing stages was suggested. Some of his later results, (Sperling, 1963), where he found that increasing the display time of several letters (with a preceding and postceding visual noise mask) led to a linear increase in the number correctly reported, were typically taken as supporting the notion of serial processing. Furthermore, a linear increase of RT in short memory search unfortunately has been assumed to falsify independent parallel models and to provide strong support for serial models (Sternberg, 1966). That these conclusions are wrong or at best misleading (Townsend, 1969a, 1969b, 1971b, 1972a) will be shown in the section on capacity. At any rate, the concept of parallel, limited capacity systems seems to have been forgotten for a number of years.

Broadbent (1958) unveiled a theoretical structure that allowed collation of a substantial body of experimental literature and that was seminal in its influence on later developments. Although not put directly in terms of parallel vs. serial processing, the hypothetical filter responsible for selection of material for further processing appeared to function in a serial-like fashion when the input exceeded the capacity of the "bottleneck."

Around 1969, several investigators rediscovered limited capacity parallel systems. For example, Erikson and Spencer (1969) used the analogy of a zoom lens to illustrate a (parallel-limited capacity) system that processes everything simultaneously but with better resolution when focused on a smaller field. Too, there is an implicit acknowledgement of the possibilities of limited-capacity parallel systems making predictions similar to typical serial systems in A. Treisman's review on selective attention (1969, p. 292). Atkinson et al. (1969) pointed out a type of parallel model mathematically identical to a type of serial model, and the writer gave a paper that discussed some rather large classes of probabilistic parallel and serial models that are equivalent (Townsend, 1969a, 1969b, 1971b). Soon thereafter, Gardner (1970, 1972) contributed an innovative discussion of these and similar issues. In a similar vein, Corcoran (1971) discussed a nonprobabilistic limited capacity parallel model.

Christie and Luce (1956) appear to have been the first to approach the parallel vs. serial issue from a mathematical point of view. Thomas (1969) has suggested some nonparametric tests that may be utilized in certain cases. The writer's own work in this area (Townsend, 1969a, 1969b, 1971b, 1972a, 1972b, 1972, 1973) is briefly summarized and related to other efforts in Townsend (1974). This brings us into the seventies and completes our necessarily laconic historical groundwork.

Goals of the Present Approach

It is our purpose to formulate the foregoing issues in an informal but hopefully rigorous fashion in the main text. It is unfortunately true that confusions and incorrect conclusions, especially concerning tests between parallel and serial processing, are still to be found in the psychological literature. The overall goal is to facilitate logical and systemic distinctions among these four issues and to provide a framework conducive to further theory building and more accurate testing. Within this larger goal is the aforementioned aim of convincing the reader, if he is not presently of this opinion, that the four issues are indeed logically distinct. Without detailing the mathematics presented elsewhere, we also shall try to gain some insight into why many of the experiments designed to throw light on seriality vs. parallelism have not accomplished this purpose. In the process of our development we shall have occasion to construct sundry models and refer to a number of experimental applications. The applications will often cluster in the areas of visual and memory search, since these are of special interest to the writer, but the concepts will hopefully have more extended reference than to these alone.

THE SERIAL VS PARALLEL PROCESSING ISSUE

Definitions of Parallel, Serial, and Hybrid Systems

To begin with, we wish to distinguish between systems that exist in the real world and the models of those systems which are abstract fabrications.[3] In a very real sense, there is no difficulty at all in telling systems apart, or there would not be if all the workings were completely open to our inspection. If two systems work differently or are constructed differently, then they are just so and that is all one may say about the matter.

The difficulties arise, of course, when we wish to make inferences about the inner workings of the system for some reason but cannot actually inspect these, because it is too difficult or because society frowns on indiscriminate slicing into certain black boxes of interest to psychology. Then it may be that a model, hypothesized to describe these workings and employed to predict input-output behavior of the system, may be similar or even identical to a model that began by picturing the system in a drastically different way. That the models may be equivalent does not mean that the systems they refer to are equivalent, but only that they may act in an equivalent manner, when we can observe what happens at the input (stimulus) and output (response) stages. This will become more clear as we progress. First, two informal definitions of parallelism and seriality are given.

Definition I. A *Serial System* is a system that processes elements one at a time, completing one before beginning the next.

Definition II. A *Parallel System* is a system that begins processing elements simultaneously; processing proceeds simultaneously, but individual elements may be completed at different times.

Suppose processing begins in either type of system at time $t = 0$ on elements (a) and (b) and that the total time (z) spent by the system actually processing (a) if it is completed first is given by z_{a1} and by z_{a2} if it is completed second. Similarly z_{b2} is the total time spent actually processing (b) when it is completed second, and z_{b1} is the comparable time if it is completed first. Figure 1a shows a schematic of these quantities when (a) happens to be completed first.

There are two features of Fig. 1a that are indispensable in defining seriality vs. parallelism. First note that in a parallel system, up until one of the elements is completed, there can be no prior designation of the *order of completion* [in Fig. 1a, (a) is completed first], but there can be in the serial system, since on each trial one and only one of the elements is selected to be first. Another way of putting this is to observe that the *serial* system can select (a) to be processed first with some arbitrary probability p; (b) of course is processed first with probability $1 - p$. The variable or parameter p need bear no relation whatsoever to the amounts of time spent processing

---

[3]It is convenient here to use the term "system" to refer to actual, physical entities. One may occasionally find "system" used in an abstract sense, more in the way we employ "model" in the present treatment.

(a) and (b) (the z's in Fig. 1) once they are in the processor. However, the order of completion under *parallel* processing must depend on the relative rates at which (a) and (b) are being processed. These concepts will be made explicit below.

Notice also that in the parallel system z_{b2} is necessarily larger than z_{a1}, but not in the serial system. This, too, is an important distinction between a parallel and serial system: The amount of time spent by the parallel system processing the element that is completed last is always equal to the total amount of time from the beginning to the

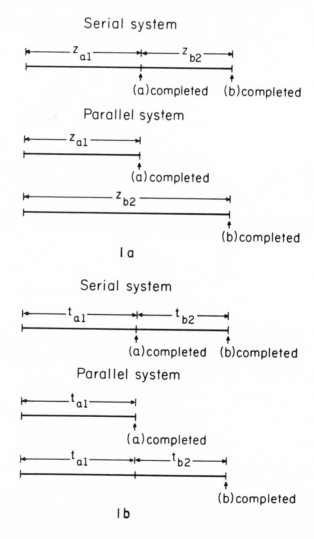

FIG. 1. 1a.—Schema showing total time spent processing (a) and (b) in a serial or parallel system when (a) is completed first. 1b.—Schema showing intercompletion times in processing (a) and (b) in a serial or parallel system when (a) is completed first.

completion of processing. But in a serial system the processing duration on the last element obviously does not include that spent on the earlier ones.

It often turns out to be helpful to discuss system performance or model predictions in terms of intercompletion times, that is, the time from the point at which one element is finished to when the next is completed. If (a) is done first (in either system), the first intercompletion time $[\text{from } t = 0 \text{ to when } (a) \text{ finishes}]$ is called t_{a1}, and if (b) is first, the first intercompletion time is t_{b1}. Similarly, the time interval from the completion of (a) to the completion of (b) is just t_{b2} and alternatively, the duration from the instant when (b) is completed first to when (a) is completed is called t_{a2}. Figure 1b shows the events of Fig. 1a but in terms of intercompletion times. Hence, in a serial system, $z_{a1} = t_{a1}, z_{b2} = t_{b2}$, but in a parallel system, $z_{a1} = t_{a1}$ but $z_{b2} > t_{b2}$, in fact, $z_{b2} = t_{a1} + t_{b2}$. The crux of the difficulty in experimentally testing between parallel and serial systems is that in being confined to input-output relationships, all we actually observe, even under optimal conditions, are t_{a1}, t_{b2} or t_{b1}, t_{a2}. The relationship of the intercompletion times to the actual processing times must be inferred. When parallel and serial models produce identical predictions for the t's, they represent systems that are behaviorally indistinguishable.

We are emphasizing parallel and serial processing in this exposition and neglecting other types because of want of space, but a few cursory remarks may be pertinent to "hybrid" systems and models.

Definition III. A *Hybrid System* is a system that processes in neither a parallel nor a serial manner (Townsend, 1969a, 1971b, 1972a).

Hybrid models have been of limited current theoretical interest, probably due in part to the difficulty in testing them experimentally. As remarked earlier, the quite special case of seriality vs. parallelism is difficult enough to discriminate experimentally. Among such hybrid models are those that represent processing as being serial part of the time and partially parallel within trials. That is, during part of a trial the elements may be worked on simultaneously, and during another part of the trial they may be worked on one at a time, each being completed before the next is begun. On the other hand, another hybrid model might suppose that on some proportion of trials processing is entirely serial, and on the remainder, it is entirely parallel. Of more recent theoretical interest have been models that can be interpreted either as parallel or hybrid (Townsend, 1972a). Rumelhart's (1970) parallel model is a special case of this class of models. In its hybrid interpretation, such a model presumes time-sharing, in that one element is worked on at a time but that element may be abandoned while the processor works on another element for awhile, after which time the processor may return to the "first" element, and so on. Strict serial processing demands that each element be completed before processing is begun on the next. We may note that in certain experimental contexts, the distinction between time-sharing and seriality may be supererogatory. In a situation where a subject must attempt to monitor two different messages transmitted to separate ears, the elements can be conceived of as the separate (ear) channels. In time-sharing or serial processing with respect to the two channels, attention switches back and forth in an all-or-none manner between channels, but a parallel processor places attention on each channel simultaneously.

A last remark concerning terminology. We shall refer to stage 1 as the state of a system from the start of processing until the first element is completed. Similarly, stage 2 is the state of a system from the completion of the first until the completion of the second, and so on; stage i is the state of the system from the completion of the $(i - 1)^{th}$ element to the completion of the ith. At stage $n + 1$ a system is once again at rest.

Practically our entire discussion will be based on the concept of *rates* of processing and *order* of completion of the elements being processed.

The concept of order of completion is, of course, natural and well-defined. Rate, however, is more fuzzy. We shall take the tack here of establishing rate as a variable expressed in specific cases as a positive number. In certain simple distributions on processing times, these rates will appear as actual parameters in the models. The rates are then related in a very natural way to mean intercompletion times and overt processing durations. However, "rate" may also be *defined* in terms of selected statistics.

For example, if the mean (expected) time to completion for (a) is $E_a(t)$, then we could *define* the rate of processing of (a) as $u_a = 1/E_a(t)$; in models based on exponentical intercompletion times, this relationship appears automatically. [4]

First, consider the serial models. Let $u_{a\,1}$ = processing rate for element (a) when it is processed first, (i.e., during stage 1) and $u_{b\,1}$ the processing rate for element (b) when it is processed first. Similarly, let $u_{a\,2}$ be the processing rate for element (a) given that it is processed second (stage), after (b) and $u_{b\,2}$ the rate for (b), when it is second, after (a). Let p be the probability that (a) is processed first. It is extremely important to note that p is, in general, independent of the processing rates in serial models. That is, the serial system may be viewed as making a selection among the possible processing orders on each trial according to some arbitrary but fixed probability distribution. In the case of two elements, the probability distribution is just p for order (a) first, (b) second, and $1 - p$ for order (b) first, (a) second.

Turning to parallel models, let $v_{a\,1}$, $v_{b\,1}$ be the processing rates for elements (a), (b) respectively, during stage 1. In probabilistic parallel systems, either (a) or (b) may by chance be completed during stage 1. If (a) has this distinction, then unless the system terminates processing for some reason, (b) will complete its processing at the rate $v_{b\,2}$. If (b) is finished first, (a) will be completed second at the rate $v_{a\,2}$. Unlike the serial models, we expect the order of processing to depend on the relative rates of (a) and (b) during stage 1, $v_{a\,1}$, $v_{b\,1}$. If $v_{a\,1}$ is much larger than $v_{b\,1}$ it may typically be predicted that (a) will finish first more often than will (b) and vice versa.

---

[4]Typically, quantitative statements concerning the u, v, and p variables are exact only in the case of models with exponential intercompletion times, that is, for models whose intercompletion times (the t's in Fig. 1) can be described by density functions of the form $u \cdot \exp(-ut)$. However, they may be approximations in other cases. One of the aims of this chapter is to indicate the existence of parallel and serial models that *are* mathematically identical and discuss the related intuitions that hold exactly for certain classes of models and approximately for others. Precise delineation of the mathematical detail is beyond the scope of this chapter. With regard to approximation, it is possible to make two models, one serial and the other parallel, give identical predictions at, say, the level of mean RT, although the full models are not equivalent on all possible statistics (see Townsend, 1972a).

Of the four issues raised in the introduction, that of parallel vs. serial processing is pivotal. The reason is that the interpretation of the other issues assumes different forms in parallel as distinguished from serial processing.

We do not have sufficient space to reiterate in depth previous results on parallel and serial models that are equivalent, and therefore indistinguishable by behavioral data. But, the resultant intuitions that relate to ideas of rates and order of processing will help elucidate the present information structure and the four issues in particular.

A Coin Tossing Example

Let us consider a coin tossing analogy. The analogy corresponds quite closely to the actual modeling situation, where parallel-serial equivalence can appear. The main difference is that in the coin case, we use discrete time but in the typical real modeling case, continuous time. One other important difference will be pointed out below.

Consider as the serial analog a coin tossing mechanism that tosses each of five coins, one at a time. It must obtain a head for each coin before going on to the next, and we assume each coin may be identified by some mark placed on it. For a given experiment, the mechanism sets up a probability distribution on the different processing (tossing) orders for the five coins. Arbitrarily assigning the letters a, b, c, d, and e as names for the coins, then any order of tossing, for example, <d, a, e, c, b>, will have some likelihood of being selected. It is assumed that there are no orders that never occur. Further, we assume that each coin may have its own, possibly unique, probability of coming up heads.

As the parallel analogue, simply assume that all five coins are tossed simultaneously, but each continues being tossed until it personally achieves a head. That is, all five coins are tossed, those coins attaining a head are removed, the remaining coins are again tossed simultaneously, and so on. The basic unit of time is that fixed interval required for one simultaneous toss.

Now, in this discrete case, the parallel system can never quite be exactly the same as the serial because on a given toss (the fixed duration of a toss defining a unit of time) more than one head can come up. In the serial case, only one head can come up during the fixed unit of time. Thus, the exact probabilistic description, and therefore the sampling distribution, cannot be the same. However, when the basic time unit or interval is squeezed down smaller and smaller, in the direction of attaining continuous time, this difference disappears for many interesting models.[5] In any case, we may compare the parallel and serial coin mechanisms in overall behavior to continuous-time parallel and serial systems.

First, it is clear that if the same coins were used first in the parallel tossing system

---

[5]We can not go into detail here but, for example, parallel models with intercompletion times that are independent across the elements at any given stage fulfil the condition that for very small intervals the probability of two or more completions becomes very small, thus making possible serial-like behavior. It should be noted that independence referred to in this footnote is *not* independence of *successive* intercompletion times or even necessarily of overall completion times (see "Independence vs. Dependence Issues").

and then in the serial system, the time in toss units until the first head appears will be significantly shorter in the parallel than in the serial case. Hence, to make this time roughly the same, the probabilities (of a head) of the parallel coins will have to be made smaller, or equivalently, the serial probabilities will have to be made larger. At each succeeding stage the total behavior of the parallel coins has to correspond to the behavior of the toss of a single coin in the serial system; either the serial coins, the parallel coins, or both must undergo some adjustment. The important point is that the summed activity of the parallel system must equal the individual activity of the serial system for each remaining number of parallel and serial coins.

The other critical aspect of the analog is the order of completions. Somehow, the probability distribution on these orders used by the serial system has to correspond to that obtained by chance in the parallel system. It is quite apparent that the order of finishing in the parallel system will depend on the various magnitudes of the head-probabilities of the coins. In the serial case, on the other hand, the actual order is entirely established by the probability distribution on the orders, independently of the coins' probabilities of turning up heads. Hence, we can try to make the serial system mimic this aspect of the parallel system's behavior by adjusting the order probabilities so that, say, the likelihood that coin "d" gets a head third equals the probability that it does so by chance in the parallel system. If its parallel probability of getting a head is intermediate among the others, this serial probability of being third would be relatively high. This probability could be easily arranged in the serial system. Conversely, the parallel head-probabilities could be adjusted to match the likelihoods associated with the order probability distribution in the serial system.

Parameter Mappings That Can Render Parallel and Serial Models Equivalent

Although we shall return from time-to-time with intuitions based on the coin example, let us turn to the continuous time case with our serial, u_{ai}, u_{bi}, and parallel, v_{ai}, v_{bi} rates ($i = 1$, 2, the stages) for elements (a) and (b); recall that p is the probability that (a) is chosen to be processed first in the serial system.

If equivalence is possible between serial and parallel *models*, then there must exist transformations or *mappings* that express the serial parameters in terms of the parallel parameters, and vice versa. Further, these mappings must ensure equivalent predictions of all possible statistics by the two models. The parameters of the serial model we will continue discussing are the rates u_{ai}, u_{bi}, and p. The parameters in the parallel model are likewise v_{ai}, v_{bi}. If such mappings can be found then, for example, typical values may be assigned to the parallel parameters and the mappings used to find the corresponding serial parameter values. This serial model then will make predictions identical to those of the parallel model.

In probabilistic continuous-time systems, the intercompletion times when more than one element is being processed in parallel will typically be shorter, assuming fixed processing rates, than if only one is being processed. In fact, we can represent this speed-up by summing the two parallel rates, $v_{a1} + v_{b1}$. Hence, to make the parallel and serial behavior alike up until the first element is completed, it must be the case that $u_{a1} = v_{a1} + v_{b1}$ when (a) is processed first in the serial system, and $u_{b1} = v_{a1} +$

v_{b1} when (b) is processed first in the serial system. That is, the sum of the processing rates for the two elements undergoing parallel processing must be the same as the individual serial rates during stage 1. But observe that *both* u_{a1} and u_{b1} must equal v_{a1} + v_{b1} in order for the behavior of the parallel and serial systems to look the same during the first stage of processing. This result suggests what turns out to be an important fact concerning the present parallel and serial models: The serial models are more general because the processing rate at stage 1 can depend on which element is being processed first. It is comparable to the greater generality of the serial coin tosser: the average waiting time to the very first head depends on which coin is tossed first. This means that the subset of trials on which coin "b," say, is tossed first will in general have a different frequency distribution and mean than will that subset of trials on which coin "e" was tossed first. The parallel tosser, on the other hand, will have the same probability distribution on every trial, that representing a series of simultaneous tosses of coins with different probabilities attached. Similarly, the continuous-time parallel system and its model (or models) will have a description of the first inter-completion time (that is, waiting time to the first completion) that depends only on $v_{a1} + v_{b1}$ on every trial and hence cannot show the diversity of behavior for this event that the serial system and models can.

The actual situation is somewhat more complex than this, since the serial systems can make the processing rates dependent not only on the element processed but also on the complete order of processing of the various elements on a given trial. Thus, in the general case of n elements there are $n!$ different serial processing rates for stage one, but only one for the parallel model. However, as processing evolves during a given trial, the parallel system gains more and more freedom, since it can make its rates depend on the previously processed elements and their order (on the same trial). During the final stage of processing the parallel system attains freedom equal to that of the serial system. To see this, observe that there are n different elements that can be processed last and $(n - 1)!$ different orders in which the other $n - 1$ elements could have finished, so there are $n!$ different rates for the last stage in the parallel as in the serial system (the serial system can have $n!$ different rates at every stage). It is reasonable that a serial system can predetermine processing order and have the potential of making processing rates depend on these orders, but the order of processing evolves by chance in probabilistic parallel systems and, hence, the parallel rates at stage 1, for example, cannot depend on what element finishes fourth. A parallel system could only attain this aspect of generality processed by serial systems by the singular property of prescience.

It would appear possible to get around this constraint by taking probability mixtures of parallel systems. That is, if $n!$ parallel systems are available and one is chosen with some probability on each trial, then one could have $n!$ different rates during stage 1 as in the serial systems. However, not only cannot this "mixed" parallel model be equivalent to the serial model, in general, but the serial model cannot generally be equivalent to the parallel. The main proviso here is that if the serial distributions are of a certain class, for example exponential, gamma, etc., then those distributions determining processing time frequencies for each element processed in parallel must be the same, and vice versa. Probability mixtures of members of a certain class of distributions are not generally of the same class as the members. To see that the mixed parallel model still cannot typically mimic the serial, observe that if we consider a single order, say (a) is first, of processing two elements, then the processing time for (a) will be given by a distribution depending on a single rate, but in a mixed parallel system, it would be given by a probability mixture of distinct-rate distributions. For similar reasons, the serial models cannot mimic mixed parallel models, except in degenerate cases or in cases where the underlying "component" distributions are assumed to be different in the parallel and serial models (see Townsend, 1972a, p. 178).

Returning to ordinary parallel systems, we see that by setting $u_{a1} = u_{b1} = v_{a1} + v_{b1}$, and $u_{a2} = v_{a2}$, $u_{b2} = v_{b2}$ the parallel and serial models look alike because the rates governing observable input-output behavior are alike. We are completely free to make $u_{a2} = v_{a2}$ and $u_{b2} = v_{b2}$ because the parallel models' freedom at the last stage, here stage 2, equals 2, the same as the serial case. However, there is one other constraint that must be present, one relating to order of processing. Roughly, the likelihood that (a) is completed first in the parallel system should be related to the magnitudes of the rates v_{a1} and v_{b1}, that is,

$$\text{Probability } \big[(a) \text{ is completed first}\big] = \frac{v_{a1}}{v_{a1} + v_{b1}}$$

But in the serial case this probability is just given by p. So for the orders to be comparable we require that $p = v_{a1} | (v_{a1} + v_{b1})$. By use of these parameter mappings, we can retrieve serial models that give behavior expected of parallel systems, and parallel models that yield behavioral predictions reminiscent of serial systems. For instance, the mapping above immediately tells what the serial parameters have to look like to mimic parallel behavior. The reverse mappings, parallel parameters written as functions of the serial parameters, are just $v_{a1} = p \times u_1, v_{b1} = (1-p) \times u_1, v_{a2} = u_{a2}, v_{b2} = u_{b2}$; note that we use u_1 to stand for the common values of u_{a1} and u_{b1}. It is important to notice though, that the direction of the mapping, parallel-to-serial or serial-to-parallel, does not by itself specify whether the models are describing activity *typically* associated with parallel as opposed to serial processing (or with either, for that matter). For example, the actual numbers for the u's in a given case may already be such as to predict behavior commonly thought of as parallel; in this case when the v's are obtained via a serial-to-parallel mapping, the resulting values will be those "typical" of parallel models and, hence, of parallel systems. However, if the numerical values of the u's are those expected of serial systems, then the v's will be specified parameters of a parallel model that yield serial-like predictions.

Can people process in parallel? Here, as in the applications section, we see that the firm establishment of one or the other way may be quite tricky. Further, the proper answer to the question will almost certainly be positive for some types of processes and negative for others. Surely the brain is capable of doing a number of complex things simultaneously. For instance, the driving of an automobile while engaged in sophisticated problem solving is obviously parallel processing, albeit by probably more or less *functionally* distinct subsystems. Another aspect is a tie-in with organization or Gestalt properties of the stimulus or task. In watching a ballet, it appears considerably easier to "pay attention" to all the dancers simultaneously when they are involved in rhythmic movements with a high degree of similarity and symmetry across individuals and continuity in time than when the dancers are performing sequences less integrated into a holistic Gestalt.

THE SELF-TERMINATING VS EXHAUSTIVE PROCESSING ISSUE

Basic Concepts

As shall become increasingly apparent, the parallel-serial distinction, being directed to how the available processing resources are deployed to the inputs, serves as a basic descriptive agent and largely determines the approaches to the other issues.

There are many occasions in perceptual and memorial experiments where the information sufficient to make a correct response is embedded in only part of the total stimulus pattern presented to the subject. In this case, if the subject's information-processing system is capable of a cessation of processing when that information has been obtained, we say it is self-terminating. Otherwise it is exhaustive: It must always process all the information available. Of course, some trials by their very nature may require exhaustive processing, but this does not enable us to call the processor exhaustive. It is the incapability of self-termination that is defined as exhaustiveness. An experimental paradigm on memory search that involves trials where self-termination can occur, and others where processing must be exhaustive, with respect to the basic input units (in this case digits), is given in the Sternberg (1966) paper, and a visual span of apprehension analog to this design is given by Atkinson et al. (1969). The "detection paradigm" formulated by Estes and Taylor (1964) and mentioned in the introduction, is basically a two-alternative forced-choice design that allows for self-termination on all trials.

General Memory and Display Search Predictions for Two Elements

Let us imagine a Sternberg (1966) (or Atkinson et al., 1969) task where on every trial either one or two letters are presented to a subject for memorization, followed by presentation of a target letter. The subject responds positively if the target is in the memory and negatively if not. On one-half of the trials, the target is in the memory set; in the other half, it is not. Accuracy is high and RT is the main dependent variable. RT includes other components besides that of the processing times, of course, but we must ignore those here. Before giving serial and parallel predictions for self-terminating and exhaustive-processing times, we need to recall some simple relations between processing rates and mean processing times.

The situation is especially nice for serial models, since the average of the sum of individual processing times is the sum of the individual (element) averages. If we take the relation of the mean processing time to the rate as the aforementioned reciprocal relationship, then the expectation or mean for, say, element (a) at stage 1 is simply

$E(t_{a\,1}) = 1/u_{a\,1}$. When processing is exhaustive and we know that *(a)* is processed first, then the total mean processing time is just $E(t) = (1/u_{a\,1}) + 1/u_{b\,2}$.

However, turning to parallel models, we have connected the rates of intercompletion times, at any given stage, to the sum of the individual rates. The intuition for this, again, is that with many elements undergoing processing simultaneously, the chances are increased that one of the elements will be finished in a relatively early time, simply by chance. Although parallel models obviously do not permit simple additivity of processing times for the individual elements, we may still retain an additivity of intercompletion times, the overall sum of intercompletion times just being the overall processing time. Thus, we dissect the total processing time, be it self-terminating or exhaustive, into the separate intercompletion times and add them up. Now we have seen that regardless of which element, (a) or (b), finishes first in the present parallel systems, the rate of this event is just $v_{a\,1} + v_{b\,1}$; so according to our reciprocal rule relating mean processing times and rates, $E(t_{a\,1}) = E(t_{b\,1}) = (1/v_{a\,1} + v_{b\,1})$.[6] However, if (a) finishes first then (b) goes ahead and completes processing at the rate $v_{b\,2}$, and if (b) finishes first then (a) continues until its completion with rate $v_{a\,2}$. Hence, the average total exhaustive completion time *given* that (a) is completed first is $E(t/(a)\text{first}) = (1/v_{a\,1}+v_{b\,1}) + (1/v_{b\,2})$ and the other is $E(t/(b)\text{first}) = (1/v_{a\,1} + v_{b\,1}) + (1/v_{a\,2})$.

Relating these developments to the Sternberg paradigm when $n = 2$, and designating "processing" as being the comparison of the target letter with each of the memory letters, we observe that an "input" to the processor is a pair of letters, the target and one of the possible memory letters.

On a positive trial, that is, the target is also in memory, if processing is *self-terminating,* the serial predictions for the two possible cases of target placement are

$$E(t \mid \text{target is } (a)) = p\frac{1}{u_{a\,1}} + (1-p)\left(\frac{1}{u_{b\,1}} + \frac{1}{u_{a\,2}}\right) \qquad (1)$$

and

$$E(t \mid \text{target is } (b)) = p\left(\frac{1}{u_{a\,1}} + \frac{1}{u_{b\,2}}\right) + (1-p)\frac{1}{u_{b\,1}}. \qquad (2)$$

The prediction for negative trials and for all trials if processing is exhaustive is

$$E(t \mid \text{target absent or processing is exhaustive}) =$$
$$p\left(\frac{1}{u_{a\,1}} + \frac{1}{u_{b\,2}}\right) + (1-p)\left(\frac{1}{u_{b\,1}} + \frac{1}{u_{a\,2}}\right). \qquad (3)$$

---

[6]This property implies that the average first-stage processing time is independent of which element finishes first; it is peculiar to a class of processes of which the exponential is a special case. Investigation of a functional equation that is necessary and sufficient for parallel-serial equivalence with independent parallel models (Townsend, 1974), shows that in more general cases, the class of serial models may still be more general than the class of parallel models. The more general limitation on parallel models is closely related to this special case limitation.

We see that when the target is (a) that self-termination is reflected in the absence of the (b) component when (a) happens to be processed first, with probability p, and vice versa when the target is (b).

To arrive at the parallel predictions we could work directly from our remarks about additivity of intercompletion times, but we may alternatively use our previously established serial-to-parallel mappings to immediately acquire them. That is, let $p = (v_{a1}/v_{a1} + v_{b1})$, $u_{a1} = u_{b1} = u_1 = v_{a1} + v_{b1}$, $u_{a2} = v_{a2}$, $u_{b2} = v_{b2}$, which converts Eqs. (1), (2), and (3) to

$$E(t \mid \text{target is } (a)) = \frac{v_{a1}}{v_{a1}+v_{b1}} \times \frac{1}{v_{a1}+v_{b1}} + \frac{v_{b1}}{v_{a1}+v_{b1}} \times$$

$$\left[\frac{1}{v_{a1}+v_{b1}} + \frac{1}{v_{a2}} \right] = \frac{1}{v_{a1}+v_{b1}} + \frac{v_{b1}}{v_{a1}+v_{b1}} \times \frac{1}{v_{a2}}, \tag{4}$$

$$E(t \mid \text{target is } (b)) = \frac{1}{v_{a1}+v_{b1}} + \frac{v_{a1}}{v_{a1}+v_{b1}} \times \frac{1}{v_{b2}}, \tag{5}$$

$$E(t \mid \text{target absent or processing is exhaustive}) =$$
$$\frac{1}{v_{a1}+v_{b1}} + \frac{v_{a1}}{v_{a1}+v_{b1}} \times \frac{1}{v_{b2}} + \frac{v_{b1}}{v_{a1}+v_{b1}} \times \frac{1}{v_{a2}}. \tag{6}$$

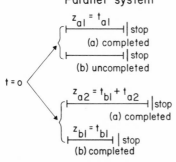

Serial system

Parallel system

FIG. 2. Self-terminating serial and parallel systems when completion of element (a) terminates processing.

So far, so good. Figure 2 shows in schematic form the operations of self-terminating parallel and serial systems in the situation when (a) is the target.

The Standard Serial Model

The ony problem with application of the foregoing formulae to real data is that there are five parameters in the serial model $(p, u_{a1}, u_{b1}, u_{a2}, u_{b2})$ and four in the parallel $(v_{a1}, v_{b1}, v_{a2}, v_{b2})$. There will in general be $(n + 1)! - 1$ parameters for the serial model and

$$n! \sum_{k=0}^{n-1} \frac{1}{k!}$$

for the parallel, for each value of n. Now, a typical experiment and data reduction may result in only $n + 1$ degrees of freedom, at each value of n, corresponding to the n serial position mean RT's when the target is present and 1 for the target-absent mean RT. And this is without considering RT components from other parts of the information processing chain. Hence, it is of substantial interest to investigate models with further constraints on their parameters. A favorite serial model results from assuming that $u_{a1} = u_{b1} = u_{a2} = u_{b2} = u$, that is, the serial rate parameter is constant across the various elements and also through the different stages of processing. Further, this homogeneity of processing rate is extended across different numbers of input elements to be processed, so that if u_1 stands for the processing rate for $n = 1$, u_2 for the processing rate when $n = 2$, etc., then the latter assumption is expressed as $u_1 = u_2 = u_3 = \ldots = u_{n^*}$ where n^* is the largest number of inputs conceived of for an experiment. This last assumption basically involves capacity notions as we shall see later.

A known fact of statistics tells us that the mean of a sum of randomly distributed times is equal to the sum of the means of the individual times. Thus, any set of distributions yielding means that are equal on the different elements, independent of order and magnitude of n, will be referred to as a standard serial model. Specific assumptions about the underlying probability distributions will, of course, yield particular members of the class of standard serial models.

The preceding assumptions yield the classical straight line RT functions as n is varied. Inserting these constrained values of the u_i in expressions (1), (2), and (3) we obtain,

$$E(t \,|\, \text{target is } (a)) = \frac{1}{u} \, (2-p), \tag{7}$$

$$E(t \,|\, \text{target is } (b)) = \frac{1}{u} \, (1+p), \tag{8}$$

$$E(t \,|\, \text{target absent or processing is exhaustive}) = \frac{2}{u}. \tag{9}$$

The resulting processing time on a negative (target absent) trial then $n = 2$ is obviously just twice what it is when $n = 1$. When processing is self-terminating, it can be seen from Eqs. (7) and (8) that the processing time on a positive (target present) trial will depend on which element is the target.

It is typical to presume that the comparison times for the different items or elements (e.g., different letters of the alphabet) used in a Sternberg task are about the same; certainly the different items, usually letters or numerals, are randomly assigned positions in the displays. We therefore use (a) and (b) to designate different serial positions. Thus, (a) is taken as serial position 1 and (b) as serial position 2. If the letters are displayed visually, serial position 1 refers to the leftmost element, and so on until serial position n is the last toward the right. If they are presented acoustically, serial position 1 refers to that element presented first, serial position 2 to that presented second, etc.

Hence, it happens that processing time will differ according to serial position on positive trials when $n = 2$ *if* self-termination is possible *and* p is not equal to $1/2$. [This can be concluded by inspection of Eqs. (7) and (8).] The latter means, of course, that the subject does *not* process (a) first just as often as he processes (b) first. The next thing to note is that the processing time averaged over serial positions, again assuming random placement of the target, is given by

$$E(t \,|\, \text{target present}) = \frac{3}{2u}. \tag{10}$$

The general formulae that give the straight lines as functions of n, again with the constrained u's, are

$$E(t \,|\, \text{target absent}) = \frac{n}{u}, \tag{11}$$

$$E\,(t \,|\, \text{target present}) = \frac{n}{2u} + \frac{1}{2u}, \tag{12}$$

where Eq. (11) clearly is the result of summing n average processing times, and Eq. (12) may be thought of as proceeding from the fact that on the average positive trial the self-terminating processor will go half-way through the n elements in order to find the target. Expressions (11) and (12) yield the famous, but rarely encountered, 2-to-1 slope ratio of negative to positive processing times, $(n/u) \div (n/2u) = 2$. We omit the expressions that correspond, in the case of arbitrary n, to Eqs. (7) and (8), since these can depend in quite complex ways on the probability distribution on processing orders of the n elements. The results up to here lead us to remark on a dilemma that has faced investigators of the Sternberg and similar paradigms: It is possible to obtain serial position effects, which suggest self-termination, and to simultaneously obtain equal-sloped positive and negative RT functions, which suggests exhaustive processing (with, for example, slopes of n/u). We shall pursue this dilemma in our section on applications to real data. We shall delay consideration of a typical self-terminating parallel model until the next section, since it ties in well with the independence-dependence issue. However, we close the present discussion by noting a parallel model that gives equivalent predictions to the present equal-u serial model. Let $v_{a1} = pu$, $v_{b1} = (1 - p)u$, $v_{a2} = v_{b2} = u$. That it does give equivalent predictions may be confirmed by plugging these values of the parallel parameters into expressions (4),

(5), and (6). More general serial-to-parallel mappings for larger values of n have been worked out elsewhere (Townsend, 1972a, 1972b).

THE INDEPENDENCE VS DEPENDENCE ISSUE

Independence of Total Completion Times

In some respects this issue is difficult to discuss. One reason is that there are many kinds of independence. The second is that the type we wish to approach has as yet been studied empirically only a little. This, as mentioned in the Introduction, is independence of total completion times of the various elements. We take especial note here that in all subsequent sections, when we speak of independent parallel processing or models, we are referring to independence of total completion times. By total completion time, we refer to the total amount of time the whole system is in operation before the element whose total completion time we are recording is finished. Putting it another way, the total completion time in a serial system is the processing time of the element whose time we are recording *plus* the sum of the processing times of the other elements whose processing precedes this designated element. In a parallel system, on the other hand, the total completion time *is* just the processing time of the element itself. Viewing Fig. 1a again, we see that our total completion time for (b) for the particular case shown, is $z_{b\,2} = t_{a\,1} + t_{b\,2}$ in the case of the parallel system, and $z_{a\,1} + z_{b\,2} = t_{a\,1} + t_{b\,2}$ in the case of the serial system. Neither the actual processing duration notation, given by the z's, nor the intercompletion time notation, given by the t's, is that needed for total completion time, so let us use x to refer to this new variable. Let x_a and x_b refer to the total completion times of elements (a) and (b) respectively. Then, we wish to learn something about how and/or why x_a affects or is interdependent with x_b.

Independent parallel models. Simply on the face of it, we might suspect that since these variables are just the processing times for the parallel models, independence would be easier or more natural to come by. Indeed, this is the case, as we may by fiat declare it so by selecting processing time probability distributions for x_a and x_b, so that they are independent; that is so that $f(x_a,x_b) = f(x_a) \times f(x_b)$ where $f(x_a,x_b)$ is the joint probability density function for x_a and x_b, and $f(x_a)$ and $f(x_b)$ are the respective marginal density functions.[7] In particular, the mathematical formulation for those simple parallel models possessing exponential intercompletion times, which corresponds to the intuitive parallel descriptions used throughout the other sections, can be easily made to do this. Let $v_{a\,1} = v_{a\,2}$, $v_{b\,1} = v_{b\,2}$, and this results in an independent parallel model. The rationale is that since the rate of processing (a) and of (b) proceeds unchanged across stages, there is no effect in completion time of one can have on the other.

Aside from the independence itself, we can observe that the average total times for

[7]Roughly, $f(x_a, x_b)$ as the joint probability density function gives the likelihood that the values x_a, x_b occur. The marginal probability density functions $f(x_a), f(x_b)$, give the likelihoods of x_a, x_b, respectively, when one has averaged over x_b, x_a, respectively. For a more precise treatment see Parzen (1960).

(a) and (b), *without* the independence assumptions, are just Eqs. (4) and (5), $E(x_a) =$ (4) and $E(x_b) =$ (5), in other words, the expressions for self-terminating means when the target is (a) or (b), respectively. However, under our independence assumptions, Eqs. (4) and (5) reduce to

$$E(x_a) = \frac{1}{v_a}, \tag{4'}$$

$$E(x_b) = \frac{1}{v_b}. \tag{5'}$$

This is the parallel independent model that will be applied to RT data from a search task in the section on applications. Its model yields accuracy predictions of the sort associated with the parallel, independent sampling model suggested by Wolford et al. (1968). However, there were no processing time assumptions attached to their model apart from that of independence. Since their main interest was accuracy results with repetitions of the target element, specific processing time distributions weren't necessary. Any model that predicts $f(x_a, x_b) = f(x_a) \times f(x_b)$, and the obvious generalization to larger values of n, will predict independence of sampling for a fixed allotted time allowed the processor. That is, if total completion times are independent then, given a fixed time t that processing is going on, the probability that (a) is completed during that time is independent of whether or not (b) is finished during the same time interval. In symbols,

$$P\left[\text{(b) is completed during time } t \,|\, (a) \text{ is completed during time } t\right]$$
$$= P\left[(b) \text{ is completed during time } t\right]$$

or equivalently,

$$P\left[(a) \text{ and } (b) \text{ are both completed during time } t\right]$$
$$= P\left[(a) \text{ is completed during time } t\right] \times P\left[(b) \text{ is completed during time } t\right].$$

Turning from the question of *independence* for a moment, we inquire if there are manipulations in the rates can cause *dependence* in parallel models. The answer is yes. Thus, a mathematical specification of parallel models gives a negative correlation when $v_{a2} < v_{a1}$ and $v_{b2} < v_{b1}$. The reasoning is that if the second stage rates are slower than the first stage rates, knowing that, say, (b) was completed during that time increases the likelihood that part of (a)'s processing time was governed by the slower rate. Thus, the chances are increased that a longer processing time was required for (a) and, hence, reduces the probability that it was completed during the fixed time t. We write this

$$P\left[(b) \text{ is completed during time } t \,|\, (a) \text{ is completed during time } t\right]$$
$$< P\left[(b) \text{ is completed during time } t\right]$$

$$P\left[(a) \text{ is completed during time } t \,|\, (b) \text{ is completed during time } t\right]$$
$$< P\left[(a) \text{ is completed during time } t\right].$$

Taking the opposite tack and setting the parallel rates so that $v_{a2} > v_{a1}$ and $v_{b2} > v_{b1}$ ensures that if one of the elements is completed sometime during a fixed time t, it is more likely that the other was also completed during that interval. That is,

$$P\left[(b) \text{ is completed during time } t \mid (a) \text{ is completed during time } t\right]$$
$$> P\left[(b) \text{ is completed during time } t\right]$$

$$P\left[(a) \text{ is completed during time } t \mid (b) \text{ is completed during time } t\right]$$
$$> P\left[(a) \text{ is completed during time } t\right].$$

It may be apparent that by trying intermediate alternatives, such as $v_{a2} > v_{a1}$, but $v_{b2} < v_{b1}$, that intermediate cases may be attained. Here, for example, the occurrence of (a)'s completion would lower the chance of (b)'s, but the completion of (b) would enhance the likelihood that (a) was also finished.

Independent serial models. Where do serial models stand on the question of independence of total completion times? Again, hammering home the point of the logical distinctiveness of the four issues, we find that serial models may yield independence or negative or positive dependencies, these three possibilities appearing as the relationships among the rate parameters are changed. In fact, it should now occur to us that we have only to employ our previous parallel-to-serial mappings to create serial models that evidence any of the three possibilities. This type of interplay crops up again and again in exploring processing structure of parallel and serial models: It is quite frequent that one investigates either the serial or parallel model, depending on which is most "natural" in some sense, simplest to work with, or both, and then employs the transformations of the variables (parameter mappings) that give equivalent results in terms of the other type of model.

Thus, to achieve an independent serial model, set $p = (v_a \mid v_a + v_b)$, $u_{a1} = u_{b1} = u_1 = v_a + v_b$, $u_{a2} = v_a$, $u_{b2} = v_b$. Note that the independence constraints are already contained in the parallel parameters and these are now incorporated into the serial structure via the mappings. To illustrate this, we can write the average self-terminating processing times in the serial version and then use the mappings to show the equivalence. Of course, equivalence of the average processing times says nothing about independence in general, but it will give us a hint about what is going on in averaged performance without deeper involvement in the mathematics. So, we rewrite Eq. (1):

$$E(t \mid \text{target is } (a)) = p\frac{1}{u_{a1}} + (1-p)\left(\frac{1}{u_{b1}} + \frac{1}{u_{a2}}\right)$$

$$= \frac{v_a}{v_a + v_b}\frac{1}{v_a + v_b} + \frac{v_b}{v_a + v_b}\left(\frac{1}{v_a + v_b} + \frac{1}{v_a}\right)$$

$$= \left(\frac{v_a}{v_a + v_b} + \frac{v_b}{v_a + v_b}\right)\frac{1}{v_a + v_b} + \frac{v_b}{v_a(v_a + v_b)}$$

$$= \frac{1}{v_a + v_b} \left(1 + \frac{v_b}{v_a}\right)$$

$$= \frac{1}{v_a}.$$

Similar operations show Eq. (2) to be:

$$E(t \mid \text{target is } (b)) \qquad = p \left(\frac{1}{u_{a\,1}} + \frac{1}{u_{b\,2}}\right) + (1-p)\frac{1}{u_{b\,1}}$$

$$= \frac{1}{v_b}.$$

It is not at all difficult to arrive at serial models that possess positive or negative correlations in total processing times by way of our parallel-serial equivalences. Given our limited space, however, we choose to take a brief look at a standard serial model with specific assumptions about the probability distribution on the intercompletion times. This is the model with a processing rate that is constant over stages, elements, and different number of input elements. It yields the average processing time predictions of the standard serial model presented in the previous section. When these assumptions are embedded in a model with exponential intercompletion times and when $p = 1$ or $p = 0$, the model becomes a Poisson process or alternatively and equivalently, the total completion times are Gamma distributed. For any value of p, it can be shown that there is a positive correlation between, say, x_a and x_b when $n = 2$. Thus, when it is known that (a) has completed processing during time t, the likelihood is increased (over what it would be if there were no knowledge of (a)) that (b) has also been finished during that same time period. This particular serial model corresponds to one of the parallel models, as far as the independence problem goes, that assumes an *increase* in processing rates across stages, with the relative values of the v's at each stage mimicking the serial probabilities of the various processing orders.

Figure 3 shows how parallel and serial rates act in cases of positive dependence and Fig. 4 shows independence when (a) is finished first. Note that to achieve independence, it is not enough simply for the serial rates at stage 2, $u_{a\,2}$, $u_{b\,2}$, to be less than the stage 1 rate, u_1; they must be less than pu_1 and $(1 - p)u_1$, respectively.

Other Types of Independence

Before leaving the topic of independence, it may be helpful to our perspective to review some of the types of independence other than that of total completion times.

Independence of number of elements. For the first, it is common to use the term independence to refer to a functional independence of the number of elements to

Parallel system

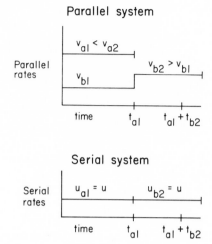

Serial system

FIG. 3. Positively dependent systems shown when (*a*) is completed first.

Parallel system

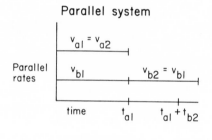

Serial system

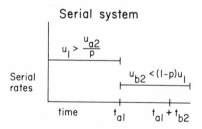

FIG. 4. Independent systems shown when (*a*) is completed first.

be processed, which has no necessary logical connections with statistical independence. If it is found that RT curves as n is varied are flat, it is said that processing is independent of n. This is okay, but it must be kept in mind that the question of how processing time and therefore RT varies as n varies is really one of capacity, as noted in the Introduction.

Donderian independence. The term ''stage'' is often used to denote successive subsystems in the human information-processing chain. Used in this more macroscopic sense, if two successive stages are additive in that the processing time of the second begins immediately when the first is completed and not before, and if they are non-interactive in the sense that variables that affect the magnitude of the processing time of one do not affect that of the other, then here also a separate type of "independence" occurs. An hypothesis that this kind of independence characterizes successive stages is termed an "assumption of selective influence" by Sternberg (1969). Two successive stages will be *dependent* in this sense if something that affects the overall average magnitude of one affects the overall average magnitude of the other (see also Pachella's discussion of this type of independence, this volume). This type of independence is statistical only in the sense that statistical analyses, as linear regression or analysis-of-variance, may be used to test it.

Independence of successive intercompletion times with element identity. Yet another kind of independence, or dependence, is statistical in a fundamental sense. Some serial models, associated with this kind of independence, which give means that are additive in the mean processing times of the individual elements (i.e., giving those serial formulae presented earlier), posit independence of successive intercompletion times. That is, the fact that (a) finishes first in exactly t msec has absolutely no bearing on how long it now takes (b) to be processed, and vice versa if (b) is completed first. Although this sense of independence at first may appear to be intimately related to that of total completion times, models possessing independence of successive intercompletion times can predict either independence of the type (i.e., of total completion times) we considered in detail earlier. Parallel models can also possess independence of successive intercompletion times with element identity. In fact, the models on which we base our discussions in this chapter assume this type of independence.

Independence of successive intercompletion times without element identity. A slightly grosser level at which the question of independence may be asked is with respect to whether the *overall* processing time of the second element is independent of the processing time of the first. This is not quite the same thing as that in the preceding paragraph. There, not only the *duration* of processing of the first is given, but also the *identity* of the element processed first. In the level referred to here, the identity is not known, only the duration of the first element's processing is known, with an averaging over the identity of the elements. It can be shown that the presence of independence of successive intercompletion times with element identification does not imply independence of successive intercompletion times when such knowledge is absent; nor does it imply dependence.

One other remark is pertinent here. The general idea of independence of intercompletion times, or successive stages in the microscopic sense used in this paper, may be applied to macroscopic successive stages. That is, it may be asked whether, for example, stimulus encoding time is statistically independent of short-term memory storage time. This question is itself "independent" or orthogonal to the question of the Donderian type of independence. Thus, an experimental manipulation that affects the overall rate of processing in the stimulus encoding stage may or may not affect the overall rate of processing in the storage stage. Either may occur without in any way relating to whether or not the magnitude of time taken by the encoding stage on a given trial affects that taken by the storage time on the same trial. For instance, the latter may show a correlation via a trial-to-trial interdependence of the two stages' deviations about their relative means. On the other hand, we could discuss models in which these two types of dependence are tied together, but since they are not *necessarily* connected they should always be treated in a logically separate manner.

In concluding this section, it is germane, as usual, to emphasize the limitations on interpretations of experimental results. A finding of independence of total completion times, for instance, although perhaps more intuitively associated with parallel models, can be predicted by serial models. Hence, under conditions where there might be some slowing down of processing by a serial mechanism in succeeding stages, it may be reasonable to postulate a serial, independent system. Conversely, there may exist processing tasks where processing is parallel but a warm-up effect occurs, inducing a speed-up of processing rates; such a system can yield positive correlations of the sort associated with serial systems.

THE LIMITED VS. UNLIMITED CAPACITY ISSUE

Basic Concepts

The capacity issue refers naturally enough to the distinction between channels or processors that take more time or make more errors as the number of inputs increases — as opposed to those that do not. This theoretical dichotomy is frequently referred to as limited- vs. unlimited-capacity processing systems.

To be sure, no real system, biological, electronic, or mechanical, ever really has unlimited capacity. All physical or biological devices or systems have an upper limit on their capacity. In fact, the term ''attention'' would be unnecessary in psychology if the mind *really* had unlimited capacity. However, it is quite helpful to entertain the possibility that within certain limits a system might perform in a constant manner (to be made more precise below) regardless of the number of inputs. For example, the possibility that some central agent responsible for monitoring incoming signals from our various modalities had unlimited capacity relative to, say, hearing, seeing, and touch was suggested to be false early in the history of experimental psychology, and the prior-entry hypothesis (Boring, 1950) (essentially a serial explanation) was used to explain how the central agent reacted to more or less simultaneous inputs over separate modalities. A current matter of interest is whether for certain types of symbol-detection tasks the visual system is capable of acting as an unlimited capacity processor (Estes & Taylor, 1964; Erikson & Spencer, 1969; E. E. Smith, this volume).

Any complete theory of processing has to include structure explaining how errors may arise. Within the present theoretical treatment, which emphasizes the possible stochastic nature of processing of individual inputs, a natural way of introducing error is through time limitations. For example, speed-accuracy tradeoff predictions can be obtained by assuming the subject establishes a criterion duration at the end of which he makes a response based on the information he has been gathering up to that time. Clearly, error rate will be inversely proportional to the value of the criterion. Similarly, experimental manipulations of the duration that the stimulus inputs are available for processing, as with the use of brief displays and backward masking, would be expected to affect error probability.

Another possibility in explaining speed-accuracy trade-offs, at least at a rudimentary level, would be to assume the subject sets a "state" criterion rather than a time criterion; that is, he might decide to quit processing after some given number of elements have been processed. More subtle versions of time-dependent decisions abound in the modern sensory and information-processing literature. A recent example of interest to which the reader is referred is the comparison of predictions by an average "waiting-time" criterion with those from a "count" criterion in psychoacoustic experiments (Green & Luce, 1972).

We will confine our attention here primarily to how variation in number of inputs affects overall processing times, assuming, as we have throughout the chapter, essentially unlimited processing time is available, relative to the processing rates. Predictions of probability correct, etc., involving truncated processing times, can be retrieved by employing the same probabilistic descriptions of the models from which processing time predictions are derived. Any assumption of error-free processing is, to be sure, only an approximation under the best of conditions. Under certain circumstances, it may be that errors reflect aberrations in mechanisms other than the processes under scrutiny (e.g., the fast-guess model, Yellott, 1971), but this would have to be empirically demonstrated. We cannot go further into these issues here, but it is becoming increasingly apparent that a thorough treatment of the error problem is overdue in memory and perceptual-scanning studies. An approach that promises to be fruitful within certain experimental contests is offered by Theios, Smith, Haviland, Traupman, and Moy (1973). Their serial model employs some specific assumptions about order of processing in short-term memory search and derives predictions about errors, reaction time, and sequential effects.[8]

Capacity at Different Levels

As noted above, the terms "unlimited capacity" and "limited capacity" are not very accurate ones. However, rather than resort to neologisms, we shall try to make clear how we believe the usual terms should be employed. Apart from the misleading semantic connotations, however, there is a more substantive problem, namely, the capacity issue may be raised with respect to any number of different levels of

---

[8]The same questions could be posed for time and noise as are posed here for n. That is, systems that have unlimited capacity with respect to time limitations or with respect to variations in the amount of noise present, at least up to a point, are in principle conceivable. For example, one could devise a system which up to certain limits could provide a variable amount of filtering action in order to maintain a constant processing time and/or constant accuracy rate. The present theoretical apparatus will have to be imbued at some point with structure for direct representation of noise effects before latency predictions concerning them can be dealt with. There is not much evidence for human information-processing systems that have unlimited capacity with respect to time, in other than the trivial sense of perhaps having much more time than they need under some conditions.

processing. Thus, unlimited capacity at the level of individual elements means that when an element is actually undergoing processing, the amount of time it requires to be processed is unchanged as the total number of input elements, n, is varied. The processing durations referred to are, of course, simply the z's in Fig. 1a. Limited capacity at this level would mean that some measure of the individual processing times, most likely the mean, would increase as n increased. At the opposite pole in the hierarchy of levels is exhaustive processing. Unlimited capacity at this level has to imply that the overall total time to complete all the elements, again probably a measure of central tendency like the mean, remains constant as n is increased. Limited capacity points to an increase in this measure. We shall use mean processing time as the desired measure.[9]

Two other related aspects must be mentioned in preparing to make specific statements. One is that fixing a type of capacity at one level may involve inexorable consequences in capacity at the other levels. Thus, we shall show that an assumption of unlimited capacity at one level may simultaneously force a limitation in capacity at higher levels, and something "better" than unlimited capacity at lower levels. "Higher" here refers to more elements, so the exhaustive level is higher than the individual element level. "Better" in the above sentence brings up the second aspect and suggests the concept of "super capacity," in that processing may actually speed up on the average at a given level as n increases; we shall use the term "super capacity" to that effect in the following.

Unfortunately, the situation is even more complicated than we have so far admitted. The additional complexity arises because the rates, which specify speed of processing of individual elements, may be related to the individual mean processing time in an intricate manner. This happens, for example, when the rates are free to change across stages during a single trial. The outcome for modeling is that a parallel and serial model may make identical predictions everywhere, including capacity effects, but the ways the predictions are evidenced via the rates of processing will typically be completely different for the two. We shall have occasion to remark on this circumstance again below.

The Standard Serial Model

We begin with our typical or standard serial model, the one with equal u's over everything. The first point to be made here is that this model has unlimited capacity at the level of individual elements, since the rates and individual mean processing times are unchanged as n varies. As was emphasized earlier, this assumption that the serial rate is constant over differing values of n is in no way a necessary concomitant of the concept of seriality: one-at-a-time processing. In the present serial model, processing is of limited capacity both at the self-terminating level and at the exhaustive level of processing, since mean processing time increases (linearly as it happens) with n for

---

[9]The reader may wish to try his hand at deriving predictions for a level we shall have to neglect here: that of minimum processing time. Egeth (1966) discusses some of these.

TABLE 1

Capacity as a Function of Model and Level

	Level		
	Individual element	Self-terminating	Exhaustive
Standard serial model with equal constant u' s	UC	LC	LC
Standard parallel UC deterministic models	UC	UC	UC
Probabilistic nonindependent model that is UC at exhaustive level	SC	SC	UC
Standard parallel probabilistic independent model with equal constant rates	UC	UC	LC

Note.—UC = unlimited capacity; LC = limited capacity; SC = super capacity.

both of these levels. These features are represented in the first row of Table 1. Another feature of this serial model that is interesting to contrast with parallel models is that the limitations in capacity for these higher levels do not depend on any particular type of probability distribution for processing times. The fact that the mean processing time is just the sum of the means of the individual elements implies this generality. Indeed, it should be clear that a deterministic serial model that assumes a processing time of exactly $1/u$ for every element gives descriptions of capacity identical to probabilistic models that assume that $1/u$ is the mean processing time for the individual elements.

Standard Parallel Models

It provides an interesting contrast to next discuss standard parallel models that also have unlimited capacity with respect to *individual* elements. Here, it *does* matter whether we are discussing deterministic or probabilistic models and systems. If processing is deterministic and processing rates for individual elements are unchanged as n increases, then the exhaustive and self-terminating processing times will also be unchanged and therefore of unlimited capacity. On the other hand, if processing is probabilistic, then whether exhaustive processing is of unlimited capacity will depend on whether correlations in total completion time exist (see the section on the independence-dependence issue) and whether the correlations are positive or negative. The deterministic parallel capacity predictions are shown in row 2 of Table 1.[10]

To produce flat exhaustive curves in nondeterministic cases it must happen that processing somehow speeds up as n increases. A fairly reasonable way to produce this is to assume that as each element finishes, the remaining elements speed up proportionately. This assumption, along with the assumption that at the *start* of processing on any given trial, each element has the same rate as if there were only one element to be processed, is sufficient to produce a flat, mean exhaustive-processing time curve as a function of n. Thus, if v is the processing rate for a single element when only one is input, then that is also the processing rate for each of n elements at the first stage of processing when n are input.

At the end of stage 1, which is itself governed by total speed or rate nv (that is, the sum of the n individual rates), assume that the new rate for each of the $n - 1$ remaining elements is $(n/n - 1)v$, that it is $(n/n - 2)$ at the third stage, and so on. The time required, on the average, for stage 1 is naturally the reciprocal of the total rate, namely, $1/nv$. Since the rate during stage 2 is $(n/n - 1)v$ for each of the remaining $n - 1$ elements, the total speed or rate is $(n - 1) \times (n/n - 1)v = nv$, and by the same principle as before, the average time for stage 2 is just $1/nv$. Following this line of reasoning we see that the overall mean exhaustive processing time will then be the sum of the times over all n stages, $1/nv + 1/nv + \ldots + 1/nv = n \times 1/nv = 1/v$, the same duration as that taken when $n = 1$, thus yielding exhaustive unlimited capacity. However, this model does not give unlimited capacity at the self-terminating or individual levels. On the contrary, it predicts *super capacity* performance on both these. This is because the average completion time for a given element is found by averaging over all the possible stages in which the given element would be completed. If it is not finished until last, it takes time $1/v$. Any other stage of completion results in less time, so the overall average is itself less than $1/v$, the time required for an element when $n = 1$. Thus individual and self-terminating processing time is super capacity, that is, decreases with n (this may be shown precisely by carrying out the averaging process and observing the resulting expressions' behavior as a function of n). Row 3 of Table 1 summarizes this model. Another characteristic of the model is that the total completion times are positively correlated.[11]

---

[10]A slight intricacy in parallel deterministic processing should be noted here. If the elements to be processed are heterogeneous with regard to how fast they can be processed, then increasing n will mean that, on the average, exhaustive times will increase, even though the rates of the individual elements do not increase as n increases. The reason is that since the longest time determines the exhaustive time, the more elements there are to be processed, the greater the likelihood that a very slow element will be included on any given trial. However, if self-terminating processing requires that only a single critical element be processed, then heterogeneity will not affect this processing time, since the probability of a slow or fast element being the critical element will be unchanged as n increases (under suitable stimulus randomization).

[11]Yet another possibility is that while the elements' total completion times are parallel and independent, the individual times consist of a series of steps that are negatively correlated with one another; when one step takes a long time, the succeeding step takes only a little time, and so on. The negative correlations in these random times could make the overall result appear deterministic.

There is a fair amount known about the case of independence of parallel total completion times and the influence of varying n on exhaustive processing times, especially when the processing time distributions are the same on all the elements. The reason is that the latter problem is really just that of computing the maximum value of a random sample of n identically distributed random variables. The maximum value corresponds, naturally enough, to the longest processing time of the n elements. The exact distribution of the maximum is usually not trivial to find. However, the case of n independently sampled, identically distributed values (e.g., equal constant v's), is perhaps the most classic of modern statistics, so it is not too surprising that something has been achieved on the mean or expected maximum as n varies (see e.g., Gumbel, 1958, p. 91). An important finding for most reasonable probability distributions on processing time for a single element is that the *largest possible* mean or expected exhaustive processing time is $E(t|$ exhaustive processing of n elements$) = E(t|$ one element$) + \dfrac{\sigma(n-1)}{\sqrt{2n-1}}$, where σ = standard deviation for $n = 1$. It follows easily from this expression that this largest possible mean exhaustive time grows at a rate slower than $\sqrt{n|2}$. The curve of such a function is increasing but at an ever slower rate. This does not imply that all exhaustive-mean predicted curves of unlimited-capacity (individual level) independent, parallel models must be positive, and negatively accelerated as the above is. However it, along with the observation that several typical distributions do just that, suggests this may not be uncommon behavior. Given an initial mean and standard deviation, it does give bounds on how much increase is possible for any larger value of n. This is apparently the rationale behind Sternberg's (1966) parallel-bound curve.

In any case, this type of system or model is typically limited capacity at the exhaustive level by virtue of the increment in processing times associated with increases in n. It is also the set of models falsified by Sternberg's (1966) data. Nevertheless, the implication in that paper that the fairly steep straight-line RT curves obtained by varying the number of elements in memory cannot be predicted by independent parallel models is wrong, as we shall show later in the present section. On the other hand, it is true, by virtue of the negative acceleration pointed out in the preceding paragraph, that typical independent parallel models that are *unlimited capacity* at the level of *individual elements* do not predict *linear* increasing RT functions.

To gain some insight into these negatively accelerated exhaustive-processing functions, assume that each of a set of memory elements is itself made up of more elementary features. Assume further that the memory elements are compared in parallel and independently with a target element but that within each memory element the features of which it is composed are serially matched against those of the target element. Now, since we are considering exhaustive processing, we ask about the finishing time of that last element to be completed. But, on the average, when all the features of the first element to be finished are done, some of the features of the others will also have been completed. Finally, when $n - 1$ of the n memory elements are done, most of the features of the last one will already be finished so only a little more time will be required to complete it. Hence, it can be seen that for each added memory element, a smaller increment to the exhaustive processing time will be added, this increment corresponding to the smaller number of unfinished features left after the next to last element is completed.

A special case of this class of models is obtained when each memory element is compared holistically with the target letter, or equivalently, only a single feature is required for comparison. In this case, we let v represent the processing rate for each element, and since this model is unlimited capacity at the level of individual elements, the rate v is constant across values of n. This model, assuming as it does exponential intercompletion times, yields the expected negatively accelerated exhaustive processing curves.

The idea here is that when processing begins at stage 1 for arbitrary n, each element rate is v (for any value of n) and by our former remarks on intercompletion times for such parallel models, the first mean intercompletion time will be $1/nv$. At the second stage, with one element completed, the total sum of parallel rates is $(n - 1)v$ so the next intercompletion time average is $1/[(n - 1)v]$ and so on until the last intercompletion time is $1/v$, yielding the exhaustive mean processing time of $1/v + 1/2v +$
$\ldots . + 1/nv = \dfrac{1}{v} \sum_{i=1}^{n} \dfrac{1}{i}$. A note on this sum that is often useful is that its curvilinearity is well approximated by $\log (n)$ and thus conforms to our previous statement about parallel independent, individual unlimited capacity, with identically distributed times having increasing negatively accelerated curves.

What happens at the self-terminating level in these models? Since processing is independent on the individual elements' processing times, no element affects any other, and so the self-terminating time is invariant as n changes. Table 1, row 4 summarizes the capacity properties of these parallel models.

Mimicking Parallel and Serial Capacity Predictions

Parallel models that mimic the standard serial model. First, consider the standard serial model (Table 1, row 1). We already possess the type of mapping strategy that produces parallel models that are equivalent to serial models when $n = 2$. This same strategy may be expanded for larger n. Complete derivations are given elsewhere (e.g., Townsend, 1972a, 1974). Here we confine ourselves to seeing what the mappings look like when all processing orders are equally likely so that all the serial p values are equal. In that case, writing the equal v values as functions of n and stage, $v(i,n)$ we have $v(i,n) = [v(1)/(n-i+1)]$, $(v(1) =$ processing rate when $n = 1)$. Since at stage i, there are $n-i+1$ elements remaining, all being processed at rate $v(i,n)$, it follows that the total rate at each stage is just $(n-i+1) \times v(i,n) = v(1)$, so that the average total time for exhaustive processing is $nv(1)$. The average time for self-terminating processing is, of course, $(n + 1/2)v(1)$, so letting $v(1) = u$ produces equivalent predictions to the standard serial model.

On several occasions in this section, a within-trial speed-up of *individual* parallel rates has been employed to some purpose; in the present case, to help mimic standard serial behavior. A possible rationale for such a speed-up is the reallocation of capacity that was devoted to a completed element to one or more of the uncompleted elements.

The preceding parallel model does not possess independence of total completion times of its elements, so it was not one of the parallel models claimed to be falsified by Sternberg (1966). This study involved the memorization of letter lists of varying (but small) size and a consequent presentation of a target letter which the subject reported as present or absent in his memorized list. However, it was then implied that the class of parallel independent models was falsified by the resulting relatively steep straight-line RT functions of n. Since the target-absent and target-present observed curves were coincident, therefore having equal slopes, it was proposed that the appropriate model was (what we are calling) the standard serial model with exhaustive processing even on target-present trials.

We now present an independent parallel exhaustive model that predicts straight line RT curves. We may not let the rates change with stage (e.g., no speed-up within trials is assumed) because this typically produces nonindependent processing. However, we can let v vary with n, writing $v(n)$. Specifically, for $n = 2$ let, $v(1) = 1/k$, for $n = 2$, $v(2) = (1 + \frac{1}{2})/2k$, and in general,

$$v(n) = \frac{\sum\limits_{i=1}^{n} \frac{1}{i}}{kn}.$$

We can easily prove the conjecture that this model predicts straight-line curves with arbitrary slope k. Recalling that the average exhaustive processing time in the case of independent parallel processing is simply the sum of the average times for each successive stage, and noting that since the rates of each individual element remain constant across stages, the total speed decreases in proportion to the number of elements completed, produces:

$$E(t) = \frac{1}{nv} + \frac{1}{(n-1)v} + \frac{1}{(n-2)v} + \ldots + \frac{1}{v} = \frac{1}{v} \sum\limits_{i=1}^{n} \frac{1}{i}$$

Substitute in $v = \dfrac{\sum\limits_{i=1}^{n} \frac{1}{i}}{kn}$

and verify the conjecture that $E(t) = kn$. Observe that $v(n)$ decreases as n increases, so that this model has limited capacity at the individual element level. This particular independent model also predicts no serial position effects, as was apparently the case in Sternberg's data. Independent parallel models can predict serial position effects by assuming unequal rates at the different positions. In the next section, we show that an independent parallel model can handle straight-line RT data with serial position effects. Now, it is not claimed that this particular model is necessarily the "true" model for these data, only that the data did not actually rule out parallel independent (limited-capacity) models.

Serial models that mimic parallel, deterministic, unlimited capacity models.
A task that is interesting to consider in the present connection was used by Neisser (1963). In these experiments, a subject holds one or more items (e.g., letters) in

memory and looks through lists to detect matches with the memory list. When they have had a great deal of practice, it is not uncommon to find that subjects can perform scans of lists of letters for memory set sizes of 1 to 10 letters, with no appreciable increase in average scan rate per display-list letter. To the extent that this can occur without a corresponding increase in error rate, some form of unlimited capacity model at the level of exhaustive processing is supported. The idea is that although when the processor comes upon a target letter, the comparisons can be self-terminating, that the bulk of the time is taken up with negative comparisons with nontarget letters. This is because most of the list letters are nontarget letters. All the latter comparisons must be exhaustive with respect to the memory list. The deterministic parallel model with unlimited capacity at the individual level makes appropriate predictions for these data (Table 1, row 2). The probabilistic parallel models that assume super capacity at the individual element level cannot be ruled out either, since there was no opportunity in those experiments to test the prediction of these models that self-terminating times should decrease with n (Table 1, row 3).

It is very critical that we be clear on the prediction of serial models with respect to flat RT functions as n varies. Serial models *can* indeed predict such functions, therefore preserving the logical and mathematical independence of capacity and parallel-serial assumptions that we have argued for. This is not to say that the serial explanations are intuitive or natural. In fact, this is one of the few situations where there is a strong intuitive argument for one of the types of processing over the other. If the curve of RT as n increases went up at all, then it would be easy to find serial models *or* parallel models that could explain the data in an intuitive fashion. But to predict completely flat functions, the serial models have to say that processing is super capacity on individual elements, that is, a speed-up takes place as n increases. And this super capacity cannot happen in a reasonable way as it could in the case of parallel processing. The parallel processing rates could be the same (as when $n = 1$) at stage 1 and then increase across stages by (perhaps) picking up excess processing capacity left over from the completed elements. But in serial processing, since the total sum of n individual times must equal that for $n = 1$, there can be no such capacity sharing. The type of speed-up across stages that works for a parallel system, for example, will not work for a serial system. Consider a serial system that takes the preceding rate and adds it to the rate for the next element. This was mentioned as a rationale for parallel models that have unlimited capacity at the individual level. Although not perhaps as reasonable as for a parallel model, such a speed-up within trials might occur due to a within-trial priming or warm-up as processing gets under way. In any event, the total exhaustive processing time would be $1/u + 1/2u + 1/3u + \ldots + 1/nu$. This, of course, is not equal to $1/u$ as it would have to be. A (unintuitive) type of speed-up that *would* work is to simply let the (supercapacity) $u(n) = nu$; that is, the rate of processing grows proportionately to n.

Serial models that mimic standard probabilistic, independent parallel models that have unlimited capacity at the level of individual elements. What kind of serial model mimics the negatively accelerated exhaustive curves as n varies, as well as the unlimited capacity aspects of the standard probabilistic parallel models

(Table 1, row 4)? The serial models making these predictions assume that overall there is an increase in processing rate as n increases but that there is a decrease in rate as successive elements are completed within a trial. Specifically, let us mimic the standard parallel model given on p. 164 (the equal-v model).

The serial model that is equivalent to this model assumes that for any value of n, $u(1,n)=nv$, $u(2,n)=(n-1)v$ . . ., $u(n,n)=v$, where $u(i,n)$ is the serial rate for any element that is processed at stage i when a total of n elements are being input into the system. Also, the probability that any given element is processed i^{th} is just $1/n$. It is fairly obvious that the increasing rate with n mimics the addition of more elements in the parallel case and that the within-trial decrease in rate mimics the slow-down in overall parallel production (i.e., the more elements that are finished, the longer the intercompletion times) as more and more elements are completed. Perhaps the reader will wish to prove further to himself that the predicted self-terminating time is indeed $1/u(1,1) = 1/v$. The serial, parallel-mimicking system that conforms to this model can be viewed as gearing up its stage 1 processing rate more and more as the number of inputs increases, but "getting tired" within a trial, slowing down to its old rate $(u(n,n) = v = u\ (1))$ for the last (n^{th}) element to be processed. Further, the equal parallel rates force the equal p's on the serial model (i.e., equally likely processing orders), so that both would predict a lack of serial position effects.

Serial position and other order effects have been neglected in this section because some studies either don't find them or preclude their appearance. The presentation would also have been substantially complicated had they been included. However, conclusions concerning predictions and rate effects will continue to hold on the average when order related phenomena are treated.

In the following section, we review the modeling and conclusions of a recent experiment and offer a general discussion of models for search experiments.

AN EXPERIMENTAL APPLICATION AND CONSIDERATION OF GENERAL MODELS OF SHORT-TERM MEMORY AND BRIEF VISUAL DISPLAY SEARCH

The Experiment

Mathematical characterization of cognitive processing and issues is all well and good but of little interest to the experimentalist unless it can be shown to aid him in the penetration of data. In this section, we take a small but representative portion of data obtained in some recent multisymbol search experiments (Townsend & Roos, 1973) and show how some of the concepts developed in the preceding sections can be applied to data. There have been few mathematically specified serial models actually fit to data, and with the exception of Rumelhart (1970) almost no mathematical parallel applications. The investigation involved behavior in a short-term memory experiment of the Sternberg (1966) variety, as well as in a brief visual display search-task previously employed by Atkinson et al. (1969). Part of the study was directed toward an attempt to formulate a qualitative model of an overall system, subsystems of which were assumed to interact in producing performance in the two tasks. Several broad characteristics of the data were very similar in the two situations, with some mildly unusual facets appearing in the memory part of the task. Two quantitative models were fit to the data of both experiments. Some general mathematical models were examined that were supported or falsified by these and like data of other experimenters. Because the visual search data were more typical of those obtained by others than the memory data, we shall take a portion of the former for detailed consideration.

To get to particulars, the data we take up were acquired in a task in which the subject had to indicate by pressing one of two buttons whether or not a letter that had been given to him visually 3 seconds earlier was in the later multiletter visual display. The first display appeared for 2 sec, and the later display appeared for 400 msec. The second multiletter display was centered horizontally in the subject's fixation area, and its size (n) varied randomly from 1 to 5 letters. On ½ of the trials the second display did contain the "target" letter, and if present, the target occupied any of the n display (serial) positions with probability $1/n$, ($n = 1, 2,...5$). This type of paradigm, run under high accuracy conditions, as it was here, was apparently first employed by Atkinson et al. (1969), although it has generic precedents in the designs of Estes and Taylor (1964) and Sternberg (1966).

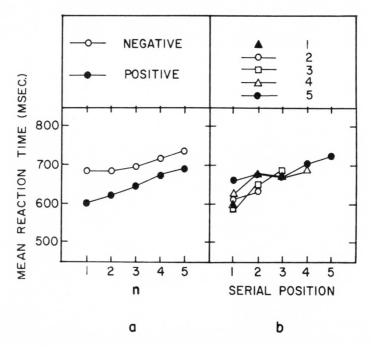

FIG. 5. 5a.—Target present (positive) and target absent (negative) mean reaction time as a function of number of letters in display. 5b.—Mean reaction time as a function of serial position (target location); the different curves are for $n = 1,2,3,4,5$.

Reaction times were recorded, and it was duly noted that errors were small and inconsistently related to n. We pause again to note that a full treatment of such experiments will ultimately have to include error prediction. But as suggested in earlier papers (e.g., Townsend, 1971b, 1972a) the problems of equivalence between models is portentous, even omitting the error dimension, and the other issues are sufficiently complex to command some sustained attention.

The three subjects employed produced results rather similar to one another including similar trends in serial position effects. It will be recalled that serial position effects are the RTs for trials when the target was present (+ trials) as functions of the position of the target. Serial position effects are obviously confined to + trials since target absent (−) trials provide no differential position RTs. Figure 5a shows the overall mean RTs as functions of n (our numerical illustration shall consider only $n = 1, 2$, and 3, although the figures show all 5 points obtained in the study), and Fig. 5b shows the serial position functions, where each separate curve is for a different n and both graphs represent group averages. The average standard error for a single point in Fig. 1a was between 5 to 10 msec, and there are 750 trials underlying each point.

A strong linear trend is obvious in the overall means, indicating limited capacity at exhaustive and possibly self-terminating levels.[12] The serial position curves indicate a tendency to respond faster, the more left the target appeared in the display.[13]

Serial and Parallel Models: Fits to Target-Present Data

We shall take a couple of "typical" models, one serial, the other parallel, and fit them to the RT+ (reaction time) data and then see how well they predict the RT- data. We shall then discuss the implications these results have for parallel and serial models in general.

The serial model. The serial model we are going to use is self-terminating and assumes that the processing rate is constant over serial positions and stages of processing but allows the rate possibly to change as a function of n [i.e., we use $u(n)$]. Hence, this model assumes equal u's for *fixed n*, but the capacity question is left

---

[12] A detailed discourse on conceivable explanations of the limited capacity nature of these and similar results cannot be taken up here. However, recent studies have shown that identification of letters may be affected by interletter similarity and by lateral masking effects in multiletter situations (Estes, 1972; Estes & Wolford, 1971; Townsend, 1971a; Townsend, Taylor, & Brown, 1971; see also the discussion by E. Smith, this volume).

It may be observed in this context, that the present definitions concerning capacity purposely do not distinguish between structural or bottleneck as opposed to energy-source types of limitations (see e.g., Kahneman, 1973). It does not seem entirely clear at present, whether a structural vs. energy nature of capacity dichotomy will turn out to be fruitful. When a parallel distribution of attention is reduced to a single element, seriality and the appearance of a "bottleneck" is obtained. Possibly, a criterion for distinguishing structural from other kinds of capacity-limiting mechanisms should be the relative lability of the distribution of capacity.

[13] In this study, the Ss were instructed to attempt to scan from left to right in order to see if serial position effects could be elicited. As they were weak or nonexistent in the Atkinson et al. (1969) experiment, it was of interest to optimize the chances that they could occur. Since they did, manipulability of this aspect of processing behavior is suggested.

open. In order to obtain a workable theory of the distribution on processing paths, it is assumed that with each position in the processing order i, there is a probability [i.e., $(p_i(n)$] that the letter in the corresponding serial position i will be processed then (i.e., i^{th}). If [with probability $1 - p_i(n)$] the ith serial position is not processed i^{th}, any of the other $n - 1$ possible serial positions is processed i^{th} with probability $1/(n - 1)$, that is, the ith processing position then has an equal probability of containing any other serial position's letter in the processing order. Note that this automatically assures that the total probability that the ith processing position contains *some* serial position is equal to 1. However, it also the case that the total probability that each serial position gets processed *somewhere* in one of the n processing positions must be 1. Since this constraint is not forced by the assumptions given so far, it was assumed for purposes of parameter estimation that for any serial position k ($k = 1, 2,...n$), the probability that k is in the nth processing position is just 1 minus the sum of the probabilities that the kth serial position is contained in one of the other processing positions (that is, in one that is less than n).

In addition to these "processing" parameters, there is a parameter, t_0, required to predict a nonzero intercept. The parameter t_0, which we call the residual latency parameter, presumably includes averaged sensory, motor, and other time contributions that are not directly related to comparing the display letters with the target. We make the usual assumption that t_0 is additive with the comparison processing times as n is varied. These assumptions about processing lead to the following formulae for serial-position mean reaction times, $t_{n,i}(i = 1, 2,...n; n = 1, 2, 3)$, where i = serial position and n = number of elements in the display:

$$t_{1,1} = t_0 + \frac{1}{u(1)} , n = 1$$

$$\left. \begin{array}{l} t_{2,1} = t_0 + p_1(2) \times \dfrac{1}{u(2)} + \left[1-p_2(2)\right] \times \dfrac{2}{u(2)} , \\[2em] t_{2,2} = t_0 + \left[1-p_1(2)\right] \times \dfrac{1}{u(2)} + p_2(2)\dfrac{2}{u(2)} , \end{array} \right\} \quad n = 2$$

$$\left. \begin{array}{l} t_{3,1} = t_0 + p_1(3) \times \dfrac{1}{u(3)} + \dfrac{\left[1-p_2(3)\right]}{2} \times \dfrac{2}{u(3)} + \dfrac{\left[1-p_3(3)\right]}{2} \times \dfrac{3}{u(3)}, \\[2em] t_{3,2} = t_0 + \dfrac{\left[1-p_1(3)\right]}{2} \times \dfrac{1}{u(3)} + p_2(3) \times \dfrac{2}{u(3)} + \dfrac{\left[1-p_3(3)\right]}{2} \times \dfrac{3}{u(3)}, \\[2em] t_{3,3} = t_0 + \dfrac{\left[1-p_1(3)\right]}{2} \times \dfrac{1}{u(3)} + \dfrac{\left[1-p_2(3)\right]}{2} \times \dfrac{2}{u(3)} + p_3(3) \times \dfrac{3}{u(3)}. \end{array} \right\} \quad n = 3$$

Note that the RT for serial position is composed of contributions from occasions when it is processed at other locations in the processing order as well as the ith location. It would not be correct to write, say,

$$t_{3,1} = t_0 + p_1(3) \times \frac{1}{u(3)} + \frac{\left[1-p_1(3)\right]}{2} \times \frac{2}{u(3)} + \frac{\left[1-p_1(3)\right]}{2} \times \frac{3}{u(3)}$$

The latter expression would result if we viewed the system as taking each serial position in turn and selecting a processing position for it. It seems more natural to assume that at each stage of processing, a serial position must be selected whose letter will be compared with the target.

The simplifying assumptions in the present serial model, namely, that if serial position i is not processed i^{th} (with probability $(1 - p_i(n)$ then any of the other serial positions are processed i^{th} with probability $1/(n - 1)$ should be viewed as an expedient to assess seriality and the magnitude of serial position effects (the latter via the values of the $p_i(n)$). There are two reasons for this. The first is that if we took the above assumption seriously, exceedingly strong consequences ensue. For instance, when $n = 3$, it follows from assuming that $\dfrac{1-p_3(n)}{2} = 1 - p_1(3) - \dfrac{1-p_2(3)}{2}$, that $p_1(3) = p_2(3) = p_3(3)$; that is, no serial position effects could be predicted. By allowing the probability of processing the kth serial position n^{th} to be 1 minus the sum that it was processed earlier, *without* regard to $\dfrac{1-p_n(n)}{n-1}$ (e.g., $\dfrac{1-p_3(3)}{2}$), we avoided this untoward result. The second reason for viewing the assumption as a convenient fit-device is that there seems to be no processing interpretation that yields nondegenerate values of the $p_i(n)$ (e.g., values such that $p_i(n) \neq p_j(n)$, $i \neq j$).

Estimation of t_0 was performed by subtracting the slope of the best fitting linear function (given for these data by $RT^+_n = 578.3 + 22.7n$) from the intercept. That is, the fit of the straight line gave an overall estimate of n which was then employed to estimate t_0. The intercept is *not* equal to t_0 for the $+$ RT's since, as we have seen, the slope of a self-terminating serial model with $u(n) = u$ is $1/u \cdot 1/2$ rather than $1/u$ and, hence, the intercept is really $t_0 + 1/2u$. This would not be quite so simple if the RT function had not turned out so straight. Our policy here is to estimate t_0 based on the assumption of a constant u, then use this to estimate the p's and reestimate the u's for each n, thus providing a test of u's constancy over n.

Once t_0 is estimated in this fashion ($t_0 = 555.6$), the average serial position processing times are computed from $t_{n,i} - t_0 = x_{n,i}$ as are the average processing times for each n, $x_n = RT_n - t_0$. The latter is used to estimate $u(n)$ as we illustrate for $n = 1, 2$.

When $n = 1$
$x_1 = x_{1,1} = RT_1 - t_0 = t_{1,1} - t_0 = 1/u(1) = 601.61 - 555.6)$ msec = 46.01 msec and hence, $u(1) = .022$ letters/msec.

Similarly when $n = 2$
$x_2 = RT_2 - t_0 = 3/2u(2) = (621.56 - 555.6)$ msec = 65.96 msec so that $u(2) = .023$ letters/msec
and when $n = 3$
$u(3) = .022$ letters/msec.

Obviously the estimates of u are quite close to one another and thus the standard serial model with $u(n) = u$ really applies to this part of the data.

Recall next that imposed constraints on the p's require that
$p_2(2) = p_1(2)$

and

$$p_3(3) = 1 - \frac{1-p_1(3)}{2} - \frac{1-p_2(3)}{2} = \frac{p_1(3) + p_2(3)}{2}.$$

The value for $p_1(1)$ is just 1, of course, but for $n = 2$, we have now, using the above constraints,

$$x_{2,1} = p_1(2) \times \frac{1}{u(2)} + \left[1-p_1(2)\right] \times \frac{2}{u(2)},$$

$$x_{2,2} = \left[1-p_1(2)\right] \times \frac{1}{u(2)} + p_1(2) \times \frac{2}{u(2)},$$

which are two simultaneous equations, linear in $p_1(2)$ and $1/u(2)$. But, we have already estimated $u(2) = .023$ letters/msec and, hence, can solve for $p_1(2)$, which turns out to give $p_1(2) = .82$. That is, the estimated probability that the letter in serial position 1 is processed first, and that in serial position 2 is processed second, is quite high (.82).

When $n = 3$, the simultaneous equations become (where we denote the estimated u's appropriately)

$$x_{3,1} = p_1(3) \times \frac{1}{u(3)} + \left[1-p_2(3)\right] \times \frac{2}{u(3)} + \left[1-p_1(3) - \frac{(1-p_2(3))}{2}\right] \times \frac{3}{u(3)},$$

$$x_{3,2} = \frac{\left[1-p_1(3)\right]}{2} \times \frac{1}{u(3)} + p_2(3) \times \frac{2}{u(3)} + \left[1-p_2(3) - \frac{(1-p_1(3))}{2}\right] \times \frac{3}{u(3)},$$

$$x_{3,3} = \frac{\left[1-p_1(3)\right]}{2} \times \frac{1}{u(3)} + \frac{\left[1-p_2(3)\right]}{2} \times \frac{2}{u(3)} + \frac{\left[p_1(3) + p_2(3)\right]}{2} \times \frac{3}{u(3)}.$$

Substituting in $u(3) = .022$ and then solving for $p_1(3)$ and $p_2(3)$ yields $p_1(3) = .99$, $p_2(3) = .87$, and hence, $p_3(3) = .93$, thus illustrating within the context of this model the high likelihood that a subject processed from left to right with occasional switches of serial positions 2 and 3.

The reader may verify by substitutions the estimated p's and u's and t_0 into the original formula that this model fits the $+$ RT data extremely well. All predictions were within one standard error (10 msec) of the observed serial position means. Even though the number of parameters is greater by one than the degrees of freedom in the data, when S_0 is included, a perfect fit is not guaranteed (for proof of this fact, see Townsend & Roos, 1973, Appendix A). Roughly, the reason is that the serial position means cannot be too different from one another without causing p and/or u to be less than zero.

The parallel model. The parallel model developed for application to the same data assumed (*1*) independent processing (the rates, v, constant over stages), but (*2*) with different processing speeds assumed for different serial positions $v_i \neq v_j$ and (*3*) with an explicit dependence of rate on n, $v_i(n)$, thus permitting a limited capacity self-terminating predictor. These assumptions resulted in a limited-capacity parallel model with the same number of parameters, when a t_0 is estimated for the residual RT effects, as for the preceding serial model. Unlike the serial model, however, this parallel model's structure is guaranteed to fit the present data since

$$x_{n,i} = \frac{1}{v_i(n)} = t_{n,i} - t_0$$

and $v_i(n)$ can be any positive number at all. Note that the expressions for $x_{n,i}$ just follow from the independent parallel assumptions giving self-terminating means of $1/v_i(n)$, when the target is placed in serial position i.

The overall mean RT here is just

$$RT_n + = t_0 + \frac{1}{n} \sum_{i=1}^{n} \frac{1}{v_i(n)},$$

the arithmetic average of the serial position means. We will not pursue the obvious fit technique here, but the reader may note that it can be done directly from the data.

At first glance, it might seem as if the obvious linearity in the data reduces the number of parameters more in the serial model than in the parallel model since there would be only one u instead of 3 (for $n = 1, 2, 3$). However, the linearity may be similarly employed in the parallel context.

Thus, linearity implies that the average self-terminating prediction (i.e., the means on target-present trials) must be proportional to n, that is,

$$\frac{1}{n} \sum_{i=1}^{n} \frac{1}{v_i(n)} = cn ,$$

where c = positive constant. But this expression implies that one of the $v_i(n)$ may be written as a function of the others. Although we haven't space to show it here, this operation reduces the number of parallel parameters to that of the present serial model with a single value of u assumed.

Let's take a brief digression to discuss a couple of aspects of theorizing related to the above model testing.

One of the arguments sometimes advanced for employing serial models would seem to be that predictions of mean processing times can be derived without detailed particular probability distributions on the element completion times. This is because of the additivity of the serial successive completion times. However, more detailed assumptions must be made if variances, for example, are to be predicted. In any case, this type of argument still appears weak, to the extent that as psychologists, we are interested in finding out how things actually work in the black box, not simply what is an adequate summarizing description. It may be feasible (but it is by no means guaranteed) to develop the mathematics and concomitant experimentation that will allow specification of ever narrowing classes of models or theories that detail the kinds of mechanisms and functions that must be present to yield behavioral data. In recent years, investigators in finite automata theory have worked out means of determining canonical sets of sequential machines that can predict observed input-output data (see e.g., Booth, 1967). Undoubtedly any type of analogous development in psychology will be an Herculean task in comparison and will likely be quite different in form. One detrimental factor is that often we must rely on summary statistics within a given experiment, rather than an entire scope of input-output sequences. Also, the sheer complexity of the human black box is almost dismaying. A somewhat ameliorative aspect is that we have an extremely rich spectrum of data, across conceivable experiments, to work with, that may provide an ever mounting set of converging operations.

Predictions of Target-Absent Data

At this point the parallel and serial models have done equally well with the RT^+ data. We could proceed to similarly fit the RT^- data, but to do so would not teach us much. Instead, we employ the parameters estimated above to predict the RT^- data, assuming the exhaustive serial and parallel models, since processing must be exhaustive when the target is absent from the second display.

The exhaustive serial prediction for a given n is just

$$RT_n^- = t_0^- + \frac{n}{u(n)}$$

which effectively becomes $RT_n^- = t_0^- + \frac{n}{u}$ because of the constancy of $u(n)$ in the RT^+ data. The corresponding prediction for the parallel model is quite hideous (the reader may refer to Townsend and Roos for the complete expression for arbitrary n). However, it was found that the exhaustive expression that is associated with rates that are constant over serial position gave quite similar predictions for our data, and hence, the following expression was used to predict the exhaustive processing times:

$$RT^- = t_0^- + \frac{1}{v(n)} \sum_{i=1}^{n} \frac{1}{i} .$$

This latter expression is found by using the techniques shown in the section on capacity (in particular see "Standard Parallel Models"). It can be seen that it was necessary to grant a different residual latency parameter to the exhaustive models, $t_0^- > t_0^+$.

The results of these predictions for the RT^- data may be viewed in Fig. 6, with mild distaste if not outright revulsion. So much for typical serial *or* parallel models being able to handle *both* RT^+ and RT^- data, assuming self-termination on $+$ trials! The large number of parameters estimated from the RT^+ data make the RT^- falsifying conclusions even stronger. For scientific purposes, the bigger the class of falsified models the better, and the smaller the class of supported models the better. If processing is really exhaustive on both $+$ and $-$ trials, then there is no discrepancy for the overall mean RT functions, but then where do serial position effects (the quite strong ones found here, for example) fit in? This outcome leads us to discuss more reasonable exhaustive alternatives below, as well as self-terminating models that can predict the present kinds of data. An alternative explanation is that serial position effects arise outside the comparison processing box, but there is as yet little or no direct evidence for this.

Bamber (1969), in discussion of same-different data, has suggested an interesting type of dual processing mechanism, one for target, the other for nontarget comparisons, that can predict equal-sloped $+$ and $-$ RT functions. One, the identity reporter, is fast and emits signals for "same" responses only. The other, a serial processor, is slow and emits signals for both "same" and "different" responses. These two

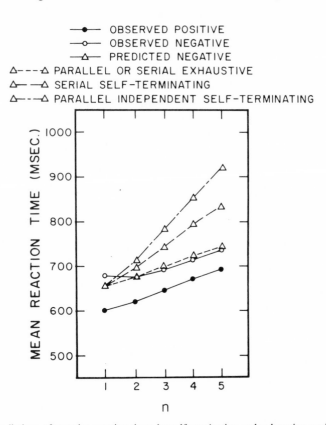

Fig. 6. Predictions of negative reaction times by self-terminating and exhaustive models based on parameter estimates from positive reaction times.

mechanisms appear to function more or less autonomously. They were able to predict the form of Bamber's results. It is of interest to consider alternative conceptualizations that do not require two separate processors, but yet allow for more latitude in thinking about processing + as contrasted with − comparisons. Specifically, Townsend and Roos proposed the hypothesis that − comparisons may take more time and/or their rates may change differently, as n varies, than do the + rates (that is, for example, $u^+(n) \neq u^-(n)$, where the superscripts refer to a match or mismatch respectively) because a unitary (single) processor is engaged in radically distinct tasks in the two cases. Measuring the fit of two things (letters) that match perfectly might require a different amount of time to achieve a certain degree of accuracy than measuring the fit of two things that mismatch to a greater or lesser extent. This notion can be discussed within either a template or feature-testing type of scheme, but is more general than either.

A Large Class of Falsified Serial Models

Not all models that allow for different rates on + and − comparisons are capable of explaining typical search results; quite the contrary. There is a large class of serial self-terminating models that cannot predict equal-sloped + and − RT curves as functions of n (Townsend & Roos, 1973, pp. 325–326 and Appendix B). This class of models is large in the sense that processing rates can vary with processing order and individual element, processing order may vary from trial to trial, − rates can differ from + rates, and the rates may vary as a function of n subject to the following constraint. The models are limited by what we have referred to as an "equal average time-increment assumption," which limits the *overall* effect that changes of rates with n can have (a capacity assumption). Basically the constraint means firstly that as n increases, the time to process a + comparison, averaged across element and processing order, remains constant. It is critical to perceive that the average time to process a + element alone (z, see Fig. 1) is being discussed, rather than the average total time to complete the positive trial. The latter duration is the self-terminating time, includes − comparisons, and may increase. Secondly, the constraint says that as n increases, the average time to process a − element remains invariant, again averaged over processing order and element. This is just like the + constraint, except that since nothing but − comparisons are processed on target-absent trials, multiplying the average − processing time by n gives the average exhaustive-processing time for that value of n. These two constraints represent a substantial generalization of the usual assumption that u is constant over everything. Aside from the point that many models are consequently falsified by most of the extant search data, it should be evident that the common feature of the falsified models is one of capacity changes in the model or system, nothing else.

There is, of course, nothing mathematically sacrosanct about equal sloped curves. If most investigators found curves with four-to-one slope ratios, then similar theorems could be proved about models that are falsified by these results. It *is* true that theoretically predicted equal-sloped curves and the class of models that is falsified by these both seem singularly simple and natural.

Three Classes of Models that Predict Equal Slopes and Serial Position Effects

With regard to variable and changing-rates kinds of models that *can* predict the dyad, serial position effects, and equal sloped + and − curves, there are two models that appear interesting to discuss; one is self-terminating, the other exhaustive. A third model employs overlapping comparison and response selection stages to achieve proper predictions. To lessen confusion, we shall intersperse this latter model between the discussion of the two models that put all the explanatory burden on the comparison process.

Within models that posit differential changes of + and − comparison rates as functions of n, either parallel or serial processing may be assumed. Further, the typically reported intercept difference between and − curves can be put in mechanisms external to comparison processing (whose effects are then clustered in t_0) or assumed to result from + and − rate differences that are present when $n = 1$ [for example, in $u^+(1) = u^-(1)$]. Because of limitations in space, we shall confine the present treatment to mentioning only the most central ideas and possible intuitions connected with the models.[14]

The self-terminating, changing-rates class of models. The first to be considered, the self-terminating changing-rates of comparison models, permit the + comparison rates to become smaller relative to the − rate, which effectively allows the ascent of the + RT function to increase and be equal to the − RT curve. For example, consider an independent parallel model of the sort fit to the data of this section, but assume in addition that although $v^-(1) = v^+(1) = v(1)$, in general, $v^+(n) \neq v^-(n)$, $n > 1$. For purposes of explication, we assume that rates are constant across element (or serial position) and processing order; these restrictions are absolutely not necessary but lead to simplification of the mathematics. The inclusion of variable rates over serial positions for the purpose of predicting serial position effects only lends added generality to the present models. Now, it turns out that if $v^-(n)$ decreases in less than inverse proportion to n, and $v^+(n)$ decreases in inverse proportion to n, that exactly equal + and − RT functions (except for the possible t_0 difference) can result. More precisely, the rates as functions of n that yield equal slopes are

$$v^-(n) = \frac{v(1)}{n} \sum_{i=1}^{n} \frac{1}{i}, \; v^+(n) = \frac{v(1)}{n},$$

where $v(1)$ is the + and − rate at $n = 1$, and it can be seen that $v^+(n)$ decreases at a faster rate than $v^-(n)$. The assumption that $v^+(1) = v^-(1)$ is not necessary, but is convenient for illustration. Although we have given the illustration in terms of simple exponential intercompletion times, the qualitative result is more general than this. As we saw, independent parallel models that assume *unlimited capacity* at the individual

[14]The first model to be discussed, the self-terminating changing-rates model, is presented in Townsend and Roos (1973). All three models, the two changing-rates models and the nonDonderian model were recently given a general mathematical characterization (Townsend, 1973). It should be pointed out that D. A. Taylor has made progress in applying a particular form of nonDonderian model to visual search data (Taylor, 1973).

level and equal rates for + and − comparisons (e.g., $v^+(n) = v^-(n) = v$, a constant) predict flat self-terminating + functions and increasing negatively accelerated − functions (see "Standard Parallel Models"). The upshot of this state of affairs is that whatever curvature the equal-sloped exhaustive − and self-terminating + curves take, the average individual comparison times for − comparisons will never evidence greater increases (that is, a slow-down in rate) than will those for + comparisons.

Turning to serial models, we find a somewhat more complex situation but a similar outcome. The treatment is too detailed to be given here, but the method and a fairly general statement of results can be found in Townsend and Roos (1973, pp. 326 – 327). Under all reasonable conditions that the writer has been able to devise, equal slopes of + and − RT functions of n are associated with + comparison rates that slow down more, or speed up less, than − comparison rates.

What might be responsible for such changes in rates in typical search experiments? One possibility that comes to mind is closely associated with speed-accuracy trade-off. In the usual experiment, the target and nontarget elements are drawn at random, but without replacement, from a fixed-sized alphabet with varying degrees of similarity among the members of the alphabet. In the present type of search task, the number of nontarget elements is increased to enlarge n, but there is always only one target element. Now, assume for the purpose of discussion that errors originate from confusions of nontargets with targets or vice versa, rather than from processes outside the comparison mechanism (e.g., the fast-guess model is of the latter type). Then the fact that in the present kind of search experiment there is always at most one target element, but the number of nontarget elements changes in order to vary n, may radically affect the relative average processing rates of + as opposed to − comparisons. Consider the fairly general case where either nontarget or target may contain both target and nontarget features on a given trial; nontargets may contain target features simply due to similarity with the target, and the target may have some nontarget features because of noise. Suppose further that feature matching between target and display (or memory) elements is all-or-none and is always performed correctly (these assumptions do not appear to be critical to the general outcome). Finally, suppose that the subject rejects an element in a self-terminating fashion as a nontarget if some criterial number of negative feature matches is attained and accepts an element as the target if some criterial number of positive feature matches is attained.[15]

[15]An aside here of some importance in the theory of feature testing relates to the number of matches or mismatches required for acceptance or rejection of the element, or pattern, in a pattern recognition context. It is sometimes assumed that exactly one mismatch is sufficient to reject the element. Obviously, if the situation is noisy, perfect accuracy cannot be so obtained; false negative responses (i.e., misses) would occur. Another assumption rather often found in the literature is that on individual elements, matching of + features must be exhaustive on target-target comparisons, the rationale being that less than complete matching by all the features may lead to false positives (i.e., false alarms). However, in a nonnoisy situation, where it never happens that features get added to the elements in the display or memory set, there will exist a subset of target features, the combination of which is unique to the target. Hence, if the subject is not merely capable of counting feature matches but also of taking note of what features match, then he can terminate when one of these subsets is completed. In many cases, there will be one or more single features that is unique to the target, and the efficient subject will be able, in principle, to terminate when he correctly matches one of these to its correspondent in the target.

In any case, the probability that any given criterial number of nontarget features is found in the target-target comparison will not increase with n, but the probability that the analogous criterial number of target features will be found in one of the $n - 1$ nontargets increases as n increases. Hence, if the subject interprets his instructions as meaning that he should maintain a low and constant error rate, he will have to change his feature criteria. Specifically, he may increase his criterion for the number of + feature matches required to accept an element as target, and this means a slow-down in the apparent + processing rate $[u^+(n)$ or $v^+(n)$ relative to the $-$ rate $(u^-(n)$ or $v^-(n)]$. The difficulty with this explanation is that one would suppose that unless the $-$ criterion is also raised, more false negatives would be found for larger n; the reason being that the $-$ criterion would be reached more often on target-present trials due to the higher + criterion. Although the number of errors in the earlier discussed experiment was too low to permit a definitive error analysis (about 1.8%), it appeared that only one of the three subjects evidenced a real increase in false-negative errors across n. In any case, to obtain precise predictions, the rates should be applied at the feature-comparison level rather than the overall element-comparison level. At this point we must move on to the next set of models; the treatment will have to be even more laconic than the immediately preceding one.

A nonDonderian class of models. In the second of the three classes of models, we entertain the possibility that the equal slopes of the + and $-$ RT functions come from two separate mechanisms, or stages in the overall processing chain, as opposed to being entirely in the comparison link. In particular, Donders' (1868) assumptions are purposely violated; namely, the stipulation that separate stages in processing do not overlap temporally but are rather distinct and additive, and, secondly, that these additive steps are independent. Two side comments are pertinent here. One is that *within* the comparison stage alone, serial processing is in accord with the additive assumption of Donders. However, the usual assumption of independence, in this case among individual element processing stages, may not hold if there is a correlation among the intercompletion times (which in the serial instance are also the individual processing times, the z's; see ''The Independence vs Dependence Issue''). Conversely, parallel processing is certainly not of a Donderian nature but can clearly yield results that manifest an appearance of additivity and independence. Thus, the non-Donderian quality of the present model is placed in the relationship between the comparison stage and *another* stage, specifically the *response selection* stage.

The present models represent the selection process as beginning during the comparison stage and as possibly biasing toward or preparing to make one or the other of the two responses, depending on the specific experimental design. In the case of search for single targets, it is plausible that before any element is processed the subject is equally disposed to making an affirmative or negative response, since the probability of a target-present trial is typically 1/2. However, as more and more comparisons are completed, the more likely it is that the set of elements on that trial does not contain the target. Thus, acting in an efficient manner, the subject's response selection mechanism may be readying to perform the ''target absent'' response until such time as either the target is located and the ''target present'' response ensues or all

n elements are processed as $-$ matches and the $-$ or "target absent" response takes place.

General but convenient mathematical models that contain these ideas (Townsend, 1973) may be constructed. This is accomplished by a decomposition of the total processing time (ignoring t_0, which now does not contain response selection but still includes the actual motor response time) into the comparison time plus the amount of time that is required to select the proper response after the comparison process is completed. The latter duration is shortened on $-$ response trials by an amount depending monotonically on how many negative elements have been processed; this number is always n on $-$ trials. The response selection duration will be lengthened by an amount depending on how many $-$ elements were processed before the target was located on $+$ trials. The interesting and critical aspect of this type of model, as far as working out predictions goes, is that the total response selection time, including that part overlapping with the comparison stage, may be written as a sum of 2 (random) variables. The first is the time required if no preselection biasing or asymmetry in readiness occurs, plus or minus that amount of time saved or wasted during the comparison stage. Thus, if no preselection biasing occurs, then the random variable Y represents the amount of time necessary to choose the response. However, on a $-$ trial, the quantity $g(n - 1)$ may be subtracted, where $g(n - 1)$ is a random function whose mean may be assumed to increase as n increases. The reason that $n - 1$ is employed rather than n is that we view the subject as going ahead with the response selection as soon as the nth element is completed, so the results of the nth comparison cannot further bias the selection mechanism. So, on a given trial the total time consumed by response selection is given by $Y - g(n - 1)$.[16] On $+$ trials, the biasing that occurs actually hurts or slows down the time to choose and then make the $+$ response. If the target is processed first, then no biasing or predisposition will have a chance to occur; otherwise, the selection time will be $Y + g(k)$, where k is the number of $-$ comparisons completed before the target is found. Again, we think that g will be larger on the average when k is larger. The $+$ response selection process thus has to compensate for the increasing predisposition toward making a $-$ response.

How does this relate to parallel $+$ and $-$ RT functions of n? The effect of the predisposition towards negative responses within trials is to increasingly slow down $+$ RT's relative to $-$ ones as n grows larger; obviously the larger n becomes, the more of a chance the bias process has to operate. We have already seen that decreasing the speed of $+$ times relative to $-$ times can equalize the slopes of the RT functions. In fact, it is possible to determine the relationship between the comparison process and the selection bias process that results in parallel or equal sloped $+$ and $-$ RT functions of n (Townsend, 1973). As in all three of the classes of models we are presently discussing, it doesn't matter at all whether comparison processing is assumed to be parallel or serial, although the exact relationship between g and the comparison rates will depend on this aspect of the model. Similarly in the present

---

[16]Observe the difference $Y - g(n - 1)$. Since $Y - g(n - 1)$ cannot be less than zero it is necessary to assume in an exact account that Y has some lower bound, say Y^*, and the $g(n - 1)$ is always less than or equal to Y^*.

class, self-termination and exhaustiveness are both compatible with its nonDonderian characteristics.

In closing our discussion of this class of models, we might make a remark about the general epistemology of the mind and brain. Although employing Donderian types of assumptions (see, e.g., Sternberg, 1969; Pachella, this volume) has been quite fruitful and will undoubtedly aid us substantially in the future, it appears likely that much of the brain's work must be carried on in parallel and in an integrated, highly correlated fashion. When we are able to go beyond relatively simple (but to be sure very complex nevertheless) processing chains we shall probably find more and more activity proceeding simultaneously. And, the fact that flat RT functions as n is varied are sometimes obtained in cognitive tasks provides fairly strong support, as noted earlier, for the proposition that consciousness can sometimes be directed to more than one thing at a time (see, e.g., Egeth, Jonides, & Wall, 1972). Finally, from a physiological point of view, some of the scanning or comparison times reported seem to be faster than known neural structure is capable of producing in a serial fashion (see, e.g., Anderson, 1973).

A class of exhaustive models that predict serial position effects. One of the most entrenched assumptions in theorization about information processing and cognitive behavior concerns the meaning of spatial and temporal effects associated with experimental placement of target stimuli. Specifically, it is generally accepted that if serial position (or comparable) effects are to be explained within a processor assumed responsible for a given task, that these serial position effects imply *self-termination*. This is false. It *is* true that self-termination, along with a non-uniform distribution of attention (parallel) or preferred processing sequences (serial) can predict serial position effects. It is also true, contrary to the usual supposition, that *exhaustive* systems can produce serial position and like effects. This section is devoted to a brief discussion of such systems and models.

As usual, we can mathematically develop both parallel or serial models that make these predictions, but we confine our present discussion to serial models. All the exhaustive serial models that predict serial position effects *and* equal sloped + and − RT functions of n have the following two properties: (*1*) a difference in the positive processing rate and the negative processing rate at a given serial position, to yield serial position effects, and (*2*) the difference in the average individual + processing times from n to $n + 1$ elements (n greater than or equal to 1) is equal to the difference in the average individual − processing times from n to $n + 1$ elements, to yield equal sloped + and − RT functions of n. We mention two special cases that appear of interest. We concentrate on how the serial position effects occur since this aspect is probably of most import for exhaustive models, and the techniques of investigating slope equality have been given earlier in the chapter.

In the first special case, it is assumed that the − rates are constant for a given value of n but that the + rate differs across the serial positions. The serial position effects will naturally directly reflect the + speed of processing on the various positions. In contrast, the second special case produces serial position effects that are inversely related to processing rates. This type of model assumes that the + rate is constant over serial positions for fixed n but that the $-$ rate is not. Since it seems unlikely that the $+$ rate is much slower than the average $-$ rate, assume that in fact the $+$ rate is faster than the $-$ rate. Then a novel and intriguing aspect of this model is that the serial position effects are given by virtue of the property that when the target is in a given position, the $-$ rate for that position does not occur (since a mismatch between target and an item in that position does not occur). Therefore, the serial position effects, revealed in the data, are actually in the *opposite* order of the $-$ processing rates. For example, suppose that the $-$ rates are slowest for the first serial position and graded up to being fastest at the last serial position; that is, there is a strong recency effect and no primacy effect. Then these models say that the serial position effects will show fastest times on target-present trials when the target is in the first serial position and slowest times when it is in the last position. Our conclusions about $-$ processing rates must then be opposite of what we observe in the data! There are other interesting exhaustive models, many of them more general than the two included here, but perhaps the latter will serve to illustrate some of the attendant flavor and intuition.

The three classes of models discussed in this section seem to the writer to contain some aspects of parsimony and plausibility. They are all capable of quantitatively explaining reported search phenomena from basically divergent assumptions. They are geared around a kind of rough approximation to a minimal systems approach, in the sense that only few mechanisms are involved and they appear to function in a fairly reasonable way. Other hypotheses, such as repeated scans through a list, may be viable in certain circumstances. Also, although the kinds of ideas discussed here seem simple from the viewpoint of what the overall system or subsystem is doing, the way what it is doing is evidenced in the mathematics may be complex at times. When there is a high degree of complexity, there is often an increased problem of parameter estimation and thus an implicit challenge to select experimental conditions and stimulus materials in such a way as to reduce the number of parameters and test the basic assumptions of the models. Experimental testing even of only those three classes of models presented here seem formidable. Including predictions for errors may help if it turns out that the small error rates reported in brief visual-display search and/or short-term memory search are related to comparison processing or, in the case of the nonDonderian model, to response selection. In any case, error predictions should certainly aid model testing in the case of long-term memory search.

We should finally mention that critical experiments are needed to see how short-term memory search differs from visual search, if at all. The learning curve for memory search RT appears to be much more extended than that for visual display search (Townsend & Roos, 1973, pp. 323–324), but evidence concerning potential differences in actual comparison processes should also be helpful. There is also the possibility that we have, most of us, overemphasized the processing of both types of comparisons, $+$ and $-$, in any search experiment. It may be efficient for the subject, in experiments involving at most the presence of a single target, for example, to look actively for a $+$ match and to disregard elements with few or no matching characteristics (e.g., features). ''Target absent'' responses might then be made after some criterion time has elapsed with no target detected. In support of this possibility is the fact that the subjects often tell of difficulty in recalling elements that were present in a list but did not match the target. To some extent, subjects may be able to tailor their processing strategies according to specific task demands.

SUMMARY

The goal of this chapter has been first to present a coherent and empirically relevant development of the issues of serial vs. parallel processing, independent vs. dependent processing, self-terminating vs. exhaustive processing, and unlimited vs. limited capacity, all of them appearing to be critical in the modeling of information-processing systems. The second goal, closely bound to the first, has been to attempt to make a strong case for the proposition that these issues are logically, mathematically, and systemically independent. Within these broad aims, many models were examined and problems of model equivalence were treated in detail. In the section on applications, an independent parallel and a typical serial model, each self-terminating, were fit to some recent search RT data, and it was found that both could predict linear target present ($+$) RT's as n (number of elements) was varied. However, if it was assumed that the same rates were applicable on target absent trials, then neither model could predict the $-$ RT's. It was shown that a large class of serial self-terminating models is falsified by contemporary data, and then several models that are capable of predicting these experimental results were discussed.

REFERENCES

Anderson, J. A. A theory for the recognition of items from short memorized lists. *Psychological Review*, 1973, **80**, 417–438.

Atkinson, R. C., Holmgren, J. E., & Juola, J. F. Processing time as influenced by the number of elements in a visual display. *Perception & Psychophysics*, 1969, **6**, 321 – 326.

Bamber, H. K. Reaction times and error rates for "same-different" judgments of multi-dimensional stimuli. *Perception & Psychophysics*, 1969, **6**, 196 – 174.

Booth, T. L. *Sequential machines and automata theory*. New York: Wiley, 1967.

Boring, E. G. *A history of experimental psychology*. New York: Appleton-Century-Crofts, 1950.

Broadbent, D. E. *Perception and communication*. New York: Pergamon Press, 1958.

Christie, L. S. & Luce, R. D. Decision structure and time relations in simple choice behavior. *Bulletin of Mathematical Biophysics*, 1956, **18**, 89 – 112.

Corcoran, D. W. J. *Pattern recognition*. Middlesex, Pa.: Penguin, 1971.

Donders, F. C. Die Schnelligkeit psychischer Processe. *Archiv für Anatomie und wissenschaftliche Medizin*, 1868, 657–681.

Egeth, H. E. Parallel vs. serial processes in multidimensional stimulus discrimination. *Perception & Psychophysics*, 1966, **1**, 245 – 252.

Egeth, H. E., Jonides, J. & Wall, S. Parallel processing of multi-element displays. *Cognitive Psychology*, 1972, **3**, 674–698.

Erikson, C. W., & Spencer, T. Rate of information processing in visual perception. Some results and methodological considerations. *Journal of Experimental Psychology Monographs*, 1969, **79** (2, Pt. 2).

Estes, W. K. Interactions of signal and background variables in visual processing. *Perception & Psychophysics*, 1972, **12**, 278 – 286.

Estes, W. K., & Taylor, H. A. A detection method and probabilistic model for assessing information from brief visual displays. *Proceedings of the National Academy of Sciences,* 1964 **52**, 446 – 454.

Estes, W. K., & Taylor, H. A. Visual detection in relation to display size and redundancy of critical elements. *Perception & Psychophysics,* 1966, **1**, 9 – 16.

Estes, W. K., & Wolford, G. L. Effects of spaces on report from tachistoscopically presented letter strings. *Psychonomic Science,* 1971, **25**, 77 – 80.

Gardner, G. T. Spatial processing characteristics in the perception of brief visual arrays. Unpublished doctoral dissertation, University of Michigan, 1970.

Gardner, G. T. Evidence for independent parallel channels in tachistoscopic perception. *Cognitive Psychology,* 1973, **4**, 130 – 155.

Green, D. M., & Luce, R. D. A neural timing theory for response times and the psychophysics of intensity. *Psychological Review,* 1972, **79**, 14–57.

Gumbel, E. J. *Statistics of extremes.* New York: Columbia University Press, 1958.

Hamilton, W. *Lectures on metaphysics and logic.* Vol. 1. Edinburgh: Blackwood, 1859.

Hunter, W. S., & Sigler, M. The span of visual discrimination as a function of time and intensity of stimulation. *Journal of Experimental Psychology,* 1940, **26**, 160 – 179.

Hylan, J. P. The distribution of attention I. *Psychological Review,* 1903, **10**, 373 – 403.

Kahneman, D. K. *Attention and effort,* Englewood Cliffs: Prentice-Hall, 1973.

Neisser, U. Decision time without reaction time: Experiments in visual scanning. *American Journal of Psychology,* 1963, **76**, 376 – 385.

Parzen, E. *Modern probability theory.* New York: Wiley, 1960.

Rumelhart, D. E. A multi-component theory of the perception of briefly exposed visual displays. *Journal of Mathematical Psychology,* 1970, **7**, 191 – 218.

Sperling, G. The information available in brief visual presentations. *Psychological Monographs,* 1960, **74**(11, Whole No. 498).

Sperling, G. A model for visual memory tasks. *Human Factors,* 1963, **5**, 19 – 31.

Sternberg, S. High speed scanning in human memory. *Science,* 1966, **153**, 652 – 654.

Sternberg, S. Memory-scanning: Mental processes revealed by reaction-time experiments. *American Scientist,* 1969, **4**, 421 – 457.

Sternberg, S., & Knoll, R. L. The perception of temporal order: Fundamental issues and a general model. In S. Kornblum (Ed.), *Attention and performance IV.* New York: Academic Press, 1972.

Taylor, D. A. Questioning the assumption of selective influence in the analysis of search and matching tasks. Paper presented at the sixth annual Mathematical Psychology Meeting, Montreal, August, 1973.

Theios, J., Smith, P. G., Haviland, S. E., Traupman, J., & Moy, M. C. Memory scanning as a serial self-terminating process. *Journal of Experimental Psychology,* 1973, **97**, 323 – 336.

Thomas, E. A. C. Alternative models for information processing: Constructing nonparametric tests. *British Journal of Mathematical and Statistical Psychology,* 1969, **22**, 105 – 113.

Townsend, J. T. Binocular information summation and the serial processing model. *Perception & Psychophysics,* 1968, **4**, 125 – 128.

Townsend, J. T. Stochastic representations of parallel and serial processes. Paper presented at Mathematical Psychologists Conference, Bloomington, Indiana, 1969. (a)

Townsend, J. T. Mock parallel and serial models and experimental detection of these. *Proceedings of the Purdue Symposium on Information Processing,* 1969, **2**, 617–628. (b)

Townsend, J. T. Theoretical analysis of an alphabetic confusion matrix. *Perception & Psychophysics,* 1971, **9**, 40 – 50. (a)

Townsend, J. T. A note on the identifiability of parallel and serial processes. *Perception & Psychophysics,* 1971, **10**, 161 – 163. (b)

Townsend, J. T. Some results on the identifiability of parallel and serial processes. *British Journal of Mathematical and Statistical Psychology,* 1972, **25**, 168 – 199. (a)

Townsend, J. T. Identifiable parallel and serial models for same-different matching experiments and a paradigm for testability at the level of mean processing times. Paper presented at the fifth annual Mathematical Psychology Meeting, La Jolla, California, August, 1972. (b)

Townsend, J. T. Solutions to a functional equation necessary for parallel-serial equivalence. Unpublished manuscript. Purdue University, 1972. (c)

Townsend, J. T. Three models for search reaction-time performance. Paper presented at the sixth annual Mathematical Psychology Meeting, Montreal, August, 1973.

Townsend, J. T. A stochastic theory of matching processes. Unpublished manuscript, Rockefeller University, 1974.

Townsend, J. T., & Roos, R. N. Search reaction time for single targets in multiletter stimuli with brief visual displays. *Memory & Cognition*, 1973, **1**, 319–332.

Townsend, J. T., Taylor, S. G., & Brown, D. R. Lateral masking for letters with unlimited viewing time. *Perception & Psychophysics*, 1971, **10**, 375 – 378.

Treisman, A. M. Strategies and models of selective attention, *Psychological Review*, 1969, **76**, 282–299.

Wolford, G. L., Wessel, D. L., & Estes, W. K. Further evidence concerning scanning and sampling assumptions of visual detection models. *Perception & Psychophysics*, 1968, **3**, 439 – 444.

Yellott, J. I. Correction for fast guessing and the speed-accuracy tradeoff in choice reaction time. *Journal of Mathematical Psychology*, 1971, **8**, 159 – 199.

5
COGNITIVE REPRESENTATIONS
OF SERIAL PATTERNS

Mari Riess Jones
The Ohio State University

INTRODUCTION

This is a sequence of chords distributed over two measures in a musical score. It is a serial pattern that has a symmetrical appearance. The spatial symmetry in this fragment is repeated and transformed by Debussy in an attempt to graphically capture lofty Gothic arches with his cathedral music, *La Cathedrale engloutie*.[1] As a time pattern this visual array is heard as a regular rise and fall, so that events within either the visual or auditory series can be anticipated by the human observer on the basis of internal relationships. That is, these events are no more randomly arranged than are the digits: 123654456321. In both cases, we are compelled to interact with the events, and it is this response to nonrandom relationships that is the subject of this chapter. Our concern is with acquisition of knowledge about perception and memory of serial regularities that do not involve semantically meaningful references. Therefore, we are not concerned with establishing the validity of Debussy's attempt to evoke an image of an external referent, such as a cathedral arch. Rather, our concern is with the human representation and use of internal relations. But the pervasiveness of internal constraints upon forms as conveyers of meaning is found throughout music, poetry, art, and artful prose. James Joyce, for example (in Levin, 1947), fractures semantic meaning so that he may play more freely with visual and temporal patterns of wordlike forms: ''O gig goggle of gigguels. I can't tell you haw! It's too screaming to

[1]For a fuller discussion of parallels between the graphic aspects of Debussy's score and architectural details see pp. 155–158 in *The piano works of Claude Debussy* by E. Robert Schmitz.

rizo, rabbit it all! Minneha, minnehi, minaaehe, minneho! [p. 733]." For those schooled in the search for direct external references of words and phrases, *Finnegan's Wake* brought criticism that prose composed of such strings lacked real "meaning." But like music, the presence of sequential regularities suggests that meaning may also reside in internal constraints. Some have distinguished internal meaning from external meaning (Birkhoff, 1933; Garner, 1962; Meyer, 1956), so that the study of human response to patterned sequences can be understood as the study of human ability to capture and retain internal meaning. This endeavor is fraught with problems of interpretation of pattern meaning, as well as with disagreements over psychological processes involved. Properly, a sequence is a pattern when it possesses regularities that permit its meaningful extension. But, immediately, the question of "meaningful" extension arises; one purpose of this chapter is to acquaint the reader with several systems of constraints that vie for the opportunity to describe meaningful extensions of serial regularities. In general, regularities fall into two categories: those that arise from the recurrence of items within a presented series (e.g., OX—OOX— —OOOX ····), and those based upon what we "know" about the events involved (e.g., ABZYCDXW· · ·). Patterns characterized by regularities of the first type are usually built from unordered symbol sets, or *vocabularies*. Patterns with constraints of the second type arise from symbol sets possessing order properties, or *alphabets*. In an interesting class of sequences, regularities play both upon a pattern's surface appearance and its alphabet. Examples of these sequences opened this chapter, for Debussy's score is built from the ordered set of tones and yet displays superficial regularity in its symmetry. The sequences 123654456321 or ABCXYZABCXYZ· · · similarly combine relations built from alphabets with regularities of the pattern's surface.

Such distinctions are useful in understanding psychological processes that underlie our "effort after internal meaning." Theoretical disagreements over the representation of internal constraints as well as the human ability to perceive and remember relations must ultimately be tempered with an understanding of the nature of the constraints themselves. In this chapter, there has been an attempt to flavor the discussions of theory and research with these considerations.

Theoretical Background

The reader will gain perspective if he is sensitized to the several streams of thought that direct current thinking in pattern processes. These are: (*a*) mathematical learning theory, (*b*) psycholinguistics, (*c*) concept attainment, and (*d*) information theory.

Mathematical learning theory, in particular the simple linear and the *N*-element pattern model, generated an interest in the probability-matching phenomenon. As this interest grew, research in sequential responding, in general, increased. A decade's research culminated in the rejection of the original models, primarily as a result of their failure to capture aspects of selective memory and hypothesis-testing in sequential strategies (see Jones, 1971, for a complete review). Current views of sequential encoding (e.g., Myers, 1970) spring from this era.

The general influence of psycholinguistics upon theory and research in sequential learning is readily traced to the thinking of Chomsky (1957). Fruitful links with both Markovian learning models and information theory were apparent in some applications of finite-state grammar generators as early as 1958 (Miller, 1958). But Chomsky and Miller (1963) have sought to enlarge psychologists' concepts of syntactic structure, and the growth of interest in artificial language learning based upon transformational rule structures (e.g., Smith, 1973) testifies to their success.

With the need to specify grammars underlying pattern regularities has also come a concern for understanding the selective mechanisms that permit a person to detect rules and seemingly ignore "irrelevant" aspects of the sequence, such as the particular symbols involved. Strategies that facilitate concept attainment in probabilistic (Bruner, Goodnow, & Austin, 1956) and deterministic (Shipstone, 1960) sequences have been studied with a concern for the memorial and cognitive capacities of the human categorizer. Patterned sequences offer a flexible and realistic medium for studying strategies of problem solving (Bjork, 1968; Johnson, 1955) and thinking (Bartlett, 1958).

Finally the reemergence of Gestalt thinking in contemporary form finds instead of the laws of pragnanz, the metrics of information theory put forth to quantify the good pattern (e.g., Attneave, 1954, 1959). Foremost in extending the concepts of uncertainty into a multivariate description of pattern structures has been Garner (1962) who has attacked serial pattern perception and learning by linking uncertainty measures to certain figure-ground correlates of expectancy.

It's mistaken to imagine that these approaches are unrelated. We find, for example, recent discussions (e.g., Simon, 1972) that emphasize conceptual aspects of pattern learning, while at the same time the complexity of pattern conception is measured with the aid of information theory.

Basic Paradigms

Our response to patterned sequences may differ, depending upon whether we are caught in the midst of an unfolding temporal pattern or are attempting to recreate a briefly presented spatial array. A sensitivity to task differences is important. Pattern prediction, pattern reconstruction and recognition, and judgment tasks vary in nature and complexity. Prediction is most demanding; the judgment task least demanding. Each has potential for providing useful information.

Prediction. A prediction task attempts to capture dynamic aspects of our response to speech or music by placing the subject within a temporal succession of events. It is demanding, for the person must (*a*) remember prior events, (*b*) discover regularities in the recalled events, (*c*) generate a timed response consistent with the regularities, and (*d*) evaluate the response in terms of the hypotheses and feedback.

With roots in both probability learning and serial anticipation learning, the paradigm itself takes the form of requiring a person to anticipate which of several (S) events in a patterned series will occur on each trial. The prediction response itself is either manual (button-press) or verbal ("one," "six").

Performance is evaluated in terms of dependent measures common in serial anticipation learning, such as trials-to-criterion or total errors. The most interesting dependent measure, however, is the serial position curve of pattern learning, which reveals prediction error frequencies at each point within a pattern. Pattern prediction learning rarely results in smooth-bowed serial position curves characteristic of anticipations of unrelated items. Instead, provocatively irregular curves result, and these challenge the theorist to make inferences about the strategies people use to predict these patterned events.

The potential of serial position analysis is illustrated by considering possible predictions to the binary (S = 2) pattern 001110011100111···· as it repeats itself in time. Because each event must be anticipated, the extent to which people detect useful regularities will be reflected by relatively low error frequencies whenever these regularities apply. Furthermore, if salient relationships change, prediction errors should pile up at corresponding serial positions. In this sequence, for example, if salient relations are strings of identical events, or event runs, such as 00 and 111, then the change from 00 to 111 should cause prediction errors. In other words, the serial position profile should look like curve R in Fig. 1, where most errors occur at the transition between the two runs. On the other hand, if people use the initial 00 as a basis for setting up a general expectancy for double-alternations, then curve E would reflect subjects' strategies. Curve E shows a majority of errors corresponding to the first disconfirmation of the alternation expectancy, which occurs on the last event in the run of three.

Thus, an advantage of the prediction paradigm is its potential for revealing details of subjective structure. Paradoxically, in order for this revelation to occur the subject is continually pressed to respond overtly as the sequence unfolds. It can be argued that

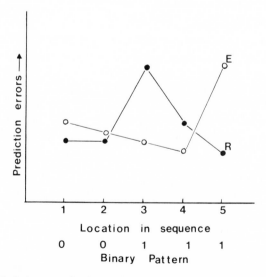

FIG. 1. Hypothetical curves reflecting prediction error profiles for the binary pattern 00111. The E curve is consistent with a double-alternation expectancy interpretation of salient relationships, while the R curve represents a simple run-encoding prediction.

forcing such a trial-by-trial record neither realistically captures the dynamic aspects of human responding to temporal patterns, nor promotes performance that is free from response interference (see Jones, 1971, for a discussion of overt prediction). Thus, complexities of the prediction task suggest the need for complementary tasks.

Pattern reconstruction. Recall requires that a person reproduce all, or part of, the sequence after presentation. Effects of overt response interference should be less disastrous than in the prediction paradigm, for in recall designs the response cannot disrupt attention to the ongoing pattern. Nevertheless, the effects of output interference at recall are well-known, so that variations of the recall paradigm as well as recognition designs are superior in reducing response interference.

Whether a pattern occurs once or repeatedly, the subject may be asked to reconstruct the entire sequence. Commonly, no requirements are imposed upon recall order, thus pattern reconstruction shares with free recall an absence of experimenter-imposed directives. Caution is recommended in treating the two settings as parallel, however; for this reason "free" pattern recall is referred to as pattern reconstruction. In part, lack of output constraints results in some misplaced fragments during recall and so contributes to a problem within the reconstruction paradigm. The nature of this problem is illustrated by considering the following digit pattern and a typical written response protocol:

Pattern:	1 2 3 6 5 4 2 3 4 5 4 3 6 5 4 1 2 3 5 4 3 2 3 4
Protocol:	1 2 3 4 3 2 5 4 3 4 3 2 1 2 3 1 2 3 4

Serial Position Score: c c c   c c c

A retention score based strictly on serial position counts only six correct responses. Obviously this person has retained more than this score reflects. Difficulties arise, however, in considering item retention regardless of position. The fragment 543, for example, appears twice in the pattern but once in the subject's protocol. Which is the subject recalling? Such misplaced fragments not only play havoc with standard scoring techniques that tally item content and item location, but also defy traditional indexes of subjective structure (e.g., Shuell, 1969).

Three solutions to recall scoring vary in sensitivity. An *all-or-none* score used in perceptual recall (e.g., Glanzer & Clark, 1963) requires scoring an entire protocol wrong if at least one error exists. Vitz and Todd (1969) have argued that *total-errors-per-pattern* is more sensitive than an all-or-none score. Errors, however, must be scored strictly according to serial location, with misplaced fragments scored as errors. In view of this, the *serial-pattern-reconstruction-curve* goes further in reflecting those pattern locations with which people have greatest difficulty. Nevertheless, applications of standard scoring techniques that score as correct the item in its proper location will be both conservative with respect to amount retained and insensitive to structural detail. Lack of sensitivity of serial reconstruction curves is illustrated with data collected in our lab, where people were asked to reconstruct digit patterns such as 123654234543654123543234 wherein progressions such as 123 or 654 always spanned three digits. Patterns were presented for reconstruction several

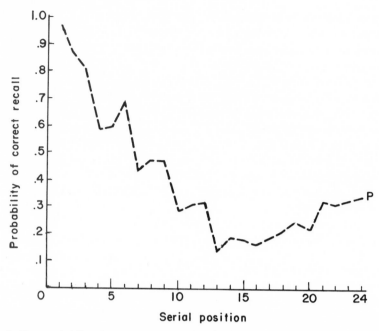

FIG. 2. Mean probability of correct recall per pattern locations for serial digit patterns formed from progressions based on 3-digit groups. Pattern reconstruction protocols over 10 pattern presentations were scored strictly according to serial position.

times, with protocols scored according to serial position. Sensitivity to serial structure should be revealed in reconstruction profiles by relatively high errors after every third digit (e.g., 4, 7, etc.), where progressions changed. Figure 2 shows mean probability of correct recall for the 24 serial positions. Sensitivity to rule changes in the patterns was minimal. Averaging over trials and subjects magnifies the dampening effect of misplacements in reconstruction protocols. The reader is urged to compare the curve of Fig. 2 with those typical of the prediction paradigm shown in Fig. 1.

Some of the sensitivity evident in prediction profiles is recaptured with a modified reconstruction task wherein people are required to recall parts of a presented pattern. A context-probe paradigm, introduced by Jones and O'Hara (1973), confronts subjects with a pattern fragment and requires reconstruction of the remainder. Not only are misplacement errors fewer, but output interference effects are also reduced in this design, so that serial position error profiles for reconstructed segments are more trustworthy and more sensitive to pattern structure.

Recognition. Recognition designs also offer relief both to the scoring dilemma and to response interference effects, for they require a subject to make one of two responses (e.g., "same," "different") to an entire pattern using confidence criteria that permit the control of response bias (e.g., Green & Swets, 1966). The recognition task is used in two ways: (*a*) The first use involves the subject in learning a set of serial patterns followed by a recognition phase in which the subject must identify the *same* patterns amidst an equivalent number of novel patterns. (*b*) In the second use, a learning phase is followed by a recognition phase in which the subject encounters only novel patterns. The subject must "recognize" which patterns are similar, in some sense, to the learning set. The first use of recognition involves processes of reproduction and identity-matching; it does not necessitate *a priori* similarity criteria. By contrast, the second application forces both the subject and the experimenter to outline similarity criteria that should govern recognition judgments. If similarity criteria involve rule structures, then the latter application has potential for tapping processes of production. When successfully applied (e.g., Kantowitz, 1971), the subjects' use of structure in forming pattern concepts can be studied.

Judgments. The subjective representation of structure is of major concern in pattern processing. Sometimes the simplest means of gathering information about subjective structure is to ask the individual about it. The subject is granted freedom to reveal a subjective scale by asking him to assign numbers or category labels, or to rank-order different patterns. If judgments are orderly, we can infer something about structural properties that determine them. Subjective scales that have received the greatest amount of attention have been those involving judgments of pattern goodness (e.g., Garner & Clement, 1963) and pattern complexity (Vitz & Todd, 1969).

In sum, each paradigm focuses upon different aspects of our interaction with a patterned environment. Our goal is to understand all facets of this interaction, for with an understanding of serial pattern processing will come insight into our response to form in music, art, and language.

THEORIES AND ISSUES

Understanding is born of meaningful interpretation of facts, not isolated bits of information. And, although we are hardly on the threshold of thorough understanding of sequential responding, several current theoretical views offer potential for drawing together the facts of pattern processing. At the same time, limitations in scope or differences in assumptions of various theories raise provocative questions for future research. Sketches of these theories are presented here with an emphasis on their basic assumptions, explanatory power, and primary evidence. The theories fall into three general categories: (*a*) modern associationism, (*b*) encoded groups, and (*c*) rule-formulation theories. The approaches differ in their emphasis upon active psychological processes and the nature of formal representations of these processes.

Modern Associationism

A basic aspect of traditional serial learning that has preoccupied adherents of stimulus-response associationism is the bowed serial position curve characterized by relatively high likelihood of recalling beginning and end members of a series, and low probability of recalling those in the middle. When order of recall is controlled, the emergence of a bowed serial-position curve reflects the course of a subject's struggle over trials to overcome confusions of item location, a phenomenon once described in terms of the "doctrine of remote associations." Current theories of memory in sequence learning must cope not only with the dual problems of serial position phenomena and the ultimate mastery of serial order, but also with a myriad of details that qualify serial learning when it becomes serial pattern learning. Many have argued persuasively (e.g., Johnson, 1972; Lashley, 1951; Restle & Brown, 1970a) that S-R associationism cannot meet the challenge of serial pattern learning. That is, the breakdown of a smooth, bowed serial-position curve into a jagged, unseemly profile with patterned events appears to qualify the doctrine of remote associations to a point where it loses meaning.

While limitations of traditional associationism appear overwhelming, Estes (1972) has resurrected elements of the old faith within the currently popular hierarchical framework. Associations develop not between adjacent serial events, but between groups of events and codes in long-term memory. Immediate memory for a series is supported by associative pulses that flow constantly between long-term codes and immediate memories. Estes' rejection of interitem associations elminates an explanation of serial recall in terms of interfering associations. Instead, memory losses come from disruptions resulting from random fluctuations in the timed associative pulses set up between memory units. These disturbances explain a subject's confusion of item location, as well as the fact that confusions are more likely with central items. So ultimately random fluctuations determine the bowed shape of immediate serial recall curves. Mastery of serial order comes from a subject's ordered rehearsal of events in memory, and it is this rehearsal process that maintains and cements serial order. Specifically, rehearsal establishes inhibitory associations that prevent responses tied to other codes from intruding during recall as learning progresses.

Primary evidence. Estes' views arise from the study of immediate recall of short strings of unrelated consonants. The extension of his model to patterned strings holds greater interest for this discussion. In this regard, a span of related items is associated with a long-term memory code. Thus, in the pattern 123654654123, events within the 123 progression are represented as a group controlled by a long-term memory code. Random fluctuations in associative pulses are limited by the establishment of a hierarchy of codes, and these constraints give rise to more recall errors at group boundaries early in learning.

Evaluation. Estes' model has great scope. It encompasses not only traditional recall of unrelated events, but also details of serial pattern learning. Furthermore, the model is unusual in its incorporation of internal timing properties of the organism. Paradoxically, it is the conception of timing that may ultimately present difficulties for this theory. This is because timing is tied to a constant flow of associative pulses and is not conceived in terms of natural rhythms. Because rhythm is extrinsic to the model, Estes relies upon a rehearsal mechanism to cement memory units. As rehearsal establishes inhibition of intruding responses, the recency of early recall gives way to serially ordered outputs. In this respect, the validity of modern associationism turns upon the tenability of a rehearsal mechanism in serial pattern learning.

Encoding of Serial Groups

Two encoding theories emphasize human representations of surface regularities in serial patterns. The two differ in their descriptions of what regularities are encoded as well as how they are encoded.

Encoded runs. Vitz and Todd (1969) tie encoding to event repetitions, or runs. A string of consonants such as XXPPPNP is assumed to be quickly cast into perceptual run codes (XX), (PPP), (N), and (P) that function in learning and memory. Pattern representation is achieved after adjacent codes are wrapped into larger units such as $[(XX)(PPP)]$, and $[(N)(P)]$, and finally into an encoded version isomorphic with a pattern's surface regularity. The relative frequency of runs within a sequence determines the ease of encoding; this is indexed by an uncertainty metric described in a later section.

Major evidence. While Vitz and Todd's model has sprung from perceptual recall and judgment tasks, there is widespread evidence that runs of events are remembered as units (e.g., Jones & O'Hara, 1973) and function as powerful determinants of prediction (e.g., Myers, 1970) in binary pattern learning. Furthermore, Vitz and Todd (1969) themselves offer impressive correlational evidence that run uncertainties may affect complexity judgments of consonant patterns.

Evaluation. The model's generality is limited to encoding born of event repetition. Thus, if people encountering a pattern such as 1221112222 cannot resist assigning integers to the runs and remembering the series as 1-2-3-4, this strategy cannot be handled by the model, for it does not presume that metric relations determine codes. And while the encoding process incorporates uncertainty and so offers a basis for describing pattern predictability, the elements upon which uncertainty is determined prevent conceptualization of learning in terms of figure-ground relations, symmetry, or rule-governed expectancies. Thus the spatial array XXXPPNPNPPXXX is evaluated in terms of the relative frequencies of (XXX), (PP), (N), and (P), not in terms of bilateral symmetry, nor its potential for generating expectancies about run progressions. In contrast, Garner emphasizes the role of expectancies in pattern learning.

A two-process approach. Figure-ground relations are important ingredients of Garner's (1962, 1970) approach to pattern processing. However, the psychological processes that play upon figure-ground relations vary with aspects of pattern presentation. Specifically, Garner and Gottwald (1968) have argued that encoded serial representations result from active expectancies that are generated at slower rates of temporal pattern presentations. But at rapid presentation rates, a perceptual process obtains that is immediate and passive. Nevertheless, according to Garner and Gottwald (1968) "Even though a distinction between perception and learning is necessary, similar principles of pattern organization operate for both $[$p. 97$]$."

Common principles of organization that relate the two processes are loosely described in terms of accent patterns determined by the placements of event runs and alternations (Preusser, Garner, & Gottwald, 1970).

Major evidence. Evidence for the role of expectancy in pattern learning is found in studies that require people to predict different arrangements of a given pattern, such as 00111 and 11100. The expectancy of double-alternations provoked by 00111 resulted in a pile-up of prediction errors on the third event in the run, 111, and slowed overall learning (Garner & Gottwald, 1967, 1968). Moreover, differences as a function of pattern arrangement were not observed if the same sequences whipped by at faster rates (Royer & Garner, 1966), lending support to a two-process theory in which active expectancies do not operate at fast presentation rates (Garner & Gottwald, 1968).

Evaluation. Garner's theory provides a useful transition from passive perceptual models such as that of Vitz and Todd to the active rule-formulation theories to be discussed next. It has greater scope than either. However, the principles of organization that link perception and learning share some of the vagueness of Gestalt laws of pragnanz, while lacking their comprehensiveness. In contrast to Gestalt thinking, for example, Garner (1970) has maintained that symmetry is not one of the formal relations that influence serial expectancies. A symmetrical pattern such as 11100111··· is easy because with repetition it develops into a powerful run arrangement, namely, 11111100···· . Nevertheless, Garner's distinctions both dramatize and circumscribe the concept of man as an expectancy-driven organism.

Rule-formulation Theories

In contrast to encoding theories in which emphasis is placed upon regularities in the presented sequences, rule-formulation theories turn on an indvidual's use of ordered vocabularies, or alphabets, and rules that relate to alphabetic properties. Both Restle (1970) and Simon (Simon, 1972; Simon & Kotovsky, 1963) propose that people actively abstract serial relations and, using alphabetic rules, generate corresponding cognitive structures. While the rules themselves are often similar, Restle and Simon differ in their descriptions of serial learning.

Restle's theory. Restle (1970) assumes people attempt a cognitive representation of patterns as rule-trees wherein rules arise from an alphabet. Some examples of rules are: (*a*) *next,* N, which shifts an event on the alphabet; (*b*) *repeat,* R, which is an identity rule; (*c*) *complement,* C, which complements an event in terms of the alphabet.[2] Thus N(1) becomes "take event 1 and move to the next event on the alphabet." With an alphabet of the digits 1 through 6, N(1) is 2. Similarly, R(1) is 1, and C(1) is 6.

Learning involves rule-testing, where each newly-acquired rule applies to more of the pattern. For example, the pattern 11226655 is described by an N rule that changes

[2]Restle's notation is in terms of *mirror-image* (M) and *transposition* (T) instead of *complement* (C) and *next* (N). In order to standardize notations throughout, I have chosen the latter two terms for these operations. A *transpose* (T) operator is introduced in a later section and has a different definition than does Restle's transposition rule.

11 to 22; but a C rule changes 1122 into 6655. A rule-tree describes this:

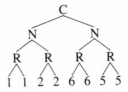

Realization of these tree structures assumes that mastery of the last half of a pattern results from recall of all events within the first half plus the highest order rule. In this case, a person must know 1122 and C to correctly anticipate 6655. Learning proceeds from acquisition of lower-order rules (e.g., R) to highest-order ones (e.g., C in this pattern).

Major evidence. The validity of the individual rules is established in serial anticipation learning of temporal light patterns, where the alphabet is a row of six equally spaced lights (S = 6). Restle and Brown (1970a, 1970b) required some people to predict the sequence 1235433234 and others to predict its spatial transform, 2346544345. Digits refer to lights in the spatial alphabet:

$$\underline{1} \quad \underline{2} \quad \underline{3} \quad \underline{4} \quad \underline{5}$$

Relations governing these and other patterns were not combined hierarchically, but indivdual rules such as N and C were studied. Mean prediction errors at each serial position over 20 pattern repetitions for these patterns is shown in Fig. 3. Profiles for both groups of subjects are similar in revealing that points of greatest difficulty corresponded to rule changes such as the break-off of 123 (N rule) at location 4. Rule shifts at locations 1, 7, and 9 also gathered more prediction errors.

Patterns generated by rule-trees often result in serial position curves that have a majority of errors associated with predicting events at the high-order rule transition. So the sequence 11226655 would bring most errors between 2 and 6, fewest between 1 and 1 or 2 and 2. Further, such patterns are easier to learn than ones with the same event groups haphazardly arranged such as 11556622.

Evaluation. Powerful evidence in favor of the individual rules outlined by Restle and Brown (1970a, 1970b) suggests that people readily encode more complex relations than surface regularities arising from event repetitions and alternations. Restle's hierarchical formulas are interesting in that, while the rules involved refer to an alphabet, the subject must apply them to the pattern surface in an increasingly burdensome manner. That is, rules at successively higher levels in a structural tree span proportionately more of the presented string. Most of the evidence in support of this version of hierarchical structures comes from studies wherein rule-levels have been confounded with serial position. In contrast, Simon's model does not envision rules applying directly to the pattern surface.

Simon's theory. The nature of a sequence as it is presented offers only guidelines for the length of a rule-span, according to Simon (1972). Thus a change from 1 to 2 in

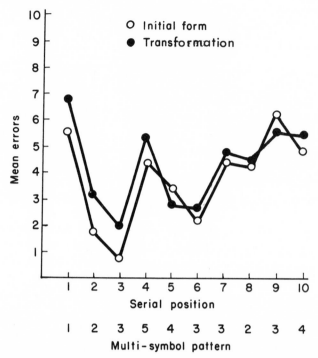

FIG. 3. Mean errors per location for subjects predicting the pattern 1235433234 and its spatial transform 2346544345. Each subject received 20 presentations of one of the two patterns. (From Restle & Brown, 1970 (*a*); reproduced with permission of the authors and the American Psychological Association.)

the pattern 11226655 establishes a periodicity, and to remember events within each periodicity the subject applies rules to a memory alphabet. Rules such as R, N, and C are possible in Simon's model, but they instruct the subject where to go in an alphabet, not how to change preceding subpatterns. Thus a person detects that R determines the relation between events within groups, so he locates 1 in the alphabet and repeats it: 11. A memory marker references the first event, 1, to which the subject returns between periods. To generate 22, N(1) instructs a shift to 2 on the alphabet, where repetition again occurs: 22. Next, 66 is generated by complementing the initial event, C(1), and repeating the resulting 6. This continues until the sequence has been generated. A person in this model is seen constantly referring to an alphabet and to the initial pattern element. What is remembered is a series of moves along an alphabet, not a string of events.

Major evidence. Support for rule discovery and pattern generation activities comes from studies that evaluated the order in which letter patterns were viewed and extrapolated (Kotovsky & Simon, 1973; Simon & Kotovsky, 1963). Features people noticed first corresponded to periodicities within the presented string. The recurrence of A in ATBATAAT···, for example, was often reported to determine a rule span. Those aspects of rule-structure that presented difficulties in pattern generation related to different memory demands. Note that the ATBATAAT···· requires the subject to operate at one alphabetic location (i.e., A · · · B). In contrast, to extend the sequence RSCDSTDE···· a subject must keep track of rules at two different memory locations (i.e., RS····ST and CD····DE). The latter sequence Simon and Kotovsky (1973) predicted to be relatively difficult, and it was.

Evaluation. Simon's ideas have potential for great scope, but they have wrestled with verification infrequently and only within letter completion tasks. The emphasis upon discovery of periodicities, however, find some parallels in the learning of digit patterns (e.g., Fritzen & Johnson, 1969). But other details of presentation that could affect discovery, such as rhythm, have been neither developed nor tested.

Finally, both rule formulation theories arise from prediction or extrapolation tasks, and neither has been extended to other paradigms. In spite of this, both approaches have potential for interesting interpretations of pattern reconstruction. If a sequence, such as 123, can be predicted by a rule, then why not simply remember the rule and where it begins (i.e., 1) and reconstruct the sequence at recall? Such theories readily lead to the expectation that pattern reconstruction should be orderly, characterized by a compulsion to begin at the beginning to recreate the sequence.

A Theoretical Overview

What is most striking in this review is the extent to which various theories become paradigm-bound. Those designed to describe ordered recall have not considered implications of their assumptions within judgment, prediction, or even reconstruction tasks. Those arising from anticipation learning have been extended to no more than variations of these paradigms. In an age of mini-models it is easy to lose sight of the possibility that information gathered from one paradigm may lend perspective to that gathered from another. Moreover, if people adjust in systematic ways to different paradigms, not only is this important in itself, but it may shed light on each set of paradigmatic strategies observed. Only the theories of Garner and Estes have seriously attempted to cross the paradigm barrier. The contrasting images of the human responder in these two approaches are familiar ones. Estes suggests an associative-inhibitory network in which the individual must rehearse to make good, while Garner finds people generating expectancies as a function of accent patterns and figure-ground relationships. And so, the very concept of man as an active expectancy-generating individual is a debatable one, and this raises one basic issue that is developed throughout the remainder of this chapter. Related issues also spring from these theoretical sketches and may serve as focal points for the evaluation of research that follows: (*a*) What is the role of rule-structure in pattern reconstruction? (*b*) How do aspects of pattern presentation, such as rhythm in temporal patterns, relate to the issue of man as an active concept-former? (*c*) What are fundamental elements of pattern structure and how may these be quantified? It's always easier to raise issues than resolve them. Some of these will remain unresolved by the chapter's end, but perhaps by then the reader will have acquired some awareness of the problems in serial pattern research.

GENERAL CHARACTERISTICS OF PATTERN PROCESSING

Instructions and the Manipulation of Pattern Recall Strategies

Imagine attempting to reconstruct the sequence ABYBCXCDW. Where would you begin? Commonly people begin at the beginning, which perhaps is not surprising at all. However, this circumstance gathers its interest from the fact that, at least on early trials, free recall of sequences with no structure does not begin at the beginning, but at the end. Rule-formulation theories, in particular, raise the possibility that people represent patterns in terms of relations that guide recall even on the first attempt at pattern reconstruction. This section evaluates the role of structure in directing recall by (*a*) comparing pattern reconstruction profiles to those of ordered recall, and (*b*) examining the role that instructions play in pattern reconstruction.

Pattern reconstruction and traditional serial recall: A comparison. Some perspective upon the role of instructions in guiding recall is given by a consideration of ordered recall. If people are specifically instructed to recall a series of unrelated items seriatim, beginning with the initial item, immediate recall reveals good memory for initial items (high primacy) and poor memory for later items (low recency). This recall profile rarely results if people are permitted to recall the same series in any order; here high recency characterizes immediate recall profiles. Furthermore, it is well-known that immediate free recall of sequentially dependent material (Deese & Kaufman, 1957) results in serial recall profiles comparable to those of people instructed to begin at the beginning. Thus, there appear to be at least two ways in which a subject may be induced to observe a particular serial order in recall: The experimenter may instruct him to order his output, or the subject may instruct himself as a result of perceived structural regularities.

The shape of pattern reconstruction profiles in the first few learning trials then is symptomatic of the manner in which pattern rules guide output. Using a set of specific rules to define structure in serial digit patterns, Jones (1973) has verified that pattern reconstruction results in recall curves with high primacy and low recency. Subjects were instructed to reproduce patterns such as 111222666555222333555444 in writing, beginning at any point they wished. Pattern reconstruction, scored by serial position, is shown for the first trial in Fig. 4. The curve is striking for its high primacy and negligible recency effects. The same sort of profile results on the first recall trial whether patterns occur as time patterns with digits occurring one-at-a-time or as spatial patterns.

While such findings are consistent with a rule-representation view, they are by no means proof. Because rule-formulation theories emphasize the role of initial pattern elements as well as the instructive character of the rules themselves, these data seem particularly compatible with extensions of theories such as Restle's (1970) and Simon's (1972). Estes' model has some difficulty in accounting for the observation that little recency appears on early recall trials, although this finding is not a crucial test of that theory. Furthermore, support for the interpretation that rules serve as instructions to guide recall turns upon accepting the null hypothesis of no difference

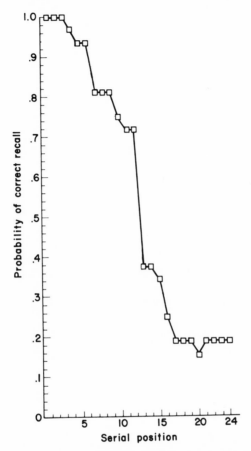

FIG. 4. Probability of a correct recall per location on the first reconstruction trial for patterns generated hierarchically from the alphabet of digits 1 through 6 and rules such as next and complement.

between ordered recall and "free" recall of structured sequences. We must seek additional sources of evidence.

The manipulation of pattern recall strategies by specific instructions. If subjects are required to recall a patterned string in an order that is inconsistent with the rule structure, then we may expect disruption of recall and a change in the shape of pattern reconstruction profiles. Pitting vague instructions against powerful structural determinants of responding is unprofitable in sequential research (e.g., Jones, 1971; Jones & O'Hara, 1973). Therefore, Jones (1974) specifically instructed subjects on what to do during the recall of temporal digit sequences. Half the subjects were told to recall the presented patterns backwards (B) beginning with the final digit, while the other half were told to order their recall in any fashion they pleased (F).

Recall profiles for both groups are shown in Fig. 5. Backward recall significantly

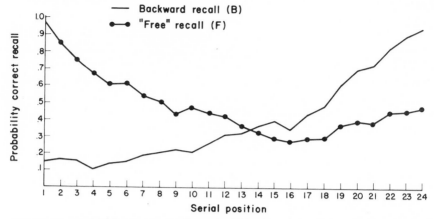

FIG. 5. Mean probability of correct recall at each of 24 serial positions of hierarchically constructed digit patterns for subjects recalling sequences backwards (B) and for subjects reproducing the same sequences in a "free" recall fashion (F) beginning at any point. Each subject received 10 presentations of a given pattern.

disrupted performance and dramatically changed the shape of the serial pattern recall curve. Only subjects using free recall revealed high primacy and low recency; the mirror-image of these profiles found with B groups supports the contention that output interferes with subsequent recall. Moreover, the findings as a whole suggest that people typically encode patterns so that they may begin recall with the first element and proceed seriatim.

Summary. The special characteristics of pattern recall clearly relate to properties that set patterns apart from other lists, namely, the relations between serial events. Theories that assume that rules operate as instructions, where the instructions depend upon the first item in a sequence, are most compatible with the findings of this section. Thus the models of either Simon or Restle, if developed within the reconstruction paradigm, would have little difficulty. Modern associationism, as developed by Estes, would encounter some problems in accounting for the shape of serial reconstruction curves upon the first recall trial. The extension of encoding aspects of approaches such as Garner's (1970) or Vitz and Todd's (1969) to serial ordering of recall, however, is not clear.

Some Aspects of Pattern Presentation: Time, Space and Other Things

Lashley (1951) observed, "In attempts to play a melody backwards . . . I find that I can do it only by visualizing the music spatially and then reading it backward [p. 129]." Unless we find a suitable strategy such as Lashley's, the requirements of backward recall are indeed taxing, as the last section illustrates. Perhaps backward recall can only be achieved by some such implicit strategy of event reordering. Further, with temporal patterns it is only cognitive remnants of the series that may be rescanned after the pattern itself has come and gone. Such is not the case with spatial patterns where rescanning can occur during a presentation. It is the scanning flexibility of vision that permits conversion of a single spatial array into one of several temporal arrangements. This flexibility suggests that visual processes may ultimately play a role in translations of time and space patterns. Perhaps, as Lashley indicates, we come to represent temporal sequences by visual images—frozen in time as cognitive spatial arrays available for rescanning. Whether or not the mechanism for translation of time and space patterns is essentially visual, the issue raised by Lashley has other implications. The notion of interchangeability of temporal and spatial order is one. Interchangeability suggests that a serial pattern is finally represented as a concept that transcends the particular aspects of pattern presentation (Lashley, 1951):

> Spatial and temporal order thus appear to be almost completely interchangeable in cerebral action. The translation from the spatial distribution of memory traces to temporal sequence seems to be a fundamental aspect of this problem of serial order [p. 128].

The concept of interchangeability of spatial and temporal order readily assimilates deceptively obvious facts. Our facility at recognizing comparable relations in auditory and visual sequences argues, for example, that finally we use a common referent and so transcend limitations of these respective modalities. The same is true of our response to spatial and temporal versions of a pattern. Ultimately our representations are selective, directed more by relationships between events than by the sound or appearance of the events themselves. However, key words in this discussion are "ultimately" and "finally," for as we attempt to abstract serial relations, we bring to bear our human limitations; and the limitations of memory and of organizing ability cannot be dismissed. Thus, in the struggle to master a serial concept, the extent to which a spatial array, for example, relieves memory and permits freedom of scanning becomes important. And, too, the relative efficiency of visual and auditory modalities in keeping track of temporal sequences may affect the speed with which an individual finally frees himself from aspects of pattern presentation. Of course, this raises a larger question, namely, does man ever free himself from the details of pattern presentation? That is, do we forget or ignore detail to arrive at a serial pattern concept? These are issues pertinent to this section, the purpose of which is exploration of effects of presentation modality and presentation dimension upon pattern processing. The view of man as striving to represent patterns as serial concepts either in terms of rules or figure-ground relations suggests that, under some conditions, pattern processing will be independent of details of sequence presentation. Specifically, we may ask: (a) Under what conditions, if any, do differences in presentation paradigms disappear? (b) What is the nature of observed differences, if any, and what do these differences imply about theories of man as an active concept former?

Presentation modality. The sequence 00011011 can be realized as a temporal pattern either by pairing 0's and 1's with different buzzers (e.g., 145 cps or 195 cps, respectively) or with differently colored lights (red or green). Using repeating binary patterns (length eight) Garner and Gottwald (1968) compared auditory with visual presentation modality in this fashion. A subject received the same pattern in each modality, presented at one of five different rates (.8, 1.6, 2.67, 4.0, and 8.0

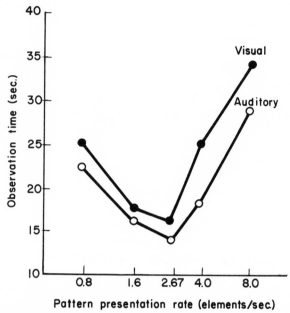

FIG. 6. Mean observation time before an attempted pattern description as a function of presentation rate and modality. The binary patterns involved were those initiated at (previously determined) preferred serial locations within each pattern. (From Garner & Gottwald, 1968; reproduced with permission of the authors and the Quarterly Journal of Experimental Psychology.)

elements/second). A subject was to "observe" the repeating sequence until he could describe it.

Average time to identify visual and auditory versions of the same pattern is shown in Fig. 6. Subjects consistently took longer to identify visual patterns than auditory ones, although differences were more pronounced at rapid rates. The data of Fig. 6 are interesting in a second respect. The functions relating observation time to rate are U-shaped for both visual and auditory presentations. Major differences in favor of the auditory mode occur at rates above the common optimum rate of 2.67 elements/second. These data suggested to Garner and Gottwald that processes that permit us to perceive a briefly presented pattern are different from those we bring to bear in more leisurely circumstances.

A methodological consideration. A methodological consideration involves the discriminability of the auditory and visual events themselves. The authors point out that discriminability between lights was not equated with discriminability between buzzers. Because interest is in the effects of modality upon perception and memory for "relatedness," and not for individual events, the lack of this control argues for some caution in interpetations.

Nevertheless, this study remains a major source of information on effects of presentation modality. The validity of the study is buttressed by the comparability of its findings with those involving unstructured sequences where similar effects in favor of auditory presentations and comparable rate-by-modality interactions obtain (e.g., Murdock & Walker, 1969).

The data lend themselves to the interpretation that modality differences arise when little opportunity exists for transforming the physical input. This occurs at fast presentation rates, where the auditory modality is superior in keeping track of sequential events. But differences as a function of presentation modality tend to disappear at slower rates, indicating that we attempt to conceptualize sequences in a modality-independent fashion if given time. The representation of auditory and visual patterns in terms of common relations is borne out in the Garner and Gottwald study by the parallel effects of pattern structure upon responding at slower rates. Performance was better with sequences that began with longer runs (e.g., 11111100) than with versions of the same pattern that began with short runs (e.g., 00111111). In the latter situations, it appeared that people generated inappropriate and disruptive expectancies about pattern alternations. Effects of expectancies were apparent only at slower presentation rates where modality differences disappeared, a finding consistent with Garner's two-process theory.

Frequently, dramatic effects of expectancies about serial structure emerge with temporal patterns. This may result from the fact that with time patterns the individual's scan strategy is controlled, leaving little opportunity for the subject to linger over strange juxtapositions of events, so disruptions by "improbable" events are readily documented. Spatial patterns are reconstructed after the entire pattern has been presented, so that effects of an "unlikely" relation are less obvious. It is useful to consider the role of presentation dimension in more detail.

Spatial and temporal patterns. A temporal pattern is one in which serial events occur one at a time. A spatio-temporal pattern is a temporal pattern in which events occur singly, but the events themselves are spatially distinct; that is, the alphabet of the temporal pattern is a spatial one, such as a row of lights. A purely spatial pattern is one in which the complete sequence is presented all-at-once. This section discusses comparisons of purely temporal patterns with purely spatial ones, as well as comparisons of spatio-temporal presentations with spatial presentations.

Complete presentation of a visual pattern has two potential advantages over temporal presentations: (*a*) relief of memory strain and (*b*) freedom of visual scan strategy. These advantages could lead people to detect structural relationships more readily in spatial patterns than in temporal ones. As it turns out, they do.

Epstein (1962) was the first to compare purely temporal presentations with spatial ones. He exposed wordlike strings of nonsense syllables all-at-once (7 seconds) repeatedly until subjects could recall the strings perfectly in writing. People recalling structured patterns were better than those recalling random control strings. Moreover, both groups displayed serial position curves with high primacy and attenuated recency effects. When the same materials were presented to subjects over time in a serial anticipation task (2 sec/item), subjects failed to detect structural relations, and a bowed serial position curve resulted. Epstein concluded that spatial presentations encouraged people to perceive the patterns as wholes while temporal presentations did not.

Control of response mode. Epstein's conclusions have been criticized (O'Connell, 1970) for failure to control response mode in his comparison of *written* recall of spatial patterns with *verbal* anticipation of temporal patterns. O'Connell, Stubbs, and Theby (1969) argued that sensitivity to structure was suppressed by overt responding during temporal presentations. However, more recent work, using written recall, has supported Epstein's original conclusion. Schwartz, Lordahl, and Gambino (1973) with binary patterns and Jones (1973) with multisymbol patterns found subjects more sensitive to structural details with complete presentations. Jones, furthermore, required half the subjects in each condition to pronounce presented elements. Overt responding did not suppress sensitivity to pattern structure in either temporal or spatial presentations.

In both the Schwartz et al., and the Jones study, the temporal patterns were, in fact, spatio-temporal patterns. Jones compared spatial digit patterns with spatio-temporal ones in which each of six digits was correlated with a given spatial location.[3] Although relatively small effects of manipulations of pattern structure occurred with temporal patterns, rather large and interesting differences as a function of structure were found with complete pattern presentation. These are worth evaluating in terms of issues directing this chapter.

Some effects of structure in complete presentations of digit patterns: A study in pattern reconstruction. The Jones study presented spatial digit patterns that were constructed hierarchically, according to Restle's tree-structure approach, with the highest-order rule modifying the first half of the sequences to yield the second half. Rule structure was manipulated by changing the nature of the highest-order rule in half of the patterns. Some of these patterns are shown in Table 1. Patterns were constructed from the digits 1 through 6, and each involved a complement (C) rule at the highest level of its structural tree. Half of the patterns shown in Table 1 were generated according to Restle's (1970) grammar, with the highest-order rule changing the first half by complementing the first digit, then its successor, and so forth. Figure 7 illustrates this construction for the sequence 1̲6̲1̲161252252526161̲6̲525525. Here the complement of each of the first 12 digits (on the base 6) beginning with 161 is taken to yield the last half of the pattern (i.e., 616· · · ·). The four patterns constructed with Restle's forward-rule-application technique are CF patterns. Each CF pattern has a matched control sequence in which the complement rule is applied in reverse direction beginning with the last digit in the first half. Thus, as Fig. 7 illustrates, 161161252̲2̲5̲2̲5̲2̲5̲525616616 begins as does its mate above, but the complement rule used to generate the second half is applied backwards (CB) beginning with 252· · · · to yield 525· · · · and so forth. Thus, lower-order rules within the tree

---

[3]Patterns based upon alphabets with interval properties are discussed throughout in terms of rules relating to these properties. No distinctions have been made between patterns based upon such alphabets defined along some physical dimension (e.g., ordered tones or spatial arrays) and those defined along a symbolic dimension (e.g., integers). The acquisition of dimensionality itself is at issue here and indeed raises interesting questions about cultural and maturational determinants of dimensionality that are as yet unresolved. An assumption upon which this chapter rests is that common relations exist between these different alphabets and that if given sufficient time to conceptualize symbolic dimensions, people will treat patterns based upon such dimensions in a fashion that parallels responding to purely physical dimensions.

Hierarchical Tree Structure

A Complement (C) Pattern

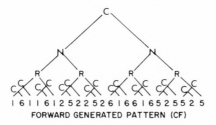

FORWARD GENERATED PATTERN (CF)

I 6 I I 6 I 2 5 2 2 5 2 5 2 5 5 2 5 6 I 6 6 I 6

INVERSELY GENERATED PATTERN (CB)

FIG. 7. A diagrammatic representation of hierarchical tree structures used to construct digit patterns based on forward application of the highest-order complement rule (CF) and backward application of the same rule (CB).

and specific digits were the same for each CF and CB pair. The two sets of patterns differ only in the nature of the highest-order rule.

Restle's theory, derived from predictions of temporal patterns, would lead to the expectation that CB patterns would be more difficult to reconstruct than CF patterns, because CB patterns compound two higher-order rules: a complement rule and an inversion rule. Further, such effects might be marked in spatial patterns where effects of higher-order rules upon the entire first halves of the sequences may be more readily detected.

Each subject received eight pattern presentations and attempted reconstruction after each. Serial reconstruction profiles for CF and for CB patterns are shown in Fig. 8. Two aspects of the curves are worthy of note. First, surprisingly, the CB patterns constructed in a fashion inconsistent with Restle's theory were easier than CF patterns! Secondly, the CF curves display high primacy and low recency, and so agree with serial position curves from spatial patterns reported by Epstein (1962). But

TABLE 1

Hierarchically-Constructed Patterns of Length 24 Involving 4 and 6 Digit (S = 6) Patterns[a]

No. of Digits	CF	CB
4	161161252252616616525525	161161252252525525616616
4	111222111222666555666555	111222111222555666555666
6	123654234543654123543234	123654234543432345321456
6	161252252343616525525434	161252252343434525525616

[a] In these patterns, the highest-order rule (C) applies forward (CF) or backward (CB).

CB patterns bring forth a bowed serial position curve. Those people reconstructing CB patterns exhibited greater recency as trials continued. Inspection of Table 1 suggests a reason. Beginning and end members of CB patterns were quite similar, a circumstance that resulted from the reversal of the C rule with these particular patterns. The CB patterns were fairly symmetrical and the effects of this symmetry were striking with spatial presentations. It not only improved recall, but it changed the shape of the recall curve. These effects were not found with temporal versions of the same patterns.

No current theory has sufficient scope to handle these findings. Few theories make specific allowances for differences in people's responses to spatial and temporal presentations, and none encompass the interactions of pattern structure with presentation dimension. Pattern symmetry is a morphological property. This means that symmetry describes the appearance of the string, not functions that tie it to an alphabet. A pattern such as 123654456321, for example, is symmetrical because of its surface appearance with similar beginning and end groups, so that the sequence can be folded in half. Theories most directly tied to relations arising from surface regularities are those incorporating perceptual processes, namely Garner's and Vitz and Todd's. Because Garner (1970) specifically rules out symmetry as a factor in

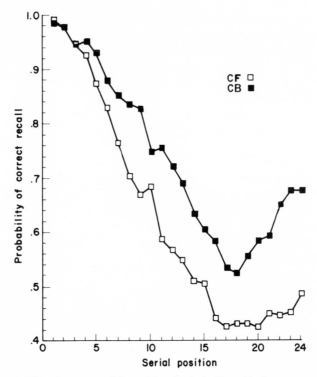

FIG. 8. Probability of correct recall for each location in the hierarchically constructed patterns shown in Table 1. Subjects received either 8 presentations of a CF pattern or 8 presentations of a CB pattern.

figure-ground relations, his theory does not adequately address these findings. And Vitz and Todd's approach ignores such overall morphological effects, subsuming symmetrical relations under ones involving identical or similar run codes.[4]

While Estes could tie morphological relations into his associative hierarchy, once this is done his theory would predict that recency effects with symmetrical patterns might appear early and decline as intruding responses are inhibited with trials; in fact, the reverse occurs with spatial patterns.

Rule-formulation theories seem obvious candidates for explanatory vehicles. But Simon's model emphasizes the growth of a concept based upon alphabetic not morphological relations. Only Restle's approach has potential applicability. This is because the rules Restle postulates operate upon the surface of a pattern, not upon the alphabet. Unhappily, rarely do Restle's hierarchical structures generate symmetrical patterns; and if they did, Restle has no provision for the effects of spatial symmetry upon the shape of serial reconstruction.

All in all, these data indicate that interesting effects arising from the interactions of alphabetic relations with morphological structure have, at present, no theoretical home. Whether the effects of symmetry arise from a scanning strategy or merely from enhancements during recall remains to be discovered. The potential of visual scanning, as Lashley has indicated, is great and warrants special consideration in building a theory to house such effects.

These findings suggest that people are less sensitive to relations within temporal sequences than within spatial ones. But, comparisons have been limited to those between spatial patterns and paced temporal sequences. If scanning of spatial sequences can permit people to pause and emphasize aspects of the structure, rhythm may offer a parallel respite in temporal presentations.

Rhythm in temporal patterns. Rhythm arises from the arrangements of relative accents in time. In pattern processing, it may be manipulated in ways that involve variations of event duration and intensity. Further, a common means of manipulating rhythm involves the insertion of pauses that determine temporal groups within a pattern. It is well-known that grouping has large positive effects upon immediate recall and learning of unstructured sequences (Bower & Winenz, 1969; McLean & Gregg, 1967; Ryan, 1969a, 1969b; Wickelgren, 1964, 1967). What is interesting about the manipulation of temporal aspects of structured sequences is that some rhythms not only fail to improve performance but actually degrade it.

To understand why this is so, consider an ambiguous light pattern 12343454·····. This temporal sequence may be presented either as 1234 pause 345 pause 4··· or as 12 pause 343 pause 454 ····. Restle and Brown (1970b) have reported that pauses in such sequences induced subjects to learn the same patterns either as progressions (e.g., 1234) or as trills (e.g., 343). But, when pauses are inserted that are not congruent with syntactic relations within a pattern, then people appear compelled by the rhythm to "learn" incorrect relations that distort overall structure (Restle, 1972).

[4]It has been common to define the redundancy that arises from bilateral symmetry in terms of repeated elements. Indeed, Staniland (1966), among others, argues that any beneficial effects that accrue to pattern symmetries are merely dependent upon identical or similar members.

Naturally, an important question is: "Why does the introduction of pauses have such a powerful effect?" Two explanations are possible: First, pauses permit the subject to rehearse prior items. Estes' (1972) theory suggests this explanation. In that theory the insertion of pauses at appropriate places in a pattern would allow the subject time to rehearse the order of prior events and so improve performance. The second explanation has pauses relating to accents within a sequence and so highlighting appropriate relations.

The rehearsal hypothesis implies that performance should improve not only with appropriate insertion of temporal pauses but also with pause duration. The second hypothesis requires an understanding of rhythm. Martin (1972) has maintained that rhythm breaks time into equal segments, each signalled by an accent. Relatively longer time segments receive stronger accents. Thus, insertion of pauses can offer a distribution of subjective stresses to events within a sequence. If an accented segment reflects a rule, it will be more readily learned and overall performance will improve relative to patterns without pauses. This hypothesis emphasizes relative timing in temporal patterns, but does not imply that increments in pause duration should improve performance, since they merely offer accents to highlight relations. If pauses highlight a rule that does not fit with adjacent pattern relations, it will nonetheless be readily learned but overall performance may suffer.

Evidence favors the interpretation that pauses determine accents. Restle (1972) found that increasing the average pause time in serial patterns had no effect upon learning light patterns, while Ryan (1969b) reported parallel results with unstructured letter sequences.

The power of rhythmic properties therefore relates to emphasis and timing and so may facilitate the discovery of relations in hierarchical patterns. An overall sense of what-goes-where would permit the early discovery of higher-order relations at the same time lower-order relations are detected. Consider a hierarchical pattern presented temporally with the stress pattern:

stress pattern: 1   3   2   4

letter pattern: ABCZYXBCDYZW

If primary stresses (1, 2) are upon letters that define the initiation of the higher-order period (i.e., from A to the second B) then people may first discover something like: ABC___BCD___. These aspects of rule-learning have not been explored. In fact, Restle and Brown (1970b) maintain that learning of multilevel pattern structures does not proceed in this fashion but begins with lower-order relations such as ABC and ZYX. Their evidence comes from serial learning of temporal patterns with no rhythmic cues. With the possibility that people respond to both temporal and syntactic relations hierarchically, there arise interesting questions about the ways in which aspects of the two structures interact to determine the course of serial learning. These questions, too, are among those awaiting resolution.

Summary. A major question posed initially in this section raises the issue of whether man achieves a serial concept that is free from details of pattern presentation. The answer appears to be yes, in some circumstances. If given sufficient time, the effects of presentation modality no longer bind the subject, suggesting that some common representation is achieved. This general finding is consistent with Garner's two-process theory. It would be compatible with other approaches as well, save for the fact that with temporal patterns the predominant effects of rhythmic and syntactic expectancies on conceptual learning are consistent neither with run-encoding (e.g., Vitz & Todd, 1969) nor with associationistic-rehearsal (e.g., Estes, 1972) models.

Garner's theory, as well as others, however, falls victim to the interaction of morphological structure with underlying alphabetic rules that affect the person reconstructing spatial patterns. Here it is provocative to imagine that the spatial continuum guides expectancies about morphological detail through scanning in the same way rhythms contribute to temporal expectancies. In general, interactions of expectancies about alphabetic relations with those involving time or space are not developed in any current theory.

Assessment of Pattern Structure

The problem of the good figure has haunted psychologists for decades; the current decade is no exception. Those who have attempted to quantify structure have rapidly come to realize that assessments of pattern complexity cannot be manufactured independently of psychological processes. So because little agreement exists about the workings of psychological processes, there are predictably a variety of candidates for a good pattern metric. Several theories we have previously discussed culminate in attempts to quantify pattern complexity. The purpose of this section is to acquaint the reader with the techniques of structural assessment, apart from theoretical specula- tions about perception or learning. But strict separation is impossible, because the first stage in assessment of structure involves defining the "relevant structural detail." A second stage concentrates upon devising a reliable yardstick for measuring the complexity of "relevant structural detail." In neither stage can the task or psychological assumptions be entirely disregarded.

With respect to the second stage, information theory has offered a tempting and apparently ready-made framework within which to cast measurements of complexity (Attneave, 1959; Evans, 1967; Garner, 1962; Staniland, 1966). Paradoxically, this appeal has resulted in more, rather than less, confusion. Confusion has stemmed from different ways of conceiving the task and of evaluating surplus information, or redundancy.

Properly, the original specification of the maximum amount of information con- tained in a message, or pattern, of length λ composed of S symbols is given by

$$H_{\max} = \log_2 S^\lambda, \tag{1}$$

which is based upon the total population of ($N = S^\lambda$) patterns possible. Any subset of patterns taken from this total will carry surplus information. The measurement of redundancy originally proposed by Shannon and Weaver (1949) emphasized the difference between maximum uncertainty based upon population size and actual uncertainty based upon the size of a sampled subset, H_s. Indeed, the difference between $H_{\max}$ and H_s ($H_{\max} - H_s$) is at the heart of many current psychological applications of redundancy (e.g., Garner, 1962). But uncertainties are determined by relative probabilities of messages within a set, and depending upon the context, this fact makes determination of H_s for sets of patterns difficult.

Often in psychological applications of information theory, the task has been ignored in assessments of redundancy (Evans, 1967). That is, a person asked to discriminate between several patterns may use entirely different aspects of the sequences than a person required to learn all n patterns in a set. In the first situation, for example, if two patterns differ in four ways instead of one, then some information about differences is surplus and may be used to advantage in pattern discrimination. But if a person must reconstruct all n patterns, lack of common pattern properties will prove a handicap. These distinctions can be reflected in terms of components of uncertainty (Evans, 1967). Notice that one way of increasing the difference between $H_{\max}$ and H_s is through enlarging the population size, N, and so inflating $H_{\max}$ if n remains the same. At the level of a psychological task, this means that patterns within a set may differ in more ways either as a result of increasing pattern length (λ) or the number of symbols (S) involved. This sort of manipulation affects *discrimination redundancy*. In contrast, with fixed sizes of population and sampled subset, similarities between the n patterns will depend upon the ways in which they have been sampled. If rigorous sampling constraints are used, the resulting patterns will be similar, and this will help the subject to learn the various patterns but will hinder discrimination. This manipulation results in *constraint redundancy,* according to Evans (1967).

Total redundancy, then, consists of two components. These are constraint redundancy, H_c, and discrimination redundancy, H_e:

$$H_{\max} - H_s \;=\; H_e \;+\; H_c \;.\tag{2}$$

Failure to consider the two-fold nature of redundancy has been a source of confusion. If $H_{\max}$ and H_s are constant, then the sum of H_c and H_e is fixed, and the total amount of redundancy associated with different subsets drawn from the same population will be equivalent. But for a fixed $H_{\max} - H_s$, different proportions of H_e and H_c may exist. From a psychological point of view this is important, since H_c and H_e have opposite effects upon performance, depending upon the task.

It is important to bear these distinctions in mind while evaluating the usefulness of information theory in indexing pattern structure. Commonly, it is through constraints upon sampling that patterns of similar structure result. But constraint redundancy indexes the *amount* of surplus information conveyed by a particular set of sampling rules, not the *form* of redundancy. That is, two different sets of sampling rules imposed on a total population may result in two different subpopulations N_1 and N_2 of equivalent size from which two samples of size n are respectively drawn. Both total amount of redundancy and amount of constraint redundancy are the same for the two sets. But if one set arose, for example, from all patterns built from four consonants that began with L and the other only from patterns initiating with X, then the form of redundancy would differ.

A popular means of imposing sampling constraints has been through finite-state grammars; methods for evaluating the information of resulting sequences have been proposed by Chomsky and Miller (1958; p. 110). A finite-state grammar (FSG) is a system with a specifiable number of states, S_0, S_1 $\cdots$ S_r, connected by paths as shown in Fig. 9. Attached to each state-to-state path is a symbol. Imagine a machine that traverses these paths moving from the initial state (S_0) to the next (S_1) and so forth. The probability of embarking upon a given path depends only upon the current state, not upon prior paths. This path-independence property makes FSGs Markovian systems. As the machine traverses paths between states, a symbol appropriate to each state-to-state transition is generated. Thus, when a trip from the initial state to the exit state (S_0') is completed, a string of symbols is left. Transversal of the double-lines of Fig. 9, for example, leaves the string NNSXG, but this represents only one of many possible jaunts through the array. Because other strings of similar appearance may also result, an interesting question is: Does the amount of redundancy arising from FSG constraints reflect the subject's use of pattern structure? Further, do people abstract the rules used to generate these sequences? These were the kinds of questions raised by Miller in 1958.

Application of finite-state grammar generators: Miller's study. Patterns generated by an FSG are, as a subset, more alike than those resulting from a random generator, and people learn to exploit these similarities as Miller (1958) has shown. He presented 9 consonant strings based on the grammar (L) shown in Fig. 9 to one group of subjects and 9 strings of matched lengths, randomly generated (R), to others. A string, typed on a card, was presented every five seconds until nine cards were before the subject. Subjects then attempted to write down all nine strings. After 10 training trials, subjects received additional training either on another set of strings from the same condition or a set from the other condition.

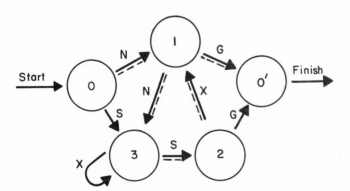

FIG. 9. Diagrammatic representation of a finite-state grammar (FSG). States are represented by numbered circles; state-transitions, by paths. Paths doubled with dashed lines illustrate the manner of generating one of many FSG strings, namely, NNSXG.

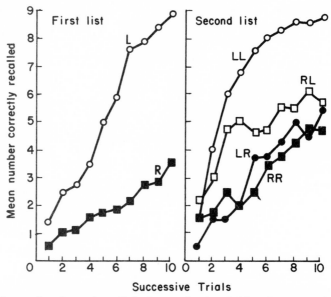

Successive Trials

FIG. 10.   Mean number of correctly recalled strings as a function of trial number, grammatical condition (L or R), and list (first or second list). (From Miller, 1958; reproduced with the permission of the author and the American Psychological Association.)

Figure 10 illustrates training and transfer with FSG (L) and random strings (R). In general, subjects were more efficient with the L strings. Moreover, people who received random strings first were at a disadvantage, relative to those trained with FSG strings, in transfer with L strings (i.e., RL vs. LL). Increments in sampling constraints, therefore, resulted in patterns that were more alike and so were easy to learn. This lends weight to Evans' analysis of redundancy and task. But the simplicity of FSG strings apparently arose not directly from the nature of finite grammar rules, but from the fact that event contingencies within resulting patterns facilitated a simple encoding strategy. Surface features of L strings encouraged people to learn a single common format and identify individual patterns by corrections to the format. For example, the similarity of NNSG, NNSXG, and NNSXXG was noted and remembered as NNS__G plus the number of X's. While Miller's interpretation has been criticized (e.g., Garner, 1962; Staniland, 1966), the criticism, for the most part, has failed to distinguish between discrimination and constraint redundancy.

The L and R strings in Miller's study differed not only in amount of redundancy but also form of redundancy. Thus, while people may not verbalize specific generative rules, their strategies suggest that learning is sensitive to structural form. To test this possibility, Reber (1969) examined pattern learning in which amount of redundancy was held constant across two different FSGs. Reber used a training-transfer paradigm similar to Miller's (1958) wherein people were required to learn by reproduction 18 training and 18 transfer-strings presented on cards in groups of three.

Thus, a person may learn a set of strings such as:

NNSG

NNSXG

.

.

.

where all sequences derive from a FSG such as that of Fig. 9. In transfer the same grammar is disguised in different symbols and novel strings; only generative rules remain invariant:

MMPYYC

PYYPYC

.

.

.

Subjects learned new pattern sets in one of four transfer conditions: (*a*) the syntax or grammar changed (Syn), (*b*) the symbols changed (Sym), (*c*) neither symbols or syntax changed (N), (*d*) both symbols and syntax changed (B). The two FSGs determined changes in syntax, while different sets of consonants signalled symbol changes. Because the grammars dictated the same amount of redundancy, any differences in transfer must arise somehow from changes in physical similarities of symbols or grammatical differences that contribute to the form of redundancy. Reber asked, ''What does a subject learn?''

If people attack patterns by learning to group on the basis of physical similarities, then either a vocabulary change or an encounter with a novel instance of the same grammar would represent an entirely different task. On the other hand, positive transfer as a function of grammar would argue for a conceptual representation independent of physical detail.

Figure 11 shows Reber's results. The crucial determinant of transfer was the nature of the grammar and not the vocabulary. Reber's hypothesis that people formed conceptual abstractions was supported. Subsequent work in the same vein that varied amount of information (e.g., Kantowitz, 1971) further supported Reber's conclusions.

These studies argue for the limited usefulness of the information metric to index effects of event contingencies determined by FSGs. In terms of a critique by Simon (1972), if an information metric is used it must be addressed to the subject's encoded units. The question becomes, do the different FSGs represent what the subject is learning? Although learning strategies obviously covary with structural detail generated by FSGs, a description of what is learned simply in these terms is untenable. Some (Braine, 1965a, 1965b; Gough & Segal, 1965) have argued that representa-

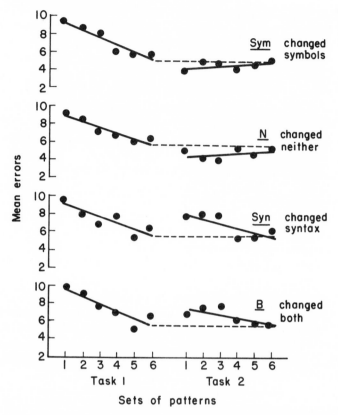

FIG. 11. Mean number of errors to a criterion on each of 12 learning sets of three strings. Eighteen training (task 1) strings and 18 transfer (task 2) strings were presented to each of 64 subjects. (From Reber, 1969; reproduced with permission of the author and the American Psychological Association.)

tions of what-is-learned in terms of finite-state grammar rules places a terrible burden upon the subject. Instead, Braine (1963) has proposed that people learn the temporal or spatial event locations in a string. But this approach does not envision that people abstract complex event contingencies such as position inversions. That is, it cannot describe learning of sequential arrangements such as: "If A then B predict C" but "If B then A predict D." But people readily learn such contingencies in temporal sequences as Jones and Erickson (1972) have shown. Other evidence, gathered from extensive work in artificial language learning, led Smith (e.g., Keeney, 1969; Smith, 1973; Smith & Gough, 1969) to argue that human sensitivity to position inversions is symptomatic of a transformational rule learning, a process antithetical both to position learning approaches and to descriptions of what-is-learned in terms of the Markovian rules of FSGs. These considerations document cautions (Evans, 1967; Simon, 1972) that task and context affect measurements of pattern complexity.

The single pattern. Information theory readily applies to the study of sets of patterns sampled from an identifiable population. Often, however, people attempt to predict or remember just one pattern. In this situation the construction of a complexity metric, in terms of information theory, requires more imagination on the part of the theorist. The relevant population of patterns that determines maximum uncertainty, H_{max}, as well as the appropriate subset for H_s, are not so easily identified when it is clear that people are governed by regularities within a single sequence. Solutions to the assessment of structure within a single pattern, therefore, are more closely bound to theoretical attempts to identify relevant populations upon which to base uncertainty statistics. Alternative messages may be tied to organizational aspects of a single pattern (Garner, 1962), or encoded elements (Vitz & Todd, 1969), or encoded rules (Simon, 1972).

Inferred alternatives: One solution to the single pattern problem. Garner (1962) identifies different versions of the pattern at hand with the relevant population of patterns upon which H_{max} depends. The subject, confronted with AAABB, conceives of different organizations: AABBA, ABBAA, BBAAA, and BAAAB. Each alternative represents a different way of starting the pattern. The more ways a pattern can be started, the greater the uncertainty associated with it. But, among these alternatives the subject imposes his own subjective constraints, thus defining a private or preference subset. Perhaps only AAABB, BBAAA, and AABBA function as real alternatives in the subject's mind, and even among these he prefers the one beginning with the longest run (i.e., AAABB). The size of the inferred subset and the relative probabilities assigned to these alternatives contribute to H_s, which is empirically determined. Garner (e.g., Royer & Garner, 1966) arrives at an uncertainty index by determining the variability people display in selecting a start-point, namely *response point uncertainty* (RPU), and it essentially reflects subjective constraint systems. While Royer and Garner (1966) have suggested that the criteria governing these constraints relate to figure-ground relations, the technique itself testifies to an important fact. This is that the way in which people define relevant alternatives for themselves can vary with the patterns and the task. Furthermore, those aspects of structure detected within a single pattern relate it to a population of patterns: As Garner (1966) notes, "How the single stimulus is perceived is a function not so much of what it is, but is rather a function of what the total set and the particular subset are. . . [p. 11]."

Encoding the single pattern. Both Garner (e.g., Preusser et al., 1970) with the single pattern and Miller (1958) with sets of FSG patterns have described the form of subjects' responses in the face of metrics that have not specifically addressed the determinants of those responses. With FSG patterns, because the vocabularies lack order, people are not encouraged to base their responses upon an underlying alphabet. Instead, the potency of event contingencies in FSG patterns, and of runs and alternations in binary patterns, is obvious. These considerations may tempt the theorist to define population alternatives in terms of relevant features within pattern surfaces; Vitz and Todd (1969) yielded to this temptation.

A person is assumed to encode a sequence into a set of run codes that vary in nature and length. Uncertainty is a function of the distribution of these encoded units within a pattern. The pattern AAABB, for example, is not easy or difficult because it calls forth five rearrangements; its difficulty stems from the fact that there are two equally-likely runs (AAA and BB) of different lengths. In this respect, patterns with more runs of different lengths (e.g., AAABBA) will be more difficult than AAABB. But patterns in which one run length predominates will be relatively easy (e.g., AABBAABB). Relations between run lengths are evaluated in terms of an information metric that assumes people further encode adjacent runs, and that at each coding level uncertainty plays a role. The final information measure of pattern complexity, H_{code}, is a summation over a hierarchy of coding uncertainties. In contrast to RPU, H_{code} permits an *a priori* parameter-free assessment of pattern complexity. Both measures are interpreted as depending on relations within the surface appearance of patterns. Neither specifically incorporate details that involve overall arrangements of runs and alternations. Thus the simplicity of AABBBBAA is explained by neither metric in terms that link symmetry to redundancy. Nevertheless, both are appropriate with binary patterns, or patterns built from unordered vocabularies, and both can account for impressive proportions of variance in judgment and recall tasks. In fact, either metric offers greater potential for reflecting complexity of patterns generated by FSGs than does redundancy defined by the FSGs themselves. But neither has been extended to describe structure within patterns built from alphabets.

Encoded relations. The problem of determining redundancy for a single pattern relates to the difficulty of specifying the effective subset of alternatives that govern H_s. Garner's solution rested with permitting the individual to define his own subset. Simon resolves that context, not the individual, constrains the alternatives open to a person. If the theorist simply focuses upon a given context, then the actual uncertainty within that setting will reflect no redundancy. Thus, Simon's approach differs from previous ones in two ways: First, he assumes that people encode sequences, in a given situation, in the most efficient fashion, using the shortest possible code. Secondly, he assumes that people encode relations that are defined on an alphabet, not on morphological properties. The first assumption permits Simon to use a basic tenet of information theory—that the amount of information in a pattern is given by the number of symbols necessary to describe that sequence. The second assumption suggests that the population is described in terms of encoded relations and that constraints upon the relations used arise from demands of a particular task. Task demands lead people to select different rules, so that a task involving binary patterns eliminates a number of rules at the outset. Simon argues that Vitz and Todd (1969) among others (e.g., Leeuwenberg, 1969; Restle, 1970) describe encoding constrained by such task parameters. Nevertheless, a general population of relations such as *next* or *repeat* are available, and depending upon the context, one or several are encoded.

The number of rules required to duplicate a pattern is equivalent to the amount of information carried by its structure. For example, a letter sequence such as ABMCDMEFM· · · · can be duplicated by a set of rules that instruct the subject to locate the letter alphabet in memory. Then, two *next* relations generate A and B respectively, by moving the marker one position each on the ordered list of letters. An M is inserted as an encoded symbol, and a *repeat* instruction finishes the description by telling the system to continue all these operations indefinitely. The number of encoded rules in this pattern description is fewer than in ABCMBCDM· · · · ·

where one more *next* instruction would result in a larger set of instructions and so a more difficult pattern.

Depending upon the properties of the alphabet, a wide variety of pattern structures can be mimicked by this coding system, including hierarchical ones. Because of the arrangement of instructions necessary to duplicate hierarchically constructed patterns, they are generated with few instructions. Thus, according to Simon, hierarchical structures should be simple patterns.

Hierarchical patterns. Foremost among the descriptions of hierarchical structures is Restle's (1970). But Restle's concern has been primarily with outlining rules and rule-combinations, and not with assessment of complexity. The grammar itself suggests that some properties of hierarchical structures must play a role in these assessments. Two main characteristics of hierarchical sequences, as Restle describes them, have to do with the relative frequency and arrangement of relations involved.

Consider the following hierarchical tree-structure that generates the digit pattern, 12126565, from an alphabet (integers 1 through 6) that has interval properties:

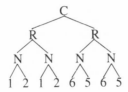

Lower-order rules are N, or *next*, and R, or *repeat*. The highest-order rule, C, complements digits in the first pattern half with respect to the alphabet. The relative frequency of rules in this structure is defined by the tree-levels, so that in this case there are 4N, 2R, and 1C rules. Moreover, these rules are not distributed haphazardly, but are regularly arranged to describe the overall sequence. Both of these factors enter into the determination of a concise set of instructions for pattern duplication, as Simon (1972) has shown. But other factors, not incorporated into Simon's approach, play important roles in determining the relative complexity of hierarchical structures. Rules differ in difficulty, with R rules being far simpler than others. To the extent that an R rule is involved in a hierarchical pattern, it will be considered a simple pattern. These, and other details involving interactions of rules with each other and with alphabet size, all contribute to pattern difficulty, but little formal attention is given to such detail. Restle, in contrast to others, has not progressed from descriptions of structural properties to an uncertainty metric. Simon's attempt in this direction places primary emphasis upon the number and arrangement of alphabetic relations, and in so doing ignores the nature of the rules themselves.

Summary. The general approach to assessments of pattern complexity has involved two stages. The first stage involves basic theoretical assumptions about the relevant aspects of sequential structure that constitute a set of real alternatives for the individual. The second stage exploits the concept of alternatives as it is developed in information theory. Uncertainty metrics have been used to assess the simple pattern as one associated with relatively small amounts of information; complex patterns are associated with large amounts of information. Most approaches find the representation of complexity in terms of uncertainty acceptable, and so few quarrels arise in the second stage. Differences occur in stage one with descriptions of appropriate alternatives and the relevant constraints that determine surplus information for the subject. It is apparent that when sampling constraints are under direct control of the experimenter and when they reflect FSG rules, both amount and form of the redundancy are used by subjects. But it is just as obvious that subjects dwell upon event contingencies within sampled patterns and not upon the Markovian rule system. And with the study of single patterns, the dominance of surface regularities is further apparent, but theorists differ in their conception of these features and the role of constraint redundancy. Some have specifically identified the elements that may determine uncertainty and redundancy (e.g., Vitz & Todd, 1969), while others have sketched a framework of alternatives within which the subject reveals his own sampling constraints (e.g., Garner, 1970). Only Simon (1972) makes the case for identification of population alternatives with alphabetic rules. And only Simon eschews redundancy by identifying it with task-imposed sampling constraints. No stage one assessment permits a distinction between uncertainties arising from surface regularities of patterns and uncertainty associated with an underlying set of alphabetic rules. And yet, it is likely that the good or simple pattern is finally a function of both morphological and alphabetic regularities.

RECONSIDERATION: A REPRESENTATIONAL SYSTEM

To recapitulate the major topics of this chapter, we have considered the role of serial structure in directing pattern reconstruction, the roles of modality and dimension in facilitating or inhibiting the encoding of pattern structure, and finally some problems involved in quantification of serial pattern structure. Several themes have emerged as theories from the opening pages were pitted against evidence. The first theme involves a useful distinction, proposed by Garner (Garner & Gottwald, 1968), between perceptual processes and conceptual processes, which has gathered some support. Serial pattern processing runs the gamut of tasks from perceptual recall to problem-solving. Active conceptualization in terms of figure-ground relations and/or alphabetic rules emerges when the task requires problem-solving and the individual has time to create expectancies that govern prediction or extrapolation; alternatively, if time pressures exist, only surface regularities may control responding. A second issue relates to the role of temporal and spatial schemas. Accent and timing, not rehearsal, are important with temporal sequences, while symmetries may direct scanning of spatial patterns. A third issue, the assessment of structure, demonstrates the importance of subjective preferences, perceptions, and task in determining maximum uncertainty and redundancy.

Groups of Rules

This final section attempts a new representation of relationships in which the rules involved may, in some circumstances, dictate beautifully symmetrical patterns, but, in others, challenge our need to add or subtract along an alphabet in memory. The rules of interest are defined with respect to positions within an alphabet.[5] They fall into two different groups referred to, respectively, as Group 1 and Group 2. Rules of Group 1 are identity (I), transpose (T), complement (C), and reflection (RL). The use of complement and reflection rules necessitate that the vocabulary not only be ordered but also possess interval properties. Rules of Group 2 are incrementing rules given by the next (N) operator and identity. A formal definition of each rule is found at the extreme right of Fig. 12. The relationships between the rules of each group are important in determining properties of patterns built from combinations of rules. These relationships are described in the product tables for each (presented in Fig. 12) and they hold for any even-numbered alphabet, size S.[6] Cells of each group table are formed from the successive application of corresponding marginal rules. The pattern of these cell entries is symmetrical about a diagonal axis, reflecting the fact that both groups are Abelian. An Abelian group is one in which rules are commutative.

Group properties are best seen through examples. Consider an alphabet of size 6 to illustrate relations of Group 1, to wit, 123 456. Group 1 rules revolve about a central axis in the alphabet. Relations that highlight this are transpose (T) and reflection (RL), as defined in Fig. 12. The transpose of 1 is 4, so that T(123), for example, maps 123 onto 456, leaving relationships between constituent events unchanged. Reflection of 1 is 3, and RL(123) is 321. Thus, reflection, while defined upon *alphabetic* positions, may result in position inversions of events along the pattern's *surface*. These rules as a group differ importantly from those already proposed in the literature, not only in their emphasis upon a central axis, but also because of their commutativity. This Abelian feature is apparent in: RLT = TRL = C; CRL = RLC = T; TC = CT = RL.

To understand Abelian properties, consider again the unit 123 in the context of the Group 1 product table. The entry in this table corresponding to row RL and column C is the product CRL, which arises from first reflecting $123 \left[RL(123) = 321 \right]$ and then applying $C \left[C(321) = 456 \right]$. But the sequence 456 is the transposition of the original unit 123. Thus, the appropriate entry for CRL is T. Commutativity is apparent if C is applied first, then RL; the result is still 456 or T(123). Products along the main diagonal reflect the fact that double application of each transform returns the system to its starting point, I. Thus C(123) is 654, and C(654) is 123. The special status of

[5]The reader with knowledge of rotation and reflection groups will recognize that the relations developed in this section parallel automorphisms of space that leave a configuration unchanged. Group 1 relations correspond to improper translations of spatial figures, while Group 2 relations are proper translations. These terms are taken from Weyl (1952), whose provocative book upon symmetry was discovered after the author had been struck with the power of these particular rules and their interrelations.

[6]These relations, with some adjustments for central axis, may also be applied to vocabulary sizes that are odd-numbered.

Group 1 Product Table

	I	RL	C	T
I	I	RL	C	T
RL	RL	I	T	C
C	C	T	I	RL
T	T	C	RL	I

Group 2 Product Table

	I	N¹	N²	N³	...	Nʲ	...	Nˢ⁻¹	Nˢ
I	I	N¹	N²	N³	...	Nʲ	...	Nˢ⁻¹	Nˢ⁺I
N¹	N¹	N²	N³	N⁴	...	Nʲ⁺¹	...	I	N¹
N²	N²	N³	N⁴	N⁵	...	Nʲ⁺²	I	N¹	
N³	N³	N⁴	N⁵	N⁵	...	I	N¹		
⋮	⋮	⋮	⋮	⋮	I				
Nʲ	Nʲ	Nʲ⁺¹	Nʲ⁺²	I	N¹				
⋮	⋮	⋮	I	N¹					
Nˢ⁻¹	Nˢ⁻¹	I	N¹						
Nˢ	I	N¹							

Formal Rule Definitions in terms of a given symbol, i

Rule	Notation	Definition
Identity	I	$I(i)=i$
Next	N	$N^j(i)=i+j$
Transpose	T	$T(i)=i+\Delta$
Complement	C	$C(i)=2\Delta+1-i$
Reflection	RL	$\Delta+1-i$ (if $i \leq \Delta$) ; $3\Delta+1-i$ (if $i > \Delta$)

Where $\Delta = S/2$ and S is alphabet size

FIG. 12. Product tables for Group 1 and Group 2 rules with formal definitions of component rules given for symbol i in rightmost panel.

the identity operator in this group is nicely consistent with its apparent psychological potency, which is found in people's responses to event runs, repeating subunits, and alternations.

The identity operator also holds a special place in the second group of rules, Group 2. Here the *next* operator, N^j, can be successively applied such that $N^j(i) = i + j$. Whenever $N^j(i) \cdot N^k(i) = N^{j+k}(i) = N^S(i) = i$, the I operation describes the product. Thus in the Group 2 table $N^s = I$ leading to identities along the minor diagonal. While N^j transforms apply to any ordered vocabulary, they form a cyclic group quite readily evoking a clock array, shown in Fig. 13 for a vocabulary of size 8. Here $N^8(1) = 1$ with very little break in continuity. The N^j operators correspond to rotations of a figure; thus, steps may be integers. Indeed with the N transforms there is the basis for relationships based upon addition and subtraction that play elaborate roles in problem-solving tasks (e.g., Bjork, 1968) as well as in music and time patterns. If N

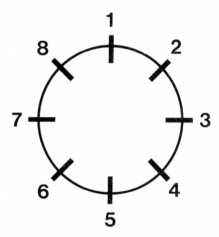

FIG. 13. Group 2 relations readily evoke a clock array, represented here with equal intervals for an alphabet of size 8.

operates in a counterclockwise or backward fashion, then j takes on negative values, but similar group relations obtain. Combinations of both types of N operators are the basis for a majority of Simon and Kotovsky's (1963; Kotovsky & Simon, 1973) letter patterns.

In general, the representation of relationships in terms of positions within various arrays suggests the potential usefulness of concepts such as symmetry in describing structures in pattern learning, perception, and problem solving. With ordered sets of tones, letters, numbers, or spatial events, the manner in which the relationships are defined emphasizes the importance of position in an alphabetic array. Note that if the subject does cognitively represent an ordered vocabulary as a spatial array with alphabetic members equidistant, then the cognitive alphabet possesses interval properties! The two groups of relations, however, may hold different meanings for the subject, depending upon the nature of the task and the manner of pattern presentations.

Some applications of group relations. Patterns constructed from these relationships can reflect different rule combinations, and a consideration of methods of combination is interesting. A common means of constructing sequences found in the work of Simon and Kotovsky (1963) emphasizes recurrent applications of a rule. Thus patterns formed from successive applications of a single rule are alternating sequences if the rule arises from Group 1, i.e.,

$$
\begin{array}{ccccccc}
123 & 654 & 123 & 654 & \quad & 1 & 4 & 1 & 4 \\
\uparrow & \uparrow & \uparrow & & \text{or} & \uparrow & \uparrow & \uparrow \\
C & C & C & & & T & T & T
\end{array}
$$

where rules ($S = 6$) operate upon the preceding unit at the points indicated above by arrows. Successive applications of an N^j translator from Group 2 does not usually result in an alternating pattern

$$
\begin{array}{ccccccc}
AB & BC & CD & & 33 & 55 & 77 \\
\uparrow & \uparrow & & \text{or} & \uparrow & \uparrow \\
N^1 & N^1 & & & N^2 & N^2
\end{array}
$$

if $S > 6$.

Thus, in both groups, the uniform application of a rule can be conveniently quantified. However, different surface regularities can result, depending upon the group to which the rule belongs.

A second means of combining relationships also transforms the preceding subunit, but several rules are involved so that the resulting structure can be given by an hierarchical tree. Consider a unit described by the complement rule, e.g., 16. The relationship of these two events remains invariant (assuming $S = 6$) throughout successive applications of rules from Group 1:

$$
\begin{array}{cccc}
16 & 34 & 34 & 16 \\
\uparrow & \uparrow & \uparrow \\
T & I & T
\end{array}
$$

It is important to note that, in fact, this pattern structure may be rewritten in terms of a hierarchical tree in which the commutativity of relations plays a major role:

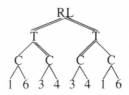

Here the distribution of rules conforms to hierarchical specifications with 4C, 2T, and 1RL rules. The identity operator is not found in this tree because the Abelian group property permits a substitution of I(34) = 34 with RL(TC) (see the double lines). That is, 34 is translated next by RL(34) to 16. Then T(16) becomes 43 and finally C(43) yields 34 once more. Patterns with true bilateral symmetry, such as 123654456321, are also readily generated with hierarchical distributions of Group 1 rules. It is this combination of relations that was exploited by Debussy (in the chords at the opening of this chapter) to describe the spatial symmetry of Gothic arches. And, it was these relations that unexpectedly emerged to direct symmetrical digit patterns in the Jones study described earlier.

Hierarchical combinations of rules from Group 2 usually yield patterns involving neither alternations nor bilateral symmetry. Consider the sequence

$$22 \qquad 33 \qquad 55 \qquad 66$$
$$\uparrow \qquad \uparrow \qquad \uparrow$$
$$N^1 \qquad N^2 \qquad N^1$$

in which the arrangement and distribution of rules conforms to hierarchical specifications. Alphabetic rules again transform the immediately preceding unit, not the whole sequence as Restle's formulas suggest, and so place a lighter burden upon immediate memory.

Both alternations and bilateral symmetry are morphological properties of patterns that, along with event runs, have powerful effects not only in conceptual learning, but also in perceptual responding. These morphological properties arise respectively from uniform and hierarchical distributions of Group 1 rules, but not from parallel formulas with Group 2 rules. Thus, patterns formed from Group 1 relations may survive the time demands often found in pattern perception, by virtue of their surface correlates. Patterns built only from Group 2 rules, or from combinations of Group 1 and 2, rarely have compelling symmetrical properties. These sequences parallel those often used in problem solving (e.g., Kotovsky & Simon, 1973), where people require time to abstract the metric relations involved.

But because relations in both groups are Abelian, some patterns can be described by several structures. The formulas give no clues as to which representational strategy is preferred, but they do lend formal justification to the individual differences found in perceptual and problem-solving tasks.

Binary patterns and patterns built from unordered vocabularies. This representation of what is learned offers a basis for understanding the potency of event runs in binary patterns. As the number of positions in an alphabet shrinks, ambiguity of relations grows. Consider a binary vocabulary (1, 2):

$$I(1) \quad = \quad R\,L(1) \quad = \quad 1 \qquad \text{and} \quad I(12) \quad = \quad R\,L(12) \quad = \quad 12$$
$$C(1) \quad = \quad T(1) \quad = \quad N(1) \quad = \quad 2 \quad \text{and} \quad C(12) \quad = \quad T(12) \quad = \quad N(12) = 21.$$

The identity operator is reinforced by its equivalence to the reflection operator: thus the potency of event runs in binary patterns. The potency of alternations is suggested by the equivalence of C, T, and N transforms for binary alphabets.

Lack of order in a multisymbol vocabulary is also accompanied by an increment in ambiguity of relations. But it is not the case that patterns based upon unordered vocabularies have no parallels to those based upon alphabets. Analyses of responses to FSG strings and artificial language systems indicate that item position in patterns from unordered vocabularies is a salient basis for relationships. Simon and Sumner (1968) have suggested that people may construct some "common alphabet" having order properties from the arrangement of elements within an initial string. A string presented all at once, such as PXBEY, for example, defines five positions from left to right so that T(PX) makes sense as EY, C(P) becomes Y, and RL(XB) is BX. Group 1 rules that dictate salient morphological regularities are more appropriate to such arrays than the counting rules of Group 2. Double application of each of T, C, and RL relations in this context still result in the identity relation [i.e., T(PX) = EY and T(EY) = PX].

This analysis suggests that a major distinction between patterns constructed by finite-state grammars and those built from ordered vocabularies is found in the basis of reference for relationships. With patterns constructed from alphabets, a person undoubtedly comes to rely upon positions within the alphabet as a basis for relations; with strings formed from vocabularies, the positions within the strings themselves may be used as reference points. Although with strings based upon unordered vocabularies, as with binary patterns, a dominant relation will be identity, it is apparent in both cases that recurrent symmetries within the strings themselves can be effectively used. The potency of position as a cue and as a basis upon which to define relations provides a provocative common ground for relating studies involving artificial language, pattern perception, and rule-learning.

Thus, it is possible that a key to what the subject is learning may be found within a more careful study of a person's representation and use of an array of positions. Perhaps by visualizing this representation spatially, a person can reconstruct serial patterns operating upon positions within the reference by means of position-defined relations.

Internal meaning. This discussion has involved an analysis of systematic and regular change. Sets of position-defined translations that leave lower-level relationships invariant amidst change have been proposed as a basis for describing what is learned. Little has been mentioned of how a person learns these relations, largely because little is known. Some properties of the relations themselves cannot help but revive the concept of man as an active translator of his environment who generates rule-governed expectancies about time and space patterns. Problems with expectancy theories that traditionally relate to quantifying expectancy may be resolved by noting that group relations permit definitions as well as suggest an impelling goal, i.e., the return to identity. The "effort after" internal meaning may ultimately be cast in such terms.

The "good" pattern revisited. With these relationships the concepts of a good figure also take on new meaning. Quantification of complexity in terms of uncertainty metrics can rest upon encoding of these rules and rule arrangements. In this conception, patterns arising from uniform (alternations) and hierarchical (symmetries) rule arrangements achieve relatively low uncertainty scores. Thus, we return to Garner's (1970) remarks about properties that determine our sense of the good pattern:

> . . . . symmetry is a usual concomitant of small subset sizes and redundancy, but not a necessary one. The important relation is that poor patterns have many alternatives, good patterns have few alternatives, and the very best patterns are unique [p. 39].

In Garner's terms, an alternating pattern such as 123654123654 will result in six distinctly different arrangements. But the hierarchically generated sequence, 123654456321 yields 12 different rearrangements and so should be judged less good. The reader may decide for himself if the symmetry of 123654456321 is so irrelevant that this pattern would be judged less good than an alternating pattern.

REFERENCES

Attneave, F. Some informational aspects of visual perception. *Psychological Review,* 1954, **61**, 183 – 193.

Attneave, F. *Applications of information theory to psychology: A summary of basic concepts, methods, and results.* New York: Holt, Rinehart & Winston, 1959.

Bartlett, F. *Thinking: An experimental and social study.* London: George Allen and Unwin, 1958.

Birkhoff, G. D. *Aesthetic measure.* Cambridge, Mass.: Harvard University Press, 1933.

Bjork, R. A. All-or-none subprocesses in the learning of complex sequences. *Journal of Mathematical Psychology,* 1968, **5**, 182–195.

Bower, G. H., & Winzenz, D. Group structure, coding, and memory for digit series. *Journal of Experimental Psychology,* 1969, **80**(2, Pt. 2).

Braine, M. D. S. On learning the grammatical order of words. *Psychological Review,* 1963, **70**, 323–348.

Braine, M. D. S. The insufficiency of a finite-state model for verbal reconstructive memory. *Psychonomic Science,* 1965, **2**, 291–292. (a)

Braine, M. D. S. Inferring a grammar from responses: Discussion of Gough and Segal's comment. *Psychonomic Science,* 1965, **3**, 241–242. (b)

Bruner, J. S., Goodnow, J. J., & Austin, G. A. *A study of thinking.* New York: Wiley, 1956.

Chomsky, N. *Syntactic structures.* The Hague, Mouton, 1957.

Chomsky, N., & Miller, G. A. Finite state languages. *Information and Control,* 1958, **1**, 91--112.

Chomsky, N., & Miller, G. A. Introduction to the formal analysis of natural languages. In R. D. Luce, R. R. Bush, & E. Galanter (Eds.), *Handbook of mathematical psychology.* Vol. 2. New York: Wiley, 1963.

Deese, J., & Kaufman, R. A. Serial effects in recall of unorganized and sequentially organized verbal material. *Journal of Experimental Psychology*, 1957, **54**, 180–187.

Epstein, W. A further study of the effect of syntactic structure on learning. *American Journal of Psychology*, 1962, **75**, 121–126.

Estes, W. K. An associative basis for coding and organization in memory. In A. W. Melton & E. Martin (Eds.), *Coding processes in human memory*. New York: Halsted, 1972.

Evans, S. H. Redundancy as a variable in pattern perception. *Psychological Bulletin*, 1967, **67**, 104–113.

Fritzen, J., & Johnson, N. F. Definiteness of pattern ending and uniformity of pattern size: Their effects upon learning number sequences. *Journal of Verbal Learning and Verbal Behavior*, 1969, **8**, 575–580.

Garner, W. R. *Uncertainty and structure as psychological concepts*. New York: Wiley, 1962.

Garner, W. R. To perceive is to know. *American Psychologist*, 1966, **21**, 11–19.

Garner, W. R. Good patterns have few alternatives. *American Scientist*, 1970, **58**, 34–58.

Garner, W. R. & Clement, D. E. Goodness of pattern and pattern uncertainty. *Journal of Verbal Learning and Verbal Behavior*, 1963, **2**, 446–452.

Garner, W. R. & Gottwald, R. L. Some perceptual factors in the learning of sequential patterns of binary events. *Journal of Verbal Learning and Verbal Behavior*, 1967, **6**, 582–589.

Garner, W. R., & Gottwald, R. L. The perception and learning of temporal patterns. *Quarterly Journal of Experimental Psychology*, 1968, **20**, 97–109.

Glanzer, M., & Clark, W. H. The verbal loop hypothesis: Binary numbers. *Journal of Verbal Learning and Verbal Behavior*, 1963, **2**, 301–309.

Gough, P. B., & Segal, E. M. Comment on "The insufficiency of a finite state model for verbal reconstructive memory." *Psychonomic Science*, 1965, **3**, 155–156.

Green, D. M., & Swets, J. A. *Signal detection theory and psychophysics*. New York: Wiley, 1966.

Johnson, D. M. *The psychology of thought and judgment*. New York: Harper, 1955.

Johnson, N. F. Organization and the concept of a memory code. In A. W. Melton & E. Martin (Eds.), Coding processes in human memory. New York: Halsted, 1972.

Jones, M. R. From probability learning to sequential processing: A critical review. *Psychological Bulletin*, 1971, **76**, 153–185.

Jones, M. R. Higher order organization in serial recall of digits. *Journal of Experimental Psychology*, 1973, **99**, 106–119.

Jones, M. R. Serial learning of temporal digit patterns. Unpublished manuscript, Ohio State University, 1974.

Jones, M. R., & Erickson, J. R. A demonstration of complex rule learning in choice prediction. *American Journal of Psychology*, 1972, **85**, 249–259.

Jones, M. R., & O'Hara, J. R. Memory interference as a function of rule-governed expectancies. *American Journal of Psychology*, 1973, **86**, 523–536.

Kantowitz, B. H. Information versus structure as determinants of pattern conception. *Journal of Experimental Psychology*, 1971, **89**, 282–292.

Keeney, T. J. Permutation transformations on phrase structures in letter sequences. *Journal of Experimental Psychology*, 1969, **82**, 28–33.

Kotovsky, K., & Simon, H. A. Empirical tests of a theory of human acquisition of concepts for sequential patterns. *Cognitive Psychology*, 1973, **4**, 399–424.

Lashley, K. S. The problem of serial order in behavior. In L. A. Jeffress (Ed.), *Cerebral mechanisms in behavior: The Hixon Symposium*. New York: Wiley, 1951.

Leeuwenberg, E. L. L. Quantitative specification of information in sequential patterns. *Psychological Review*, 1969, **76**, 216–220.

Levin, A. *The portable James Joyce*. New York: Viking Press, 1947.

Martin, J. Rhythmic (hierarchical) vs. serial structure in speech and other behavior. *Psychological Review*, 1972, **79**, 487–509.

McLean, R. S., & Gregg, L. W. Effects of induced chunking on temporal aspects of serial recitation. *Journal of Experimental Psychology*, 1967, **74**, 455–459.

Meyer, L. B. *Emotion and meaning in music*. Chicago: University of Chicago Press, 1956.

Miller, G. A. Free recall of redundant strings of letters. *Journal of Experimental Psychology*, 1958, **56**, 485–491.

Murdock, B. B., Jr., & Walker, K. D. Modality effects in free recall. *Journal of Verbal Learning and Verbal Behavior*, 1969, **8**, 665–676.

Myers, J. L. Sequential choice behavior. In G. H. Bower (Eds.), *The psychology of learning and motivation: Advances in research and theory*. Vol. 4. New York: Academic Press, 1970.

O'Connell, D. C. Facilitation of recall by linguistic structure in nonsense strings. *Psychological Bulletin*, 1970, **74**, 441–452.

O'Connell, D. C., Stubbs, C. L., & Theby, M. A. Facilitation of recall by structure in serially presented nonsense strings. *Psychonomic Science*, 1968, **12**, 263–264.

Preusser, D., Garner, W. R., & Gottwald, R. L. Perceptual organization of two-element temporal patterns as a function of their component one-element patterns. *American Journal of Psychology*, 1970, **83**, 151–170.

Reber, A. S. Transfer of syntactic structure in synthetic languages. *Journal of Experimental Psychology*, 1969, **81**, 115–119.

Restle, F. Theory of serial pattern learning: Structural trees. *Psychological Review*, 1970, **77**, 481–495.

Restle, F. Serial patterns: The role of phrasing. *Journal of Experimental Psychology*, 1972, **92**, 385–390.

Restle, F., & Brown, E. R. Serial pattern learning. *Journal of Experimental Psychology*, 1970, **83**, 120–125. (a)

Restle, F., & Brown, E. R. Organization of serial pattern learning. In G. H. Bower (Ed.), *The psychology of learning and motivation: Advances in research and theory*. Vol. 4. New York: Academic Press, 1970. (b)

Royer, F. L., & Garner, W. R. Response uncertainty and perceptual difficulty of auditory temporal patterns. *Perception & Psychophysics*, 1966, **1**, 41–47.

Ryan, J. Grouping and short-term memory: Different means and patterns of grouping. *Quarterly Journal of Experimental Psychology*, 1969, **21**, 137–147. (a)

Ryan, J. Temporal groupings, rehearsal, and short-term memory. *Quarterly Journal of Experimental Psychology*, 1969, **21**, 148–155. (b)

Schwartz, B. J., Lordahl, D. S., & Gambino, B. Effect of sequence structure on recall. *Journal of Experimental Psychology*, 1973, **98**, 212–213.

Shannon, C. E., & Weaver, W. *The mathematical theory of communication*. Urbana: University of Illinois Press, 1949.

Shipstone, E. I. Some variables affecting pattern conception. *Psychological Monographs*, 1960, **74**(17, Whole No. 504).

Shuell, T. J. Clustering and organization in free recall. *Psychological Bulletin*, 1969, **72**, 353–374.

Simon, H. A. Complexity and the representation of patterned sequences of symbols. *Psychological Review*, 1972, **79**, 369–382.

Simon, H. A., & Kotovsky, K. Human acquisition of concepts for sequential patterns. *Psychological Review*, 1963, **70**, 534–546.

Simon, H. A., & Sumner, R. K. Pattern in music. In B. Kleinmuntz (Ed.), *Formal representation of human judgment*. New York: Wiley, 1968.

Smith, K. H. Effect of exceptions on verbal reconstructive memory. *Journal of Experimental Psychology*, 1973, **97**, 119–139.

Smith, K. H., & Gough, P. B. Transformation rules in the learning of miniature linguistic systems. *Journal of Experimental Psychology*, 1969, **79**, 276–282.

Staniland, A. C. *Patterns of redundancy: A psychological study*. Cambridge, England: Cambridge University Press, 1966.

Vitz, P. C. & Todd, T. C. A coded element model of the perceptual processing of sequential stimuli. *Psychological Review*, 1969, **76**, 433–449.

Weyl, H. *Symmetry*. Princeton, N.J.: Princeton University Press, 1952.

Wickelgren, W. A. Size of rehearsal group and short-term memory. *Journal of Experimental Psychology*, 1964, **68**, 413–419.

Wickelgren, W. A. Rehearsal grouping and hierarchical organization of serial position cues in short term memory. *Quarterly Journal of Experimental Psychology*, 1967, **19**, 97–102.

Acknowledgement

The author is indebted to colleagues and students for constructive criticisms of an earlier version of this essay. Special thanks are due to Earl Hunt, Barry Kantowitz, David Stockburger, and Donald Fischer. The support and encouragement of Bob Jones and Ute Duncan, as well as the meticulous secretarial assistance of Marian Fish also contributed substantially to the completion of this manuscript.

6
THE PERCEPTION OF PRINTED
ENGLISH: A THEORETICAL
PERSPECTIVE[1]

Edward E. Smith and Kathryn T. Spoehr
Stanford University

Much of what we know, we discover by listening or reading. This seemingly innocuous statement has a strong implication for cognitive psychologists: To understand how adults acquire information, we must understand the processes that underlie the perception of speech and the perception of printed material. In the present chapter we deal with the reading problem and review the current work on letter and word perception. This research has been somewhat fragmented, with some investigators dealing exclusively with unstructured letter strings, others with the perception of isolated words, and still others with the effects of meaningful context on word perception. Given such schisms, a major purpose of this chapter will be to provide some integration of these different approaches to the perception of letter strings by emphasizing what we believe to be their common ground. In particular, we will argue that: (*a*) All research on letter-string perception is fundamentally concerned with how a perceiver extracts information from an input string and then interprets this information in terms of what he already knows, and (*b*) theories of letter-string perception differ primarily in how they conceptualize the processes and units involved in extracting and interpreting information.

Before beginning our review, it is useful to specify the boundary conditions and biases of the approach we will take. First, we need some sort of general definition of perception. We will assume that perception can be conceptualized as the processes involved in arriving at a categorization or interpretation of an input. This conception

[1]We are indebted to the members of a Seminar on Visual Information Processing held at Stanford during the Winter Quarter of 1973. Many of the people in this seminar contributed valuable ideas which have found their way into this chapter. Also, we thank Barry Kantowitz, Judy Kroll, and Leon Manelis for their comments on this manuscript. This research was supported in part by a United States Public Health Grant MH-19705.

seems to us to be in keeping with the concepts underlying truly general theories of perception, for example, Bruner's (1957) theory of perceptual readiness, or the theory of signal detectability (e.g., Swets, Tanner, & Birdsall, 1961). But while our general viewpoint may be broadly based, the actual domain of the experiments we cover will be restricted to what might be termed studies of letter-string perception. More precisely, this review includes studies of the perception of letter strings where these strings consist of (*a*) unrelated letters (e.g., BSTL), or (*b*) related letters (e.g., BLOST), or (*c*) words (e.g., BLAST). Typically such studies have employed printed letter strings, rather than handwritten ones, and accordingly we will concern ourselves only with printed English. Other reasons for deemphasizing the perception of handwritten English is that very little is known about this topic, and the little that is known suggests it is a more complex topic than the perception of printed material (e.g., Selfridge & Neisser, 1960). This deemphasis should not mislead us in the conclusions we draw about the perceptual processing of printed English, as there is evidence (Corcoran & Rouse, 1970) that printed and handwritten letters are processed by different mechanisms.

Another boundary condition is that we will deal mainly with experiments and theory that are part of the psychological literature and generally exclude research from the field of Education. The latter source, though clearly of great importance, is literally of voluminous proportions and any attempt to review it is beyond the scope of this chapter. Finally, this review will be biased in that our approach will be a theoretical one. We will present the relevant empirical findings in the context of the major theoretical positions, and our consideration of particular experimental results is frequently motivated by what they can tell us about some important theories. It seems to us that this approach holds more potential for integration than one that catalogs all empirical findings and then tabulates how many are consistent with each proposed theory.

So much for ground rules. With regard to organization, this chapter will be divided into four sections. The first is a preliminary one, as it deals with some fundamentals that set the groundwork for later sections. The next three sections are concerned with the perception of unrelated letters, related letters and words, and words in context, respectively. We will argue in these sections that certain theoretical distinctions, regarding processing stages and units, are basic to all three topics.

SOME BASIC CONSIDERATIONS

In this section we will first present a general two-stage hypothesis about grapheme (i.e., letter) perception which we will use as an organizational device throughout this chapter. We will then provide evidence on the role of feature analysis in this two-stage mechanism. Finally, we will use this two-stage hypothesis to structure our discussion of appropriate perceptual tasks for studying grapheme perception.

A General Two-Stage Hypothesis

To integrate the research of interest we deem it necessary to propose a general hypothesis that can serve as a framework for the models that will actually be considered. Our basic hypothesis holds that the perception of a letter string includes two distinct and sequentially organized stages: (*a*) an extraction of information from the input string (hereafter called the Extraction stage), and (*b*) an assignment of this information to some stored category (the Interpretation stage). We further assume that the information extracted in the first stage is in the form of visual features (we discuss this shortly), and that a category contains a description of both the visual features and the acoustic-articulatory features of some familiar language symbol, like a letter. Finally we assume that the Interpretation stage may contain as many as three sequentially organized component processes. The first of these we will call a matching process, and it involves a comparison of the features of the input to those of the relevant categories. The second Interpretation process is a decision operation which selects that category that offers the best visual match to the input. Lastly there may be a translation process which converts the visual categorization into an acoustic equivalent. It should be noted that not all theories of grapheme perception assume all three of these Interpretation processes.

An example of our two-stage hypothesis is given in Fig. 1 for the simple case where the input string or array consists of a single letter, the letter R. Figure 1 indicates that the output of the first stage would be a feature description of the input letter in terms of line segments, angles, and curves. The matching process of the Interpretation stage involves a comparison of this input description to stored visual representations of all 26 possible letters (categories), or some other means of allocating the extracted features to the relevant alternatives. The output of this matching process is some restricted set of categories, where each of these categories contains features that match those of the input to some degree. These categories are the most likely candidates for the subject's best estimate about what the input actually is. The Interpretation stage's decision involves a selection of one category from the candidate set, where this selection is made in accord with some decision rule. For example, the decision rule might be "pick the candidate that has the most features in common with the input, and, if this still leaves more than one candidate, pick the one that occurs most frequently in English." The output of this process, a single category, may then be translated into its acoustic equivalent. We note that this basic hypothesis is consistent with our definition of perception, with general theories of perception, and

INPUT   EXTRACTION STAGE   INTERPRETATION STAGE

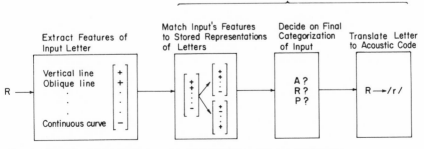

FIG. 1. Example of perceptual processing involved in perceiving a single letter.

with all of the more detailed models of letter and word perception that we will consider. Indeed, all of these more detailed models may be characterized by the assumptions they make about the processes and units involved in the Extraction and Interpretation stages.

One aspect of Fig. 1 deserves further comment, and this concerns the notion of perceptual units. Since Cattell's (1886) early work there has been a great deal of concern about the nature and size of the functional unit in letter-string perception. But despite this concern, the concept of perceptual units has often been treated in an unsystematic fashion. Our two-stage hypothesis depicted in Fig. 1 distinguishes between the perceptual units operative in Extraction and those in the various Interpretation processes. In the sample case shown in Fig. 1, Extraction operates on the features of a letter, and all the Interpretation processes operate on letter categories. Thus in this case we would say that the functional unit of Extraction is the feature of a letter (or letter position), while the unit or category of Interpretation is a letter. Later, when we consider word perception, it will become clear that there may be variations in the size of the unit of Extraction, of Interpretation, or of both.

The Case for Feature Analysis

We have already assumed that information is extracted from graphemes in the form of visual features such as horizontal or vertical lines. The most common alternative to this approach in discussions of pattern recognition (see Lindsay & Norman, 1972, and Neisser, 1967) is to assume that input letters are compared to stored, holistic representations, called templates, of the possible alternative categories. The template that best matches the input on a point-for-point basis is then chosen as the categorization of the input. Logically, however, feature analysis and template matching represent two points on a pattern-recognition continuum rather than opposite approaches to the problem (Bledsoe & Browning, 1966), because feature detectors can be thought of as mini-templates which match parts of, rather than entire, input characters. Our reasons for assuming feature analysis are motivated mainly by the widespread acceptance of a feature-extraction device among the modelers we will consider, and by some well known empirical findings that we now turn to.

Perhaps the most compelling evidence for feature analysis is derived from a series of physiological investigations by Hubel and Wiesel (1962, 1963, 1965). Recording from cells in the visual cortex of the cat, Hubel and Wiesel (1962) found cells that were activated only by edges of lines that occurred in specific orientations and positions. Hence these cells were essentially functioning as detectors for a very specific type of line segment. For other cortical cells, however, activation depended on orientation but not position. Hubel and Wiesel suggested that these latter cells might be reflecting activity from any of the previously noted more specific cells. Thus the latter cells were also functioning as line-segment detectors, but the information extracted by these detectors is at a somewhat more abstract level. These results are of great importance for letter perception because line segments at a particular orientation are very likely candidates for critical features of letters. Of course more than just line segments are needed to characterize some letters, as angular and curvature properties are also important. Again the physiological evidence is supportive as, for example, Hubel and Wiesel (1965) have found cells that respond to particular angles. All in all, these findings offer a definite means by which the feature analyzers of letter shapes may be realized at a physiological level.

The rest of the evidence for feature analysis is behavioral. Consider first an illustrative finding from a situation where a single letter is presented tachistoscopically and the subject makes an incorrect identification of it. If the initial stage of letter perception involves a characterization of the input in terms of a base set of features, then an erroneous choice could share some features with the correct alternative. As expected, errors have repeatedly been found to be similar to the correct alternatives (e.g., Keele & Chase, 1967; Townsend, 1971a). Moreover, Lindsay and Norman (1972) have recently shown that one may propose some *a priori* specification of the distinctive features of a letter, and then use this specification to predict the actual error patterns in tachistoscopic report. Another source of evidence for feature analysis is provided by the search experiments of Neisser (1963). Neisser required subjects to search for a target letter in a long list of letter strings and found that the rate of search was slower when the nontargets contained similar features to the target than when the target and nontargets shared few features. Thus the search for a *Z* was slower when the nontarget letters were also composed entirely of line segments than when the nontargets were circular letters, while the opposite obtained when the target was the letter *Q*. While other studies have replicated and extended Neisser's basic result (e.g., Chase & Posner, 1965), there is still no real consensus on what the actual features are that subjects use in identifying letters.

Tasks

We now want to bring to bear our two-stage hypothesis on some methodological issues. Generally speaking, the experimental situations used to study grapheme perception may be divided into (*a*) tasks in which the letter string is briefly exposed tachistoscopically (i.e., so brief as to preclude eye movements) and the dependent variable is an accuracy score, and (*b*) tasks in which the letter string is exposed sufficiently long to insure accurate responding and the dependent measure is reaction time (RT). We shall refer to these situations as accuracy and RT tasks, respectively. Regarding these tasks, there are two issues to be considered. First, there is the fundamental question of whether both accuracy and RT tasks are measuring the same process. Second, there is the problem of what specific variants of the two tasks are most suitable for studying perception. We deal with these issues in turn.

Accuracy and RT as converging measures. The question of whether accuracy and RT tasks reflect the same processes can only be answered within the context of some theory about the processes of interest, and so we consider an answer to this question in terms of our two-stage hypothesis. For RT tasks our hypothesis predicts that performance on even a single letter reflects the sum of the times needed for *S* to complete each of the two sequentially organized processing stages. Consequently an increase in RT due to an experimental variation indicates an increase in the duration of Extraction, or Interpretation, or both (assuming that stages having to do with executing a response have been held constant). Hence an RT task directly reflects the durations of the two stages of interest. We now want to argue that an accuracy task also reflects the durations of Extraction and Interpretation, but here the situation is a little less straightforward. To make this argument, we assume that in order for a subject to accurately perceive an input letter he must execute the two processing stages during that time interval when the physical input or its icon (Neisser, 1967; Sperling, 1960) is available. It follows that variations in accuracy (that result from experimental manipulations) reflect variations in the probability that the subject had sufficient time to execute the two stages. That is, brief tachistoscopic exposures limit accuracy by limiting Extraction and/or Interpretation time. Thus if an experimental variation leads to a decrease in accuracy it is because the variation led to an increase in the time needed for Extraction, or Interpretation, or both. By this line of reasoning both RT and tachistoscopic accuracy-tasks reflect exactly the same constraints—the processing-time demands of Extraction and Interpretation as a function of experimental variables—and the two tasks may serve as converging operations (see Garner, Hake, & Eriksen, 1956.)

It is important to note that this convergence of accuracy and RT tasks is based on the assumption that brief exposures limit accuracy by limiting processing time. There are alternatives to this limited-processing-time assumption. One alternative is that brief durations may limit perceptual accuracy by limiting the energy or information (features) in the input (Eriksen & Eriksen, 1971). This suggests that there should be little convergence of results between accuracy and RT studies of letter recognition, for the latter type of experiment imposes no limitation on the available features. But, as Eriksen and Hoffman (1972) have demonstrated, there is in fact a remarkable convergence between the results from the two tasks when they are carried out along similar lines, and our subsequent review will further document this. Hence the limited-information assumption will not be considered further. Another alternative to our limited-processing-time assumption is that tachistoscopic durations limit accuracy by limiting the time needed for Extraction, but the time needed for Interpretation is unaffected by brief durations because this stage can be carried out in the absence of sensory information. While this appears to be a reasonable alternative our subsequent review will indicate its drawbacks, namely, that some effects on tachistoscopic accuracy for related letter strings cannot possibly be due to Extraction and must reflect Interpretation. Thus our initial limited-processing-time assumption will be maintained.[2]

Perceptual tasks and response problems. Consider now the question of what specific tasks are most suitable for studying grapheme perception. The basic issue here, and it applies to both RT and accuracy tasks, is that there must be some sort of response stage that follows Extraction and Interpretation, and we do not want our results to primarily reflect variations in this nonperceptual stage. Take a classic example. Miller, Bruner, and Postman (1954) tachistoscopically presented strings of eight letters and had their subjects attempt to report all eight letters. The strings varied

---

[2]While most experimental results indicate that RT and accuracy tasks converge, it should be noted that some studies (e.g., Wheeler, 1970) have reported differential results for the two measures.

in the extent to which they approximated the statistical structure of English, and Miller et al. found that perceptual accuracy increased with approximation-to-English. But as Baddeley (1964) and others have pointed out, this effect may well be due to a response stage. Specifically, in the Miller et al. total-report task a response stage might include maintenance of the perceived letters in short-term memory and guessing for missing letters, and it is plausible that short-term memory capacity increases with approximation-to-English and/or that subjects guess in accordance with the statistical structure of the language. If either of these possibilities hold, then Miller et al.'s results may tell us little about the nature of the Extraction and Interpretation stages but may instead reflect the response stage. Baddeley (1964), in fact, demonstrated the validity of this response-stage argument by showing that Miller et al.'s approximation-to-English effect obtained even when a string was exposed for two sec, a duration long enough to insure accurate perception of all the letters in the string.

Note that the problem with the Miller et al. study would be equally severe had they used a total-report RT paradigm in which the subject was timed from the onset of the stimulus array until he started reporting the letters. In this type of situation it appears that part of the response stage involves a preparatory implicit vocalization of the string (Eriksen, Pollack, & Montague, 1970; Klapp, Anderson, & Berrian, 1973). If the time for this implicit vocalization decreases with the pronounceability of the string, then an approximation-to-English effect on RT could occur simply because higher approximations-to-English are more pronounceable and hence easier to vocalize implicitly, rather than because they are easier to process perceptually.[3]

Some of the problematic aspects of a tachistoscopic report task can be eliminated by using a partial-report procedure, where the subject is cued to report only a part of the letter display (e.g., Sperling, 1960). But while partial report may substantially reduce short-term memory factors, it does not really eliminate guessing factors as the subject must still select a response from a large set of alternatives. This guessing problem may be of little consequence when the array consists of unrelated letters (since the probability of being correct by guessing is so low), but it is of substantial import when the letters are related.

The solution to the guessing problem in both accuracy and RT tasks is straightforward and well-known. Use some sort of forced-choice response procedure. Several different variants of this procedure are now popular and all of them minimize short-term memory factors (to some extent) as well as guessing factors. One variant, used in both accuracy and RT tasks, is the same-different procedure where the subject either indicates whether all of the presented letters are the same or different (e.g., Beller, 1970; Robinson, Brown, & Hayes, 1964), or whether two simultaneously presented letter strings are the same or different (Posner, 1969). Here, there is no way for the likelihood of correct guesses to be different over experimental conditions, nor

---

[3]While we have used approximation-to-English experiments to demonstrate some points about a response stage, we do not mean to imply that there is no effect of approximation-to-English on perceptual stages. Indeed, when these experiments are performed with a more adequate methodology, perceptual effects of this variable have been obtained (e.g., Mewhort, 1967).

is there much room for short-term memory factors to operate if all the information is presented simultaneously. Another popular forced-choice procedure for accuracy tasks is a recognition procedure developed by Reicher (1969). In this situation, right after the termination of a briefly presented string, two alternative letters are presented, one above and one below a probed-for letter position in the string, and the subject chooses which alternative occurred in the string. Again, the forced-choice aspect eliminates differential guessing as a contributor to the results, while short-term memory effects are reduced (though not entirely eliminated) because the interval between termination of the string and presentation of the recognition alternatives is brief and recognition is always a single letter. A related procedure is the detection task developed by Estes and his students (e.g., Estes & Taylor, 1964). In this procedure the subject is given two alternative target letters at the start of each trial, and he then determines which of these two targets actually occurs in a briefly flashed string.

While we have described the recognition and detection procedures in the context of an accuracy task, it is possible to use these two procedures in a RT task, or to record both RTs as well as accuracy in a tachistoscopic task (e.g., Estes & Wessel, 1966; Wheeler, 1970). However, the RT procedure that most investigators have employed to study grapheme perception is a slight variation of the detection procedure. Specifically, only one target is specified and the subject's task is to respond "yes" if the target occurs, and "no" otherwise (e.g., Atkinson, Holmgren, & Juola, 1969; Sternberg, 1967). We shall refer to this as the Yes-No RT task. If, in this kind of situation, the input string is appreciably long and only Yes RTs are recorded, then we have the search RT task developed by Neisser (1963).

This is quite a proliferation of tasks and a summary is useful. Table 1 contains a breakdown of the tasks considered where the major task dimensions are type of dependent measure (accuracy vs RT) and type of response procedure (report vs

TABLE 1

Summary of Tasks Used to Study Letter String Perception

Dependent measure	Response procedure			
	Report	Forced-choice		
		Target and test simultaneous	Target precedes test	Target follows test
Accuracy	Total Report (e.g., Miller et al., 1954) Partial Report (e.g., Sperling, 1960)	Same-Different (e.g., Robinson et al., 1964)	Detection (e.g., Estes & Taylor, 1964)	Recognition (e.g., Reicher, 1969)
RT	Total Report (e.g., Eriksen et al., 1970)	Same-Different (e.g., Posner, 1969)	Yes-No (e.g., Atkinson et al., 1969) Search (e.g., Neisser, 1963)	

forced-choice). Table 1 also shows another task dimension that can be used to distinguish among forced-choice procedures. To illustrate this dimension, in Reicher's (1969) procedure the tachistoscopically flashed array may be considered the test item, the two alternatives that follow the array may be considered targets, and the subject's task is to ascertain the presence of a target in the test item. Using this terminology we can see that (a) in the same-different procedure the target and test items are presented simultaneously; (b) in the detection, Yes-No, and search procedures the target is presented before the test item; and (c) in the recognition procedure the target is presented after the test item.[4] It is also worth noting that our accuracy vs RT dichotomy is something of an artificial distinction for dependent measures. For while RT tasks were once thought to reflect error-free processing, recent work on the speed-accuracy tradeoff indicates that error frequency, even when less than 5%, must be treated in conjunction with RT in order to give an adequate picture of the processing involved (Pachella, 1972).

We will generally assume that results obtained with any of the forced-choice procedures in Table 1 are relatively free of memory and guessing factors, and so provide a basis for conclusions about perceptual processes. However, strong conclusions can only rest on converging results from different paradigms. While this by no means exhausts the methodological issues raised by choice of task, it is sufficient for our purposes.

PERCEPTION OF UNRELATED LETTERS

We are now ready to consider critical findings and theories about the perception of unrelated letters. We will first present a set of findings that have attracted a great deal of interest, and then consider several models that attempt to handle them. These models will be conceptualized in terms of our two-stage hypothesis and it will be argued that the basic difference among these models is a matter of whether they emphasize the Extraction stage or the Interpretation stage in accounting for empirical effects.

Critical Findings in the Perception of Unrelated Letters

The first finding of concern is a simple one—perceptual performance on an array of letters decreases with the number of letters in the array. This result is strikingly robust. In accuracy tasks, it has been obtained in: (a) total report paradigms (e.g., Sperling, 1960), when performance is measured by percent correct rather than total number of letters correctly reported; (b) detection paradigms (e.g., Estes & Wessel, 1966, Wolford, Wessel, & Estes, 1968); and (c) recognition paradigms (e.g., Reicher's, 1969, comparison of one vs two letters or anagrams). Similarly, the detrimental effect of array length has also been demonstrated in RT tasks using the:

[4]Note that in Table 1, the Yes-No and Search RT tasks are defined in terms of a target item preceding the occurrence of a test item. This of course is a description of the Sternberg (1966) paradigm. Sternberg's task is usually assumed to reflect primarily retrieval from short-term memory, rather than perceptual processes, and consequently we do not consider it here.

(a) same-different paradigm (e.g., Eichelman, 1970; Posner & Taylor, 1969); (b) yes-no paradigm (e.g., Atkinson et al., 1969; Sternberg, 1967); and (c) search paradigms (e.g., Neisser's, 1963, comparison of search rates through items containing either 2, 4, or 6 letters).

The above constitutes an impressive array of converging findings, but it is crucial to point out that the detrimental effect of array length is obtained only when the letters have some features in common. That is, array length impairs perceptual performance primarily when the letters are confusable. This, and other confusability effects, constitute the second set of critical results that have had a major impact on current theories. Most of these findings have been obtained in Estes' detection-accuracy paradigm and the results indicate that: (a) detection accuracy is greater for nonconfusable arrays (that is, arrays in which targets and nontargets share few or no features) than for confusable arrays (Estes, 1972); (b) detection performance, whether measured by accuracy or latency, declines with array length for confusable arrays, but is virtually unaffected by this variable for nonconfusable arrays (Estes, 1972); and (c) detection performance, measured by accuracy or latency, improves with the number of times a target actually occurs in a confusable array, while there is no effect of this variable in nonconfusable arrays (Estes, 1972).

The last set of results that deserve mention now are Sperling's (1960) findings on partial report. One of Sperling's main results was that tachistoscopic accuracy was greater in partial report with immediate cuing than in total report. While we have previously suggested that this effect is really due to short-term memory factors (see p. 237), some theorists (e.g., Rumelhart, 1970) have assumed it is a perceptual effect, and for this reason we mention it here. Another pertinent finding of Sperling was that, when cuing was immediate, the accuracy of partial report was unaffected by the number of noncued letters. While this finding appears to be in conflict with the previously mentioned detrimental effect of array length (for confusable letters), the conflict may be superficial. For if array length is defined as the number of relevant letters, i.e., letters that must be relatively fully processed, then there is agreement that performance declines with relevant array length, while the number of irrelevant letters may have little effect on performance.

Extraction-Type Models

In attempting to account for the above results the models of Rumelhart (1970) and Estes (1972) rely heavily on the Extraction stage, while the work of Eriksen and Spencer (1969), Shiffrin and Gardner (1972), and Gardner (1973) emphasize the Interpretation stage. In view of this, we will treat the two classes of models separately, first focusing on Extraction-type models.

Rumelhart's (1970) limited capacity model. Rumelhart's (1970) model offers an explicit description of the Extraction stage. Each of the N letter positions of the display is assumed to act as an input channel. During exposure of the display, features of each of the letter positions are registered in an icon, and this feature information then decays exponentially once the display has terminated. While available, the features in the icon are extracted one at a time, but all letter positions are worked on at the same time. For example, in a three-letter display the first feature extracted may be in the first letter position, the second feature extracted may be in the third position, the third feature in the first position, and so on. Since feature extraction is sequential and all letter positions are active at the same time, the probability of extracting a particular number of features from a particular input position decreases as array length increases. That is, the feature-extraction capacity allottable to a particular letter decreases with the number of letters, and it is for this reason that the model is referred to as a Limited Capacity model.

To proceed further with this model, Rumelhart posits an attention parameter, θ_i, for the Extraction stage, where θ_i is the probability that the feature being processed belongs to the ith position in the array. That is,

$$\theta_i = \frac{\omega_i}{\displaystyle\sum_{i=1}^{N} \omega_i}, \tag{1}$$

where ω_i is a weight that corresponds to the attention which the subject focuses on the ith position of the array. As for the Interpretation stage, it is implicitly assumed that an extracted feature is compared with each category description and increments a counter for every category it matches. A criterion value of c matching features is needed to categorize an input letter. Thus the Limited Capacity model manifests our distinction between Extraction and Interpretation at the level of a single feature: As soon as each feature (the unit of the first stage) is extracted, it is allocated to one of the alternative letter categories (the unit of the second stage). Note further that Rumelhart's conception of the Interpretation stage includes a decision as well as a matching process, since the presence of a criterion for each category acts as a decision rule.

Consider now how this Limited Capacity model accounts for the empirical findings mentioned earlier. We have already noted that the Extraction capacity per letter decreases with array length, so clearly the model correctly predicts the obtained performance decline with array length on confusable arrays. The model can further predict that, in a paradigm like Estes' detection task, nonconfusable arrays will be better perceived than confusable arrays. This prediction obtains because the criterion needed for a match, c, can be a lower value for nonconfusable than confusable arrays, and consequently fewer features need be processed in perceiving the elements of a nonconfusable than of a confusable array. The same consideration suggests that certain experimental variables, like array length or the number of times a target actually occurs in a detection trial, will have less of an effect on nonconfusable than confusable arrays. But it appears that such effects should not be eliminated entirely when nonconfusable arrays are used (Gardner, 1973). In this latter respect the model clearly seems faulty, and we will later return to this problem. Finally the model handles Sperling's (1960) partial report results in terms of the attention parameter. The cued letters in a partial-report paradigm are given greater attention than the noncued letters, and this will result in greater accuracy on the subset of cued letters than on a comparable subset in a total-report paradigm. Further, if the weights assigned to the cued letters are far greater than those assigned to the noncued letters, then the noncued letters will usurp little of the feature-extraction capacity and the number of such letters will have little effect on performance.

Estes' (1972) interactive channels model. A second model that attributes differences in perceptual performance primarily to the Extraction stage is the Interactive Channels model proposed by Estes (1972). Estes' Extraction and Interpretation stages bear some similarity to Rumelhart's. Letters are analyzed by feature detectors, with all letter positions active at the same time, and each extracted feature is immediately allocated to its matching categories. However, in Estes' Extraction stage, an attempt is made to analyze all of the letters at once for all possible features. That is, Rumelhart's serial-processing assumption is replaced by one of parallel processing. However, there is still a limitation on processing, where this limit is the number of feature detectors available at any given location on the retina. The greatest number of detectors for a given feature, such as a vertical line, is concentrated at the fovea, with the density of detectors decreasing as the distance from the fovea increases. Since a single detector can extract only one single feature of a multiletter display at a time, correct identification of a letter depends on a number of appropriate detectors in its immediate vicinity not being tied up in extracting features from another nearby letter in the display.

The consequences of this type of system can best be seen in a detection paradigm. An accurate detection can be made in one of two ways. If enough feature detectors are available in the vicinity of the target letter, feature extraction and the matching process of Interpretation will be complete and there will be a match between the input and the category that represents one of the targets, causing a speedy detection. In some cases, however, there will not have been sufficient feature extraction to allow the input to match entirely one of the target categories, and the subject must then execute a decision process. Specifically, he must select input positions whose features are consistent with the target alternatives and decide which is most likely to be the target. This decision process is assumed to be relatively slow and inaccurate, and hence there will be more errors and longer detection times when the decision process is required than when the matching process yields a definitive categorization. Thus the distribution of feature detectors across the retina determines a ratio of fast, complete-match detections to slow, error-prone decisions, and this predicts both accuracy and RT data.

The Estes model is quite successful in predicting the experimental data of interest. Consider a detection task in which the nontarget items are highly confusable with the target. The model correctly predicts that performance will decrease as the number of items in this type of confusable array increases, because of the increased competition for feature extraction between the distractors and the target. The competition becomes particularly critical near the periphery where there is a low concentration of detectors. Since there is an increased chance of the target appearing in the periphery with larger array size, there will be a larger proportion of slow detection responses (i.e., responses that are based on both decision and matching processes), and accuracy will decrease with array size. In the case of nonconfusable displays, the distractor letters will tie up few, if any, of the feature detectors necessary for feature extraction and complete matching, and detection performance will necessarily be better than on the confusable displays. Moreover, since there is little competition between the target and nontarget letters in the nonconfusable arrays even at the periphery, the model correctly predicts little or no effect of array size on detection for the nonconfusable displays. Clearly, all of these arguments and predictions apply to tasks other than the detection paradigm, and so the Interactive Channels model can readily handle the effects of display size and confusability in general. As for Sperling's (1960) findings on partial report, Estes (1972) simply attributes them to a short-term memory process subsequent to perception.

Interpretation-Type Models

It has recently become clear that there are certain findings that seriously challenge the validity of Rumelhart's (1970) two critical assumptions about the Extraction stage—the assumptions that there is a limited capacity for extracting features and that some letter positions are given more attention than others. Partly as a result of this, researchers have developed a new model, referred to as the Unlimited Capacity model, which attempts to explain most perceptual effects via the Interpretation stage. Let us first describe these recent findings, and then the model of interest.

Findings on capacity and attention. We have noted that detection performance on nonconfusable arrays is unaffected by array length (Estes, 1972). This same invariance of perceptual performance over array length has recently been reported in several same-different and yes-no RT tasks (Beller, 1970; Connor, 1972; Egeth, Jonides, & Wall, 1972). This null finding weighs heavily against Rumelhart's assumption of a serial feature-extraction process, for such an assumption leads to the prediction that array length will always have some effect on performance.[5]

Rumelhart's assumptions about feature analysis also seem inconsistent with the findings of Eriksen and Spencer (1969). These authors tachistoscopically presented individual letters in sequence, and varied the interval between successive letters from 5 to 3000 msec. The subject was required to determine whether or not a target letter occurred in the display. If feature-extraction capacity is limited, then accuracy should have increased with the interval between letters; this is because with longer intervals the subject would have had more time to either complete processing on each letter or shift his attention to the next input. However, Eriksen and Spencer found that performance was unaffected by the inter-letter interval, thereby giving more evidence against the limited-capacity and attention assumptions.

Perhaps the most devastating evidence against the limited-capacity and attention assumptions is provided by the experiments of Shiffrin and Gardner (1972). Using Estes' detection task, Shiffrin and Gardner's main experiment compared two presen-

---

[5] The null finding at issue also appears to be evidence against any parallel feature-extraction process that assumes a fixed capacity that must always be distributed over the elements in the array. For, as Townsend (1971b) and others have pointed out, such a process also predicts a decrease in perceptual performance with array size. A more expanded discussion of this issue can be found in Townsend's preceding chapter (this volume).

tation conditions. In one condition, four elements were presented simultaneously for some fixed amount of time, say 40 msec. In the other condition the four elements were presented sequentially, with a brief interval between elements, and each element was exposed for 40 msec. Thus in the sequential condition the total exposure time was four times greater than that in the simultaneous condition, and clearly a Limited Capacity model would predict greater accuracy in the sequential condition. In fact, for both confusable and nonconfusable displays, there was no significant difference between the two presentation conditions, and whatever difference there was actually favored the simultaneous over the sequential condition.

So Rumelhart's (1970) limited-capacity and attention assumptions predict three effects—a decrease in performance on nonconfusable arrays with array length, an increase in accuracy with inter-letter interval in the Eriksen-Spencer (1969) task, and greater detection accuracy with sequential than simultaneous presentation—and not one of these effects has been obtained. These results (or lack of them) led Eriksen and Spencer (1969) and Shiffrin and Gardner (1972) to consider a model in which feature-extraction capacity is not limited by the size of the array (within reasonable limits) since each letter position is processed as an independent channel. According to such an Unlimited Capacity model, when array size causes an effect on performance, as it does with confusable arrays, the effect is due to some Interpretation process. While the papers of Eriksen and Spencer (1969) and Shiffrin and Gardner (1972) have been most influential in this theoretical development, the fullest exposition of the model is contained in a paper by Gardner (1973).

The Unlimited Capacity model. Following Gardner (1973) we will describe the model in the context of a detection paradigm, where the subject must determine which of two target letters occurred in a briefly flashed letter string. It is first assumed that the features of each letter in an array are extracted independently of the features of other letters in the array. Thus, the Extraction stage is carried out simultaneously for all letters, and the capacity of this stage is unlimited by the size of the array within the limits of the resolving power of the eye. But of course the Extraction stage is still limited by the brief exposure time, and so the features extracted from a particular letter may either be erroneous or insufficient with respect to uniquely characterizing the letter. This will create difficulties for the subsequent Interpretation stage. The first Interpretation process is matching, which is assumed to result in each letter position being characterized by the subject's estimate of what letter occurred at that position, e.g., B in first position, T in second position. These estimates are referred to as "end states," and once determined, a decision process operates on them to decide which of the two target letters actually occurred. The crucial aspect of the decision process is the nature of the decision rule, and Gardner proposes a simple rule for the detection situation: If at least one of the end states indicates a particular target, and none indicate the other target, then respond with the indicated target; in all other cases, guess at random between the two possible targets.

Gardner (1973) has shown that this Unlimited Capacity model is consistent with the major findings obtained in detection studies. Let us start with the effects of array size for confusable arrays. In this case, the nontargets are similar to the targets, and there is a substantial probability that the features extracted from a nontarget position will incorrectly lead to an end state that indicates the wrong target. Given the decision rule described above, such an incorrect end state will result in the subject either deciding on the incorrect target or guessing, and both of these outcomes decrease overall performance. Since the probability of arriving at an incorrect end state increases with the number of end states to be considered (i.e., array size), it follows that detection accuracy will decrease with array size when the letters are confusable. For nonconfusable arrays, there is little probability that features extracted from a nontarget position will lead to a wrong end state. Consequently, accuracy should be greater on nonconfusable than confusable arrays. Further, since the probability of an incorrect end state is low, there should be little effect of array size with nonconfusable arrays, and there may even be no effect when the probability of an incorrect end state is effectively zero. As for Sperling's (1960) partial-report effects, supporters of the Unlimited Capacity model would simply attribute such effects to post-perceptual factors like short-term memory processes (Shiffrin & Gardner, 1972).

In addition to being compatible with the findings just mentioned, this model is, of course, also consistent with the negative results of Eriksen and Spencer (1969) and Shiffrin and Gardner (1972). Gardner (1973) has further pointed out that correct predictions about RTs in the detection task can also be derived from the Unlimited Capacity model, and, hopefully, the model can be easily extended to cover tasks other than detection. The potential generality of the model is further indicated by the fact that its central assumption of unlimited capacity makes contact with related research on attention. Researchers working on various aspects of attention, including Herman and Kantowitz (1970), Keele (1973), and Kantowitz (this volume) have argued that attentional limitations reflect processes subsequent to feature extraction, which is quite consistent with the unlimited-capacity conception of extraction.

One other aspect of the Unlimited Capacity model is worth commenting on. This model seems strikingly similar to an earlier model of pattern recognition, Selfridge's (1959) Pandemonium System. In Pandemonium a hierarchy of processes is posited, where lower-level processes extract features from the input array and higher-level processes interpret this information. The extraction process is assumed to be unlimited by the size of the array and the Interpretation stage involves both matching and decision processes. While Selfridge (1959; Selfridge & Neisser, 1960) did not discuss the role of confusability in Pandemonium's operations, presumably this model would make predictions very similar to those of the Unlimited Capacity model. One apparent difference between the two models, however, concerns the nature of the decision rule. While we described the Unlimited Capacity model in terms of a simple, task specific rule, the kind of decision rule that is most appropriate for Pandemonium is one that considers how much each alternative (for each input position) is favored by the feature information. But the Unlimited Capacity model can certainly be altered so as to incorporate a more complex and general decision rule.

Overview of the Models

Table 2 summarizes the main points covered in this section. The various theoretical positions are classified with respect to their implications for three perceptual processes, including feature extraction, matching, and decision making. Al-

TABLE 2
A Summary of the Letter-Perception Models in Terms
of Their Assumptions about Perceptual Processes

Models	Perceptual processes		
	Feature extraction	Matching	Decision
Limited capacity (e.g., Rumelhart, 1970)	Extract sequentially with attentional variations	Match to features of letter category	Decide on basis of criterion
Interactive channels (e.g., Estes, 1972)	Extract simultaneously with limitation on number of detectors	Match to features of letter category	Decide on basis of second and incomplete matching process
Unlimited capacity (e.g., Selfridge & Neisser, 1960; Eriksen & Spencer, 1969; Shiffrin & Gardner, 1972; Gardner, 1973)	Extract simultaneously with unlimited capacity	Match to features of letter category	Decide on basis of explicit rule for task

though all theories posit that the unit of Extraction is a feature of a letter, there are clear differences among their conceptions of the feature-extraction process. The Limited Capacity model assumes sequential processing with attentional variations, while the Interactive Channels and Unlimited Capacity models assume parallel processing. The latter two models are differentiated at this stage in that Estes' model assumes that array size can limit feature extraction because of the distribution of detectors over the visual field, while the Unlimited Capacity model assumes that extraction is in no way limited by the number of items. All of the models are, however, quite similar in their conception of the matching process. All agree that the unit of matching is a letter category and that matching is done on a feature-by-feature basis.[6] Differences between the models arise again at the level of the decision process. Rumelhart handles the decision aspects of letter perception by means of a variable criterion for the number of features that must be matched. For Estes, the decision process is only necessary when complete matching has not occurred, while the Unlimited Capacity model assumes that a decision process always occurs. The explicit decision rules are a crucial component of the latter model.

Since the above discussion merely describes the various models, some evaluation is in order. Recent findings (like those on confusability, reported in the last section) clearly favor the Interactive Channels and Unlimited Capacity models over Rumelhart's but do not seem to discriminate between Estes' assumptions and those of

[6]It should be noted that some recent research has challenged the viewpoint that the matching process considers only specific visual features. As one example of this, Posner (1969) has argued that the matching process involves an abstracted form of visual information, referred to as a schema or a prototype, and Reed (1972) has further extended this idea. As another example, Jonides and Gleitman (1972) have suggested that the matching process is partly based on conceptual information, in that a perceiver may consider whether an input item is a letter or digit in trying to match it.

the Unlimited Capacity model. Perhaps the latter two models are far more similar than is indicated by our calling one an Extraction-type and the other an Interpretation-type model, for a certain amount of arbitrariness is part of any classification. But it may be that Estes' model and the Unlimited Capacity model are indeed fundamentally different, and that future experiments will be able to distinguish between them, or to indicate how their best components can be combined to formulate an even stronger theoretical statement.

PERCEPTION OF WORDS AND OTHER STRINGS OF RELATED LETTERS

When discussing models of letter perception the theoretical distinction we emphasized was that between Extraction and Interpretation. The question of units was not of much issue, as most theorists assumed that the relevant units for the Extraction and Interpretation stages were letter features and letters, respectively. In considering word perception, however, the unit question is critical, and it merges with our Extraction vs Interpretation distinction. Most models of word perception assume that the unit of at least one perceptual process is larger than a single letter (referred to as a higher-order unit), and the major distinction among the various models is whether they assume that such higher-order units play a role in Extraction or only in Interpretation processes. This issue clearly arises when the various models attempt to account for the finding that words are more perceptible than unpronounceable nonwords (e.g., Neisser, 1967). Accordingly, we will begin our review with this finding and its implications. We will then consider several models of word perception, which posit either higher-order Extraction or Interpretation units, and will assess how well each of them can explain the word-nonword findings and related results. Finally, we will consider the role of perceptual strategies and the problems such strategies raise for any model of word perception.

One cautionary note is necessary before beginning. Models of word perception often pay little attention to the details of feature extraction. Such negligence, however, is not a cause for much concern, since word-perception models are extensions of letter-perception models, and the latter have already been shown to be quite systematic in their treatment of feature extraction.

Perceptual Differences Between Words and Nonwords

Experimentation on the problem of how people perceive letters in words goes back to Cattell (1886). Cattell was interested in determining how many individual letters could be reported from a briefly presented array. His results were striking in that the subjects' performance depended on the characteristics of the entire array and not just on the individual letters. That is, the subjects could report only three or four unrelated letters, but as many as two short words that were not semantically and syntactically related to each other (Cattell, 1886). Cattell was thus the first to find superior perceptual performance for words than for comparable strings of unrelated letters. The problem with accepting Cattell's result has to do with his use of the full-report technique since, as mentioned earlier, the use of this procedure leaves open the possibility that the results are due either to guessing or to short-term memory factors. Surprisingly, more than eighty years elapsed before the superiority of words over nonwords was determined to be a perceptual effect, when Reicher (1969) demonstrated this result in his forced-choice recognition procedure. The superior perceptual performance with words has since been replicated several times in tachistoscopic accuracy experiments (e.g., F. Smith, 1969a; E. Smith & Haviland, 1972), and in RT studies using a same-different procedure (Eichelman, 1970; Kreuger, 1970b) or a search procedure (Kreuger, 1970a).

It is important to note that in most of the above studies, while the nonwords were comparable to the words with respect to component letters, the nonwords were less pronounceable than the words. Thus the word-nonword difference really demonstrates that a word is more perceptible than a less pronounceable nonword, where pronounceability may be assessed by subjective ratings or some other independent means. This suggests that pronounceability, rather than "wordness," may be the key factor responsible for the word-nonword difference. Numerous experiments provide some support for this suggestion by demonstrating that the perceptibility of nonwords increases with pronounceability in accuracy tasks (e.g., Baron & Thurston, 1973; Gibson, Pick, Osser, & Hammond, 1962) and same-different RT tasks as well (e.g., Egeth & Blecker, 1971). But before one accepts that pronounceability is *the* critical difference between words and nonwords, note that the words and nonwords used in most experiments also differ in another important way. Words conform to the orthographic structure (or spelling rules) of English whereas nonwords typically do not, and there is evidence from tachistoscopic tasks that the perceptibility of nonwords increases as they increasingly approximate the orthographic structure of English (Mewhort, 1967—see footnote 3). Hence the contrast between words and nonwords involves differences in the factors of wordness, pronounceability, and approximation-to-English. Different models of word perception have different conceptions about which of these factors is most important, and so further consideration of the critical factor in the word-nonword difference must await our treatment of the specific models. For now, we are simply interested in what implications the very existence of the word-nonword difference has for models of word perception.

For our purposes the most crucial aspect of the word-nonword effect is that it cannot be explained by the models of letter perception considered earlier. To see this, consider again the type of empirical effects these earlier models deal with and the nature of their theoretical mechanisms. With regard to empirical effects, letter-perception models focus on array size and letter confusability. But in a typical study of the word-nonword effect (Reicher, 1969), both of these variables are constant for words and nonwords, since the nonwords are anagrams of the words. At the level of theory, none of the letter-perception models considers a mechanism that is sensitive to the relations between the letters in an array, yet such a mechanism seems to be exactly what is needed to account for the word-nonword effect. Thus we need to revise our letter-perception theories so that they can account for the basic facts of word perception.

A useful starting point for understanding these revisions is to note that words provide a perceiver with more information than just the simple descriptions of the component letters, and that this additional information is aiding the subjects in identifying the words. Viewing this notion in the light of the Extraction-Interpretation distinction, it appears that the additional information may come into play in the form of higher-order, multi-letter, processing units at either of the two stages or both. At the Extraction stage, for instance, words may provide additional information during Extraction in the form of shape features that are characteristic of words but not of unrelated letter strings (Pillsbury, 1897), or in the form of shape features characteristic of spelling regularities but not arbitrary letter clusters. These proposals lead to models of word perception that propose higher-order units for the Extraction stage, in that they assume that features can be extracted from units larger than an individual letter. On the other hand, the extra information in words may affect the Interpretation stage by allowing the subject to use his vocabulary (i.e., lexical knowledge) in perceiving a test word even when the features extracted are insufficient to identify each letter. This type of proposal leads to word-perception models that assume that higher-order units are operative in the matching or decision processes of Interpretation. A third possibility, which also attributes the effect of additional information in words to an Interpretation process, involves the observation that words have pronunciations that are constrained by the phonological rules of English. If acoustic translation plays a role in word perception, then the processing of words should be facilitated by the subject's knowledge of these rules, and we are led to a model that assumes higher-order units are operative in the translation process. The remainder of this section will deal with these three possibilities in turn.

Extraction-Type Models

The simplest word-perception model based on the Extraction stage is one that posits that words have features of their own, and that the subject extracts these features in addition to letter features. Hence, assuming that feature extraction is a parallel process of relatively unlimited capacity, more features can be extracted from a word than from a nonword during a unit time interval, and therefore words should be perceptually superior to nonwords. The most commonly cited example of a word's unique feature is its shape (Pillsbury, 1897). If word shape is an effective aid to the perception of words, then we must assume that subjects can distinguish between items on the basis of gross physical properties such as the pattern of ascenders (letters that extend above the line of print) and descenders (letters that extend well below the line of print). The difficulty with this approach is that it presupposes a kind of type, such as lower-case print, where ascenders and descenders exist and are easy to distinguish. However, F. Smith (1969b) and F. Smith, Lott, and Cronnell (1969) have shown that subjects can read through material printed in randomly intermixed type styles and sizes as quickly as they can read through standard lower-case print. This finding seems devastating to the assumption that words are recognized, in part, on the basis of word-shape features.[7] Similarly, the word-nonword difference has been obtained for stimuli printed in capital letters (Reicher, 1969; E. Smith & Haviland, 1972) where word-shape features are minimized.

Notice that the same evidence that argues against the word-shape explanation argues against the hypothesis that the shape of word subunits (e.g., Gibson's, 1965, spelling patterns) provides additional perceptual information. Moreover, in order for multiletter spelling groups to provide additional features, it is necessary that the input string be parsed into subunits before any of the letters are identified. This parsing problem (which we will return to in our treatment of subsequent models), taken in conjunction with the empirical data cited above, argues against the feasibility of many Extraction-type models of word perception.

Before moving on from these models, we should point out that it is possible to have an Extraction-based model of word perception that does not assume higher-order units of feature extraction. Specifically, one may posit that the features extracted from a word are the usual letter features, but the fact that the letter string consists of a word allows the subject to let the outcomes of prior feature tests determine which subsequent features are extracted (Wheeler, 1970). This type of theoretical approach, however, does not seem promising in view of the previously presented findings (e.g., Shiffrin & Gardner, 1972) which indicate that feature extraction is not characterized by selectivity. Also, Reicher (1969) has shown that words are more perceptible than nonwords, even when the two types of items are randomly intermixed from trial to trial, making it difficult for subjects to selectively extract features that will help them identify words. For these reasons, we will not consider this model further.

Interpretation-Type Models: Higher-Order Units in Matching and Decision Processes

We will briefly consider a simple Interpretation model (Wheeler, 1970) that proposes higher-order decision units and then discuss the more powerful models of F. Smith (1971) and Rumelhart and Siple (1974) which assume higher-order matching units. All of these models give a special status to word units, and we will then consider some problems that arise as a result of this, along with some possible models that emphasize units other than words.

Higher-order decision units: The Sophisticated Guessing model. Wheeler (1970) has proposed another model that involves only a simple extension of the letter-perception models considered in the previous section. Wheeler argues that a word is processed as an array of independent letters up to and including the matching process. If we assume that matching is imperfect or incomplete, the outcome for each

---

[7]The exact findings of F. Smith (1969b) and F. Smith et al. (1969) are hardly beyond question, however, since it is not uncommon to find an effect of type style on reading speed (Haber, personal communication, 1973).

position in the word is a set of possible end states or candidates for that position. The subject then decides among the candidates at each position, and it is in this decision process that the higher-order units play a role. For if the subject believes that an array forms a word, he may incorporate this knowledge into his decision rule by choosing only those candidates that together form a word. For example, suppose that a test item in a tachistoscopic accuracy task is the word RUT. Suppose further that after matching, the candidates for the first position are R and A, those for the second position are U and D, and those for the third position are T and F. If the subject makes his decision by choosing candidates that together form a word, he will inevitably end up with RUT, which is the correct item. Now suppose that the test item was the nonword RTU and the same two candidates are associated with each critical letter (U and D are now the candidates for the third position). Here, the subject cannot incorporate word constraints into his decision rule, and consequently he is less likely to end up with the correct item. Thus the model predicts that perceptual performance should be better with words than nonwords. In a similar vein, the subject's knowledge of the constraints of English orthography and phonology may give rise to pronounce-ability and approximation-to-English effects in letter-string perception.

This simple model is really just an instance of a general model that is referred to in the literature as Fragment Theory (e.g., Neisser, 1967; Newbigging, 1961) or Sophisticated Guessing (e.g., Broadbent, 1967). The general model merely assumes that feature extraction and matching processes limit the possibilities to some set of candidates, and then a decision is made among these candidates in accordance with some constraints or biases. However, in the typical application of this model (e.g., Broadbent, 1967) it is assumed that the matching process operates on words, rather than letters, and that the biases that enter into choosing among candidates are frequency or expectancy biases. But, in any event, Wheeler's proposal seems to incorporate the general idea of Sophisticated Guessing.

Two experimental results cause problems for Wheeler's Sophisticated Guessing model. The problems arise because Wheeler's arguments suggest that if the subject were given constraints to use with nonwords that equalled those he had available for words, the word-nonword difference should disappear. In fact, Reicher (1969) and E. Smith and Haviland (1972) equated constraints for words and nonwords and found that the word-nonword difference was unaffected by this manipulation. Both of these studies used tachistoscopic recognition tasks. Reicher (1969) equated constraints by presenting the two target letters before as well as after stimulus presentation; hence, the subject should have been able to use this prior information to restrict the candidates in his decision process, and this restriction should have been equal for words and nonwords. E. Smith and Haviland (1972) equated constraints by equating words and nonwords for distributional and sequential redundancy; thus, a comparable decision rule could be used in considering candidates for both words and nonwords. Both of these "equating" manipulations were found to affect the overall level of performance, but not the critical word-nonword difference. These findings appear to offer critical evidence against the Sophisticated Guessing model's explanation of the word-nonword difference.[8]

Higher-order matching units: The Feature Redundancy model. In the previous model the unit of matching was a letter. Such a model of word perception may be referred to as mediated, in the sense that word perception is mediated by letter perception. Since the earliest work on reading (Cattell, 1886; Huey, 1908) there have been arguments (many of them introspective) against such mediation. One alternative is to argue that word perception is direct in that the unit of matching is a word. This is the position taken by F. Smith (1971) and Rumelhart and Siple (1974) who have independently proposed what we will call the Feature Redundancy model.

Let us start with F. Smith's arguments. Smith's key assumption is that a reader develops sets of discriminating features for entire words, just as he does for individual letters. For example, if a set of seven distinctive features define the letter B and another set of seven distinctive features define the letter E, then the feature set of the word BE is simply the two component sets considered simultaneously plus some positional information. Thus the Extraction stage in Smith's model is the same as that in any model of letter perception that posits simultaneous processing. But, and this is the crucial point, the feature set for an *n*-letter word is more than just *n* feature lists, since the features of a word are redundant in the same way that the letters of a word are redundant. This means that fewer features need be extracted in order to match an *n*-letter word than *n* unrelated letters. That is, the array of features plus positional information that visually defines a word category provides *more* information than needed to distinguish the 50,000 words that the average reader can identify on sight, and consequently it is not necessary for a reader to extract every feature for every position in order to interpret properly a given input word. Instead it may be necessary to match, for example, only three out of seven possible features in each position, in order to categorize the item as a whole. Thus, in many positions, fewer matching features are needed than would be necessary for categorizing that letter in isolation, and the total number of matching features needed to categorize a word is far less than the number required to categorize each of its component letters. Assuming that nonwords are typically categorized on a letter-by-letter basis, it follows that words should be better perceived than nonwords.

Rumelhart and Siple (1974) develop this notion of feature redundancy in more formal fashion and also include a separate decision process in their theory. The higher-order units of the matching process will suffice to explain the word-nonword difference, while aspects of the decision process can be used to handle other word-perception findings. Let us deal with this model in some detail.

Unlike other modelers, Rumelhart and Siple start by defining the functional visual

---

[8]One might want to argue that the results of Reicher (1969) and E. Smith and Haviland (1972) do not necessarily discredit Wheeler's Sophisticated Guessing model. It could be the case that in these studies the subject did not consider the experimentally given constraints until after he had executed his decision process. This argument, however, runs into problems for it predicts that in these paradigms there should not have been any effect of the constraints, yet such effects occurred. Alternatively, one could argue that the constraints affected a process prior to decision, but the implications of this are unclear. All of this is to concede that it would be premature to dismiss this model.

features in the extraction and matching processes. To make this theory manageable they use items printed in a special type font, such that each letter is composed entirely of straight lines of various orientations and lengths. Given this, it is possible to define a set of distinctive or functional features for each letter or word. To illustrate the processing assumptions in the model, consider the case where a word is presented. The Extraction stage follows Rumelhart's (1970) earlier formulation of letter perception and assumes a decaying visual iconic storage system from which features of letter positions are extracted. In addition, the probability of extracting a particular functional feature, given that it appears in the word presented, increases with the length of the physical line segment that represents it. Once the features have been extracted, a matching process ensues. Here the set of functional features extracted, F, is matched to feature descriptions of stored word categories, exactly as in F. Smith's (1971) formulation. This matching process often fails to yield a unique categorization of the stimulus and instead produces a set of word categories as likely candidates for the categorization of the stimulus. The subject's task is now to make a decision among these candidates and Rumelhart and Siple offer an explicit rule on which to base this decision. To understand the rule, some terms must be defined: r_i is the correct response for stimulus s_1, $P(s_i)$ is the subject's *a priori* probability that s_i will be presented, and $C(F)$ corresponds to the members of the candidate set where these members are now being viewed as possible responses. Given this, the decision rule is presented in Eq. (2):

$$P(r_i) = \begin{cases} P(s_i) & C(F) = \phi \\ \\ \dfrac{P(F/s_i)P(s_i)}{\Sigma P(F/s_j)P(s_j)} & r_i \subset C(F) \text{ and } C(F) \neq \phi \\ \\ 0 & r_i \not\subset C(F) \text{ and } C(F) \neq \phi. \end{cases} \qquad (2)$$

Thus, only the alternatives consistent with the extracted features are considered as possible response candidates, i.e., $P(r_i) = 0$ when $r_i \not\subset C(F)$ and $C(F) \neq \phi$; in the absence of suitable information the subject guesses in accordance with his *a priori* or subjective probability, i.e., $P(r_i) = P(s_i)$ when $C(F) = \phi$; and when suitable information is available, the subject chooses his response in accordance with a Bayesian rule, i.e.,

$$P(r_i) = \frac{P(F/s_i)P(s_i)}{\Sigma P(F/s_j)\,P(s_j)} \qquad \text{when } r_i \subset C(F) \text{ and } C(F) \neq \phi.$$

The Rumelhart and Siple model goes beyond that of F. Smith in two ways. First, it posits a decision process, subsequent to matching, that emphasizes subjective probabilities and that permits the model to predict certain frequency effects that have not yet been considered. Second, it defines the functional features of letters and words, and this permits the model to give explicit quantitative predictions about differential perceptibility for different types of items. However, it is worth emphasizing that the present model would explain the word-nonword difference in exactly the same manner as Smith's model, i.e., higher-order units may be used for matching words while nonwords are generally matched on a letter-by-letter basis.

Rumelhart and Siple have been able to test their model, particularly the decision component, against data collected from human subjects in a variety of tasks, by simulating various experimental situations by computer. The initial test of the model involved the comparison of computer and human data on a task requiring recognition of three-letter sequences. These three-letter items could be either words, nonsense syllables, or strings of unrelated letters, and the human subjects were required to make a three-letter full report of each item after it was presented tachistoscopically. Of particular interest were a set of findings summarized by Broadbent (1967) that related the subjects' tachistoscopic accuracy and the word frequency of the stimuli in printed English. In one test of the model, error responses for both the computer and human data were classified according to the frequency in printed English of the actual stimulus and the frequency of the response. It was found that for both the model and human subjects, the frequency class of an erroneous response depended on the frequency class of the actual stimulus, due to a tendency for subjects to give somewhat more high-frequency error responses to high-frequency stimuli than to low-frequency stimuli. The model had similar success in predicting the distribution of correct responses across categories defined by frequency, letter predictability, and letter confusability. For both the humans and the simulated data, performance tended to increase with increasing string frequency, increasing letter predictability, and decreasing letter confusability. In a second simulation of frequency effects in perception the model predicted that with words as stimuli, words having intermediate frequency of occurrence in English would be better reported if they also contained improbable letter sequences. This finding is in line with the data collected by Broadbent and Gregory (1968).

While the above constitutes an impressive array of predicted effects, it should be noted that most of these effects have been obtained only in total-report paradigms, and some of these effects to do not occur in better-designed perceptual experiments. For example, the frequency effect completely disappears when a forced-choice paradigm is used (e.g., Baron & Thurston, 1973; Pierce, 1963). Hence some of the above simulated effects may well reflect guessing or report biases. The reason why Rumelhart and Siple predict these effects so well seems to be that the locus of these effects in the model is the decision process, and it may be that this process really represents an implementation of a report strategy rather than a perceptual decision process.

The Feature Redundancy model of Rumelhart and Siple does, however, predict one interesting effect that clearly appears to be perceptual. This is the finding by Reicher (1969) and Wheeler (1970) that tachistoscopic recognition accuracy is greater for a letter in a word than a letter presented alone. Rumelhart and Siple, as well as F. Smith, predict this effect because of the feature redundancy present in word categories. Recall that this feature redundancy is such that in many positions of a word, the number of matching features needed for categorization of the word is less than that needed to categorize the component letter. However, successful prediction of the Reicher-Wheeler effect may turn out to be more a liability than an asset for the Feature Redundancy models, for two recent experiments (Johnston & McClelland 1973; Mezrich, 1973) have shown that the effect in question actually reverses when slight changes are made in the paradigm. But this is not the most severe problem for Feature Redundancy models. Rather, the greatest difficulty for such models arises when one considers how they deal with the effects of pronounceability and approximation-to-English on the perceptibility of nonwords. It is time to treat these problems in depth.

Problems with feature redundancy models. Although the Feature Redundancy models of F. Smith and of Rumelhart and Siple are successful in predicting the word-nonword difference and numerous frequency effects, several issues, both logical and empirical, cause problems for this type of model. First, by assuming that words, and not single letters, are the categories to which input feature-information must be matched, these models require that complete feature descriptions of every word in the subject's vocabulary be maintained in memory. The problem is magnified by the fact that subjects can easily identify words in a variety of type fonts, and this requires that a complete feature description of each item be maintained for every type font the subject is likely to encounter. The problem is further confounded by the beneficial effects of pronounceability and orthographic structure on the perceptibility of nonwords. Such results indicate that the so-called word-nonword difference is really a matter of degree. This creates problem for the Feature Redundancy models, which assume that the difference in question is an all-or-none phenomenon. For these models imply that either a feature set of the input exists in memory, making perceptual performance quite good, or no such set exists and performance is quite poor. In other words, if feature redundancy is incorporated only at the level of a word, then there is no room in the model for gradations between nonwords.

F. Smith (1971) has attempted to counter the problem raised by continuous variations in the perceptibility of nonwords. He argues that a Feature Redundancy model can account for these results by inserting another process in the Interpretation stage for cases where an immediate match cannot be made on the basis of visual features alone. This extra process involves, in part, determining the pronunciation of the input item, and Smith calls this ''mediated identification'' to contrast it with the direct identification that is possible for most words. The mediation process is assumed to proceed more rapidly for items that closely resemble the structure of English, thus making them easier to identify. However, no matter how rapid the mediation process, it would clearly be the case that performance based on a mediated identification should be poorer than performance based on a nonmediated or direct identification, since less processing is necessary in the latter case. Hence the critical prediction is that there should be some perceptual advantage of words over nonwords, even for the best of all possible nonwords. This prediction has been disconfirmed in an important series of studies by Baron and Thurston (1973). These authors used two types of tasks. In one, right after the termination of a briefly presented word or nonword, four alternatives (words or nonwords) were presented, and the subject indicated which alternative had been presented. In the other task, after termination of a briefly presented test word or nonword, the subject indicated which of four alternative letter pairs corresponded to the first and last letters of the test item; here the alternatives remained constant throughout the experiment. Both types of experiments included nine subjects and at least 1000 trials per subject, and both indicated that nonwords that conformed to the orthographic and phonological rules of English were perceived as accurately as words. These results not only disconfirm a prediction from Smith's model but further highlight the logical problem encountered by the Feature Redundancy models. In order for such models to incorporate the Baron and Thurston result, the modelers would have to assume that subjects have complete feature descriptions in their memories for pronounceable nonwords that they have never seen before!

Feature redundancy in other higher-order units. The major difficulty with the Feature Redundancy models we have just described seems to lie in the fact that the categories to which input must be matched are entire words. This gives these models a certain inflexibility in handling the Baron and Thurston (1973) results or the results obtained on approximation-to-English. An alternative is to assume that the categories stored in memory are not words but some smaller linguistic unit that could be used equally easily in identifying both meaningful and nonsense items. One such unit has been suggested by Gibson (1965), and it is called the spelling pattern. A spelling pattern was originally defined as a group of letters that has an invariant pronunciation in English, given its position (e.g., beginning or end of word) within a word and the letters surrounding it. In the nonsense string GLURCK, the groupings GL, UR, and CK form three spelling patterns because they can be assigned pronunciations in English, while in the string CKURGL, the CK and the GL are no longer spelling patterns because they cannot be pronounced in the positions in which they appear. Gibson and her associates have shown that the presence of spelling patterns improves the subject's ability to name nonsense items, decreases his latency in naming the item, and improves his tachistoscopic accuracy in reporting or recognizing the item (Gibson, Osser, & Pick, 1963; Gibson et al., 1962).

More recent work by Gibson (Gibson, Shurcliff, & Yonas, 1970) makes it clear that the spelling pattern is intended as a visual unit. Thus one could propose a Feature Redundancy model that is basically the same as that of F. Smith (1971) or Rumelhart and Siple (1974), except that the unit of the matching process is a spelling pattern rather than a word. Though such a model has not been explicitly proposed, it is compatible with Gibson et al.'s (1970) arguments and merits some consideration. The model is consistent with at least some of the studies reporting a perceptual superiority of words over unpronounceable nonwords. This is because many words tend to contain more multi-letter spelling patterns than unpronounceable nonwords and consequently there are fewer units to be matched in a word than a nonword. Similarly, this model might, in some cases, also be able to predict the perceptual equality of words and pronounceable nonwords, since the two types of items might be identical with respect to spelling patterns. This model could also explain the approximation-to-English effects, since as this variable increases there is an increasing tendency for multiletter spelling patterns to occur in the string. It is unclear, however, how this model would handle the word-letter effect obtained by Reicher (1969) and Wheeler (1970) or the frequency-type effects simulated by Rumelhart and Siple (1974). But, as mentioned earlier, these effects are not very robust and, consequently, are not of crucial importance in evaluating the model.

Two possible criticisms of this type of spelling-pattern model may be raised, one empirical and the other logical. The empirical problem is that while a spelling pattern is defined in terms of orthographic and phonological rules, it may reflect nothing more exotic than simple letter-cluster frequency (Anisfeld, 1964). Gibson et al. (1970) have presented strong evidence against this frequency interpretation. They determined tachistoscopic report accuracy for nonwords containing only multiletter spelling patterns (e.g., GLURCK) and those that did not (e.g., CKURGL) and showed that simple frequency counts of bigram and trigram frequencies were relatively poor predictors of performance.

The logical difficulty with the type of spelling-pattern model that we have been considering is more severe. The problem is that this model assumes that humans are capable of parsing letter-strings into spelling-pattern units before the letters have been categorized. For if recognition of an item involves matching incoming feature information with stored spelling-pattern descriptions, the subject must have some means of determining which letter positions are to be compared to the stored categories before any categorization of the input has taken place. This parsing problem was noted and discussed by Neisser (1967). He suggested that a subject's expectancies may provide a basis for parsing an as yet uncategorized item into structural units, and Aderman and Smith (1971) provided evidence for this role of expectancy. However, expectancy is a very limited solution to the parsing problem because it is out of the question for a reader to have an explicit structural expectancy about every word he will encounter. What is needed is a general solution to the parsing problem, and this would consist of a set of rules which could parse any input string into spelling patterns before the letters are categorized. No such set exists, and it is not at all clear how such a set could be defined.[9]

There is an alternative to spelling patterns as visual categories that still allows the subject to use units smaller than an entire word and also offers the needed set of parsing rules. This is a Feature Redundancy model in which syllables form the basic higher-order visual categories. Spoehr and E. Smith (1973) have demonstrated that syllables do form an effective unit in the perception of written material and have

---

[9]Note that the kind of parsing problem we have been discussing is severe whenever one posits that the unit of either the extraction or matching process is larger than a letter but smaller than a word. In those cases where the relevant units are either single letters or words, the parsing process may utilize either inter-letter or inter-word spaces in its operation, and here there will be less ambiguity in determining which part of the input is to be matched against stored categories.

proposed a parsimonious set of parsing rules that can be used to divide any letter string into syllable-like units. These parsing rules, which will later be considered in detail, represent an improvement over the spelling-pattern approach but leave a certain amount to be desired. The problem with these parsing rules is that, although the subject does not have to categorize every letter before making his parse, he must be able to discriminate between the vowels and the consonants in the string. It may be possible to do this on the basis of a few gross features (such as the fact that most lower-case vowels are round), but the relevant experimental evidence indicates that a vowel-consonant distinction cannot be made until after the letters have been categorized (Posner, 1970).[10]

Let us summarize our main points about Feature Redundancy models. Two such models (F. Smith, 1971; Rumelhart & Siple, 1974) assume that the word is the basic higher-order unit for matching and that the feature redundancy in words permits them to be perceived more readily than nonwords. While these models have some strong points in their favor, they run into troubles when confronting perceptibility variations in nonwords. We suggested that one resolution of these difficulties would be to maintain the basic Feature Redundancy model but with the spelling pattern as the unit of matching, rather than the word. This suggestion led to a parsing problem which remains unresolved. Finally we noted that the parsing problem can be ameliorated if one replaces the spelling unit with a syllable unit, but that some serious parsing difficulties still remain.

Interpretation-type Models: Higher-order Translation Units

All of the models treated thus far consider only visual characteristics in arriving at an interpretation of the input. As a consequence, these models ignore an important property of the English orthographic system: the fact that it is alphabetic rather than ideographic or syllabic. This means that a reader of English does not have to learn separate characters for each word or even each syllable in the written language, as is implied by the Feature Redundancy models, but can get from the orthographic representation of the language to a phonological representation by employing a relatively small set of spelling-to-sound correspondence rules that map individual letters or letter clusters into phonemes (Venezky, 1967). In view of the alphabetic nature of English, both linguists (e.g., Mattingly, 1972) and psychologists (e.g., Sperling, 1967) have suggested that, when faced with a visual input in a reading or word-recognition task, English readers regularly translate letter strings into an acoustic or phonological code during the process of word perception. The assumption that such a grapheme-phoneme translation process takes place in word perception is in agreement with the evidence suggesting that short-term memory storage is acoustical in nature (e.g., Conrad, 1964) and the evidence showing that lexical information can be accessed on the basis of a phonological code (Banks & McCarthy, 1972). But

---

[10]It is possible that some of the parsing problems we have discussed would be eliminated if one adopted an analysis-by-synthesis approach (e.g., Neisser, 1967) to word perception. However, at the present time the synthesis approach to visual word perception is still a pregnant metaphor rather than a systematic theory, and for this reason we do not develop the synthesis argument further.

such findings in no way require that the translation process occur during word perception, as translation could be part of a subsequent short-term memory system. So it is first necessary to demonstrate that some truly perceptual effects implicate a translation process.

Evidence for higher-order translation units and a Spelling Pattern model. At this point we will not introduce new findings that necessitate a translation process, but rather argue that such a process is consistent with findings already noted. Specifically, many of the perceptual findings that we have mentioned in this section can be summarized by a simple generalization that implicates a translation process—perceptual performance on a letter string increases as the pronounceability of that string increases. This generalization "explains" the following results: (*a*) Words are more perceptible than unpronounceable nonwords (e.g., E. Smith & Haviland, 1972); (*b*) completely pronounceable nonwords are as perceptible as words and more perceptible than unpronounceable nonwords (Baron & Thurston, 1973); (*c*) the perceptibility of a letter string increases as the string increasingly approximates the structure of English (e.g., Mewhort, 1967), since more structured letter strings are inevitably more pronounceable; and (*d*) the perceptibility of a string is greater if the string contains multi-letter spelling patterns than if it does not (Gibson et al., 1962), since pronounceability has been shown to increase with the presence of spelling patterns. Thus, in some respects, the simplest theoretical route to follow is to construct a word-perception model that explicitly takes pronounceability into account by positing a translation process.

To illustrate how a translation process would explain some of these findings, let us consider a model suggested by the early work of Gibson et al. (1962). In this model, the Extraction stage would operate on the features of a letter. In the subsequent Interpretation stage, the component letters are first matched to single-letter categories and next grouped or parsed into spelling patterns. These spelling patterns are then translated into a phonological representation, unit-by-unit. It follows directly from this model that the effect of spelling patterns in the Gibson et al. (1962) studies is the result of translation processing. That is, if the input string can be parsed into a small number of multi-letter spelling patterns, the translation process will have only a few higher-order units to operate on, and perceptual performance will be relatively good. On the other hand, if the input string must be given its acoustical encoding in a letter-by-letter fashion, as in the case where no multi-letter spelling patterns can be formed from the string, the translation process will have more units to operate on, and perceptual performance will be relatively poor. The other pronounceability findings are similarly explicable to the extent that pronounceability variations can be well-described by spelling-pattern variations.

One point that should be stressed about this type of model is that parsing and translation follow letter-by-letter matching of the input string. This circumvents one of the principal objections to the assumption of spelling patterns as processing units namely, the lack of a realistic parsing process. By first identifying the individual letters, the subject has the information he needs to employ a general parsing system that divides the input string into higher-order units like spelling patterns or syllables, where such units now become the input to a translation process. The only translation-based model of word perception that incorporates such a general-purpose parsing system is the Vocalic Center Group model proposed by Spoehr and Smith (1973).

Higher-order translation units and the Vocalic Center Group Model. In the Vocalic Center Group (VCG) model, Spoehr and Smith (1973) assume that when a word is presented, features of each letter position are first extracted and then matched to individual letter categories. The categorized information is then placed in a sensory store. The function of this store is to maintain the visual information long enough for some orthographically dependent parsing process to segment the letter string into higher-order units, called VCGs, so that a subsequent translation process can assign an acoustical code to each unit. It is not until the translation process is completed that perceptual processing is assumed to be over.

The critical ingredients of this model are the VCGs and the parsing process that produces them. Both of these notions are based on the work of Hansen and Rogers (1965). A VCG is defined as a letter sequence that contains one vocalic element, a single vowel or a dipthong, and from zero to three consonants or semi-consonantal elements preceding or following the vocalic element. This unit, which is quite similar to a syllable, was derived from the speech-production work of Liberman and his associates at Haskins Laboratory (Liberman, Ingran, Lisker, Delattre, & Cooper, 1959). Their work suggests that a VCG is the smallest pronunciational unit within which all of the phonemic constraints can be fully specified, and this makes a VCG a very reasonable unit for a translation process. The parsing process that generates these VCGs is presented in Table 3. To see how the parsing rules operate, let us take the word PARSING and apply the rules in Table 3 to it.

Under Rule 1, we first mark the positions of the vowels, the A and the I in this example. Aplying Rule 2, we group the initial P with the A, and the final NG with the I. This leaves only the medial consonant cluster, RS, to be parsed. Since the pattern of internal vowels and consonants is VCCV, we apply Rule 3b to the RS and

TABLE 3
Vocalic Center Group Parsing Process

Rule 1.	Mark Positions of Vowels
Rule 2.	Unitize Initial Consonant(s) with Initial Vowel and Final Consonant(s) with Final Vowel
Rule 3.	Parse Intermediate Consonant(s) According to Following:

a. . . .	VCV	. . .	$\longrightarrow$	. . . V + CV . . .
b. . . .	VCCV	. . .	$\longrightarrow$	. . . VC + CV . . .
c. . . .	VCCCV	. . .	$\longrightarrow$	. . . VC + CCV . . .

Rule 4.	If Previous Rules Yield an Inappropriate Result, Reparse Intermediate Consonant(s) According to the Following:

a. . . .	VCV	. . .	$\longrightarrow$	. . . VC + V . . .
b. . . .	VCCV	. . .	$\longrightarrow$	. . . V + CCV . . .
c. . . .	VCCCV	. . .	$\longrightarrow$	. . . V + CCCV . . .

get the division PAR plus SING, where both units constitute VCGs. The only other aspect of the parsing rules that deserves mention is that reparsing rules are also included in Table 3. These reparsing rules, summarized under Rule 4, were intended for the cases where Rule 3 produces VCGs that do not match a stored phonological code for a word, but thus far it appears that they have little import for word perception (see Spoehr & Smith, 1973).

We turn now to evidence for this VCG model. Perhaps the simplest prediction is that any letter string that forms a single VCG should be better perceived than one that does not. In particular, a nonword that forms a VCG (e.g., BLOST) should be more perceptible than a comparable string without the vowel (e.g., BLST), for the former string can be translated as a single unit while the latter may have to be translated on a letter-by-letter basis. Spoehr and Smith (1972) have confirmed this prediction in a tachistoscopic recognition-accuracy task. A similar prediction from the model concerns only words. It is that words containing only one VCG should be better perceived than those containing two VCGs. (For many cases this amounts to the prediction that one-syllable words should be better perceived than two-syllable words.) Again, Spoehr and Smith (1973) have confirmed this prediction in a tachistoscopic recognition task. In another experiment, a total-report tachistoscopic procedure was used to compare words that varied with respect to the number of VCGs they contained. A detailed analysis of the results indicated that the perceptual accuracy scores for two successive letters were more correlated if the letters were both part of the same VCG than if they were drawn from two different VCGs. This result suggests that a VCG is indeed treated as something of a perceptual whole, but the result must be interpreted with caution since it was obtained in the artifact-prone, total-report paradigm.

The above results were all obtained in experiments explicitly designed to test the VCG model, but the model is also consistent with most of the previously mentioned findings in this section. The reader will recall that we were able to summarize these findings by the generalization that pronounceability enhances perceptibility. In terms of the VCG model, some of these pronounceability findings can be explained by the number of translation units created by the unitization or parsing process. Thus the unpronounceable nonwords used in many experiments (e.g., Baron & Thurston, 1973; E. Smith & Haviland, 1972) did not contain vowels, and this would explain why they were less perceptible than either words or pronounceable nonwords. But other pronounceability findings (e.g., Gibson et al., 1962) cannot be explained in this fashion, since both pronounceable and unpronounceable arrays contained vowels and formed comparable numbers of VCGs. To explain such results we need to consider some aspect of the model other than the number of VCGs. This other aspect is the ease with which the translation process can be applied to various types of strings. Specifically, we assume that the more the input string conforms to the phonological rules of English, the faster the translation process operates.

Spoehr and Smith (1972) provide some experimental results that bear on the above assumption. Using a tachistoscopic recognition task, they compared performance on three types of items: (*a*) consonant strings, (*b*) unpronounceable nonwords that contained a vowel but violated some phonological rules, and (c) pronounceable nonwords. Both the unpronounceable and the pronounceable nonwords contained a single VCG. Hence considerations based only on the number of translation units would predict that both these types of items should be better perceived than the consonant strings, and this prediction was confirmed. However, if one further considers conformity to phonological rules, there is the prediction that the pronounceable items should be better perceived than their unpronounceable counterparts, and this prediction was also confirmed. (While we have interpreted these results in terms of the VCG model, we should point out that they can also be considered as simple demonstrations of the generalization that perceptibility increases with pronounceability.)

In addition to the empirical base for the model, Spoehr (1973) has provided support for it in a computer simulation called EYEBALL. EYEBALL, a computer program written in LISP, is composed of three principle routines which correspond to the (a) feature extraction plus matching processes, (b) unitization or parsing process, and (c) translation process, in the original model. Input to EYEBALL is in the form of a feature matrix containing the visual features of each letter in the input string along with positional information. The first processing routine of the program extracts feature information from the input array in a completely parallel manner and then categorizes each letter position according to a Pandemonium-type (Selfridge & Neisser, 1960) best-guess strategy. The identified visual forms are stored in the sensory store and allowed to decay in an exponential fashion (Rumelhart, 1970) while the VCG parsing rules are applied to form higher-order units. The translation process of the current simulation assigns phonemes to letters on a one-to-one basis, and the resulting phonemic code is used as the output.

EYEBALL has been successful in duplicating the effects found in human data which are explained primarily through parsing mechanisms. For example, Table 4 shows the performance of EYEBALL on the one- and two-syllable words presented to actual subjects by Spoehr and Smith (1973). The simulated data are in close agreement with the obtained data also shown in Table 4, and statistical tests show no significant differences between the two. EYEBALL performs equally well in simulating the word-nonword effect. In this case (see Table 5) a comparison was made between the simulated and human data on the word and nonword items used by E. Smith and Haviland (1972). As Table 5 indicates there was again a close correspondence between the two sets of data.

However, one major short-coming of EYEBALL, and of the VCG model in general, is that the mechanisms by which the translation process forms a phonological code are poorly specified. The EYEBALL solution of assigning phonemes to letters on a one-to-one basis is obviously simplistic since some phonemes in English are represented orthographically as a cluster of letters. Even in cases where a single letter corresponds to a single phoneme in the acoustic encoding of a string, the letters around it will determine which phoneme it represents (e.g., the letter A in the words HAT and HATE is mapped into different phonemes), and this type of consideration does not even enter into EYEBALL.

TABLE 4
Comparison[a] of EYEBALL Simulation and Obtained Data[b]

	One-syllable words		Two-syllable words	
Letter position	Obtained data	EYEBALL	Obtained data	EYEBALL
1	.69	.69	.62	.64
2	.74	.69	.69	.66
3	.70	.71	.62	.64
4	.69	.68	.63	.61
5	.69	.66	.65	.65

[a] Comparison is in terms of probability of a correct letter report as a function of letter position in one- and two-syllable words.
[b] Obtained data are from Spoehr and Smith (1973), Experiment II.

TABLE 5
Another Comparison[a] of EYEBALL Simulation and Obtained Data[b]

Words vs Nonwords	Before rule-learning[c]		After rule-learning[c]	
	Subjects	EYEBALL	Subjects	EYEBALL
Words	.75	.76	.85	.82
Nonwords	.68	.69	.78	.76

[a] Comparison is in terms of probability of a correct letter recognition for redundant words and nonwords.
[b] Obtained data are from E. Smith and Haviland (1972), Experiment I.
[c] Midway through this experiment, subjects learned rules that equated the words and nonwords for redundancy.

Even given a workable translation process, the VCG model, like all other models of word perception, has its problems. The basic problem for the VCG model is that translation may not be an obligatory process for accurate perception of visually presented language materials. Introspective reports during reading indicate that people frequently access the meaning of items on the basis of purely visual information, without being aware of constructing any phonological code. In addition, there are results by Gibson et al. (1970) which show that deaf subjects make as much use of spelling patterns in perceiving letter strings as do hearing subjects, even though deaf subjects presumably know less about the relationship between spelling regularities and the spoken form of the language. Furthermore, Baron and Thurston (1973) present evidence that subjects were just as good at deciding which member of a pair of homophones had been presented tachistoscopically as they were at deciding which of a pair of non-homophones had been presented. If subjects had been constructing an acoustic code as a means of recognizing the items in this experiment, they should have made more mistakes when given alternatives that sounded alike. Of course the latter argument assumes that a subject discards his visual categorization once he has translated it into an acoustic one, and this assumption may be erroneous. But in any event, there does seem to be some evidence accumulating that acoustic encoding need not be employed by subjects in order to perform word-recognition tasks, and this constitutes the basic drawback of the VCG model.

Overview of the Models

We have argued throughout that word-perception models can be classified by the assumptions they make about processing units, and a summary of this classification is presented in Table 6. Most Extraction-based models assume that features of an entire word or of a spelling regularity may be extracted, and hence they posit a unit of Extraction that is larger than the feature of a single letter. This implies that Extraction-type models further assume that the unit of the matching process is also larger than a single letter, else it would make little sense to extract higher-order features. Turning to Interpretation-based proposals, the Feature Redundancy models of F. Smith (1971) and Rumelhart and Siple (1972) assume that the unit of Extraction is the feature of a letter while the unit of the matching process is a word. Other variants of the Feature Redundancy model differ only in that they posit a unit of matching that is larger than a letter but smaller than a word, for example, spelling patterns. In contrast, in the Sophisticated Guessing model suggested by Wheeler (1970), processing units larger than a letter only play a role in a decision process that follows the matching process. Similarly, in translation models like a spelling-pattern translation model or the VCG proposal of Spoehr and Smith (1973), higher-order units only become operative after matching has been completed and parsing and translation processes commence.

The above demonstrates that the models may be classified with respect to their different assumptions about processing units, but these differences should not obscure what is the fundamental commonality among all the models. All word-perception models assume that at least one processing unit is larger than a letter, and then use this assumption to explain most of the basic effects obtained in word-perception tasks.

Perceptual Strategies

If word-perception models are basically correct in explaining findings via higher-order processing units, it stands to reason that these findings should be eliminated if the subject can be induced to use only individual letters or their features as units. We shall refer to a shift from a higher-order unit to a single-letter unit as a change in perceptual strategy, and we now present evidence that such a strategy change leads to an elimination of the basic word-perception findings.

One study that clearly demonstrates this strategy change is Aderman and Smith's (1971) investigation of the spelling-pattern effect. Aderman and Smith manipulated the subject's strategy by manipulating his expectancy in a recognition-accuracy task. One group of subjects was led to expect only spelling-pattern items, which should have fostered the strategy of using higher-order units. These subjects showed the typical finding of better performance on spelling-pattern items than on items contain-

TABLE 6
Assumed Processing Units for the Various Perceptual Processes

Models	Processes			
	Extraction	Matching	Decision	Translation
Extraction-based	Features of word or spelling regularity	Word or spelling regularity		
Feature redundancy (F. Smith, 1971; Rumelhart & Siple, 1974)	Features of a letter position	Word (or other stored category)	Word (or other stored category)	
Other variants of feature redundancy	Features of a letter position	Spelling regularity		
Sophisticated guessing (Wheeler, 1972)	Features of a letter position	Letter	Word	
Spelling-pattern translation (Gibson et al., 1962)	Features of a letter position	Letter		Spelling Pattern
VCG translation (Spoehr & Smith, 1973)	Features of a letter position	Letter		VCG

ing unrelated letters. A second group of subjects, however, was led to expect items consisting of unrelated letters, and this should have induced a strategy of using individual letters as processing units. For the latter subjects there was no spelling-pattern effect. These results support the notions that the typical spelling-pattern effect is due to higher-order processing units and that a strategy change to a smaller processing unit can eliminate the effect.

This type of strategy change can also explain some interesting results of Hershenson (1969, 1972). In these studies, Hershenson has shown that the approximation-to-English and spelling-pattern effects can be reduced or eliminated by means of certain procedures. These procedures have included familiarizing the subject with the test items (sometimes the subject even knows exactly what item will be presented) and emphasizing accurate perception of individual letters. It is quite possible that these procedures, which emphasize the individual letters in an array, lead the subject to use a strategy in which processing units are individual letters. If this is the case, then one would expect the obtained reduction of the approximation-to-English and spelling-pattern effects. This same kind of explanation may also prove valuable in accounting for Gibson, Tenney, Baron, and Zaslow's (1972) recent failure to find a spelling-pattern effect in a search task where the target was always an individual letter, and in James and Smith's (1970) enigmatic lack of a word-nonword effect in a similar search task.[11]

This strategy argument can also be applied to recent studies of the Reicher-Wheeler effect by Massaro (1973) and Thompson and Massaro (1973). Under certain task conditions these investigations demonstrated a reversal of the Reicher-Wheeler

[11]The null results of Gibson et al. (1972) and James and Smith (1970) in the letter-search task may, however, depend on more than just unit size, as Kreuger (1970b) has found a word-nonword effect in such a task.

effect, that is, they found that a single letter was more perceptible than a letter in a word. To obtain this effect, Thompson and Massaro used only four critical letters, these letters either occurring alone or as the medial consonant in one of four word frames. This limited set of alternatives could have induced the subjects to attend mainly to the medial position in each word. Again, the nature of the critical task conditions was such as to foster a strategy in which processing units are individual letters, and given such processing units, the obtained results merely demonstrate the well-known finding that the accuracy of letter perception decreases with array size.

However, there are other reversals of the Reicher-Wheeler effect (noted previously) that cannot be explained by strategy changes that involve only a variation in unit size. Rather, recent experiments by Mezrich (1973) and Johnston and Mc-Clelland (1973) implicate strategy variations of a more fundamental nature. Mezrich noted that in the Reicher-Wheeler task subjects say they treat words as wholes and encode them as verbal or even meaningful units when they are presented. On the other hand, these same subjects report that the single-letter presentations lend themselves to being treated as visual patterns having no particular verbal or semantic characteristics. Thus it seems that subjects elect to use a strategy that encodes words as verbal units, but that makes decisions on the single letters on the basis of a nonverbal, pattern-match strategy. Mezrich attempted to eliminate the nonverbal strategy for single letters by requiring the subjects in a tachistoscopic recognition paradigm to vocalize (i.e., make a full report of) the entire stimulus before choosing one of the single letters in the forced-choice portion of the response procedure. Both the words and the individual letters therefore had to be processed via the verbal strategy. When performance was compared on the forced-choice recognitions for the words and single letters, the Reicher-Wheeler effect reversed. The Johnston and McClelland study provides additional evidence that the original Reicher-Wheeler effect was due to the use of a nonverbal strategy for the single letters. In this experiment, again a tachistoscopic recognition study, the experimenters simply removed the mask that typically follows presentation of an item and found that performance on words was no longer better than performance on single letters. They reasoned that a pattern mask is treated as a nonverbal form, and hence mainly masks those forms which were processed as purely visual forms, namely, the letters.

These experiments indicate that subjects have a range of perceptual strategies open to them, and that even what seems to be a minor procedural variation may have dramatic effects on the outcome of the experiment. If subjects are able to change their processing strategies as easily as these studies indicate, then we must be careful in assuming that there is only one correct model for word recognition. Rather, several of the models discussed in this section may be correct for certain situations. It may be for this reason that our review of the word-perception models was unable to come up with a model that would neatly fit all experimental findings. The task then remaining would be to specify the circumstances under which humans switch from one strategy or model to another.

PERCEPTION OF WORDS WITH CONTEXT

In moving from studies of letter perception to those of word perception we encountered a fundamental theoretical problem. Words, in contrast to unrelated letters, contained some extra information and our problem was one of how to relate or combine this extra information with the feature information offered by the input. This combination problem was solved by the notion of higher-order processing units. We now want to consider the effects of meaningful context on word perception, and once again we must confront a combination problem. In this case, context is providing a source of information beyond that involved in the perception of isolated words, and our major concern is how to combine the contextual and the perceptual information. In line with this concern, we will present some illustrative findings of the beneficial effects of context on the perception of single words, and then consider Morton's (1969) account of these findings in terms of his Logogen model.

Context Effects

A series of experiments performed about ten years ago (Morton, 1964; Tulving & Gold, 1963; Tulving, Mandler, & Baumel, 1964) document the effects of meaningful context on word perception. We can illustrate the basic findings by an examination of the Tulving and Gold study. Using a total-report accuracy task, these authors determined perceptual performance on a single target word, which had been preceded by either relevant or irrelevant contextual information of varying amounts. The contextual information was given prior to the tachistoscopic task. When relevant, it consisted of part of a sentence frame that could be finished with the target word; when irrelevant, it consisted of part of a sentence frame that was semantically incompatible with the target word. As examples, consider the target words COLLISION and RASPBERRY. Relevant contexts for COLLISION would be IN A TERRIBLE HIGHWAY (4-word context) or THREE PEOPLE WERE KILLED IN A TERRIBLE HIGHWAY (8-word context). These same two contexts would be considered irrelevant 4- and 8-word contexts for the target word RASPBERRY.

The main results of the Tulving and Gold study were simple: The perceptibility of the target word increased with the amount of relevant context, and decreased with the amount of irrelevant context (see also Tulving et al., 1964). A subsequent analysis of the Tulving and Gold data provides an additional finding of interest. The magnitude of the beneficial effect of relevant context on the target's perceptibility was predictable from the probability that a subject could correctly guess the target word given only the context. This later result suggests a simple guessing explanation of the main findings. That is, on some percentage of the trials the subject extracted and interpreted enough perceptual information to recognize the target word without the aid of context, while on the remaining trials he did not process a sufficient amount of perceptual information and so responded (guessed) on the basis of context alone. While such an explanation may be possible for the study at hand, a total-report task, the explanation seems far too simple to be of general use in understanding how readers utilize context in word perception. A far more interesting and potentially useful explanation of the Tulving and Gold results is offered by Morton's (1969) Logogen model.

The Logogen Model

The basic ingredient in the Logogen model is, unsurprisingly, the Logogen. A Logogen is a stored representation of a word which can accept inputs relevant to that word. More precisely, a Logogen is a device for accepting relevant perceptual (either visual or auditory) and contextual information about a word and combining these two sources of information so that their cumulative effect may be registered by some sort of internal counter. When the counter for a particular Logogen has tabulated a certain threshold amount of information, the word represented by the Logogen becomes available, from whence it may either emerge as an overt response or be transferred back to the Logogen as part of a rehearsal circuit.

Before considering how this model handles the context effects discussed earlier, let us flesh out more of the model's details, for this will make its relation to previously considered models more explicit. A Logogen for a particular word, e.g., MAN, may be characterized by three qualitatively different sets of features. First, there are the visual features for the word or its constituent letters; next, a set of defining acoustic features; and finally, a set of syntactic and semantic features. When the word MAN is presented visually some of its visual features will be extracted and allocated to the appropriate Logogen—the one which represents MAN—in exactly the same way that we have repeatedly described the extraction and matching of visual features. The matching features will increment the Logogen counter for MAN. If the word MAN had been preceded by some relevant context, e.g., HE WAS KIND TO THE DYING_____, then some syntactic and semantic features of MAN could have been derived from the context, and these features would also have had the effect of incrementing the counter for MAN. In this case, the resulting count would certainly be more likely to exceed the threshold than if MAN had not been preceded by context. Thus the processing of visual features is basically the same as that described in, for example, the Feature Redundancy model of the previous section, and what has been added is a device that allows the perceiver to combine his visual and contextual information.[12]

The above example shows how this model predicts the effect of context. When a target word is presented alone, the visual features available may not be sufficient to raise the Logogen's counter above threshold; but if this same target word had been preceded by a relevant context, then some syntactic and semantic features derived from the context would have already contributed to the target's Logogen's count. Tulving and Gold (1963) and Tulving et al. (1964) further reported that the beneficial

---

[12]The Logogen model can also be made consistent with a view of word perception based on translation processes. Here, it would be assumed that the Logogen for a word accepts only auditory and contextual information, and that visual inputs would be translated to acoustic form before their information could be accumulated with contextual sources.

effect of context increases with the amount of relevant context. This finding is consistent with the Logogen model because a longer relevant context should increase the number of semantic features that are derivable, which in turn should increase the counter for the target Logogen even more. Similarly, Tulving and Gold's reported correlation between the beneficial context effect on target word perceptibility and the probability of correctly guessing the target is also compatible with the Logogen model. The guessing probability may well measure how many of the target's semantic features can be obtained from the context, and, if so, this measure should be highly correlated with the perceptibility of the target in context. The only other finding to be explained is that the perceptibility of a target decreases with the amount of irrelevant context. This can be explained in terms of competing Logogens. The semantic features extracted from an irrelevant context raise the counts of some irrelevant Logogens for words other than the target, which makes these competing Logogens readily available as erroneous choices should they contain some visual features in common with the target.

Morton (1969) has further demonstrated how this model can handle some of these context effects in a quantitative manner. Using Morton's formulation, let P_s, P_c and P_{sc} represent the probability of a correct response to a target word, given only the stimulus, only the context, or both the stimulus and the context, respectively. Morton shows that,

$$\text{Logit } P_{sc} = \text{Logit } P_s + \text{Logit } P_c + \text{Log } (N-1), \tag{3}$$

where $\text{Logit } P_i = \text{Log } [P_i/(1\text{-}P_i)]$, and N equals the number of alternative responses available to a subject. Morton then proceeds to demonstrate that this equation provides an adequate fit to Tulving et al.'s (1964) obtained context results. In one way, Eq. (3) makes apparent the simplicity of the Logogen model, for it indicates that at a certain theoretical level, the contributions of perceptual and contextual information are independent. This constitutes a rather simple yet elegant solution to the problem of combining the two types of information.

Alternative Approaches to Context Effects

Other well-known approaches to understanding context effects in word perception (e.g., Kolers, 1970; Levin & Kaplan, 1970) are in marked contrast to the Logogen model. The Logogen model posits theoretical units (Logogens) the size of words, while other approaches (e.g., Levin & Kaplan, 1970) often call for larger syntactic units. Similarly the Logogen model assumes what some (Morton & Broadbent, 1967) have termed passive analysis of perceptual and contextual sources, whereas other approaches (e.g., Kolers, 1970) stress an active synthesis of these sources. Perhaps one reason for these differences is that investigators like Kolers and Levin and Kaplan have studied context effects in situations approximating real reading. That is, they have used paradigms in which the target item for report might be an entire sentence, and in which syntactic and semantic analysis is required in order for comprehension to take place. Thus they have been interested in the mutual contextual effects on all components of the sentence. It is possible that in such a situation the subject engages in more active perceptual processing and uses units larger than a word. However, it is at least equally possible that the data in such situations reflect processes other than just perception—for example, they may reflect comprehension processes—and it is the latter that are characterized by active synthesis of large units. In any event, there is little more we can say about this issue, given the present state of the art.

SUMMARY AND CONCLUSIONS

We began with a two-stage hypothesis of letter-string perception that distinguished between Extraction and Interpretation stages, where the latter includes the processes of matching, decision making, and translation. After providing some justification for our emphasis on feature-based processes, we used this two-stage hypothesis to structure our arguments about what constitutes an appropriate task for studying grapheme perception. With all of this as background, we reviewed the major models of letter perception. This review revealed the importance of our Extraction-Interpretation dichotomy, for it proved to be the major theoretical distinction among current models. Rumelhart's (1970) Limited Capacity model and Estes' (1972) Interactive Channels model both emphasized the Extraction stage in explaining certain key experimental results (e.g., the effects of array size on performance), while the Unlimited Capacity Model proposed by Gardner (1973) and others explained these results primarily by a decision process of the Interpretation stage. A consideration of additional data on confusability effects and sequential vs simultaneous presentation argued against Rumelhart's particular model, but did not resolve the Extraction vs Interpretation issue.

We also used the Extraction vs Interpretation distinction to organize our review of the word-perception models. We argued that while the letter-perception models generally assume that the units of Extraction and Interpretation are the size of individual letters or their features, models of word perception posit higher-order units for Extraction, Interpretation, or both. We first considered those word-perception models that explained basic effects (e.g., the perceptual difference between words and unpronounceable nonwords) by positing higher-order units of feature extraction. These models were treated only briefly because there is little supporting evidence for their assumption that words or spelling regularities have distinctive shape features beyond those of their constituent letters. We then turned our attention to Interpretation-based models. Here, the first model explored was Wheeler's (1970) variant of the Sophisticated Guessing model, which holds that higher-order units are operative only during the decision process. We indicated that certain experimental findings provide evidence against such a model. The next class of theories considered were the Feature Redundancy models. These models accounted for experimental findings by assuming that while extraction units were features of letter positions, the unit of the matching process was a word. Both F. Smith (1971) and Rumelhart and Siple (1974) proposed such models, and the latter model also included a decision process that mediated some well-known frequency effects.

We next argued that though these Feature Redundancy models of word perception are quite powerful in handling word-nonword and word-letter differences, there is a fundamental problem with them. They have difficulty in accounting for systematic differences among nonwords. To get around this difficulty, we explored Feature Redundancy models that assumed higher-order matching units that were smaller than a word, e.g., spelling patterns. This type of model soon encountered another critical problem, one of parsing the input's features so that they could be matched to the appropriate higher-order unit, and no simple solution to this problem was apparent. Lastly, we considered translation models which posit that higher-order units come into play only at the time of translation. We first illustrated such a model with spelling patterns as translation units, and then described Spoehr and Smith's (1973) VCG model. The latter model posits syllable-like units (VCGs) as translation units and offers an explicit parsing process for forming such units. While this model can handle much of the data on word perception, a fundamental problem for it is that not all situations may require a translation process. Thus, none of the models covered could handle all of the empirical effects, though the Feature Redundancy and translation models seemed to be the most promising. We suggested that this failure of the models might reflect the operation of perceptual strategies and showed how strategic changes in unit size could drastically affect the results obtained.

Finally, we dealt with some theoretical notions about how relevant, meaningful context facilitates word perception. The major formulation here is Morton's (1969) Logogen model, which was shown to be consistent with several well-documented context effects. This model is compatible with most of the word-perception models, but goes beyond them in specifying how perceptual and contextual information can be combined so as to produce a cumulative effect.

In conclusion, we have shown that our two-stage hypothesis, in conjunction with the notion of processing units of various sizes, is capable of describing a large number of empirical results and theoretical formulations. This capability argues for the generality of our approach to letter-string perception. However, this attempt at generality may have incurred some cost. For one thing, our characterization of specific models in terms of our two-stage hypothesis may sometimes obscure certain commonalities among the models. Another matter is that some of our postulated processes (i.e., decision and translation) may not strike a true perceptionist as "real" perceptual processes. But, in spite of these drawbacks, we have opted for generality in the hope (it is really little more than that) that this type of approach may yet provide a basis for a general model of how people perceive alphabetic material.

REFERENCES

Aderman, D., & Smith, E. E. Expectancy as a determinant of functional units in perceptual recognition. *Cognitive Psychology*, 1971, **2**, 117–129.

Anisfeld, M. A comment on "The Role of grapheme-phoneme correspondence in the perception of words." *American Journal of Psychology*, 1964, **77**, 320–326.

Atkinson, R. C., Holmgren, J. E., & Juola, J. F. Processing time as influenced by the number of elements in a visual display. *Perception & Psychophysics*, 1969, **6**, 321–326.

Baddeley, A. D. Immediate memory and the "perception" of letter sequences. *Quarterly Journal of Experimental Psychology*, 1964, **16**, 364–367.

Banks, W. P., & McCarthy, M. M. Acoustical confusions in visual word recognition. Paper presented at the meeting of the Psychonomic Society, St. Louis, November, 1972.

Baron, J., & Thurston, I. An analysis of the word-superiority effect. *Cognitive Psychology*, 1973, **4**, 207–228.

Beller, H. K. Parallel and serial stages in matching. *Journal of Experimental Psychology*, 1970, **84**, 213–219.

Bledsoe, W. W., & Browning, I. Pattern recognition and reading by machine. In L. Uhr (Ed.), *Pattern recognition*. New York: Wiley, 1966.

Broadbent, D. E. Word-frequency effect and response bias. *Psychological Review*, 1967, **74**, 1–15.

Broadbent, D. E., & Gregory, M. Visual perception of words differing in letter digram frequency. *Journal of Verbal Learning and Verbal Behavior*, 1968, **7**, 569–571.

Bruner, J. S. On perceptual readiness. *Psychological Review*, 1957, **64**, 123–152.

Cattell, J. M. The time taken up by cerebral operations. *Mind*, 1886, **11**, 220–242.

Chase, W. G., & Posner, M. I. The effect of visual and auditory confusability on visual and memory search tasks. Paper presented at the meeting of the Psychonomics Society, Chicago, October, 1965.

Connor, J. Effects of increased information load on the parallel processing of visual displays. *Perception & Psychophysics*, 1972, **12**, 121–128.

Conrad, R. Acoustic confusion in immediate memory. *British Journal of Psychology*, 1964, **55**, 75–84.

Corcoran, D. W. J., & Rouse, R. D. An aspect of perceptual organization involved in the perception of handwritten and printed words. *Quarterly Journal of Experimental Psychology*, 1970, **22**, 526–530.

Egeth, H. E., & Blecker, D. Differential effects of familiarity on judgements of sameness and difference. *Perception & Psychophysics*, 1971, **9**, 321–326.

Egeth, H. E., Jonides, J., & Wall, S. Parallel processing of multielement displays. *Cognitive Psychology*, 1972, **3**, 674–698.

Eichelman, W. H. Familiarity effects in the simultaneous matching task. *Journal of Experimental Psychology*, 1970, **86**, 275–282.

Eriksen, C. W., & Eriksen, B. A. Visual perceptual processing rates and backward and forward masking. *Journal of Experimental Psychology*, 1971, **89**, 306–313.

Eriksen, C. W., & Hoffman, J. E. Some characteristics of selective attention in visual perception determined by vocal reaction time. *Perception & Psychophysics*, 1972, **11**, 169–171.

Eriksen, C. W., Pollack, M. D., & Montague, W. E. Implicit speech: A mechanism in perceptual encoding? *Journal of Experimental Psychology*, 1970, **84**, 501–507.

Eriksen, C. W., & Spencer, T. Rate of information processing in visual perception: Some results and methodological considerations. *Journal of Experimental Psychology Monograph*, 1969, **79** (2, Pt. 2).

Estes, W. K. Interactions of signal and background variables in visual processing. *Perception & Psychophysics*, 1972, **12**, 278–286.

Estes, W. K., & Taylor, H. A. A detection method and probabilistic models for assessing information processing from brief visual displays. *Proceedings of the National Academy of Sciences*, 1964, **52**, 446–454.

Estes, W. K., & Wessel, D. L. Reaction time in relation to display size and correctness of response in forced-choice visual signal detection. *Perception & Psychophysics*, 1966, **1**, 369–373.

Gardner, G. T. Evidence for independent parallel channels in tachistoscopic perception. *Cognitive Psychology*, 1973, **4**, 130–155.

Garner, W. R., Hake, H. W., & Eriksen, C. W. Operationism and the concept of perception. *Psychological Review*, 1956, **63**, 149–159.

Gibson, E. J. Learning to read. *Science*, 1965, *148*, 1066–1072.

Gibson, E. J., Osser, H., & Pick, A. D. A study in the development of grapheme-phoneme correspondence. *Journal of Verbal Learning and Verbal behavior*, 1963, **2**, 142–146.

Gibson, E. J., Pick, A. D., Osser, H., & Hammond, M. The role of grapheme-phoneme correspondence in the perception of words. *American Journal of Psychology*, 1962, **75**, 554–570.

Gibson, E. J., Shurcliff, A., & Yonas, A. Utilization of spelling patterns by deaf and hearing subjects. In H. Levin & J. P. Williams (Eds.), *Basic studies on reading*. New York: Basic Books, 1970.

Gibson, E. J., Tenney, Y. J., Barron, R. W., & Zaslow, M. The effect of orthographic structure on letter search. *Perception & Psychophysics*, 1972, **11**, 183–186.

Hansen, D., & Rodgers, T. S. An exploration of psycholinguistic units in initial reading. In K. S. Goodman (Chm.), The psycholinguistic nature of the reading process. Symposium presented at Wayne State University, Detroit, May 1965.

Herman, L. M., & Kantowitz, B. H. The psychological refractory period effect: Only half the double stimulation story? *Psychological Bulletin*, 1970, **73**, 74–88.

Hershenson, M. Stimulus structure, cognitive structure, and the perception of letter arrays. *Journal of Experimental Psychology*, 1969, **79**, 327–335.

Hershenson, M. Verbal report and visual matching latency as a function of the pronounceability of letter arrays. *Journal of Experimental Psychology*, 1972, **96**, 104–109.

Hubel, D. H., & Wiesel, T. N. Receptive fields, binocular interaction and functional architecture in the cat's visual cortex. *Journal of Physiology*, 1962, **160**, 106–154.

Hubel, D. H., & Wiesel, T. N. Shape and arrangement of columns of cat's striate cortex. *Journal of Physiology*, 1963, **165**, 559–568.

Hubel, D. H., & Wiesel, T. N. Receptive fields and functional architecture of monkey striate cortex. *Journal of Physiology*, 1965, **195**, 215–243.

Huey, E. B. *The psychology and pedogogy of reading*. Cambridge, Mass.: MIT Press, 1968. (Originally published: MacMillan Co., 1908.)

James, C. T., & Smith, D. E. Sequential dependencies in letter search. *Journal of Experimental Psychology*, 1970, **85**, 56–60.

Johnston, J. C., & McClelland, J. L. Visual factors in word perception. *Perception & Psychophysics*, 1973, **14**, 365–370.

Jonides, J., & Gleitman, H. A conceptual category effect in visual search: 0 as letter or digit. *Perception & Psychophysics*, 1972, **12**, 457–460.

Keele, S. W. *Attention and human performance*. California: Goodyear, 1973.

Keele, S. W., & Chase, W. G. Short term visual storage. *Perception & Psychophysics*, 1967, **2**, 383–386.

Klapp, S. T., Anderson, W. G., & Berrian, R. W. Implicit speech in reading reconsidered. *Journal of Experimental Psychology*, 1973, **100**, 368–374.

Kohlers, P. A. Three stages of reading. In H. Levin & J. P. Williams (Eds.), *Basic studies on reading*. New York: Basic Books, 1970.

Kreuger, L. E. Search time in a redundant visual display. *Journal of Experimental Psychology*, 1970, **83**, 391–399. (2)

Kreuger, L. E. Visual comparison in a redundant display. *Cognitive Psychology*, 1970, **1**, 341-357. (b)

Levin, H., & Kaplan, E. L. Grammatical structure and reading. In H. Levin & J. P.Williams (Eds.), *Basic studies on reading*. New York: Basic Books, 1970.

Liberman, A. M., Ingram, F., Lisker, L., Delattre, P., & Cooper, F. S. Minimal rules for synthesizing speech. *Journal of the Acoustical Society of America* 1959, **31**, 1490–1499.

Lindsay, P. H., & Norman, D. A. *Human information processing: An introduction to psychology*. New York: Academic Press, 1972.

Massaro, D. W. Perception of letters, words, and nonwords. *Journal of Experimental Psychology*, 1973, **100**, 349–353.

Mattingly, I. G. Reading, the linguistic process, and linguistic awareness. In J. F. Kavanagh & I. G. Mattingly (Eds.), *Language by ear and by eye: The relationships between speech and reading*. Cambridge, Mass.: MIT Press, 1972.

Mewhort, D. J. K. Familiarity of letter sequences, response uncertainty, and the tachistoscopic recognition experiment. *Canadian Journal of Psychology*, 1967, **21**, 309–321.

Mezrich, J. J. The word superiority effect in brief visual displays: Elimination by vocalization. *Perception & Psychophysics*, 1973, **13**, 45–48.

Miller, G. A., Bruner, J. S., & Postman, L. Familiarity of letter sequences and tachistoscopic identification. *Journal of General Psychology*, 1954, **50**, 129–139.

Morton, J. The effects of context on the visual duration threshold for words. *British Journal of Psychology*, 1964, **55**, 165–180.

Morton, J. Interaction of information in word recognition. *Psychological Review*, 1969, **76**, 165–178.

Morton, J., & Broadbent, D. E. Passive vs. active recognition models or Is your homunculus really necessary? In W. Wathen-Dunn (Ed.), *Models for the perception of speech and visual form.* Cambridge, Mass.: MIT Press, 1967.

Neisser, U. Decision-time without reaction-time: Experiments in visual scanning. *American Journal of Psychology*, 1963, **76**, 376–385.

Neisser, U. *Cognitive psychology.* New York: Appleton, 1967.

Newbigging, P. L. The perceptual redintegration of frequent and infrequent words. *Canadian Journal of Psychology*, 1961, **15**, 123–132.

Pachella, R. G. Memory scanning under speed stress. Paper presented at the meeting of the Midwestern Psychological Association, Cleveland, May, 1972.

Pierce, J. Some sources of artifact in studies of the tachistoscopic perception of words. *Journal of Experimental Psychology*, 1963, **66**, 363–370.

Pillsbury, W. B. A study in apperception. *American Journal of Psychology*, 1897, **8**, 315–393.

Posner, M. I. Abstraction and the process of recognition. In G. H. Bower & J. T. Spence (Eds.), *The psychology of learning and motivation.* Vol. 3. New York: Academic Press, 1969.

Posner, M. I. On the relationship between letter names and superordinate categories. *Quarterly Journal of Experimental Psychology*, 1970, **22**, 279–287.

Posner, M. I. & Taylor, R. L. Subtractive method applied to separation of visual and name components of multi-letter arrays. *Acta Psychologia*, 1969, 30, 104–114.

Reed, S. K. Pattern recognition and categorization. *Cognitive Psychology*, 1972, **3**, 382–407.

Reicher, G. M. Perceptual recognition as a function of meaningfulness of stimulus material. *Journal of Experimental Psychology*, 1969, **81**, 274–280.

Robinson, J. S., Brown, L. T., & Hayes, W. H. Test of effective past visual experience on perception. *Perceptual and Motor Skills*, 1964, **18**, 953–956.

Rumelhart, D. E. A multicomponent theory of the perception of briefly exposed visual displays. *Journal of Mathematical Psychology*, 1970, **7**, 191–218.

Rumelhart, D. E., & Siple, P. The process of recognizing tachistoscopically presented words. *Psychological Review*, 1974, in press.

Selfridge, O. G. Pandemonium: A paradigm for learning. In D. V. Blake & A. M. Vittey (Eds), *The mechanisation of thought processes.* London: H. M. Stationery Office, 1959.

Selfridge, O. G., & Neisser, U. Pattern recognition by machine. *Scientific American*, 1960, **203**, 60–68.

Shiffrin, R. M., & Gardner, G. T. Visual processing capacity and attentional control. *Journal of Experimental Psychology*, 1972, **93**, 72–82.

Smith, E. E., & Haviland, S. E. Why words are perceived more accurately than nonwords: Inference vs. unitization. *Journal of Experimental Psychology*, 1972, **92**, 59–64.

Smith, F. The use of featural dependencies across letters in the visual identification of words. *Journal of Verbal Learning and Verbal Behavior*, 1969, **8**, 215–218. (a)

Smith, F. Familiarity of configuration vs. discriminability of features in the visual identification of words. *Psychonomic Science*, 1969, **14**, 261–262.

Smith, F. *Understanding reading.* New York: Holt, Rinehart & Winston, 1971.

Smith, F., Lott, D., & Cronnell, B. The effect of type size and case alternation on word identification. *American Journal of Psychology*, 1969, **82**, 248–253.

Sperling, G. The information available in brief visual presentations. *Psychological Monographs*, 1960, **74**, (11, Whole No. 498).

Sperling, G. Successive approximations to a model for short-term memory. *Acta Psychologica*, 1967, **27**, 285–292.

Spoehr, K. T. Linguistic processes in the perception of letter strings. Unpublished doctoral dissertation, Stanford University, 1973.

Spoehr, K. T., & Smith, E. E. Perceptual units and parsing processes in word perception. Paper presented at the meeting of the Psychonomic Society, St. Louis, November 1972.

Spoehr, K. T., & Smith, E. E. The role of syllables in perceptual processing. *Cognitive Psychology*, 1973, **5**, 71–89.

Sternberg, S. High-speed scanning in human memory. *Science*, 1966, **153**, 652–654.

Sternberg, S. Scanning a persisting visual image versus a memorized list. Paper presented at the meeting of the Eastern Psychological Association, Boston, April, 1967.

Swets, J. A., Tanner, W. P., & Birdsall, T. G. Decision processes in perception. *Psychological Review*, 1961, **68**, 301–320.

Thompson, M. C., & Massaro, D. W. Visual information and redundancy in reading. *Journal of Experimental Psychology*, 1973, **98**, 49–54.

Townsend, J. T. Theoretical analysis of an alphabetic confusion matrix. *Perception and Psychophysics*, 1971, **9**, 49–50. (a)

Townsend, J. T. A note on the identifiability of parallel and serial processes. *Perception & Psychophysics*, 1971, **10**, 161–163. (b)

Tulving, E., & Gold, C. Stimulus information and contextual information as determinants of tachistoscopic recognition of words. *Journal of Experimental Psychology*, 1963, **66**, 319–327.

Tulving, E., Mandler, G., & Baumal, R. Interaction of two sources of information in tachistoscopic word recognition. *Canadian Journal of Psychology*, 1964, **18**, 62–71.

Venezky, R. L. English orthography: Its graphical structure and its relation to sound. *Reading Research Quarterly*, 1967, **2**, 75–106.

Wheeler, D. D. Processes in word recognition. *Cognitive Psychology*, 1970, **1**, 59–85.

Wolford, G. L., Wessel, D. L., & Estes, W. K. Further evidence concerning scanning and sampling assumptions of visual detection models. *Perception & Psychophysics*, 1968, **3**, 439–444.

7
THE MECHANICS OF THOUGHT[1]

Earl B. Hunt and Steven E. Poltrock
The University of Washington

I. INTRODUCTION

Cogito ergo sum. To Descartes thinking was a fact which implied existence. We wish to turn this reasoning around and ask what the fact of our existence implies about our thought processes. Specifically, we shall introduce a way of thinking about very complex problem solving. The previous chapters have shown that even when we deal with relatively simple stimuli and responses, such as pushing a button in response to a tone, a good deal of theory is required to account for the observations that can be made. Here theory will be stressed even more strongly. "Thinking" can cover activities that vary from choosing the next move in a chess game to choosing a spouse. "Covering the literature" in such a diverse field would require several volumes. What we shall do instead is to present a way of theorizing that can be applied to thought processes and, at the same time, is compatible with our knowledge of performance on the simpler tasks described earlier in this book.

Our approach is a variant of the "computer simulation" approach first stated by Newell, Shaw, and Simon (1958) and since amplified by them and many others. In its purest form, the computer simulation approach views thought as a process of symbol manipulation. Therefore an appropriate model of the thought process must be stated in a language for symbol manipulation. Furthermore, in order to qualify as a scientific theory, a model must be precise. This presents us with a problem, since mathematics

[1]The preparation of this paper was made possible by the support of the National Science Foundation, Grant GB 25979. We would like to thank our colleagues at the University of Washington and elsewhere for the considerable help they have given us, and in particular to acknowledge the assistance provided by Mari Jones, Barry Kantowitz, Elizabeth Loftus, and Phillip Milliman. Finally, our intellectual debt to the ideas of Allen Newell and Herbert Simon will be apparent throughout this paper.

is our most precise language, but conventional mathematics is not well suited to describe symbol manipulation. The reader who doubts this is invited to write a set of equations describing the process of replacing the letters "rat" by "mouse" in a body of text, while avoiding the problems introduced by words such as "apparatus" and "cooperation." Newell, Shaw, and Simon solved this problem by moving from the notation of conventional mathematics to the notation of computer programming. A computer program is an ordered set of explicit rules for manipulating symbols. The interaction between these rules may be very complex. In fact, it is often necessary to execute the program on a machine in order to discover just what the rules imply. This does not pose a problem, since we have such a machine: the digital computer. To return to psychology, suppose that we wish to write a set of rules describing exactly how a person solves a problem. We can do this by writing a program that expresses our ideas about what the person is doing "inside his head." If the program is simple enough, we will be able to understand its actions by examination. In particular, we will want to determine whether the program reaches the same solution to problems presented to it as does the person whose thought we are explaining. In addition, if we can observe any intermediate steps that the person takes, we want to be sure that the program takes the same steps. If the program is so complex that we cannot determine these things by examination, then we may exercise the program on a digital computer, simply to see what our theory implies. Note that in doing so we have *not* committed ourselves to the notion that the human being's thought processes are in any way physically similar to the computer's physical techniques for symbol manipulation. The correspondence in which we are interested is solely between the logic of the program and the logic of mental symbol processing. A physical explanation for thought is quite outside the scope of our concern.[2]

Let us consider a concrete example. A number of investigators have studied the eye movements of chess players as they examine the board, prior to choosing their move.[3] After an initial scan, players appear to form mental groups of related pieces, scanning back and forth to determine the relationship between pieces within each group. As part of a larger effort to simulate chess play, Simon and Barenfeld (1969) wrote a program to analyze board positions. This program also forms groups of related pieces. It does so by selecting a key piece (e.g. the King, or a piece in center board position) and determining the relationship between the key piece and other pieces about it. "Relationship" was defined in chess terms — "attack," "defense," etc. This can be done by scans up and down the board from the key piece. For example, to determine which pieces directly attack the King, one need only to (*a*) determine whether there are any hostile Knights within two squares of the King, and then (*b*) scan down all open rows, files, and diagonals as far as the first piece. This sequence of actions implies a sequence of eye movement patterns, and thus provides an

---

[2] We qualify this by saying that we would not want to espouse any theory whose basic mechanisms were ruled out on the grounds of physiological evidence.

[3] There are several ways this can be done. One technique is to have the subject wear a contact lens with a small mirror. An infrared light can be reflected from the mirror to the board, at the point of gaze, and be tracked on suitably sensitive film.

hypothesis about eye movements that can be tested against observable behavior. The hypothesis is not vacuous, because there are other ways in which the same information could be obtained. For instance, a computer program could be written to scan the board in reading order and, as each piece was encountered, to determine its relation to all other squares on the board. Configurations of pieces could then be extracted after the board scan, but the order of their extraction would be quite different from the order implied by the method we first described.

Having led the reader this far, we ought to indicate the success of the effort. Figure 1 shows (*a*) a chess position, (*b*) the eye movements of a strong chess player examining the position, and (*c*) the order in which the Simon and Barenfeld program examined pieces on the position. There is clearly a nontrivial correspondence between eye movements and program movements. In subsequent research (Chase & Simon, 1973; Simon & Gilmartin, 1973) Simon and his associates have shown that

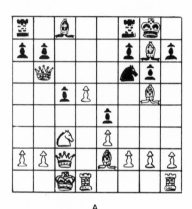

A

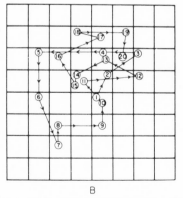

B

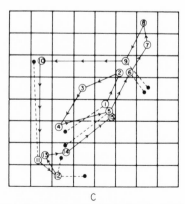

C

Fɪɢ. 1. (A) A middle game chess position. (B) A record of eye movements for the first 5 seconds. (C) Simulated eye movements during orientation of the PERCEIVER program (after Simon & Barenfeld, 1969).

the configurations of pieces detected by the program are closely related to the codings good human players use in describing and remembering chess positions.

II. EXTENDING THE SIMULATION PROGRAMMING IDEA TO THE COMPUTER SYSTEM MODEL

In the chess example the concept of a computer program was used as an abstract tool, a language if you will, for constructing a psychological model. There was no commitment to any of the concepts that have proven useful in the design of actual computing systems. The reader may have noticed that this is in decided contrast to the approach taken in several other chapters in this text (especially those by Kantowitz, Pachella, and Pew), where the authors seem to have had in mind a physical device as a psychological model. The difference in the approach is due to the difference in task demands. In the laboratory tasks, subjects typically had to respond rapidly. Chess, however, is a task that detaches man from his environment. The game is played at a notoriously slow pace, without interruptions. Each player knows where the relevant stimuli will appear, and when. In chess play the "real" information processing takes place as the player evaluates a position, and not as he recognizes the names of the pieces on the various squares. Quite different information-processing problems would have to be dealt with if we tried to simulate the decision processes of an automobile driver. The concepts of evaluation and choice of move would still be valid, but we would have to explain how the person is able to deal with a rapidly changing, unpredictable world. We can summarize the distinction between these tasks by saying that the driving task has a *real time requirement* and the chess task does not. More generally, a real time requirement exists if a person must respond to an environmental change almost as it happens. A second, closely related distinction between tasks is the distinction between *single channel* and *multichannel tasks*. This distinction refers to the predictability of the locus of important environmental changes. Chess is clearly a single channel task; the player knows that all important events will occur on the board. Driving a car is just as obviously a multichannel task, especially when you consider the need to respond to a variety of visual and acoustic signals. More succinctly, in a single channel task the person can predict where important changes in the environment will occur and restrict his attention accordingly. In a multichannel task the prediction can be made only probabilistically.

When the idea of simulation is extended to real-time and multichannel tasks, we can no longer ignore questions about how the simulation program is to be executed on a physical machine. Figure 2 illustrates the interaction of an hypothetical computer and its environment. The machine receives input from several sources. In order to determine its responses, the machine must compute some function of its current input. It may be aided in doing this by reference to its library (in humans, its memory) of previously presented information. Such information will be of two basic types: programs that can control the machine, and data files (records of the past) that the machine and its programs may consult in order to compose the "best" response to the current input.

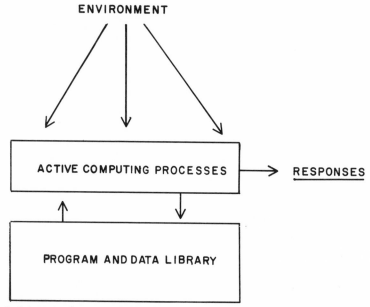

FIG. 2. Schematic of processes in real time computing.

There are many real computers that act in this way. The machinery to run a computer-controlled chemical plant is a good example, and so is the computer used to handle airline reservations and make flight status reports. Our point is that human beings, in fact all animals, face exactly the same general information-processing problem as do these real-time multichannel computing systems. Computer Science has developed some descriptive concepts to apply to the machinery. We claim that the same concepts can usefully be applied to highlight questions about the psychology of human information processing. To illustrate our point, we shall list four major concepts and illustrate how they apply both to computing and to psychology. We shall then step back and examine the psychological application of each concept in more detail.

Data Types

One of the most basic things you can ask about an information-processing machine is how it stores information. Every computer has one or more ways in which this is done. Each representation of information is called a *data type*. For example, most large computers have different representations of real and integer numbers. At the most elementary level, the machine's operations can be split into two groups, operations for moving information from one place to another and operations that manipulate information content expressed in a given data type. Examples of the latter are ''Add two real numbers'' and ''Subtract one integer from another.'' Again considering things only at an elementary level, a program is a sequence of these primitive operations.

The psychological analog of a data type and an operation on a data type is, at first, most unclear. By logic alone, we know that something like a data type must exist, for the assertion "There is a data type in the brain" can be understood to mean "There is some consistent way in which information is coded in memory." Of course, there must be. The physical substrate of the code is properly a question for physiology, so we shall be little concerned with this. The logical question is "What information is stored in the basic code?" A favorite answer is that we store records of sensory images. We shall argue in the next section that this is insufficient. Our point here is just that the code must exist.

System Architecture

A computer system consists of separate "boxes," with different and somewhat autonomous functions. The way in which these components are connected may exert a profound effect on the operation of the entire system. To take a simple example, early computer systems typically consisted of a card reader, a memory, an arithmetic processor, and a printer. All of these devices were attached to the processor and could only communicate with each other through it. Thus data could not be printed out from the memory while cards were being read in, since the processor could only do one thing at a time. It was quickly discovered that such a system was inefficient, for the rapid electronic components often stood idle while the slower electromechanical devices were active. In more modern computing systems the card readers and printers are attached directly to the memory (with some technical exceptions that need not concern us here), so that input, output, and computation can all occur at the same time. This permits the system to be computing the nth job in a sequence, while reading cards for the $n + 1$st, and printing the results of the $n - 1$st job. By rearranging components we avoid bottlenecks.

However the human system is wired, it is surprisingly good at avoiding embarrassing bottlenecks. At least, this is so in the normal human environment. Within the psychology laboratory it is fairly easy to produce bottlenecks that are often most revealing of the system architecture. In a dichotic listening task different stimuli are presented to each ear. Typically if speech a is presented to the right ear, and speech b is presented simultaneously to the left ear, only speech a or b will be heard. As a first approximation, we can think of the speech reception areas of the brain as a single processor that switches its attention back and forth from one ear to another. Further experimentation has shown that this simple model is not quite correct (see Kantowitz, this volume, or Broadbent, 1971, for details), but it does illustrate the point. We regard the brain, too, as having specialized memory and processing areas. In order to fill out the computer analogy we must specify what these components are, and how they are functionally connected. Such a description is called a description at the *system architecture* level. In Section IV we shall discuss a particular system architecture model.

Programming

A computing system is of little value to a user unless there is some way to issue commands to the machinery. In order to do this there must be a language in which the user can state what is to be done, and which can then be translated, by some automated process, into a sequence of elementary machine operations. Again illustrating from real machines, virtually every major computer system on the market today is prepared to accept a program written in the FORTRAN language. This language permits the user to make statements such as

$$A = B + C$$

which, rather transparently, states that the variable A is to be set equal to the sum of variables B and C. The programming language is not strictly part of the machine[4], but it is a very important component in determining the capability that the system has in interacting with its environment. The language is at once a way of talking about a user's problem and a way of commanding the machinery to execute a specified sequence of actions. The ideal language is one that can satisfy the requirements placed on it by both these tasks. The user should find the language natural, and there should be a direct correspondence between constructs in the language and the operation of the machine.

The parallel to the use of "programming languages" in the psychology of cognition is exact. A model of human thought must be described in some sort of notation. This notation is a description of how the psychologist believes the human computer solves a particular problem. The basic constructs of the notation should have an interpretation in human action, and the notation should be sufficiently rich to permit precise description of the complexities of human thought.

We can illustrate how a language is used to describe psychological processes by discussing a notation system that has been proposed for thought but which, we believe, does not work. This is the "stimulus–response" notation developed by Hull, Spence, and many others during the 1930s and 1940s. Its basic concept is the notion of a bond between a stimulus, S, and a response, R. We write S → R, where S and R are observable stimuli and responses, respectively. The arrow indicates that R has, somehow, become associated with S, so that presentation of S will (possibly probabilistically) cause the subject to produce R. The S → R pair has a clearcut psychological interpretation, in the conditioned response, so stimulus–response notation may be useful for describing such responses. Unfortunately, the S–R notation fails miserably when it is tested for its ability to describe the actions involved in a complex thought. Consider the situation in a free association experiment where the stimulus is the word "Mother." If the response is "Father," the S–R theory has little trouble explaining this as a highly learned association between two words. If the response is a bizarre one, say "Purple," then it is necessary to postulate a sequence of internal, mediating stimuli (the small s's and r's, for those familiar with the theory) which eventually lead to the production of an internal stimulus to which the external response "Purple" has been conditioned. Given the actual stimulus and response, and the context of the situation, it is probably always possible to construct a reasonable stimulus–response chain for any free association. The manner in which this is to be done, however, is not specifiable within the S–R notation. (At least, it has

---

[4]A programming language is not strictly part of a machine. However, the mechanisms permitted in the language will place requirements on the machine structure (Hopcraft & Ullman, 1969).

never been done satisfactorily.) Thus the S–R notation fails a crucial test of its adequacy as a programming language for cognition; it is imprecise. Probably the most important conceptual notion in Newell et al.'s (1958) original paper on simulation was their idea that an actual computer programming language, which would, of necessity, be precise, could also be rich enough to describe thought. We shall return to this idea in Section V, where we offer a notation (also due to Newell and Simon) for cognitive psychology that appears to have a number of advantages as a simulation language.

There is a simple point about programming languages that, surprisingly, is sometimes lost. The assertion that a particular language is an adequate notation for the study of cognition does not mean that one therefore has a correct model of thought. It is quite possible to state an inadequate theory in an adequate notation. Think again of the analogy to FORTRAN. This is a fine notation for expressing statistical computations, but it is easy to write a FORTRAN program that incorrectly computes an analysis of variance! Subsequently we shall use our notation to write simulation programs for various tasks. In evaluating this work the reader should try to separate questions concerning the accuracy of the particular simulation being discussed and the adequacy of the notation to express the class of models under discussion.

File Structure

Real-time computing systems often refer to data banks in order to determine how to handle a current request for services. Again illustrating, whether an airline computer will honor a request for a seat depends upon the status of the reservation records for the flight in question. Furthermore, as soon as an action is taken by the system, it is necessary to alter the files to record that action. The airline computer should reserve each seat not more than 1.1 times! In order to do all this the files must be organized so that appropriate information is easy to retrieve from them. File organization requires some sort of indexing system that permits the system to locate rapidly information that is likely to be needed. It may be acceptable to allow some files to be lost, simply because the indexing system does not contain any way to access them, if these files are so unlikely to be wanted that the cost of keeping an index is not justified.

The psychological analogy to computer memory file organization is the organization of information in our memory. It is self-evident that we cannot recall, at will, any piece of information we know. What we can recall at any given time will depend very much on how we are asked the question. In computer terms, an entry will be made into our file indexing system by means of certain entry keys. These keys will combine with the indexing system to determine what memorized information we retrieve. The appropriate combinations of keys and indexing will determine whether a memory search is simple, difficult, or impossible. To make this point we invite the reader to perform the following tasks:

1) Think of a word beginning with "k."
2) Think of a word whose third letter is "k."
3) Write down your telephone number.
4) Write down the telephone number at the house in which you lived two houses ago.

The first and third tasks were, no doubt, trivial. In computer terms, your memory files are set up to retrieve this sort of information. The second task probably required some effort, even though there are actually more words with k as a third letter than there are with k as the first letter. We wager that a not insignificant number of readers will find the fourth task impossible. Yet surely you knew the answer once! We do not believe that you have lost the information itself. We do believe you have lost the indexing information that allowed you to locate the information in your brain.

The organization and modification of long-term memory is clearly a central topic in psychology, but it cannot be said that research has shed a great deal of light on the problem. In fact, Anderson and Bower (1973) have suggested that until recently no psychological model of memory was very much better than that proposed by Aristotle! Computer Science has had to deal with the question of how memory might be organized, partly in order to construct artificial intelligence devices for logical inference, problem solving, and question answering. The simulation approach has probably had more influence in the development of ideas about long-term memory organization than it has had in any other area of psychology.

III. DATA TYPES

Any statement of a formal scientific theory must begin with a definition of the meaning of the theory's primitive symbols.[5] To state a theory of cognition we must define symbols that will represent the indivisible elements of cognition, as we conceive them. This means that we must state the classes of basic symbols that exist in memory, the experiential events they represent, and the rules for manipulating each class of symbols. We call these classes of symbols the *data types* of the theory.

The most obvious answer to the question "What does memory contain?" is to assume that memory contains representations of the sensory images of past experiences. We "know" intuitively that we can produce images from stored information. Most readers will have no trouble in visualizing an image of the last person to leave the room. (If they examine their image a bit more, however, they may find that there are details missing that they simply cannot produce.) Secondly, a sensory-image theory of memory implies a continuity between human **and** animal memory, and this is surely desirable. Finally, it is easy to show that imaging may play an important role in human thought. Many problems in memory and cognition appear to be solved by mental manipulation of an imaged model of the problem under discussion. Imaging also appears to mediate recall in many situations (Paivio, 1971).

Most theorists accept the idea that some of our memories are stored as images, but the proposition that images are a sufficient data type for thought has been seriously questioned. It is hard to see how thoughts about concepts such as "duty" or "honor" can be imaged. Mathematicians manage to think about imaginary numbers and spaces with dimensionality greater than three. In order to explain such behavior within a

---

[5] A mathematical system, as opposed to a scientific theory, does not even have to do this. In a mathematical system the symbols themselves are specified and the rules for forming well-formed expressions from them are stated, but no interpretation of the symbols need be offered. A scientific model, then, is an interpretation of a mathematical system.

purely sensory-image theory of memory, it is necessary to assume that the data being imaged is not the idea itself, but rather the language used to describe it. In the higher-dimensional space example, the mathematician might "image" the phrase *an n-dimensional vector* in order to represent a point in *n* space. Recall would thus consist of an arousal of an image of the descriptive phrase, followed by an interpretation of the phrase in the light of other stored knowledge about phrases. This explanation of memory is a fairly widely held one. Basically it asserts that all information is stored in sensory image form, but that the image may be either one produced by the physical sensation of the stimulus or by the sensory image of a linguistic string describing the stimulus. This is called the *dual coding* hypothesis. It is intended to offer a plausible explanation for the occurrence of complex thought, without assuming a discontinuity between human and animal memory. In addition, and this is no small point in our favor, it is consistent with our intuitive experience of recall.

Pylyshyn (1973) has presented a strong case against the dual coding hypothesis. We find much of his argument directly applicable to computer simulation. Pylyshyn begins by observing that the reality of the imagery phenomenon cannot be questioned, but that this fact does not compel one to assume that the information in memory is itself an image. We are forced to report verbal or visual images when we recall information from memory, simply because we have no other language for describing our own mental processes. Therefore we are unable to discriminate between the direct arousal of a stored image and the arousal of non-imaged information that can be used to re-create the image, by some imperceivable process. Therefore the image vs. non-image controversy about memory cannot be solved on the basis of introspective report. Pylyshyn argues further that there is indirect evidence for the existence of some form of non-image memory. Much of his case rests on the fact that we do not always recall perceptual details, and that when our memory is faulty, it is not faulty in any way directly related to the geometry of the stimulus.

> When our recollections are vague, it is always in the sense that certain perceptual qualities or attributes are absent or uncertain—not that there are geometrically definable pieces of a picture missing [Pylyshyn, 1973, p. 10].

Pylyshyn concludes that at least some information is stored in propositional form, as a "statement about a property of an object," rather than as a sensory image either of an object or its description.

In most simulations of thought processes it has been implicitly assumed that information is represented in the brain by a list of properties, i.e., in Pylyshyn's propositional form of knowledge. The effect of this assumption upon problem solving can be seen by examining one of the most famous programs in simulation and problem solving, the General Problem Solver (GPS) developed by Newell and his associates (Ernst & Newell, 1969; Newell, Shaw, & Simon, 1959; Newell & Simon, 1961, 1972). We shall briefly describe the problem solving methods used in GPS and then contrast them to the problem solving methods used by another artificial intelligency program, the ARTIFICIAL GEOMETER (Gelernter, 1959), which differed from GPS in its problem representation.

GPS is a program for manipulating primitive objects, called *states*. Formally, a state is an ordered list of pairs of the form (attribute, value). The equation

$$A + A = 2 \cdot A$$

might be represented as

number of left side place holders=2

number of left side variables=1

list of left side constants=( )

list of left side operators=(+)

number of right side place holders=2

number of right side variables=1

list of right side constants=(2)

list of right side operators=(·).

Clearly, further information could be specified. The example is intended only to illustrate the point that each object is represented by a list of propositions about it. To initiate problem solving, GPS is provided with three classes of information: (*a*) a definition of the propositions that may be made about a state, (*b*) a list of operators that may be applied to states to change their form (for example, in algebra the "commutativity of +" operation changes an expression of the form $x + y$ to $y + x$), and (*c*) an *operator-difference* table, which lists which operators affect which types of propositions. In the example given above, the operator-difference table would contain the entry indicating that commutation affects propositions about order of variables in an expression. [6]

Having provided the program with this general information, the user presents a specific problem to GPS by stating a current state and a desired state. The program proceeds to find a sequence of operators that will produce the desired state by using a technique called *means-end analysis*. First the difference in the propositions describing the current and desired state are compared. If no difference can be found, GPS assumes that the problem is solved. Assume that a difference exists. The program searches for an operator that will reduce this difference, by consulting the operator-difference matrix. An attempt is then made to apply the operator to the current state, and thus presumably make it more like the goal state. In some cases, however, the chosen operator cannot be applied directly, for its application may be contingent on certain propositions being true about the current state. When this happens the program establishes the subproblem of altering the current state so that the desired operator can be applied. This problem can be attacked *recursively*, i.e., GPS uses itself as a

---

[6]It is possible to write a program that will develop the operator-difference table from the definition of propositions and operators (Quinlan & Hunt, 1968).

subroutine to attack a subsidiary problem, and then uses the solution to the subsidiary problem as a step in the main problem solution.

We could illustrate GPS precisely by demonstrating how a problem in logic, algebra, or trigonometry would be solved, but in doing so we would have to deal with many more details of the programming procedure.[7] The flavor of a GPS solution may be captured by considering the following "traveling professor" problem.

The professor is in his office in Seattle and wishes to give a lecture to an audience in Chicago. GPS reasons as follows:

1. Consider the propositions about the geographic locations of the offices. What is the difference between them? Distance, measured in hundreds of miles. What reduces large distances? An airplane. An airplane should be applied to the professor, in order to change his location.

2. Do the propositions required for "airplane application" apply to the professor's current position? No, to take an airplane one must be at an airport. What is the difference between current location and the airport? Distance measured in miles. What reduces intermediate distances? An automobile.

3. Do the propositions required for automobile application apply to the current location? No, to take an automobile one must be in a parking lot. What is the difference between the current location and the parking lot? Distance measured in feet. What reduces distance in feet? Walking. Can walking be applied? Yes.

4. Apply walking, then driving, then flying.

At this point, the professor will be at the airport at Chicago, and GPS will have solved all the subproblems developed thus far. The program then tests to see if the problem is solved and finds that it is not — the professor is not in exactly the right location. A new subproblem, moving from the airport to the lecture hall, is established and solved as in steps 1, 2, and 3.

Means-end analysis is an appropriate name for this technique because an operation is chosen to affect a specific subgoal. The problem solving method is quite general; one cannot immediately think of any problem to which it is not applicable.[8] The difficulty that GPS has with a particular problem will depend upon the aptness of the propositions chosen to describe the different states. In the traveling professor problem we dealt only with geographical location. Suppose we had also specified that the number of chairs in a room was an important property, even more important than distance. The program could have been fooled into believing that the first thing to do was to add chairs to the professor's office, so that the meeting could be held there, before it discovered that the professor had to leave the office. More generally, a problem will be difficult if a GPS program has to spend a great deal of time and effort

---

[7]The GPS approach to problem solving is discussed in great detail by Ernst and Newell (1969) and Newell and Simon (1972). The latter reference considers GPS as a simulation of human thought. Formal comparisons of the GPS method to other computer oriented problem solving methods are given by Nilsson (1971) and Hunt (1974a).

[8]Problems that GPS cannot solve do exist and can be specified formally (Chang, 1970). The general nature of these problems is that they require an indirect proof; for example, the proof of a lemma before proceeding to prove the problem directly. Intuitively, such problems should be difficult for humans.

removing irrelevant differences, or if a necessary intermediate step in a problem requires production of a state less like the goal state than the original starting state. Newell and Simon (1972) observe that the latter type of problem is also quite difficult for people.

About the time that GPS was published, Gelernter (1959) reported a program for solving problems in plane geometry. This program, the ARTIFICIAL GEOME-TER, is of considerable interest because it uses a basically different form of internal representation; it manipulates images. (Strictly speaking, it manipulates digital definitions of visual images, but this need not concern us.) The program is not intended to represent a direct simulation of human thought. Nevertheless, many people find intuitively that its actions form a more accurate simulation than the property manipulations of GPS. In terms of power, the program gives an excellent account of itself on a high school geometry test. The program is of interest to us for two reasons: its use of a different internal representation of data and its use of a different problem solving method, called the *subproblem generation* method.

In order to understand the GEOMETER, it is necessary to realize a fact that many high school students never grasp: Euclidean geometry as such has nothing to do with lines and figures. It exists as a purely abstract formal system, and any formal proof in geometry must be constructed by progressive application of axioms, or theorems proven from axioms, in the formal, symbolic system. However, it is well-known (both by the high school student and Euclid) that there is a correspondence between the statements of plane geometry and the physical relationships between lines and points on a plane. Like virtually every human geometry student, the GEOMETER makes use of this correspondence to suggest lines of proof.

The program begins with a set of known true statements, a statement to be proven, and a set of rules for inferring the truth of new statements from the truth of old statements. These rules fall into two classes: (*a*) the rule stating that corresponding parts of congruent triangles are identical and (*b*) a set of rules for inferring that triangles are congruent, or that lines and angles are identical. Although means-end analysis could be used in the formal system, the GEOMETER attacks a geometry problem in a very different way. First it establishes a series of subproblems which, if they were to be solved, would imply solution of the main problem. The program then uses the "givens" of the problem to "draw a diagram" representing the problem. It establishes which of the subproblems are true in the diagram and restricts its attention to them. Subproblems are solved in the same manner.

Consider the problem of proving that the diagonals of a parallelogram bisect each other. An appropriate diagram is shown in Fig. 3. The initial statements are

> QUADRILATERAL ABCD
> TRIANGLE AED, AEB, ADB, BEC, DEC, BDC
> TO PROVE: AE=EC and DE=EB.

The original problem requires the solution to two subproblems, AE = EC and DE = EB. Like the clever student, the program is capable of noting that the solution

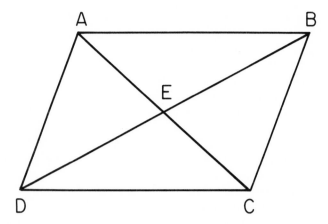

FIG. 3. Diagram for problem of proving that the diagonals of a parallelogram bisect each other.

to one of them is also a solution to the other, so we will consider only the solution of
AE = EC. A solution will be achieved if AE and EC can be shown to be corresponding line segments of two congruent triangles. From purely formal considerations we
know that to do this one of the following congruencies must be proven.

$$(1) \quad \triangle AED \cong \triangle DEC$$
$$(2) \quad \triangle AED \cong \triangle BEC$$
$$(3) \quad \triangle AEB \cong \triangle DEC$$
$$(4) \quad \triangle AEB \cong \triangle AED$$

The problem will be solved if any of (1) through (4) is chosen, so which one is easiest
to prove? We can phrase this in a negative way; the program certainly should not attempt to prove any congruencies which, in fact, are false. But how to detect this without going through the proof? This is where the diagram is used. By a process of crude
measurement, the program examines the diagram and notes which pairs of triangles in
(1) to (4) are mechanically ("visually") congruent. Formal proofs of congruencies
are attempted only for those pairs of triangles that pass this test. In the example, this
heuristic restricts the program's attention to pairs (2) and (3). Like GPS, the
GEOMETER then attempts to solve the subproblems recursively. In this particular
case there are several ways in which congruencies can be determined, e.g., by
proving either that a side, angle, side or a side, side, side equality exists. The diagram
can be examined to determine where these relations are true, thus establishing new
subproblems. Eventually a "subproblem" will be encountered which is on the list of
given facts. When a given fact is encountered the GEOMETER notes which
subproblems have been proven, and then continues, until the proven subproblems
imply proof of the original problem.

The GEOMETER solution method of selecting subproblems and forming inferences from solved subproblems is greatly facilitated by what is sometimes called a
"goal tree." A goal tree is a connected set of nodes where each node represents a
subproblem. A partial example for this problem is shown in Fig. 4. The highest node

of the tree is attached to the original problem. Immediate subproblems of the original problem are attached to nodes directly below the first node. Note that these are linked together by an arc. This is done to indicate that they are in an AND relation to the higher node, since all the subproblems must be solved if the higher-order problem is to be considered solved. The four subproblems of AE = EC are listed below its node. These subproblems are not linked by an arc, since they are in an OR relation to the subproblem generating them; solving any one of them is sufficient to solve the main problem. When a known statement is encountered as a subproblem it is marked solved. If it is linked to the node above it with an OR relation or if it is the last subproblem in a set of AND subproblems, the node above the solved subproblem is marked solved. This process is repeated until either no more problems can be marked solved or until the highest node can be marked solved. In the latter case the main problem is solved, and the program is done. In the former case the program selects an unsolved subproblem and generates a series of sub-subproblems from it, then either continues to generate more subproblems or, if a known statement is encountered as a second subproblem, modifies the goal tree as just described.

Means-end analysis is inherently tied to the propositional form of data representation. Subproblem generation might use either an image or propositional notation. Clearly the distinction between image and proposition is important for computer problem solving. Is it similarly important for human problem solving? We think it is. To support our contention, we describe briefly computer simulations of performance

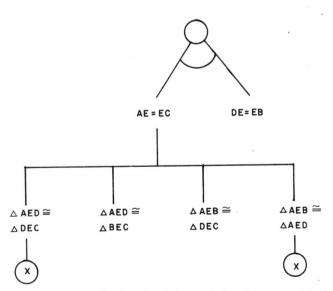

FIG. 4. Goal tree for problem in Fig. 3: *AND* relations are indicated by an arc; *OR* relations are not linked. Paths ending in Ⓧ indicate goals that are not true in the diagram.

on two types of intelligence test items. In one of the simulations it was found that the level of performance depended on the type of representation. In the other simulation it became obvious that both types of representation were needed to perform well on a test of an allegedly unitary cognitive ability.

Raven's Progressive Matrix Test (Raven, 1958) has sometimes been asserted to be a pure measure of the general factor in intelligence (Jensen, 1969). This test presents the subject with a 3 × 3 matrix of visual patterns, with the lower right-hand element missing. The items in each row and column are "discoverable" according to some general rule about relations between successive row and column members. A set of possible replacements for the missing element is shown to the subject, who must choose one of them. A simple example is shown in Fig. 5. Other problems are much harder. Hunt (1974b) pointed out that an intermediate level of performance on this test can be obtained by regarding the known eight items as forming a visual scene, and then applying well-known perceptual processes, such as continuation of lines or inference of symmetry, to define the missing element. Superior level performance on the test can only be obtained by representing matrix elements as lists of propositions describing them. Hunt showed that given a correct propositional description of test items, means-end analysis could be applied to solve all problems in the short form of the Raven Test.

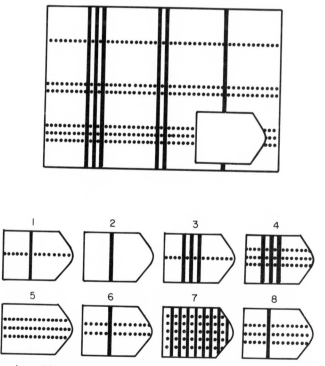

FIG. 5. Practice problem from Set I of the Advanced Progressive Matrices.

Baylor (1971) simulated the information processing required to solve problems in Guilford's Block Visualization Test. In this test the subject is told how a plain cube is to be painted, and then cut. The subject must then answer a series of questions about the colors painted on the smaller blocks which have been cut from the original one. An example problem is

"The four narrow sides of a one inch by four inch by four inch block are painted red. The top and bottom of the block are painted blue. The block is then cut into sixteen one inch cubes.

    1. How many cubes have both red and blue faces?

    2. How many cubes have one red and two blue faces?

    3. How many cubes have no painted faces?''

Baylor based his simulation upon a careful study of the remarks made by a graduate student while solving Block Visualization tasks. Although the test is supposed to be a measure of spatial deduction, Baylor found that two representations were required to mimic the problem solving of this subject. One, the S-representation, was a set of propositions about blocks, faces, and cuts in general. Further propositional information about the length, width, and cuts of the specific cube in question were extracted from the problem description. This information was then used to produce a "visual image," or I-representation, of a particular cube. The propositional information about cuts was next transformed into a sequence of operations upon the image, producing an image of a number of smaller blocks. Upon receiving a question, the program translated it into a series of propositions, and then examined the images of the blocks to determine which of them satisfied the propositions.

Quite aside from the convenience of the propositional notation for computer simulation, is there any evidence that this notation is a psychological fact? We believe there is. Posner (1969; Posner & Keele, 1970) and Reed (1972) performed a very similar sequence of experiments, but with quite different stimuli (either dot patterns or cartoon faces). First they exposed classes of stimuli created by systematically distorting a prototype stimulus. The prototype itself, however, was not exposed. Next they showed subjects a series of new and old stimuli, including the prototype. Both experimenters found that the prototype stimulus was highly likely to be "recognized" as a member of a class even though it had not been seen previously. This implies that what the subjects stored was not a sensory image of the actual stimulus, but rather a set of propositions about the stimuli seen. The propositions would also apply to the prototype and, hence, it would be recognized as old. Therefore the Posner and Reed studies are consistent with the position that nonverbal stimuli are not stored solely as sensory images. This finding is particularly impressive because of the differences in the stimuli and procedures used in two logically very similar studies.

The Posner and Reed work can be challenged by the argument that the subjects stored a sensory image of a verbal description of the stimuli. This, of course, would be consistent with the "dual code" hypothesis of the S–R theorist. Evidence against this belief has been obtained by Franks and Bransford (1972). In an earlier study these investigators had found that if a complex idea is presented in a series of short sentences, then a longer sentence containing several components of the idea is likely to be judged as familiar, even though it has not actually been seen (Bransford & Franks, 1971).

Suppose the subject is shown

THE BIG ROCK ROLLED DOWN THE HILL.
THE HUT WAS TINY.
THE ROCK CRUSHED THE HUT BY THE LAKE.

A sentence that might be falsely recognized as familiar is

THE BIG ROCK CRUSHED THE TINY HUT.

since this contains the propositions of the original idea. Of course, this study can be made consistent with a sensory-image theory of memory by reversing the argument previously made about the Reed and Posner studies. We simply assume that what was stored was a visual image of the objects and events described by the original verbal stimuli. Subsequently a sentence will be recognized as familiar if it describes the stored visual image. This is particularly likely in the Bransford and Franks study, since their verbal stimuli lend themselves to vivid imagination.

Franks and Bransford attacked this idea by using sentences containing ideas that would be hard to image. An example is

AN ARROGANT ATTITUDE WAS EXPRESSED.
THE ATTITUDE EXPRESSED IN THE SPEECH LED TO CRITICISM.
THE CRITICISM WAS IMMEDIATE.

Nevertheless, the same result observed in the Bransford and Franks study was again found. We conclude that the stored information was the set of propositions made, but not in their original verbal form.

From this evidence we are convinced that there is at least some justification for the common assumption of computer simulation builders, that the internal human data representations are propositions about objects, rather than sensory images of the objects. This is good, because if this assumption could not be justified, a great deal of the work on simulation would be of questionable relevance to psychology.

IV. A SYSTEM ARCHITECTURE FOR COGNITION

At this point we have described some of the processes that we believe are the basis of cognition, and the types of data representation on which these processes could operate. To complete our model of the cognitive system, we must specify the memory stores that contain the various data types, the processors that interface with the memory stores, and the interconnections between these components. In short, we must specify the system architecture.

Our approach to the development of a system architecture will be based on Hunt's (1971, 1973) *Distributed Memory* model. As its name implies, in this model the brain is assumed to be organized so that information is distributed into a number of distinct memory areas. Each memory area has a limited capacity to store and/or process the information it contains. Furthermore, each area can communicate its information to certain other areas. A schematic of the Distributed Memory model is shown in Fig. 6. The model proposes four memory systems: a series of sensory buffers, a short-term memory (STM) for information received in the last few seconds, an intermediate-term memory (ITM) for information active over the past few minutes, and an essentially permanent, limitless long-term memory (LTM). The buffer and STM concepts are quite common ones in modern cognitive psychology [see, for example, Neisser (1967), Broadbent (1971), or Atkinson and Shiffrin (1968), as well as several other papers in this volume]. These memory areas are essential for the processing of "immediate" information, but have a limited impact on what we colloquially call complex thought, so we shall deal with them only briefly.

When information first strikes an organism it must be converted from its external physical form, such as variations in light or acoustic energy, into an internal code. Assume that it produces a *sensory feature code,* consisting of a collection of features extracted from the sensory input and specific to that sensory mode. The sensory feature code, held in the outermost buffer, is the first of a series of hierarchically organized codes, progressing from genetically determined features to culturally meaningful symbols. To gain the flavor of the idea, consider the steps involved in recognizing words on a printed page. First, figure must be detected from ground; then lines must be located and organized into closed figures; then letters and words must be identified. The process involves only visual features until the "letter" stage is reached, and is probably mainly dependent on these features until the "word" stage, at which point the name code pointing to a meaningful unit in LTM will be aroused. Although the process is not a conscious one until the word stage, there is clearly some

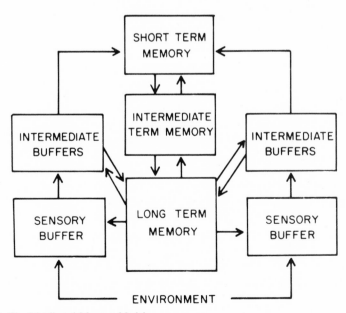

FIG. 6. The Distributed Memory Model.

involvement of memory for learned forms in earlier stages. The buffer system provides a series of way stations that can hold progressively more meaningful stimulus codes, finally resulting in the appearance of complex codes representing consciously perceived items in STM.

STM is thought of as a memory for the very limited number of items (one to nine) that are the focus of immediate attention. Auditory coding appears to be very much involved in STM. Indeed, some theorists have argued that STM consists of those auditory codes that are maintained in an active state by rehearsal (Atkinson & Wescourt, 1974). Hunt (1973) referred to the items in STM as *lexical* codes, since these are the "dictionary" entries from which more complex sentences of thought must be constricted. The defining property of a lexical item is that it is recognizable in isolation, as, for instance, is the auditory code of a word. There is a great deal of experimental evidence for some sort of STM. Most of the psychological studies require only that the subject be able to recall a particular lexical item recently placed in STM, and possibly the order of entry of an item relative to other items in STM. It is clear that people have this capability, providing that no more than seven or so items are to be held in STM at any one time, and provided that they are permitted to hold these items by rehearsal. Order of recall is usually fairly accurate, but there is little evidence for other organizing of the data.

At first thought, one would think that more information would have to be held in STM in order for us to be able to do the complex things we do. In an abstract sense, though, this is not true. Any machine, including a biological one, must learn about its environment by receiving a temporally ordered string of the basic commands that it can recognize. This is equally true if the commands are depressions of buttons on a control panel or pronunciations of words from a dictionary. A simple machine (e.g., an automobile) will respond to each command in isolation. A sophisticated machine (e.g., a human) is capable of constructing a complex command from a "sentence" of basic commands, each of which is to be interpreted in the context of the total string of commands. We may refer to such a device as a linguistic machine.

One of the basic goals of mathematical linguistics is the determination of those machine characteristics required by a linguistic device capable of interpreting grammatical strings of varying degrees of complexity (Chomsky, 1963; Hopcroft & Ullman, 1969). It is easy to show that the only basic discriminatory capacities the machine must have are the capacities to recognize the basic commands and to note their order of appearance. It can also be shown that, in order to handle languages of much less complexity than a natural language, some form of STM is needed. Still further reflection on the problems posed for a machine capable of comprehending natural language leads us to one of the important conceptual contributions of the simulation effort, the need for an intermediate-term memory structure.

In the distributed memory model intermediate-term memory can be thought of as a storage area that holds currently developing ideas, perhaps for a period of several minutes or even hours, while STM is a memory for very recent stimulus codes and

LTM a repository for developed ideas.[9] There is at best only tangential experimental evidence for ITM. We will argue that this structure is needed on logical grounds alone. Our argument rests heavily on the approach to natural language comprehension advocated by Schank (1972, 1973) and his associates.

We begin with the commonplace observation that a linguistic utterance can seldom be understood except in the context in which it is made. In order to achieve such understanding, mental structures representing the contextual situation must be readily available. The presence of these structures permits sorting and selection among relations indicated by the stream of lexical items passing through STM. Consider the following account of a bit of American history:

> A detachment of British infantry had been posted to the Boston Commons. Some of the unrulier elements of the crowd began to threaten them, making the officers increasingly nervous. At the height of the speechmaking the crowd pressed forward. The soldiers fired, and several fell dead.

It is highly likely from this account that "several of the unrulier elements," rather than several British soldiers, fell. Resolution of the ambiguity is not so clear in the next example, where the interpretations of Anglophobe and Anglophile may differ:

> As soon as the company fell into marching ranks for the return to Boston, minutemen began to fire from concealed positions. Whenever the soldiers turned to fire on their tormentors, several fell dead.

In the second case "several" could sensibly be interpreted to mean either minutemen or British soldiers. The point of the illustration is that language comprehension is a complex problem solving task, in which pieces of a sentence are fitted into a gradually developing network of ideas. The network, at any given time, stands ready to be modified by new input, but it also stands ready to guide the interpretation of that input.

Schank summarizes this by saying that language comprehension is based upon the expectation of particular types of input. Expectation may operate at several levels. There are certainly syntactic expectations; at some points in a sentence one knows what class of word is likely to follow. Semantic expectations are much more interesting. If we read the above description of the 1775 Boston Massacre aloud and hesitate after "soldiers fired," we wager that even people who do not know their history will expect to receive words describing the effect of the firing. What Schank has done is to formalize the intuitive ideas of expectation and cognitive link (Schank, 1973) to the point that the ideas can be programmed to give a reasonable account of comprehension and expectation (Schank, Goldman, Rieger, & Riesbeck, 1973).

---

[9]Parenthetically, by the definitions of distributed memory, virtually all psychological studies of "memory" are of ITM, for easily 90% of our literature on human memory deals with events that happened only minutes before memory is tested.

Schank postulates the existence of four classes of "objects of thought": picture producers (PP), acts (ACT), picture aiders (PA), and action aiders (AA). The PP and ACT categories represent things that are, loosely, reasonable concepts without modification, while the PA and AA categories contain appropriate modifiers. The four basic categories are themselves subcategorized. For example, PPs include human, animate, inanimate, and nonliving things. A conceptualization is a specification of the relationships indicated between categories. The simplest, for instance, is when an *actor* (a PP that can take an action) is linked to a specific ACT. Within-category restrictions determine the relations that may exist. For example, "speak" is an ACT that can be linked as an action only to PPs for human objects.

Every specific concept in memory can be defined by the relationships into which it can enter and the relationships that it requires be fulfilled. Schank (1973) uses a rather complicated notation; for our purposes we may define a "comprehended utterance" to be a network of nodes, in which each node represents a basic concept, and in which the arcs between the nodes represent the connections between the concepts. The arcs, therefore, must be labeled.[10] We illustrate from two scenes from Tolstoy's *War and Peace*.

At one point in the novel, we find that

Denisov proposed to Natalia.

Let us assume that this sentence is spoken and trace the progressive development of structures in STM and LTM, coordinated in the spirit of Schank's model.[11] Figure 7 shows the step by step construction of the concept conveyed by the sentence. First *Denisov* is recognized as a PP referring to a specific male. A PP in isolation clearly requires an ACT (Schank's symbolization for this is PP $\Leftrightarrow$ ACT), but at this point only the left hand argument of the double arrow is available. Next *proposed* is discovered. This word is a label for several ACTS, all of which are compatible with

---

[10]Such a structure is called a *directed, labeled graph*. More formally, a directed graph is a set of triples, $< A,R,B >$, in which A and B are members of the set of concepts, called respectively the *head* and *tail* of the triple, and R is a member of the set of relations between concepts.

[11]"In the spirit" is necessary, rather than "as dictated by," because any particular example of Schank's proposal depends both on the rules for conceptual linkage, which are general, and the interpretation of particular words as referring to concepts with a specific conceptual structure. For example, we have interpreted "propose" in a certain way. Someone who assigned a different conceptual meaning to the word would develop a different comprehension. This represents a general problem about computer simulation theories. In any specific application they thoroughly mix up general ideas about symbol manipulation in cognition and specific ideas about the interpretation of given symbols. This makes it very difficult to test the theory in any specific situation, since if the simulation does not work one does not know whether to blame the general theory or the specific interpretation. This problem is made especially difficult by the fact that people will have varying difficulty in solving logical problems stated with familiar or unfamiliar content, even though the problems are identical at a symbolic level (Wason & Johnson-Laird, 1972). Such an observation, of course, is anathema to a logic based theory of problem solving. It also suggests that if computer simulation models are to be completely successful it will be necessary to define a specific procedure for extracting a person's interpretation of the situation from observations about his behavior. A start in this direction has been made by Waterman and Newell (1972) in their proposal for a computer program that extracts a subject's representation of a problem from a "first level" protocol describing his behavior. It is too early to evaluate the success of this effort.

Denisov as an actor. (At another point in the novel, Denisov proposes an attack on the French left.) The situation is as shown in Fig. 7b. One of the meanings of propose is "X offers marriage to Y," where X is a male and Y a female person. When *to Natalia* is encountered, it becomes clear that the appropriate conceptualization is of a marriage proposal, and the ITM structure is completed (Fig. 7c). Note that the preposition "to" is not needed, although it could be used as a clue to syntax. A program modeled after Schank's theory could easily handle a terse telegram, *Denisov proposes Natalia.*

A strong psychological assumption of the model is that paraphrases are regarded as being psychologically equivalent. Suppose that the conceptual representation of the verb *dance* is "PP$_1$ and PP$_2$ move accompanied by music." This implies that no distinction would be made between *Denisov danced the mazurka with Natalia* and *Natalia danced the mazurka with Denisov,* since the two sentences will have equivalent conceptual representations. Of course, *Natalia* and *Denisov* could not be changed in the *proposed* example, because this would change the conceptual structure. The example corresponds with intuition, and also with observations from the laboratory. A number of experiments have shown that if ideas are presented to people at separate times, but in different grammatical forms, then the people are unlikely to notice the change, but that they are quite sensitive to changes in meaning (Barclay, 1973).

Schank's stress on the role of conceptualization and predictive analysis in speech comprehension is mirrored by a number of other studies of various aspects of computer comprehension of natural language. Wilks' (1973a, 1973b) work on mechanical translation and Winograd's (1972, 1973) work on machine execution of commands phrased in natural language are typical. Both programs attempt to extract a propositional statement from a sentence and respond to it, rather than establishing a mechanical correspondence between input and output. This forces both Wilks and

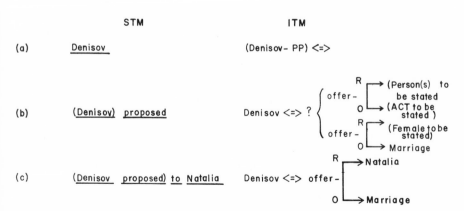

FIG. 7. Example of the construction of a conceptualization. The ambiguity at (b) is resolved by the naming of a female person *and* by the failure to name an ACT in (c). R indicates a relation of reception between an ACT and a PP; O indicates the verb-object relation.

Winograd to maintain partially developed conceptual graphs and to interpret a given utterance in the light of what the program knows about the current state of the world. Anderson and Bower (1973), after a very careful review of representation schemes for ideas in memory, state that they do not see any way to avoid using meaning structures held in an intermediate-term memory area. In spite of such arguments, the concept of ITM remains curiously ephemeral. On the one hand, it has to be there. On the other hand, the hard-headed empiricist can properly observe that no one has developed experimental operations that differentially affect ITM, STM, and LTM. Thus we have no empirically convincing observation of ITM's reality. We suggest that finding such evidence is possible and would be a rewarding activity for a clever experimenter.

Long-Term Memory

The final box left in the distributed memory model is the permanent data store-LTM. Virtually every modern theory of memory asserts that such a storage area exists. Theorists are also generally agreed (although on very little evidence) that information does not actually drop out of LTM, although access to it may be lost. An excellent analogy is to a library that never has books removed from its shelves but where index cards may be lost.

In discussing LTM we must distinguish between architectural hypotheses, which address questions about the data communication within LTM and between LTM and other components of the system architecture, and data structure hypotheses, which address questions about the logical organization of information in LTM. Computer simulation is a natural tool for dealing with data structure hypotheses, and some of the relevant work is dealt with in Section VI. Computer simulation has been much less used to investigate architectural hypotheses. On the other hand, psychologists with a rather different orientation have conducted many studies that could be seen as tests of various LTM architectural hypotheses. A complete simulation model would have to come to grips with some of their major findings. We shall mention a few of the most important.

There is a very large body of clinical, neurophysiological. and experimental evidence indicating that LTM contains separate processing areas for speech and patterned nonspeech information (Gazzaniga, 1970). Simulation studies have, in general, ignored this fact and worked only with the asserted propositional form of information. The situation is complicated by Day's (1973) discovery that there are marked individual differences in the extent to which people rely on speech or nonspeech processes in situations where the stimuli permit a choice. Like most of experimental psychology, the simulation approach more or less assumes that there will be a general explanation for mental phenomena. The work on speech processing suggests that it may be necessary to use quite different stimulations to mimic the thinking processes of different individuals.[12]

In computer terminology, information in LTM can be read by the STM and buffer

---

[12] For further elaboration of this point, see Hunt, Frost, and Lunneborg, 1973.

memory systems. This must be the case, since otherwise we would be unable to recognize sound patterns as phonemes or words in our learned language. "Reading," in this situation, evidently means bringing the LTM memory code to a sufficient state of excitation so that it forces its way into either a buffer or STM area. Indeed, Craik and Lockhart (1972) have argued that STM itself is best conceived of as the set of LTM items currently in the highest state of excitation, rather than as a separate box in the head. Whatever the merits of this argument, it appears that (*a*) the reading process is not necessarily a conscious one, (*b*) that it occurs in parallel for different parts of the buffer system, and (*c*) that the act of reading information in LTM affects the reading of related information. All these points were made in a study by Lewis (1970). His subjects shadowed the information input to one ear during a dichotic listening task. Repetition of the information in the attended ear was disrupted if semantically related information (e.g., synonyms) were input to the other ear. This means that the subjects must have responded to the meaning of the nonattended information, even though the information was not consciously processed and, in the terminology of the distributed memory model, never entered STM.

In contrast to reading, writing information into LTM may only take place through the STM–ITM system. This conclusion is suggested by experiments by Bower and Winzenz (1969), in which they presented stimuli in such a way that the subject structured them in one form during presentation. For instance, by pausing in presenting the information, a sequence of digits can be structured as

$$1,4,9 \qquad 6,3,2,1 \qquad 4,8 \qquad 7,5$$

Subjects learn such sequences after a few repetitions. On the other hand, it is very difficult to learn the sequence if the grouping is changed, e.g., to

$$1,4 \qquad 9,6,3 \qquad 2,1,4 \qquad 8,7,5$$

on each trial.

Bower (1970) has presented a complete review of these and other studies, all of which indicate that if linguistic material is to be recalled with any degree of accuracy it must be structured into related groups of information. Furthermore, such structuring requires time and space. In the theory, this is what ITM is for.

Whether these findings are restricted to linguistically meaningful material is not at all clear. There is some evidence that nonlinguistic visual material is "written" directly into ITM and LTM without an intervening holding and organization period in STM. (Is STM perhaps a property of the linguistic processor?) This is consistent with the observation that humans have an excellent capacity for recognition of nonlinguistic pattern information, even after a very brief exposure to it. Literally hundreds of faces can be recognized as having been seen before, after only a single exposure (Shepard, 1967). On the other hand, recall of such information is difficult to demonstrate. It might be that Pylyshyn's argument about propositional structures is correct, and that we can only recall information that contains an entry in the propositional information system. This, in turn, may require ITM processing. To continue the library analogy, perhaps any peripheral memory can write into LTM, but only ITM can manipulate the indexing system.

V. PROGRAMMING CONCEPTS

Production Systems

A computer is useless without a method for programming it. If we are going to regard the brain as a computing device, then we must postulate something that is functionally analagous to the instruction cycle of an electronic computer, yet physically compatible with what we know of the brain's physical functioning. To do this, we shall make use of a particular programming technique called *production systems,* which was first developed for use with computer languages and which Newell and Simon (1972) have brilliantly applied to the analysis of human problem solving. Our discussion differs from Newell and Simon's in that we shall emphasize "psychological" interpretations of programming actions, whereas Newell and Simon (1972, p. 804) note that such an interpretation is possible, but concentrate attention on the formal details of the method. Our concern will produce a number of technical differences between the Newell and Simon production system model and our own.

Let us write S for a structure in STM, and $I_i (i = 0,1 \ldots)$ for a structure in ITM. A *production* is a rule of the form

(1) $S; I_0, I_1, I_2 \rightarrow S'; I'_0, I'_1, I'_2; A.$

It is interpreted as

"If the structure in STM has the form of S, and the structures in ITM have the form $I_0, I_1,$ etc., place structure S' in STM and structures $I'_0, I'_1,$ etc. in ITM, then take action A."

The expression "in the form of" must be amplified. We consider the structures of a production as being general structures stored in LTM. A general structure is a sort of template, as $X + Y$ is a template for the particular structure $3 + 2$. The left-hand side of a production is said to be recognized if STM and ITM contain a specific example of the template. When the contents of STM and ITM are changed, whatever substitutions are required to match the specific examples in STM and ITM with the templates on the left side of the production will be carried over to produce specific structures from the templates on the right hand side.[13] For instance, suppose the task is to add two numbers. The production rule is

(2) $x + y; 0 \rightarrow \text{sum } (x, y); 0$

which states that if the form $x + y$ is recognized in STM, it is to be replaced by the sum of $x + y$. In a concrete case, $3 + 2$ would be replaced by 5.

This example implies the need for the concept of *variable types.* (This should not be confused with the *data type* concept discussed in Section III.) A production system

---

[13]More formally, let S and I be structures in STM and ITM containing variables $x_0, x_1 \ldots x_k$, and let x_i/t_i be the operation of replacing variable x_i by term t_i. A substitution $\pi = x_0/t_0 \ldots x_k/t_k$ is the operation of replacing the indicated variables in the substitution by terms. Let $S\pi$ be the resulting structure. In a specific application, a production is the operation

$$S\pi; I\pi \rightarrow S'\pi; I'\pi; A\pi$$

structure cannot be filled in by any substitution of lexical items; otherwise we would have such inanities as "2 + Annabel." Each variable in a structure must specify the class of lexical items that can serve as substitutions. We shall introduce special notation for variables of a particular type as we need them.

We shall also use the concept of a *primitive function*. A primitive function is an action that either tests to determine whether a particular relationship holds between two items in STM or ITM, or that finds an item in LTM that stands in a specific relationship to an item in STM or LTM. For example, we shall use the function *ident* (X,Y), which maps any pair of terms of the same type into the possible logical terms, TRUE and FALSE. Another example is the function *next* (X,Y) where X is an item and Y is a list containing X. The value of the function is the item succeeding X on Y, e.g., the value of *next* (b, alphabet) is c. Since use of a primitive function entails an *ad hoc* psychological assumption, every effort should be made to use as few such functions as possible within a given production system. Of course, a function that is "primitive" to one production system may imply a complex sequence of actions in itself.

What happens if the contents of the STM–ITM system matches the left-hand side of two or more productions? We shall intentionally leave this partly unspecified, to permit variations in problem solution at different times. There is one situation in which we want recognition to be biased toward choice of a particular production. Suppose that there are two productions, P_1 and P_2, with left-hand sides L_1 and L_2, respectively. We say that L_2 is less general than L_1 if L_2 can be derived from L_1 by substitution of terms for variables in L_1. For example, 3 + 2 is less general than X + Y. If L_1 and L_2 both match the STM–ITM system, then L_2 should be recognized in preference to L_1.[14]

Now let us consider a psychological interpretation of the production system technique. Productions are rules for (cognitive) actions. The rules themselves reside in LTM. There is sometimes a temptation to regard LTM as being similar to a computer's memory, i.e., a passive store for large amounts of information. We conceive of LTM in a different way, as an active pattern recognizer that continually "watches" the STM–ITM system in an attempt to match the left-hand side of production systems, thus activating them. This conceptualization represents a major difference from the use of production systems in computer science. In computing, production systems are *ordered* sets of productions. In the distributed memory model, production systems are probabilistically ordered, in the sense that the activation of one production will leave STM–ITM in a certain class of states, thus

[14]We will not go into a detailed justification of this rule. Studies in artificial intelligence indicate that it is required for efficient problem solving (Quinlan & Hunt, 1968). A simple illustration shows how useful it is. A production system for doing mental arithmetic might well contain the following productions

$$P_1 \qquad X \cdot Y; \rightarrow \text{product } (X, Y);;$$

$$P_2 \qquad 10 \cdot Y; \rightarrow Y0;;$$

which allows rapid multiplication by 10.

increasing the probability that another specific production in the set of productions will be applied. Since LTM is basically a probabilistic pattern recognizer, there always exists some chance of breaking the "normal" order of production application. Breaks will, in turn, be biased to occur at certain points and in certain ways.

The rest of this section illustrates how the production system technique can be applied to study psychological problems. Newell and Simon offer similar demonstrations in their studies of symbolic logic, chess, and cryptarithmetic. Because of the complexity of the tasks studied, it is difficult to use their work for pedagogy. We have chosen to look at simpler tasks, but in each case to tasks that build on each other, in the sense that each one requires a more complex simulation than the task preceding it. Lest we be misunderstood, we stress again that our illustrations are intended to demonstrate the method, and not to make a point about the "true" psychological model for the tasks analyzed. For each of the three tasks described below there is a fairly extensive literature on both experimental findings and theoretical explanation. We make no attempt to survey such works.

Simple Reasoning about Pictures

Coordinating visual and verbal statements is certainly a common human activity. We can obtain information about reality either by hearing a description of a scene or by direct exposure to it. In order to decide if a scene and its description are in agreement the internal representations derived from speech and observation must be compared.

Clark and Chase (1972) have studied human performance in a task that isolates the comparison process in what, at first, appears to be its pure form. The scenes they studied were very simple, consisting of either a picture of an asterisk ("star") over a plus or vice versa. We symbolize the two scenes as (*/+) or (+/*). Clark and Chase showed their subjects a sentence describing such scenes on the left-hand side of a computer display screen, and the scene itself on the right-hand side. Thus normal reading order would lead the subject to read the description, then look at the scene. The subject's task was to indicate whether or not the sentence accurately described the scene. Sentences were constructed from the eight grammatical combinations of (star, plus) (is, is not) (above, below) (plus, star). Typical sentences, then, were "Star is above plus" and "Star is not below plus." Each sentence can be described by stating the *subject* (star or plus, which also determines the object), the *preposition* (above or below), and the presence or absence of *negation*. In order to complete the task, a person must first create an internal code of the sentence, then encode the picture, and finally compare the two. By analyzing the latencies for reading plus decision, and showing how the latencies varied with the form of the sentence and its relation to the picture, Clark and Chase were able to argue for the following model:

1) A sentence is encoded in terms of preposition, subject, and negation.

2) The preposition is recalled, and it determines how the picture is viewed.

3) The picture is coded by finding the appropriate subject for the preposition.

4) To determine truth or falsity, the subjects of the two representations (picture and sentence) are compared and a variable is set to TRUE if the subjects are identical.

The sentence representation is then examined for the presence of NOT. If NOT is present, the current value of the variable is negated.[15]

In order to present these ideas as a production system some added notation is required.

ϕ = An empty string in STM or ITM.

x = Any string of items in STM, including a null string.

y = Any structure of items in ITM, including a null structure.

OP = A variable type that may take the values ABOVE or BELOW.

A = A variable type that may take the values PLUS or STAR.

(+/*) = STM representation of the visual image "Plus above star."

(*/+) = STM representation of the visual image "Star above plus."

L = A variable type that may take the values TRUE or FALSE.

$ident$(x,y) = A primitive operation that is TRUE if its arguments are identical, FALSE otherwise.

$\neg$ = The negation operation.

Table 1 contains a production system sufficient to simulate the Clark and Chase paradigm. The productions in this table are divided into three sets: productions for encoding the sentence, encoding the image, and comparing the two codings to determine the response. The productions do not predict the Clark and Chase data; they were chosen to reproduce it. Because the simulation was designed only to deal with this specific situation it was possible to make two restrictive assumptions. It has been assumed that the entire linguistic string can be placed in STM and that, once the subject of the sentence has been determined, the object may be disregarded. The latter assumption is true because all the sentences used in the study have an identical grammatical structure. Clearly neither assumption is true in general. We note, though, that dealing with more general linguistic structures would not present any problems that could not be handled, in principle, by a production-system approach. Schank's analysis of comprehension could be written as a production system.

Although the production system in Table 1 was chosen in a conscious effort to follow Clark and Chase's model, an interesting fact about the model turns out to be a consequence of any production system. The model assumes that the encoding stages are separate and sequential; in the production system they must be. It also follows, from both the Clark and Chase model and the production-system approach, that the time required to make a particular judgment will depend upon the grammatical form and the truth value of the sentences used. Not all productions are required to encode all sentences. Table 2 shows the productions required as a function of grammatical form. From this table it can be seen that sentences containing NOT should require more time in both the sentence encoding and comparison stage. We might also expect to find a difference between sentences involving ABOVE and BELOW. The theory itself does not dictate the direction of this difference, although Clark and Chase have argued that BELOW should take longer to encode than ABOVE, because of

---

[15]There is some evidence in the Clark and Chase data, and in related work by Trabasso, Rollins, and Shaughnessy (1971) that the index should be set to TRUE initially, and then changed each time a mismatch is detected.

TABLE 1

Production System for Clark and Chase's Sentence – Picture Comparison Experiment

Production	Comment
I. Encoding of sentence	
P1. Ax; $\phi \rightarrow x$; A	If first symbol of STM is an object and ITM is empty, move object name to ITM.
P2. NOT x; $y \rightarrow x$; y NOT	If first symbol of STM is NOT, move NOT to end of the structure in ITM.
P3. OP x; $y \rightarrow x$; OP y	If first symbol of STM is an OP symbol, move it to front of the structure in ITM.
P4. A; $y \rightarrow \phi$; y	If STM contains a single object name, remove it.
P5. ϕ; OP $y \rightarrow$ OP; y	If STM is empty and the first symbol of the structure in ITM is an OP, move the OP name to STM.
II. Image encoding productions	
P6. (A_1/A_2) ABOVE; $y \rightarrow A_1$; y	If an image and the term ABOVE are in STM, replace the contents of STM with the image's upper object name.
P7. (A_1/A_2) BELOW; $y \rightarrow A_2$; y	Similar to P6, except for use of BELOW and the lower object name.
III. Comparison operations	
P8. A_1; $A_2 y \rightarrow$ Identical (A_1, A_2); y	Compare the object name in STM to the first object name in ITM.
P9. L; $\phi \rightarrow \phi$;ϕ; output (L)	If STM contains a boolean variable (i.e., either TRUE or FALSE) and ITM is empty, output the value of the variable.
P10. L; NOT $y \rightarrow \neg$ L; y	If STM contains a boolean variable and the first symbol in STM is NOT, negate the STM variable and remove NOT from ITM.

psycholinguistic considerations that do not concern us. Table 3 shows some relevant comparisons from Clark and Chase's study. Clearly the greatest difference between sentences is due to the presence or absence of NOT. A smaller, though consistent, difference is due to the ABOVE–BELOW distinction.

TABLE 2

Conditions under which the Sentence Encoding Productions of the Clark and Chase Paradigm Are Required

Conditions of use	Productions
1. Productions used for all sentences	. P1, P3, P4, P5, P8, P9
2. Production used only if sentence contains ABOVE	P6
3. Productions used if sentence contains BELOW	P7
4. Productions used if sentence contains NOT	P2, P10

TABLE 3

Times to Encode and Compare Sentences and Pictures
(Rearranged from Data by Clark and Chase, 1972)

Sentence contains	TRUE	FALSE
ABOVE	1744	1959
BELOW	1875	2035
NOT ABOVE	2624	2470
NOT BELOW	2739	2520

It might be argued that this comparison is faulted, simply because sentences containing NOT have an additional morpheme, and thus take longer to read. There are some reasons to disbelieve this, both because of the size of the difference and because a related series of experiments by Trabasso, Rollins, and Shaughnessy (1971) indicate that an appreciable difference in the processing time of logical statements cannot be explained by a small difference in the number of words. Nevertheless, it would be best to challenge the question directly. This was done in our laboratory, in an unpublished study by Hunt and Ellis. Recall that in the basic Clark and Chase paradigm both sentence and picture are exposed simultaneously, with the picture to the right of the sentence. Hunt and Ellis separated these stages. First a sentence was exposed, until the subject indicated he understood the sentence by pressing a button. A picture was then exposed immediately, and the subject compared the remembered sentence to the picture. The production system model assumes that there will still be a difference at the second (judgement) stage, since production P10 will be called only if the sentence contained a NOT. Figure 8 shows the results; clearly the judgement time was affected by the form of the sentence, even though the sentence had been read before the picture was exposed.

One of the ways in which one shows that a hypothetical construct in psychology is useful is to show that measures of it enter into meaningful relationships with other, better established, measures. In psychology systematic individual differences can be observed in almost every interesting task. In particular, Hunt, Frost, and Lunneborg (1973) have found that reaction time measurements taken in "basic" cognitive tasks are related to intelligence as measured by conventional psychometric tests. If our combination of the distributed memory and production system approach is correct, then surely the time required to activate a production should be an important part of an individual's ability to process information. Therefore it ought to display some relationship to psychometric intelligence. A second part of the Hunt and Ellis study addressed this point. They used two groups of subjects: college students who scored in the highest or lowest quartile of a test of verbal intelligence. An estimate of the time required to activate production P10 can be obtained by subtracting the time required to make comparisons after sentences that did not contain NOT from the time required to make comparisons after sentences that did contain NOT. As Fig. 8 shows, this estimate is substantially greater for subjects with (comparatively) low verbal intelligence. This is consistent with the findings in a number of related studies in our laboratories, in showing that low verbal intelligence is generally associated with slower information manipulation in short-term memory.

In summary, analysis of the Clark and Chase study suggests that the processes that encode the physical environment need not retain all information from the physical environment. The production system of Table 1 retains only one of the visual elements during image encoding and does not retain the object of the sentence. The reaction time data of Table 3 suggest that the nature of the stimulus determines the processing that it receives. Productions 2 and 10 are applied only to those sentences containing the word NOT, resulting in longer reaction times for these sentences. The Hunt and Ellis study indicates that one of the factors that affects the time to process a production is also related to verbal activity, perhaps in a causal relationship.

Verification Based on Knowledge

Meyer (1973) observed that the verification of statements about common knowledge is very similar to the Clark and Chase paradigm. What happens if a person is asked to judge the truth of sentences like "Apples are edible"? The sentence must be

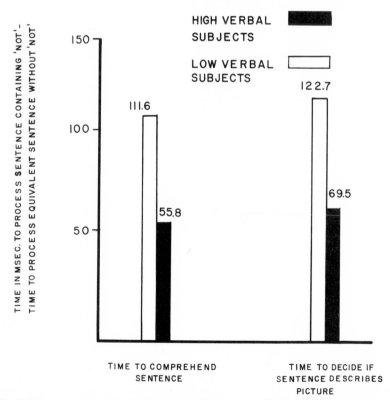

FIG. 8. Time to process negation during process of sentence encoding and picture examination (Hunt & Ellis, unpublished).

analyzed to determine its assertion about the relationship between apples and edibility, the facts about that relationship must be retrieved from memory, the two representations must be compared, and finally a response must be computed. If this is, indeed, a reasonable description of the psychological processes involved, then a formal model should closely resemble a formal model of behavior in the Clark and Chase paradigm. On the negative side, verification of sentences from memory is a much more complicated situation. The biggest problem is that the nature of the verifying information is not clear. The experimenter and subject see the same visual display, but the experimenter cannot know how information is stored in the subject's brain. Therefore it is necessary to choose the sentences to be verified in such a way that the same memorized information must be retrieved for each sentence, regardless of the sentence's linguistic structure. A second problem is that we must be careful of the linguistic structure itself. It is easy to show that the ''man in the street'' will not always interpret a logical sentence as a logician would (Wason & Johnson-Laird, 1972). Nevertheless, a subject in an experiment will respond to his own, not the experimenter's, interpretation of a sentence.

Meyer attempted to avoid the above problems by training adult subjects to verify *particular affirmative* (PA) and *universal negative* (UN) sentences. A PA sentence asserts that at least one member of set X is also a member of set Y. An example sentence is ''Some doctors are women.''[16] A UN statement is a denial of the corresponding PA; it asserts that no members of class X are members of Y, e.g., ''No doctors are women.'' The truth value of both statements is determined by the same information. The PA sentence ''Some X are Y'' is true if and only if the sets of X and Y objects have a non-empty intersection. Naturally, the corresponding UN, ''No X are Y,'' is false.

Meyer's experimental task was, logically at least, identical to Clark and Chase's, except that the pictures were present only in the mind. Subjects sat before a screen on which PA or UN sentences about common objects were displayed. The subject responded (presumably after consulting memory) by indicating if the sentence was true or false. The response latency was recorded. As all questions could be answered without deep thought (as in the examples above) there were very few errors.

The production system we propose for this task is very similar to that proposed for the Clark and Chase study. We need to use the symbol $\cap$ (intersection), and its negation, $\overline{\cap}$. These play the same logical role as did the visual symbols ($+/*$) and ($*/+$) in the previous discussion. The encoding productions are given in the first part of Table 4.

[16]Wason and Johnson-Laird (1972) discuss the effects of some common reinterpretations of logical statements upon deductive reasoning. The PA sentence ''Some X are Y'' is a good example of this point. Wason and Johnson-Laird observed that a common ''naive'' interpretation of this is ''Some X are Y, but some are not.'' If this is so, an untrained subject might assert that ''Some girls are females'' is false, while to a logician it is clearly true. More formally, a PA sentence is true if the intersection of X and Y is not empty. This condition is met if X is a subset of Y. From the Wason and Johnson-Laird report, we conclude that this interpretation is not always accepted by (nonlogician) native speakers. The problem does not seem to have arisen in Meyer's experiment, probably because he used subjects who received considerable training to familiarize them with the task.

TABLE 4

Production System for Meyer Study

Production	Comment
1. NO x; $\to x;\urcorner$	Negatives are processed last.
2. SOME x; $\to x$;	Linguistic encoding productions
3. X ARE Y; $y \to$ X,Y;$\cap$ y	
4. X,Y; $y \to intersect$ (X,Y); y	Memory search production; *intersect* (X,Y) is a function with value $\cap$ if the memory representations of X and Y intersect, $\emptyset$ otherwise.
5. S_1 ; S_2, $y \to ident$ (S_1,S_2); y	S is a variable which may have value $\cap$ or $\emptyset$.
6. L ; 0 → 0; 0; *output* (L)	Comparison productions
7. L ;$\urcorner y \to \urcorner$L ; y	

Application of productions 1–3 will produce the STM–ITM data structures

    X,Y ; 0   for PA sentences

and

    X,Y ;$\urcorner$ for UN sentences.

Production 4 triggers a search of memory, given two variable terms. The nature of the search need not be specified here, since the same search process will apply regardless of whether or not a PA or UN term has been received, i.e., the search itself depends only on the identity of the X and Y terms. Finally, productions 5–7 control the comparison and response production processes.

   We again eschew any claim to originality; the production system proposed is essentially a restatement, in the modified Newell-Simon terminology, of Meyer's explanation in justifying his study. How well does it fit the data? Two important qualitative predictions can be made. The most obvious is that there will be a negation effect, since an additional production is required at both the encoding and comparison stages in order to process UN statements. Meyer has confirmed this prediction. He found that it required an average of 200 msec longer to process UN as compared to PA sentences. A subtler prediction is that the time for a memory search will not be (directly) affected by the logical status of the statement, but rather will depend solely on the identity of the X and Y terms. Meyer argued that if this is true, then there should be no interaction between the type of sentence (PA, UN) and any change in X-Y relation that was known to change memory search time. In previous research Meyer (1970) had shown that the set relationship between X and Y is such a variable. Specifically, suppose subjects are asked to determine whether X and Y do intersect. For added simplicity, let us confine ourselves solely to a situation in which the answer is always "YES," i.e., in situations in which there is an intersection. The time required to determine this depends upon whether X is a subset of Y (e.g., collies, dogs), a superset (dogs, collies), or whether the two sets overlap (doctors, women). Figure 9 shows Meyer's results for verification of PA and UN sentences when set relationship is varied. The figure indicates that the set relation effect is *roughly* parallel for PA and UN sentences. In fact, the interaction between sentence type and set relation is not significant. On the other hand, one hesitates to accept the null hypothesis, since the set relation effect was 70% greater (109 msec vs. 63 msec) for UN than for PA sentences. In addition, Meyer reported a number of additional analyses (which we will not detail) all of which were consistent with the hypothesis that relative difficulty between two memory searches, X,Y and X*,Y*, increases if the terms are presented in UN rather than PA sentences. The interaction effect is best described as small but persistent.

This result is compatible with the production system model proposed here, providing we introduce one further assumption: that the memory search, symbolized here by the function *intersect,* is itself a production system that uses the ITM–STM system. The efficiency of the search will thus depend upon the extent to which space is available in working memory. If the search is called in order to answer a PA question,

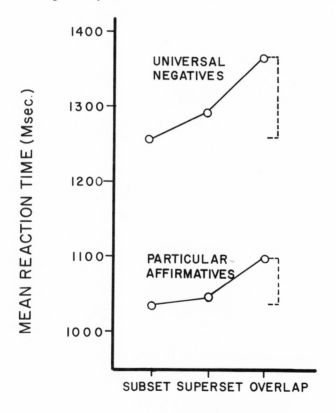

FIG. 9. Mean RT for particular affirmatives and universal negatives as a function of set relation. Dashed braces indicate the comparative magnitudes of the set-relation effect for the two types of proposition (reproduced from Meyer, 1970).

all ITM is available except the space (or, alternatively, effort) required to maintain the symbol ∩ . If the search is called to verify a UN statement, space must be reserved for twice as many symbols, ∩ and ⌐. This difference might not affect simple memory searches, but could alter the efficiency of the search process if an extensive investigation of memory was required.

To conclude this section, it appears that generally similar production systems can handle the sentence verification task, regardless of whether the verification is by reference to visually presented or memorized information. Dealing with memorized information introduces two new considerations: the need for a memory search and the possibility that the memory search competes with the verification process for STM and ITM resources. In Section VI we consider a task that throws more light on how the search itself might proceed.

The Series Completion Task

At this point we have discussed, somewhat vaguely, how computer simulation can be applied to very complex tasks, such as chess or language comprehension, and then described very precisely simulations of two tasks that, although they do involve cognition, certainly do not involve great mental effort. The reader may have been impressed by the number of *ad hoc* assumptions that had to be introduced even to explain the simple task of deciding whether a star is or is not above a plus. This, of course, is one of the advantages of computer simulation. It forces the theorist to make all the assumptions about a task precise. When this is done it often becomes clear that what was seen as simple is really not so simple.

We will now try to bridge the gap between analyses of simple tasks that can be done ''in the style of simulation,'' but without a computer, and the analysis of very complex tasks, for which the analysis itself cannot be understood without actually running the computer program. We will do this by dealing with a problem of ''intermediate'' complexity, the task of discovering rules for generating sequences of symbols. Since the task probably represents the limits of complexity of a model that can be understood without pointing to computer output, many readers may prefer to skim this section, as it is of necessity much concerned with detail. Other readers, however, may find it instructive to observe how much detail is required in a substantial computer simulation effort.

The class of tasks with which we shall deal are, roughly, the most difficult of the numerous serial pattern recognition tasks reviewed by Jones in Chapter 5 of this volume. The particular task to be studied was originally developed by Thurstone for use in intelligence testing. The subject is shown a sequence of k letters and asked to continue the sequence for one or more letters, ''using the same rule.'' For instance, what is the next letter in the sequence

(3)   a b c d e f ____?

Virtually every adult would agree that the answer is ''g.'' As we shall illustrate, much more difficult problems can be developed.

Formally, in a series completion problem one is given a sequence, $s_0, s_1 \ldots s_{n-1}$

of n symbols drawn from some previously defined alphabet, and asked to predict the $n+1$st symbol. The problem solver is assured that, in fact, the entire sequence has been generated by a rule, f, such that for all k,

(4) $s_k = f(s_0, s_1 \ldots s_{k-1})$.

The rule f will, itself, be concocted from some set of simpler rules, $r_0, r_1 \ldots r_p$ which are presumed to be known to the problem solver. The problem is generally solved by describing f in terms of these more primitive functions. For example, in the trivial problem represented by sequence (3), f can be defined in terms of the *next* relation,

(5) $s_k = \begin{cases} \text{a if } k = 0 \\ next(s_{k-1}) \text{ if } k > 0. \end{cases}$

A more complex problem, which comes nearer to capturing the effort involved in most series completion items, is

(6)   a n b o c p ____

We urge that the reader try to solve this problem before reading onward. After a brief conscious effort, in which at least some problem solving steps are clearly defined, it will be discovered that the sequence can be defined by the rule

(7) $s_k = \begin{cases} \text{a} & k = 0 \\ \text{n} & k = 1 \\ next(s_{k-2}) & k > 1 \end{cases}$

There are two basic ways in which psychologists can approach the study of problem solving behavior in this situation. One is to attempt to find a way of describing the generating rule, f, so that the complexity of the description is related to the psychological effort required in discovering f. The other alternative, which is of more concern to us, is to ask what sort of problem solving steps are required to construct an answer. To connect the two approaches, the first approach seeks to find the "internal language" in which a pattern generating rule is framed, while the second seeks to find a mechanism for forming sentences in the internal language. Simon and his associates have done several studies of series-completion problem-solving behavior (Kotovsky & Simon, 1973; Simon, 1972; Simon & Kotovsky, 1963; Simon & Lea, 1972). Our approach is patterned closely after theirs. Before plunging into the details of our analysis, we would like to point out two psychologically important ways in which the series completion task is markedly different from the other tasks we have analyzed.

The first is that performance on this task is far from perfect. We can make a clearcut distinction between problems that are solved incorrectly and problems on which the subject simply gives up. A measure of the difficulty of a series completion problem can be derived from the number of errors encountered on the problem, or from latency scores. Kotovsky and Simon (1973) found the correlation between measures to be so high that either measure adequately represents problem difficulty.

A second point is even more important. "Thought" in the serial completion task is not spontaneous. It is organized. The series completion task is one that most people report as requiring conscious effort. This, in turn, leads the typical person to a good deal of introspection about how his problem solving processes should be organized. Such a concern with the organization of thought is typical of most people's approach to difficult problems, as is evidenced by the amount of concern for organization voiced by Newell and Simon's (1972) subjects, when asked to "think aloud" while solving problems in chess, logic, and cryptarithmetic. Turning to our familiar analogy, computer problem solving, we find a similar distinction on examining programs for solving "easy" or "difficult" computational problems. A program for an easy computational problem, such as finding the mean of a set of numbers, is composed almost entirely of operations that deal directly with data—reading it in, altering it, and printing the results. A program for a hard operation, such as translation from a complex language like FORTRAN or ALGOL into machine operations, contains a substantial number of operations whose purpose is *not* to deal with data, but rather to organize a number of "simpler" subprograms so that they deal directly with data and in the correct order. Simon (1969) has speculated that this sort of difference between devices to accomplish easy and hard tasks is characteristic of all information processing, whether carried out by mechanical, electrical, or biological devices. As the reader will observe, we accept his speculation.

With these remarks in mind, let us take a closer look at the series completion task. A series is typically composed of *periods* of m letters, such that the pattern description rule f can be established by finding a simple rule for each letter in the period. Each rule consists of a relation and a letter position in the prior period or an earlier position in the same period. Let us call this the *base* letter, and the letter being defined the *target* letter. Each target letter can be produced by applying the relation to the base letter. In the first period of the sequence, the rule may not be applicable because the base letters have not yet been defined. In this case, the letter is called an *initial base letter*, and its definition is a part of the pattern description rule f. For example, consider the sequence

(8)   a b m c d m e f m _____

This sequence has a period length of three letters. Let the letters in a period be denoted s_0, s_1, s_2, and the letters in the preceding period be p_0, p_1, p_2. The generating rule is

(9) $s_0 = \text{next} (p_1)$
       $s_1 = \text{next} (s_0)$
       $s_2 = \text{same} (p_2)$
       Base letter $s_0 = $ a
       Base letter $s_2 = $ m.

To solve the problem it is first necessary to discover the period length, and then the rules used to generate target letters within the period. In order to do this, the problem solver must have access to a store of simple relations, such as *next,* out of which the period generating rule is to be composed. Simon (1972) has made the useful observation that virtually all the problems studied by psychologists involve series that can be generated using the primitive terms *same, next,* and *predecessor,* defined on any ordered set of symbols, and the relations *sum, difference,* and *k's complement,* defined on the integers. Since we will be concerned only with the alphabet, we consider only the first three relations. Kotovsky and Simon (1973) observed further that *same* is detected more readily than *next,* and *next* more readily than *predecessor.* Therefore we shall assume that the problem solver has stored in LTM an ordered set,

(10) $R = (same, next, predecessor)$

which can be accessed "from front to back" when searching for a solution. The same authors also noted that relations between adjacent pairs [e.g., the *next* relation between the first two letters in (8)] are detected more readily than relationships between nonadjacent pairs [e.g. the *same* relation between every third letter in (8)]. These are the psychological facts upon which we shall build our theoretical super-structure.

The next capability we require in the problem solver introduces a fundamentally new concept, as compared to the programming concepts used in the simpler situations. This is the idea of a "closed procedure," i.e., the notion that a production system can transfer control to a subordinate system and resume control when the subordinate system has completed its task. We note with interest that the same device has been introduced in Newell and Simon's analysis of cryptarithmetic, symbolic logic, and chess problems. The notion is a very powerful one. Unfortunately it brings with it a host of unanswered (and usually unaddressed) questions about how the brain, and in particular the memory system, keeps track of the interplay between "calling" and "called" production systems. We speculate that most of the communication is done by placing data and results in STM, and our theoretical proposals below reflect this decision. On the other hand, we have not dealt with all the problems of memory management that the introduction of the closed procedure concept requires.

The structures that we have permitted in STM and ITM have thus far been ordered sets which were always accessed from first to last element. To deal with the series completion task we require a mechanism for addressing the kth item directly. We will do this by the use of indices (indicated by I,J,K,L,M) to refer to addressing element s_i, s_j, etc. from set S. We have assumed that the operation of accessing an element will cause the END symbol to be stored in STM if the index exceeds the set size. The presence of indices in the production does not mean that we literally believe people have indices "in their heads." Indices are used as counting processes for notational convenience only. Indeed, in some cases the information-processing equivalent of counting could be achieved simply by looking at the letter string, e.g., to see if a particular letter is in the first or second half of the string. We argue that subjects indeed use such devices, but that the indexing operations we describe are equivalent at the information processing level. Several indices are required to solve series completion problems. It appears unrealistic to assume that they are all continuously in the limited capacity STM. Instead we shall assume that indices may be held perma-nently (i.e., for the duration of the problem) in ITM, with the current value being copied into STM as that index is to be used.

TABLE 5

Production System to Control Solution of Letter Sequence Problems

A1.	; →	;	; Read Sequence
A2.	; S →	; S	; Determine Periodicity
A3.	x, FOUND ; y →	x, FOUND ; y	; Describe Pattern
A4.	; y →	; y	; Output Answer

A number of ordered sets are required in ITM. These will be indicated by capital letters other than (I,J,K,L,M) e.g., R as in Eq. (10). Besides R, the important ITM sets are S, the set of known letters in a serial completion problem, and Z, the ordered set of rules defining how to compute the letters within a given period. As before, the elements of ordered sets will be referred to by lower case letters, indexed by the order of their appearance within a set. Thus r_0 is *same*, the first relation in set R, while s_2 is the third letter in a letter sequence problem, and z_1 is the rule defining the value of the second letter in a period. If the subscript is a lower case letter, its numerical value will be defined by the appropriate index. On occasion we shall want to refer to some

TABLE 6

Production System to Determine the Periodicity of a Letter Sequence

B1	; S→(J←0); S,R	Initialize the structure of relations and set the associated index.
B2.	J; S,R→r_j;S,R,J; (J←J+1)	Obtain the next untried relation
B3.	r;y→r;y; Test hypothesis 1	Test whether all letters in each period are related by r.
B4.	r,FOUND;y→r;y; Return	If a hypothesis is correct, return to the controlling program
B5.	r,NOT FOUND;y→r,(M←2),(K←1);y	Initialize the hypothesized period (M) and the test letter position (K)
B6.	r,M,K;y→r,M,K,(K>M);y	Have all letters in a period been tried?
B7.	r,M,K,TRUE;y→r,M,K;y;(M←M+1),(K←1)	If so, try another period.
B8.	r,M,K,FALSE;y→r,M,K,FALSE,(M>½ sequence);y	Have all period lengths been tried?
B9.	r,M,K,FALSE,FALSE;y→r,M,K;y;Test Hypothesis 2	If not, test whether letters M apart starting with position K are related by r.
B10.	r,M,K,FALSE,TRUE;y,J→J;y	If all periods have been tested, then try a new relation.
B11.	r, NOT FOUND,M,K;y→r,M,K;y;(K←K+1)	When a hypothesis fails, try another test letter.

unspecified member of a particular ordered set. In this case we shall use the corresponding lower case letter. By this convention, then, r would refer to any relation in the set R. With these lengthy preliminaries out of the way, we can now begin the description of the system.

TABLE 7

Production System to Test Hypothesis 1, that Relation r Applies to all Letters in each Period

C1.	$r;y \rightarrow r,(K \leftarrow 0),(I \leftarrow 0);y$	Initialize indices for letter counts in a period (K) and in the sequence (I)
C2.	$r,K,I;S,y \rightarrow r,s_k,K,I;S,y;(K \leftarrow K+1),(I \leftarrow I+1)$	Obtain the first letter of a period.
C3.	$r,a,K,I;S,y \rightarrow r,a,s_i;S,y,K,I;(K \leftarrow K+1),(I \leftarrow I+1)$	Obtain the next letter.
C4.	$End,x;y \rightarrow x,FOUND;y$	If all letters have been tested, then the hypothesis is true and the period length is found.
C5.	$r,a_1,a_2;y \rightarrow r,a_1,r(a_1),a_2;y$	Predict the next letter in the sequence
C6.	$r,a_1,a_2,a_3;y \rightarrow r,a_3,ident(a_2,a_3);y$	Is the prediction correct?
C7.	$r,a,TRUE;y,K,I \rightarrow r,a,K,I;y$	If so, then prepare to get the next letter.
C8.	$r,a,false;y,K,I, \rightarrow r,a,K;y,I$	If not, then retrieve the letter count.
C9.	$r,a,K;S,R,J,I \rightarrow r,a,ident(K,1),K;S,R,J,I$	If this is the first period, then test the count to see whether the relation worked for any letters
C10.	$r,a,TRUE,K;y,I \rightarrow r,NOT\ FOUND;y;Return$	If not, the hypothesis fails.
C11.	$r,a,FALSE,K;y,I \rightarrow r,a,FALSE,K,I;y,(M \leftarrow K)$	If the relation worked, then set the period to the number of letters for which it worked and set the count to test the next period.
C12.	$r,a,FALSE,K,I;y \rightarrow r,K,I;y;(K \leftarrow 0)$	
C13.	$r,a,K;y,M,I \rightarrow r,a,K,M;y,M,I$	If this is not the first period, then retrieve the period length and test whether the relation satisfied all letters in the period.
C14.	$r,a,K,M;y \rightarrow r,ident(K,M),K,M;y$	
C15.	$r,TRUE,K,M;y,I \rightarrow r,K,I;y$	If the relation worked, then test the next period.
C16.	$r,FALSE,K,M;y,M,I \rightarrow r,NOT\ FOUND;y;Return$	If the relation failed, then the hypothesis fails.
C17.	$r,x,FOUND;y \rightarrow r,FOUND;y$	If the hypothesis is confirmed, then eliminate the indices and
C18.	$r,FOUND;y,M \rightarrow r,FOUND;y,(z_1 \leftarrow r,0),\ .\ .\ .\ ,(z_m \leftarrow r,m-1),M;Return$	store the rules in the Z structure of ITM.

TABLE 8

Production System to Test Hypothesis 2, that Relation r Applies to Letters
in Position K with Period M

D1.	$r,M,K;y \rightarrow r,M,K,(L \leftarrow K+M);y$	Initialize an index to the position of the test letter.
D2.	$r,M,K,L;S,y \rightarrow r,s_k,M,L;S,y,K$	Obtain the Kth letter
D3.	$r,a,M,L;S,y \rightarrow r,s_l,a,L;S,y,M;(L \leftarrow L+M)$	Obtain the corresponding letter of the next period.
D4.	$End,x;y \rightarrow x$, FOUND;y	If all letters have been processed, then the hypothesis is confirmed.
D5.	$r,a_1, a_2,L;y \rightarrow r,a_1,a_2,r(a_1),L;y$	Apply the rule to the first letter to predict the second.
D6.	$r,a_1,a_2, a_3, L;y \rightarrow r,a_2, L,ident(a_2, a_3);y$	Is the prediction correct?
D7.	$r,a,L,FALSE;y \rightarrow r,NOT\ FOUND;y$	If not, the hypothesis fails.
D8.	$r,NOT\ FOUND;y,M,K \rightarrow r,NOT\ FOUND,M,K;y$;Return	
D9.	$r,a,L,TRUE;y,M \rightarrow r,a,M,L;y$	If the prediction is correct, then prepare to test the next period.
D10.	$r,x,FOUND;y,M,K \rightarrow r,FOUND,K;y,M$	If the hypothesis is confirmed.
D11.	$r,FOUND,K;y,M \rightarrow r,FOUND;y,(z_k \leftarrow r,K),M$;Return	then store the rule and return.

A Production System for the Series Completion Task

Tables 6 through 11 present a production system capable of solving many Thurstone-type serial completion problems. The reader is probably struck with the complexity of the system. Indeed, this is one of our points. We shall now describe the system loosely, indicating what each subsystem does and commenting on how the new theoretical constructs are used.

Productions A1–A4 (Table 5) are executive functions. Their role is to control the order of execution of lower level production systems that deal directly with the problem data. (As every programmer knows, executive procedures are the hallmark of complex programs.) The first subsystem called by the executive program determines the length of the period in a sequence. Reading the sequence has been assumed as a primitive capability. When the period length has been found, the executive initiates a pattern description subsystem. This system's goal is to complete Z, the ITM structure describing the pattern generation rule within a single period. Control is then passed to a process that uses the pattern generation rule and the known part of the sequence of symbols to complete the letter sequence, thus producing an answer.

The procedure for determining periodicity (Productions B1–B11, Table 6) deals directly with problem data. The "generate and test hypothesis" method of problem solving is the algorithm used (Newell & Simon, 1972). At each step a particular relation and period length are assumed, and the letter string is examined to see if the assumption holds. The order of generation of hypotheses is thus quite important.

Relations are chosen, in order, from the list R of primitive relationships. Given a relation, r, the first hypothesis tested is that the relation holds between all pairs of adjacent letters. The (tentative) length of the period is defined by the first pair of adjacent letters for which the relationship does not hold. A period of 3 would be found in the sequence

(11)   a a a b b b c c c _ _ _.

The actual testing of a relationship is accomplished by a "procedure call" to a set of productions designed specifically for examining the letter string. This is again an example of one problem solving system using another in its service, and it raises the

TABLE 9

Production System to Describe the Pattern

E1.	$r,\text{FOUND};y \rightarrow ;y$	Clear STM.
E2.	$;S,R,J,y \rightarrow (K \leftarrow 0);S,R,(J \leftarrow 0),y$	Initialize indices for the relations and letter positions.
E3.	$K;y,Z,M \rightarrow \text{Empty}(z_k),K,M;y,Z,M$	Find the first letter unaccounted for.
E4.	$\text{FALSE},K,M;y \rightarrow \text{ident}(K,M),K;y$	Are all accounted for?
E5.	$\text{TRUE},K;y \rightarrow ;y;\text{Return}$	If all are accounted for, then the description is complete.
E6.	$\text{FALSE},K;y \rightarrow K;y;(K \leftarrow K+1)$	Otherwise, try the next letter.
E7.	$\text{TRUE},K,M;S,y \rightarrow s_{k+m},K,M;S,y$	Obtain the letter of the 2nd period.
E8.	$a,K,M;S,R,J,y \rightarrow a,K,M,J;S,R,y$	Obtain the next
E9.	$a,K,M,J;S,R,y \rightarrow r_j,a,K,M;S,R,J,y;(J \leftarrow J+1)$	untried relation.
E10.	$r,a,K,M;y \rightarrow r,a,(L \leftarrow K+M-1);y,K$	Set an index to obtain the
E11.	$r,a,L;S,y \rightarrow r,a,s_{\ell};S,y,L$	preceeding letter.
E12.	$r,a_1,a_2;y \rightarrow r,r(a_1),a_1,a_2;y$	Does the relation predict the
E13.	$r,a_1,a_2,a_3;y \rightarrow \text{ident}(a_1,a_2),r,a_2;y$	unaccounted for letter?
E14.	$\text{TRUE},x;y,M,K,L \rightarrow M,K,L,x;y,M$	If so,
E15.	$M,K,L,x;y \rightarrow (M>L),M,K,L,x;y$	store the relation and
E16.	$\text{TRUE},M,K,L,r,a;y,Z,M \rightarrow y,Z,M;(z_k \leftarrow r,L)$	the position of
E17.	$\text{FALSE},M,K,L,r,a;y,Z,M \rightarrow ;y,Z,M;(z_k \leftarrow r,L-M)$	the letter to which it is applied.
E18.	$\text{FALSE},x;y,K,L \rightarrow K,L,x;y$	If not, then try the
E19.	$K,L,x;y \rightarrow \text{ident}(K,L),K,L,x;y$	corresponding letter
E20.	$\text{FALSE},K,L,x;y \rightarrow x,L;y,K;(L \leftarrow K)$	in the first period.
E21.	$\text{TRUE},K,L,r,a;y,M \rightarrow a,K,M;y,M$	
E22.	$\text{END},x;y,Z,M \rightarrow ;y,(Z \leftarrow 0),(M \leftarrow M+M)$	If all relations have been tested, clear the pattern description and try doubling the period.

TABLE 10

Production System to Output the Answer

F1.	$;S,R,J,Z,M{\rightarrow}M;S,Z,M$	Retrieve periodicity from ITM
F2.	$M;S,Z,M{\rightarrow}M;S,Z,(p_o{\leftarrow}s_o),\ldots,(p_{m-1}{\leftarrow}s_{m-1}),M$	and store the first period in structure P of ITM.
F3.	$M;S,Z,P,M{\rightarrow}(K{\leftarrow}0),(I{\leftarrow}M),M;S,Z,P,M$	Initialize indices to count letters in the period (K) and in the sequence (I).
F4.	$K,I,M;y{\rightarrow}ident(K,M),K,I;y$	When one period has been
F5.	$TRUE,K,I;y{\rightarrow}K,I;y;(K{\leftarrow}0)$	output, prepare to output the next period.
F6.	$FALSE,K,I;y{\rightarrow}K,I;y$	
F7.	$K,I;S,Z,P,M{\rightarrow}z_k,K,I;S,Z,P,M$	Obtain the next pattern description element consisting of a relation (r) and letter position (L).
F8.	$r,L,x;y,P,M{\rightarrow}r,p_l,x;y,P,M$	Obtain the specified letter from the preceeding period.
F9.	$r,a,x;y{\rightarrow}r,a,r(a),x;y$	Apply the relation to the letter.
F10.	$r,a_1,a_2,K,I;y,P,M{\rightarrow}a_2,K,I;y,P,M;(p_k{\leftarrow}a_2),(K{\leftarrow}K+1)$	Store the generated letter in structure P replacing a letter from the previous period.
F11.	$a,K,I;y{\rightarrow}(I{>}sequence),a,K,I;y$	If the generated letter is
F12.	$TRUE,a,K,I;y{\rightarrow}K,I;y;(I{\leftarrow}I+1),$Output a	beyond the sequence, output it.
F13.	$FALSE,a,K,I;S,y{\rightarrow}s_i,a,K,I;S,y;(I{\leftarrow}I+1)$	If not, then obtain the corresponding letter from the original sequence.
F14.	$a_1,a_2,K,I;y{\rightarrow}K,I,ident(a_1,a_2);y$	Compare the generated letter and the letter from the sequence
F15.	$K,I,TRUE;y{\rightarrow}K,I;y$	If they are the same, generate the next letter, but if they are
F16.	$K,I,FALSE;y{\rightarrow};$;Output failure	different, the description fails.

question of how the two systems are to communicate. Here we have assumed direct communication through STM but allowed the lower order subroutine to alter ITM structures without notifying the higher order subroutine. Analogies to mechanisms in various programming languages will certainly occur to the experienced computer programmer. Our point, as in most of this section, is not to propose that the computing techniques are precise psychological models, but to point out that the problems that gave rise to the development of these techniques exist in both human thought and machine computation.

Suppose that no relation can be found to hold between two or more successive pairs of adjacent letters. The hypothesis testing routine will so indicate to the period finding system, by placing a NOT FOUND symbol in STM. The next hypothesis to be tested is that r is applicable but to nonadjacent pairs of letters. The degree of the nonadjacency would then establish the period length. This step would detect that the *same* relationship holds between every third letter in the sequence

(12)   a b m c d m e f m _ _ _.

As in the case of the adjacency hypothesis test, the actual examination of the letter string is carried out by a subsystem.

If either of the hypothesis testing subprocedures succeeds, the period detecting system returns control to the executive program, having placed a FOUND signal in STM and constructed a partial description of the period generating rule in the ITM structure Z. If neither hypothesis testing procedure succeeds, a new relation is selected from R and a new set of hypotheses tested. If R is exhausted without success the problem cannot be solved.

Before examining what happens after periodicity is established, let us consider the hypothesis testing subprocedures. Productions C1–C18 (Table 7) are required to test the intuitively simple hypothesis that a relationship, r, holds between all successive adjacent pairs of letters in a period. The period length m is determined by the number of adjacent letters for which the relation holds. Actually most of these productions are concerned with manipulation of indices, rather than with handling of problem data. Therefore it is an open question whether these rules assume some psychological reality or are forced upon us by notation. The product of the hypothesis testing routine, a partially completed answer structure, Z, in ITM, is of interest. We noted that in processing sequence (12) ("three a's, then three b's, etc.") the *same* relation would be detected between two adjacent pairs of letters. This would be described by placing nothing in position $z = z_0$, since the rule to describe the first letter of the period would not yet be established, and then by placing *same* (0) in z_1 and *same* (1) in z_2. The period would then be completely defined as soon as the base letter, z_0, was established.

Productions D1–D11 define the hypothesis testing procedure based on nonadjacent letters (Table 8). In activating this process the executive system assumes that there is a relation between letters in the same position within adjacent periods. Therefore, if the period is of length m the relationship will appear between letters m units apart. As before, information about the rule discovered would be placed in structure Z. For instance, in processing

(13)   a b y a b x a b w a b _ _ _.

the *same* relation would be detected between the first and second "a." This substantiates the hypothesis that the period length is three, so Z must have the structure

(14) $Z = (z_0, z_1, z_2)$.

Furthermore, it is known that

(15) $z_0 = same$ (0)

Once periodicity is determined the executive system transfers control to the

"Describe pattern" system specified in productions E1–E22 (Table 9). The job of this system of productions is to complete the pattern description stored in structure Z. Suppose z_i has not yet been specified. Relations are selected, in order, from R and used to test a dependence of S_i on S_{i-1}. If one is found to hold, then z_i becomes $r(i - 1)$. If a relation fails to define a dependence between adjacent letters, then the relation is tested between the ith position of the current and preceding period. Formally, if k is the period length, an attempt is made to find a relationship such that $s_i = r(s_{i-k})$. We will write r alone to indicate that the base letter for a target is located in the preceding period. To grasp the flavor of this method, consider that sequence 13 would eventually be described by

(16) Z = (same, same, predecessor)

in which all relations are defined for base letters that are in the equivalent positions in the preceding period. However, if we replace "b" with "a" in (13), the description would become

(17) Z = (same, same(0), predecessor)

The production system fails if this step cannot be completed successfully.

Suppose a complete period description is constructed. In order to use it, the problem solver must know Z and, assuming an m-length period, the first m elements of S, to establish the base letters. Given this information the second period can be constructed from the first, the first from the second, and so forth. The necessary steps are outlined in productions F1–F16 (Table 10). Structure P initially holds the first m letters of S, and as each letter is generated it is stored in structure P, replacing the corresponding letter of the previous period. The rules stored in Z are applied to P to construct a period. The constructed sequence is then compared to the actual sequence in S, if this information is available, or output as the continuation of the letter series problem. Note that this allows the system to check its answer.

Comparison to Data

How well does this complicated system succeed in mimicking human behavior? Table 11 shows, in order of difficulty as measured by a latency score, the 15 letter sequences investigated by Kotovsky and Simon, and the pattern description generated by the production system in response to them. Eleven of the 15 problems are correctly solved. The system detects that its answer is incorrect for 3 of the problems. These problems are among the most difficult for people. Problem 3, which is easy for people, is impossible for the production system. The reason is that this problem can be answered only by finding a relationship between nonidentical positions in successive periods. The model could be complicated to handle such problems, but we have not done so. No new concepts would be required. Problem 14 is of some interest, since the production system erroneously detects a period of three, whereas the actual period is six. This problem is evidently quite hard for people.

As in all previous cases, the production system represents an attempt to develop a model that is at once general and capable of producing known results. Kotovsky and Simon, using a similar approach to computer simulation, wrote 11 different programs

TABLE 11

Letter Sequences in Order of Difficulty and the Pattern Description
Produced in Response

Letter Sequence	Pattern Description
1. cdcdcd	Z_0 = Same Z_1 = Same
2. aaabbbcccddd	Z_0 = Next(3) Z_1 = Same(0) Z_2 = Same(1)
3. abmcdmefmghm	Unable to describe pattern
4. abyabxabwab	Z_0 = Same Z_1 = Same Z_2 = Predecessor
5. mabmbcmcdm	Z_0 = Same Z_1 = Next Z_2 = Next(1)
6. rscdstdetuef	Z_0 = Next Z_1 = Next(0) Z_2 = Next Z_3 = Next(2)
7. urtustuttu	Z_0 = Same Z_1 = Next Z_2 = Same
8. jkqrklrslmst	Z_0 = Next Z_1 = Next(0) Z_2 = Next Z_3 = Next(2)
9. defgefghfghi	Z_0 = Next Z_1 = Next(0) Z_2 = Next(1) Z_3 = Next(2)
10. atbataatbat	Report failure
11. npaoqapraqsa	Z_0 = Next Z_1 = Next Z_2 = Same
12. qxapxbqxa	Report failure
13. wxaxybyzczadab	Z_0 = Next Z_1 = Next(0) Z_2 = Next
14. aduacuaeuabuafu	Report failure
15. pononmnmlmlk	Z_0 = Next(2) Z_1 = Predecessor(0) Z_2 = Predecessor(1)

before developing one that would solve all the problems of their study. The value of the production system analysis lies more in its ability to relate the analysis of "hard" problems, such as series completion problems, to simpler cognitions, such as those studied by Clark and Chase, and even to information processing in psychomotor performance and word recognition. Of course, the production system needed to handle a hard problem is more complicated than one needed to handle an easy one, but this is hardly surprising. The point is that the principles of the various micro-models are the same.

On the other hand, it has proven necessary to introduce a number of new concepts to handle performance in the more cognitive tasks. The principal new concept is that of the subprogram, which, as we have noted, brings with it a host of questions about memory. In fact, the subprogram notion is not unique to the study of cognition. If the reader will look back at Chapter 1, it will be found that Pew introduces basically the same notion in analyzing more complex motor actions. This does not rid us of the problem that the subprogram concept brings with it. How do the various active subprograms communicate? Computer programmers have had to deal with this problem for some time (Gries, 1971; Knuth, 1969). Unfortunately the solutions taken in computer science seem to be very much bound by hardware and thus are unlikely to serve as psychological models. This has been a very little studied problem in psychological theory. Devising experimental paradigms to investigate it would seem to be a particularly difficult challenge.

The reader may also have been struck by the fact that, as a problem becomes more complex, there is a great increase in the amount of shuttling of information back and forth between STM and ITM. At least on an intuitive level this seems likely to be a real psychological phenomenon. When one is working on a complex problem it is likely that only a few bits of data are directly the focus of attention at a particular moment. On the other hand, relatively large amounts of data must be held "on the tip of the tongue." We again see that ITM is a logical necessity without supporting experimental evidence.

Concluding Remarks on Programming

We have used the language of production systems to describe the cognitive processes required to solve four classes of problems. We could have used words, computer programs, or flow diagrams. Successful application of the production system approach does not in itself prove anything about the nature of the models or the problems, since the production system notation can be applied successfully to any describable task. So why have we persisted in using this notation?

We think that production system descriptions of cognition are important to psychologists for several reasons. The first and most important reason is a conceptual one. The activation of a production can be interpreted in terms of the recognition by an active LTM of the current STM and ITM structures. Logically, recognition takes the form of a successful pattern match between the templates of a production in LTM and the contents of STM and ITM. Furthermore, an important part of the information stored in our brains is best described as procedural information, i.e., information describing when and how to do things. The "when" part of procedural information is a pattern recognition rule, defining the situation (STM and ITM contents) in which a certain action should be taken. The "how" part of the information is a definition of the action, in terms of the movement of chunks of information in STM and ITM.

Our second reason for preferring the production system notation is that a production system description forces a precision not required for a written or flow-chart description. Every one of the various information-processing models described in the reports on which this paper is based skipped over at least one point that had to be dealt with in writing a production system. In particular, primitive functions and variable types, which were implied but not mentioned in the original reports, had to be assumed in order to complete the production system. In addition, at each step of the solution process it was necessary to account precisely for the contents of STM and ITM. Such accountability could permit the psychologists to discard quickly a model described in the production system notation which requires the number of elements in STM or structures in ITM to exceed reasonable limits.

A third reason for using the production system notation is that it provides a single manner of description that can be used to construct models of virtually any human information-processing task. We have applied the notation to describe human behavior in relatively complex problem solving tasks. The same notation could have been used in the opening chapter, to describe motor performance, or in virtually any of the other chapters of this text.[17]

The production system notation is a way of describing models, not a psychological theory. Two different production systems could be written to describe the same data. Our approach in developing production system descriptions of problem solving models has been based on the psychological structure of the distributed memory model. Another model of psychological structure might have yielded equally successful descriptions. The fact that we have precisely defined our assumptions in describing the problem solving models does not imply the correctness of these assumptions. Many certainly are not correct and will be shown to be defective either by new experiments or by more penetrating theoretical analyses. However, clearly stating an erroneous assumption is better than no statement, even if it may be more discouraging to the theorist.

VI. DATA STRUCTURES AND LONG TERM MEMORY

Introduction

In programming, primitive data entries are grouped into *data structures* which express relations between different pieces of information. The mind must have similar structures, for our thoughts are not randomly connected to each other. But what are they?

Simulation approaches to this question fall into two broad classes. In the "ap-

---

[17]We do not maintain that any psychological phenomenon could be expressed in a production system. Concepts of motivation seem especially hard to express with this notation.

proach from psychology'' the investigator first postulates a structure that can account for some laboratory observations about long-term memory. Usually the structure will be fairly simple, e.g., a list or set. Next an attempt is made to generalize the data structure to explain interesting, nonlaboratory tasks. This may require considerable complication of something that began as a simple model. We can contrast this progression to the ''approach from Artificial Intelligence.'' Here the first step is to construct a computer program that does some task that everyone would agree involves intelligence. Deductive information retrieval programs are the best illustration. If such programs are told that ''It is raining,'' and ''John is outside,'' then they will answer ''Yes'' to the question ''Is John wet?'' The data structures used by these programs are likely to be complex. From the psychologist's viewpoint, the programs are interesting demonstrations, but there is no chance of testing them as psychological models, since they contain too many intertwined and *ad hoc* assumptions. If the theory embodied by the program is to be tested at all (and it often is not), it is necessary to specialize the program to a manageable miniature situation, where only a few of its assumptions determine its behavior. Typically when this is done the reduced theory is demonstrated to be found wanting, and so must be altered to handle the observations from the laboratory. Hopefuly these alterations do not destroy the complete program's ability to perform on the initial interpreting task.

Another useful distinction is between programs that deal with different types of long-term memory. Arguing strictly from the psychologist's view, Tulving (1972) postulated the existence of *semantic* and *episodic* memory. Semantic memory refers to our conceptual knowledge of the world. It contains facts—whales are mammals, birds fly—stored as relations between concepts. Episodic memory, by contrast, refers to a sort of autobiography of events that have happened to us personally. There is no guarantee that the two types of memory utilize the same data structures. Tulving noted that psychological variables, such as frequency, repetition, and interference, appear to have different effects on the two types of memory. Generally episodic memory is sensitive to disruption while semantic memory is not. Of course, there must be a continuity between the two types of memory, since semantic information must have been episodic at one time.

Quillian's Approach to Semantic Memory

The seminal work on psychological simulation of semantic memory is contained in two papers by M. R. Quillian (1968, 1969), which describe how a computer might be said to ''understand'' a conversation. There is a decided similarity between this goal and Schank's (see Section IV) goal with speech comprehension. If we say that Schank is concerned with the construction of comprehension, then Quillian is concerned with the structure of the long-term memory required to guide the construction. Quillian chose as an operational definition of comprehension the ability to paraphrase a natural language statement. This, in turn, implies the ability to coordinate terms in the statement with the meaning of the referents of these terms in semantic memory.

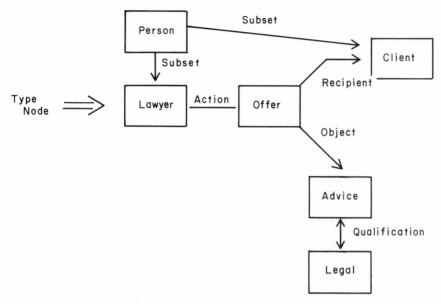

FIG. 10. Fragment of a semantic net defining *Lawyer* (adopted from Quillian, 1969).

Quillian decided to represent semantic memory as a finite, labeled graph (see Section IV), in which each node represented a basic term and each arc represented a relationship between terms. Figure 10 (adopted from Quillian, 1969) shows a graph for the term *lawyer,* which stands in a *subset* relation to *person.* In addition, *lawyer* is connected to the term *client* (also a subset of *person*) by the relation *give.* This is a three argument function which requires a donor, an object, and a recipient. The particular thing given by a lawyer, of course, is *advice,* which must be further qualified by its *type, legal.* Quillian's program could examine a semantic net to determine that a "woman's lawyer" is a "person who gives advice (legal) to a woman in return for payment."

Quillian introduced three ideas that have very much influenced all later work in this area.[18] The most obvious of these is the use of a labeled graph to represent memory and to recover the meaning of a word in context. Quillian regarded the "full meaning" of a word as the totality of the direct and indirect relations it had with other words. This would define all possible meanings of a term. To retrieve meaning in context, Quillian proposed a variety of ways to restrict the number and type of links to be examined; for instance, meaning might be defined by the shortest path between two words in a sentence. Quillian's third contribution was the distinction between a *type* node and a *token* node. The logic of this distinction is similar to the logic of using

[18]Given the dates, the reader may wonder how Quillian's work could have had such rapid influence. Quillian's 1966 dissertation was widely known in the "invisible college" of research workers in Artificial Intelligence, and many of his ideas had been discussed before then.

words to define other words in a dictionary. Every term is assigned a single node, called the *type* node, to serve as its definition. In Fig. 10, *lawyer* is a type node. In addition to its single type node a term may have any number of *token* nodes, when it is used in the definition of some other word. Tokens are logically references to types. Again referring to Fig. 10, *advice* is a token node in the subgraph, since it is used to define *lawyer*. The type node *advice* points to the token node of *advice,* so that if it is necessary to define *advice* in the process of defining *lawyer,* then this can be done. While the definition of a term is not stored with a token node, a qualification on the definition may be. Thus, in Fig. 10 *advice* is not defined, but it is noted that whatever the definition of *advice* may be, it must be qualified to be *legal advice* in the context of the term *lawyer.*

Quillian's original programs were directed at the comprehension of language by machine. His programs were capable of doing interesting things, usually associated with the correct retrieval of a term's meaning in a given context. For example, a program for examining a semantic net could detect the appropriate definition for *strike* in *the umpire called a strike* or *the union called a strike,* by examining the paths between the term *strike* and either *umpire* or *union.* The sheer complexity of Quillian's programs, and the number of *ad hoc* assumptions they contained, prevented any direct test of his ideas about semantic nets as a psychological theory. Accordingly, the theory was specialized by Collins and Quillian (1969, 1972) to permit an experimental test. The specialization dealt with two ideas, the subset–superset relation, which indicates what things are examples of classes, and the idea of a *cognitive economy.* Cognitive economy refers to the assumption that the type node of each set name has stored with it the "major" defining properties of the set, and that these properties are inherited by each member of the set unless they are specifically denied. For example, the properties "has wings" and "flies" would be stored with the set name *bird* and not with the type node of each individual bird. Exceptions can be made for specific birds (e.g., penguin or ostrich). An example of a proposed simplified cognitive structure is shown in Fig. 11.

To test this structure Collins and Quillian made an additional assumption, that moving from one node to another in the chain takes time. They then reasoned that in answering a question about possession of a particular property by an object (e.g., Can a canary fly?), a person must proceed mentally from *canary* to *bird,* in order to detect that a canary is a subset of a set of things that can fly. Now suppose the question is "Can a canary breathe?" By reference to Fig. 11, we see that to answer this question the search must proceed two links, up to *animal,* and thus more time should be required than in the first case. To test this point, Collins and Quillian constructed an intuitively satisfactory limited semantic network and calculated the relative times it ought to take to answer different questions. In general the results were as they had predicted them. For example, it takes about 70 msec longer to answer the question "Does a canary have skin?" than it does to answer the question "Can a canary fly?"

The Collins and Quillian results evoked considerable comment, both on theoretical grounds and because of questions about their experimental procedures. In their study Collins and Quillian did not allow for the associativity of different set names,

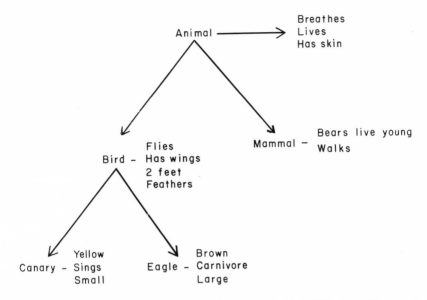

FIG. 11. A simplified semantic network. Properties are stored with the highest possible concept.

i.e., the frequency with which terms like "canary" are given as responses to higher-order set names, such as "bird" or "animal," or the reverse. Logically, their theory has trouble with certain types of intermediate concepts. For instance, although people know that "a dog is a mammal" it takes longer to answer this question than to answer the question "Is a dog an animal?" A number of attempts have been made to modify the network model to meet these objections and handle new data. One of the most interesting of these modifications is due to Elizabeth Loftus (1973). Her model provides us with a chance to coordinate our discussion of programming concepts with the discussion of semantic memory.

Loftus' basic experimental situation deals with the production of examples of a set, rather than answering questions about the properties of an object. In a typical task a person might be asked to "name a bird" as rapidly as possible. Logically, this requires three steps. First the name "bird" must be associated with its concept, the node *bird* in the semantic net. Next the nodes linked to *bird* as examples must be found. Finally, the names of the located nodes (*canary, eagle,* etc.) must be determined and pronounced. The important amplification here over Collins and Quillian's ideas is Loftus' introduction of the idea of a dictionary of "name codes" which must be referenced to interface speech and the semantic net. In addition, the name codes themselves have properties; for instance, they all begin with certain letters.

We shall now present a slight reworking of Loftus' basic ideas about semantic nets. We shall then consider how a production system for examining semantic nets might replicate the results of some of her experiments. Our interpretation of Loftus' ideas are summarized in Fig. 12, which shows a fragment of semantic memory, including both concept nodes and name nodes. Suppose a person is asked to produce the names of birds. First the name BIRD would be stored in STM and the concept *bird* would be located. This would, in turn, provide a list of pointers to some of the subsets of *bird*. We will assume that these concepts are placed in ITM. Thus if the full concept of *bird* contains pointers to, in order (*bluejay, sparrow, pigeon, partridge, eagle*), the initial concept stored in ITM might contain only (*bluejay, sparrow, pigeon*). The first item on this list, *bluejay*, would be removed from ITM to STM and, once there, replaced by its name code, BLUEJAY. The name code could then be produced by accessing its appropriate phonetic properties.

A modification of this situation reveals something about semantic memory. Freedman and Loftus (1971) asked subjects to "think of an example of X which begins with the letter Y." For example, think of a bird beginning with C. The problem, as stated, requires that the concept *bird* be located and its exemplars scanned until one is found whose name code begins with C. The situation is further complicated if the two pieces of defining information are separated temporally, by instructing the subject to

"Name an X" (pause) "that begins with Y."

According to our model, the period during the pause could be used to move some exemplars of X from LTM to ITM, so that exemplar names will be ready for comparison with the starting letter as soon as it is indicated. It should take longer to "name something that starts with Y" (pause) "that is an X," since knowing only the starting letter does not provide enough information to move useful data from LTM to ITM. Empirically, it does take longer to produce an example in the letter-concept condition than in the concept-letter condition.

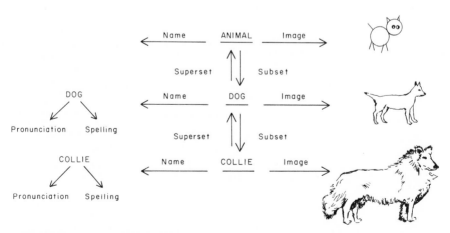

FIG. 12. Fragment of a semantic net.

We shall now develop a production system based on this analysis. It will become apparent as we do so that the informal analysis did not reveal all the assumptions about memory that are required. Some new variable types are required. The letter C will refer to an unspecified name code, the letter N to an unspecified concept, and the letter P to an unspecified property. Thus CANARY could be substituted for C while *canary* would be substituted for N, and C_1 (read "the first letter is C") for P. The following primitive functions will be used for memory searches:

$cn(C)$ retrieves the concept associated with name C

name(N) retrieves the name associated with concept N

first(C) produces the property that is the first letter of name code C.

These functions can be thought of as searches along arcs emanating from the node in semantic memory corresponding to their argument.

We shall again need the idea of indices, as in the discussion of series problems. Indices (denoted by the letters, I,J,K in STM) will be used to keep track of searches of ordered sets of items. Suppose S is such an ordered set in LTM, e.g., S = (*eagle, hawk, owl*). Successive executions of the production

(18) $s,I; S \rightarrow s_i,I;S; (I \leftarrow I + 1)$

would place eagle, hawk, and then owl in STM.

Table 12 presents a set of productions that can handle either the property-concept or the concept-property conditions of the Freedman and Loftus study. To illustrate how these productions apply, we shall go through an example using the property-concept condition. Suppose that the task is to think of "Something that starts with P . . . that is a bird." Further assume that the ordered set of subcategories associated with

TABLE 12

Production System for Semantic Memory Search

Production	Comment
P1 $P;\phi \rightarrow P; \phi$	Cycle if only property name is known.
P2 $C,x;y \rightarrow x,(I \leftarrow 0);cn(C),y$	On receiving a name code, place the associated concept in ITM and set index to zero.
P3 $P,I;N \rightarrow P,name(n_i),I;N;(I \leftarrow I+1)$	Given an index and a property in STM and a concept in ITM, fetch the name of the next exemplar, place it in STM, and update the index.
P4 $P,C,x;y \rightarrow P,first(C),C,x;y$	Given name code and property in STM, fetch first letter of name code.
P5 $P_1,P_2,x;y \rightarrow ident(P_1,P_2),P_1,x;y$	Given two properties in STM, compare them.
P6 $TRUE,P,C,x;y \rightarrow ;;output(C)$	Given that TRUE is in STM, output the name in STM.
P7 $FALSE,P,C,I;y \rightarrow P,I;y$	If FALSE is in STM, continue.

bird in LTM is (*ostrich, penguin, sparrow, hawk*). The successive states of STM and ITM will be

STM	ITM	Production	Comment
P	; ϕ	1	Cycle until more information is received.
BIRD, P	;ϕ	2	Can find needed concept.
P,O	;*bird*	3	Concept found.
P,OSTRICH,1	;*bird*	4	Find first name, change index.
P,O,OSTRICH,1	;*bird*	5	Begin check of name properties.
FALSE,P,OSTRICH,1	;*bird*	7	Properties do not match.
P,1	;*bird*	3	Begin check again.
P,PENGUIN,2	;*bird*	4	Index modified again.
P,P,PENGUIN,2	;*bird*	5	Second check of name properties.
TRUE,P,PENGUIN,2	;*bird*	6	Correct answer.
OUTPUT = PENGUIN			Make response.

Note that if the stimuli were to be reversed ("BIRD . . . P") the system would not have had to cycle, as *bird* could have been retrieved while waiting for "P."

The production system of Table 12 is a formal restatement of Loftus' (1973) network model. She has reported further work to us, which we have not discussed, which indicates need for some modifications. All of the changes of which we are aware could be handled within the production system distributed memory framework. Clearly, we see a good deal of compatibility between the ideas of propositional representation of information, network data structures, distributed memory architecture, and programming by use of productions. Before we become too euphoric about how our ideas fit together, it will be useful to examine another model of semantic memory, for this model leads to quite a different view of problem solving and memory search.

Instead of thinking of a network, imagine semantic memory to be an *n*-dimensional Euclidean space, with each dimension of the space representing a way in which objects vary. A semantic space for animals, then, might have the dimensions of size and predator-prey relations. Concepts such as *bear* and *weasel* are thought of as being located at points in the space. A generalized concept, such as *mammal,* would also have its assigned point. One could certainly include such a spatial representation in a computer program to simulate problem solving with semantic information, although to our knowledge this has not been done. Perhaps it should be, for there is a good deal of experimental support for the semantic space model. The space itself can be defined by simple experimental operations. Rips, Shoben, and Smith (1973) obtained subjective ratings of the difference between animal concepts by asking, for example, questions such as "If *lion* is arbitrarily two units from *tiger*, how far is *lion* from *giraffe?*" (This is not exactly their experimental procedure, but it is close enough to illustrate the nature of their data.) By appropriate mathematical manipulation, one can use such ratings to assign each term to a position in an n-dimensional space, such that the distance between any two terms will be proportional to the differences between the terms, as assigned by the raters (Carrol & Chang, 1970; Shepard, 1962). Rips et al. found that their rating data were matched by a two-dimensional space defined by size and predator-prey contrast. General terms, such as *mammal* and *animal,* were included in the rating and, therefore, could be assigned a location. In a separate study Rips et al. found that the time required to answer sentences of the form "Is an S a P" (e.g., "Is a sparrow an animal?") could be predicted from knowledge of the distance between the S and P terms. In general "false" answers were faster if the distance was large, whereas "true" answers were faster if the distance was small. To give the flavor of this finding, we predict from it that people will be more rapid at answering the question "Is a robin a bird?" than "Is a goose a bird?"

Rumelhart and Abrahamson (1973) illustrated the application of semantic spaces to problem solving by asking people to solve analogy problems involving animal terms. The task was to choose the appropriate term in questions such as "Lion is to wolf as goat is to . . . cat, chimpanzee, gorilla, pig." Rumelhart and Abrahamson reasoned that if the semantic space model is correct the chosen term will be located at the same point relative to the third term (goat in the example) as the second term is to the first. Therefore it should be possible to predict the choices made in analogy problems by knowing the subjects' semantic space for the terms involved. In fact, there was a very high correlation between predicted and observed answers. Note that this analysis of thought is "problem solving by examination of a physical model," and as such is more akin to the use of a diagram in the ARTIFICIAL GEOMETER (see Section III) than to the manipulation of propositions, which has characterized most of the programs we have discussed.

Semantic network models are particularly embarrassed by the finding that the further two points are from each other, the more rapidly people can respond that one is not related to the other. For example, it takes less time to deny the statement that *A robin is a car* than it does the statement *A robin is a mammal*. A semantic network theory would predict the opposite, since denial requires that all paths emanating from a node be traced to their ending. On the other hand, it is not clear how a semantic space model can be amplified to explain reasoning other than by similarity or analogy. We appear to have two different models, each of which is supported by a somewhat different body of experimental data, and neither of which handles the observations generated by the other model.

Summary Comment on Semantic Memory

After reviewing the literature through 1966, one of us concluded that computer oriented studies of memory simply had not brought about the revolution in our thinking that some enthusiasts had promised (Hunt, 1968). Only four years later another reviewer said that this conclusion was too negative (Frijda, 1972). Today's situation is dramatic. Quillian's artificial intelligence studies introduced the terminology of semantic networks, labeled graphs, types, and tokens into psychology. Collins and Quillian demonstrated that the relation between artificial intelligence and psychology need not stay at a metaphoric level. Loftus and other experimental psychologists have sharpened the Collins and Quillian model and extended it to cover other paradigms. Here we have tried to show how one can combine semantic nets with the computer oriented concepts of earlier sections, as a step toward a complete simulation of problem solving.

The fact that there is an alternative to the semantic net model presents a challenge. Can we find experimental evidence to distinguish between these two models? If we can, then we must find a way to work the appropriate model of semantic memory into programs that attempt to simulate complex reasoning.

Reasoning and Semantic Memory

Can a platypus swim? Most of our readers will, correctly, answer "yes." Why? Because we know that a platypus is a duck-billed, web-footed, egg-laying mammal, and web-footed things swim. Much of our knowledge is based on inferences from facts we know directly. This is quite clear when we deal with simple inferences. It does not strain the capacity of a city dweller's brain to assert that *An osprey can fly* once he knows that an osprey is a bird. On the other hand, no one claims that a person "knows" all the possible inferences from directly obtained knowledge. A discussion of human problem solving must address the question of how much people amplify their personal observations.

There are several computer oriented approaches to semantic inference. Our discussion of the General Problem Solver could as well have been presented under this heading as under a discussion of manipulation of propositions, since knowledge about symbolic operations is certainly an important part of problem solving. Within artificial intelligence studies a number of fairly powerful programs for proving mathematical theorems have been developed. These utilize the *resolution principle* technique of inference (Robinson, 1965), which depends on the precise logical meaning of disjunction and negation. We know of no serious proposal that resolution be regarded as a model of human reasoning, and we mention these programs only to alert the reader to their existence, and to point out that not all computer programs that attack intellectual tasks can be considered to be psychological models.

Far more realistic simulation models for inference have been designed by Abelson (1973; Abelson & Reich, 1969) and Colby (cf. Colby, 1973, for a review of his work). Abelson and Colby approach their work from the psychological viewpoints of theories about personality processes, rather than from the computer scientist's logical viewpoint. Both Abelson and Colby argue that a person's beliefs are structured around a few themes, and that whether or not a person will accept a statement as true will depend on whether or not the statement can be shown to be consistent with the statements already accepted as part of an appropriate theme. This method of inference gives an overall direction to the process of proving something, and thus makes possible some lengthy inferences. It also means that the simulation program might fail to make a correct inference, if a suitable theme was not found. Finally, there is no requirement that the rules of inference be either a complete or valid system of logic. In fact, Colby has intentionally used themes and rules of logic which he felt were typical of those he observed in his practice as a psychiatrist!

Abelson (1973) offers the following example of how a theme-based inference program might approach politics. The hypothetical program is designed to simulate the reasoning of an extremely conservative American "Cold Warrior." The question asked of the program is *Did Red China build the Berlin wall?* Assume that the program has the relevant theme

(1) *Communist nations commit actions which*

(2) *if not counteracted by Western show of force*

(3) *produce discomfort to the West.*

We further assume that the program knows that *Red China is a communist nation* and *Berlin wall cuts West off from East Germany.* A simple theme program, such as the one programmed by Abelson and Reich (1969), would accept China's building the wall, on the grounds that such an action is an acceptable specification of a relevant theme. Abelson points out that a more sophisticated program should have sufficient knowledge of logistics and geography to reject the idea that China, herself, built the wall, but that it might assert that "China would approve the construction of the wall, and may have urged East Germany or Russia to build it." One can easily think of ways that semantic nets would be useful in constructing programs that would reason in this way, although we again caution that actually constructing the program might uncover hidden problems.

Work such as Abelson's and Colby's is difficult to evaluate, since it is hard to see how such complex models can be validated other than by an appeal to their plausibility. Colby (1973) has amplified on a suggestion presented years ago by the mathematician Turing, to show that we can at least require that "plausibility" be based on a sampling of experts' intuition. He recorded an "interview" (via teletype between psychiatrists and either real patients hospitalized for paranoid schizophrenia or his program to simulate such a patient. He then asked a number of other psychiatrists to identify interviews between the real and the simulated patient. The psychiatrists were unable to do this. To make sure that this was not due to the psychiatrists' unfamiliarity with computers, Colby issued a similar challenge to members of the Association for Computing Machinery, with similar results.

Episodic Memory: Discrimination Nets

Semantic memory can be observed but is massively resistant to alteration. Episodic memory is more amenable to scientific study, since psychologists can create incidents in the laboratory and then test subjects' recall of them. The advantages of this in terms of experimental control are well-known. In the terminology of computer simulation, each experiment must establish some sort of data structure inside the subjects' long-term memory. By using controlled situations, we hope to determine how the various aspects of the incident creating the data structure determine the organization of memory. How data structures are formed and used at recall have been studied in a series of simulations based upon an information-processing theory of the learning of rote associations between stimulus and response which was first embodied in Feigenbaum's (1961) EPAM (elementary perceiver and memorizer) program.

Assume that the individual items of interest are coded perceptually as lists of features. The task is to form a data structure for storing the several stimuli in an experiment, differentiating them for later recall and recognition, and associating them with a response term. For simplicity, think of an experiment in which the task is to associate arbitrary trigrams with numbers. Each trigram will be represented by a list consisting of the first, last, and middle letter. Thus TRQ would have the internal representation (T,Q,R). To differentiate such trigrams EPAM uses a *tree graph*, similar to those described briefly in Section III. Figure 13 shows the components of such a graph. Links between nodes in a tree graph represent the predecessor-successor relation. The graph is further structured by having (*a*) a single node, called the *root*, which has no predecessor, (*b*) a single predecessor for every other node, with no node being its own predecessor, directly or indirectly, and (*c*) a set of *leaf* nodes, which have no successors. In the subsequent discussion, leaf nodes will be associated with some stimulus or response term external to the graph, while the nonleaf nodes will be associated with tests for the presence or absence of a particular stimulus feature.

EPAM assumes that the learner builds a discrimination tree to distinguish objects and to associate the objects with responses. For example, suppose the task was to learn the following pairing of nonsense syllables with digits

QRT—4	QRA—0
AKP—1	APA—2
QRQ—3	KLT—6
ZXK—5	QAY—7.

A discrimination net summarizing this list is shown in Fig. 14a. The eight leaf nodes

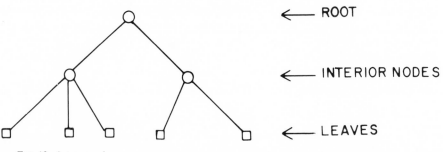

FIG. 13. A tree graph.

identify each stimulus uniquely and indicate the appropriate response. (In some work with EPAM the response is indicated as a set of directions for searching another discrimination net that distinguishes the response terms from each other. We need not go into this detail at present.) Small changes in instruction primarily affect the rules for building the tree. For example, Hunt (1962) analyzed the "concept learning" situation, where several stimuli are grouped with the same response term, in accord with some rule for describing the stimuli. An example is

QRT—1   AKP—0   APA—0
QRQ—1   QSY—0   KLT—0
QRA—1   ZXK—0

A discrimination tree can represent the grouping rule, as shown in Fig. 14b.

Several experimental studies have shown that the complexity of the discrimination tree is a rough predictor of the difficulty of the task in both paired associates learning (Simon & Feigenbaum, 1964) and in concept learning (Hunt, Marin, & Stone, 1966; Neisser & Weene, 1962). Many further details of learning can be predicted in given situations by introducing added assumptions about how the discrimination trees are

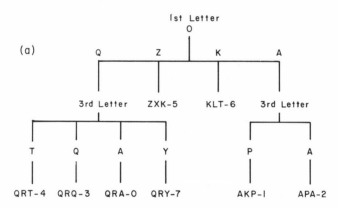

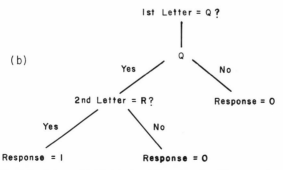

Fig. 14. Discrimination tree for (a) paired associates learning (b) concept learning as illustrated in the text.

built, but the details of the predictions depend upon the nature of the added assumptions. (See particularly the Simon and Feigenbaum study for a discussion of rote learning, and G. F. Williams', 1971, study of hypothesis formation in concept learning.)

Discrimination trees may also be used in the analysis of complex, nonlaboratory cognitive tasks. These applications are of interest, for they represent something that is seldom done, precise extension of laboratory concepts to "real life" tasks. They are also of interest because each study involves the ordering of what, in Tulving's terms, would be semantic memory at the time it is used, although it was clearly acquired as episodic information. Clarkson (1963) found that a bank trust officer's sorting of stocks into "disregard" and "appropriate purchase for this account" categories could be simulated by a program that classified stocks by means of a decision tree. Similar work has been done by Kleinmuntz (1968) in studies of neurological diagnostic procedures.

A more structured application of the concepts of EPAM is represented by Simon and Gilmartin's (1973) study of the very complicated data processing required to reproduce a chess position from memory. In this experimental task (used by several investigators) the subject is shown a board position, then asked to turn away from it and reconstruct the position on an empty board. This requires that a representation of the position be held in STM. Since STM is severely limited in capacity, it is important that this representation be an efficient coding. Chase and Simon (1973) and others have found that experienced players reproduce positions more accurately than do novices, because they recognize subpatterns involving several pieces (e.g., a castled king), and thus can fill STM with subpattern codes instead of specific piece positions. At the reconstruction stage the subpatterns are interpreted in order to position the pieces. The possibility that the experienced player simply has a better short-term memory can be ruled out by conducting a control experiment, in which the position to be reconstructed is a "random" position (often an illegal one), rather than a position that has arisen from actual play. The random positions typically do not contain game-relevant subpatterns of pieces. Experienced players are no better than novices in reconstructing such positions.

Simon and Gilmartin (1973) constructed a model of the process of subpattern memorization and recognition, by including the same procedures Feigenbaum had used to simulate rote learning in a simulation called MAPP, which reproduced chess positions. In its learning phase the program was given a large number of sensible patterns of pieces, taken from the published chess literature. It developed a discrimination net from these patterns. In the experiment simulation phase, MAPP first searched the position to be reconstructed to find roughly half a dozen familiar subpatterns. The names of these subpatterns were stored in an "STM" section. The names of the subpatterns were then used to construct the "recalled" position. Simon and Gilmartin found that this reconstruction was very similar to the reconstructions formed by humans. The program's accuracy was midway between that of a class A and a master player. By restricting the size of the discrimination net (thus forcing

MAPP to confuse some patterns) less accurate, but still human-like, reconstruction was observed.

An important point to realize in assessing this work is that Simon and Gilmartin did *not* study chess playing. They studied perception and memory for meaningful stimuli, taking advantage of the fact that there exists a task, chess, which has associated with it a well-defined vocabulary, a complex, meaningful visual display, and a population of people who have been motivated to learn both the language and the display to varying degrees of familiarity. Thus chess presents psychologists with the unusual opportunity to study a complex task that has varying degrees of meaningfulness for different individuals.[19]

The progression from EPAM to MAPP illustrates a most important use of simulation. Principles originally developed to account for laboratory learning phenomenon, and to some extent tested in the laboratory, were applied *precisely* to account for behavior in a very complex situation. Surely this is a more impressive demonstration of a continuity between the laboratory and the field than the usual loose analogies one finds in many elementary textbooks.

A Richer Associationism

Discrimination networks share with classical associationism the assumption that every episode we can recall is, basically, a conglomeration of associations between stimuli and responses. This assumption is too limiting. We seriously question whether a single, all-purpose association is sufficient to represent the different bonds that develop between elements of our thought. The episodes in our lives, and the actors in those episodes, must be linked together in memory in particular ways. To demonstrate our point, consider the recollection of this thought:

Yesterday I fed my dog while walking through the mountains on snowshoes.

Certainly our memory of this specific event is not a random potpourri of bonds between self, dog, meat, mountains, and snowshoes. Each is linked to the other in an appropriate relationship. There is an agent, *self,* linked to the two actions of *walking* and *feeding.* These actions, in turn, are linked to the other concepts in a certain way. As before, we will assert that a finite, labeled graph is required to represent this episode. A possible data structure is indicated in Fig. 15. This graph indicates that there was a basic act, *feeding,* executed by a certain agent, at a specific time (itself part of a larger episode), and involving certain other objects in a unique relationship. The reader will no doubt have noticed a similarity between the hypothetical long-term memory structure depicted in Fig. 15 and the ITM structures discussed in considering Schank's (1973) approach to the comprehension of language. The resemblance is intentional.

---

[19] Of course, chess play itself has been studied. In addition, there is a flourishing literature on the development of computer programs that play chess, without regard to whether or not they simulate human play. A somewhat dated but still excellent discussion of basic concepts is found in Newell, Shaw, and Simon (1963).

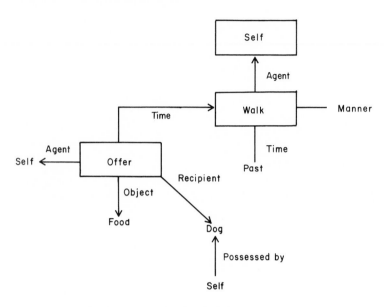

F<small>IG</small>. 15. Diagram of recollection *I fed my dog while walking on snowshoes.*

Labeled graphs are as attractive for describing episodic memory as they were for describing semantic memory. Their application, then, must be disciplined, since it is hard to imagine any recollection that could not be represented by some form of labeled graph. A meaningful theory must assert that only some labeled graphs are models of memory. The situation is somewhat analogous to our views about linguistics. We could say "Human communication is expressed in strings of words," but this is not an adequate linguistic model. Instead, a goal of formal linguistics is to specify the rules to which a string of words must conform if it is to be an acceptable sentence in a human language. In the present instance we are not satisfied by saying "Long-term memory represents thoughts as finite, labeled graphs." We need some rules to characterize the permissible, *well-formed* graphs.

In a remarkably wide-ranging volume, Anderson and Bower (1973)[20] argue that memory consists of *propositions,* which they define to be *facts* occurring in a *context.* A *fact,* in turn, exists when something is *predicated* about a *subject.* To use a classic case, "Socrates is mortal" states that Socrates is an element of the set of mortal beings.

A simple fact can be described as a tree, where the root of the tree is the fact itself, and the successor nodes refer to the subject and predicate. With this in mind, let us consider again a paraphrase of an earlier example, in which *I fed the dog while snowshoeing in the mountains yesterday.* Figure 16(a) shows the fact *I fed the*

---

[20]Rumelhart, Lindsay, and Norman (1972) have presented somewhat similar studies of the use of labeled graphs to represent LTM data structures, but with less concern for the well-formedness property. Lindsay and Norman (1972, Chapter 11) offer a nontechnical discussion of their ideas.

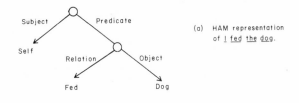

(a) HAM representation
of I fed the dog.

(b) HAM representation of
I fed the dog yesterday
while snowshoeing in the
mountains.

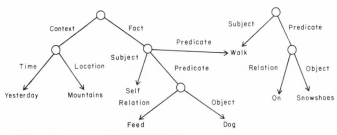

Fig. 16. HAM representation of episodic memory.

dog, a simple predication that places *self* in the relation *feeding* to the object *dog.*
Figure 16(a) is an oversimplification, though, for it does not state when the feeding
was done. The more complex representation of the entire sentence is shown in
Fig. 16(b). The hypothetical LTM structure is supposed to ignore the particular
grammatical constructions in the sentence and represent the meaning only. Therefore two acts, *feeding* and *walking,* are predicated about the subject. Furthermore, the predicate *walking* is itself a subject of a predication, for the walking was
done in a certain manner, *with snowshoes.* Finally, we must establish a context (time
and place) for the entire fact. The combination of fact plus context defines an episode
(i.e., something occurred at a particular time and place) and it is this episode, not the
fact it contains, that is associated with the top-most node in the tree structure of Fig.
16(b).

Anderson and Bower provide a set of rules for adding to graph structures so that the
resulting network is well-formed. We illustrate by describing a few of their rules.

(1) *Rule PO.* Two nodes, *a, b* which refer to concepts not currently in the graph
may be added to the graph by linking them together as facts in a subject-predicate
relation headed by a third node, *c.* The concepts *a* and *b* must satisfy any semantic
case restrictions. For instance, if concept *b* is the verb *speaks,* concept *a* must refer to
a human. Graphically, this rule states that a subgraph of the form

may be added to the graph at any time. Note that the total graph need *not* be connected. This is equivalent to the assumption (missing in Quillian's semantic memory theory) that some episodes in memory have no indicated relationship with other episodes.

(2) *Rule P1*. A predication may be made about any node *a* already in the memory structure. Graphically this means that if some node *a* exists in the structure, it is possible to connect it to another node, *b*, in the subject-predicate relation via a third node, *c*, which now represents the fact of this predication. Note that *a* could itself be a fact node, so that we might predicate a statement about a fact, e.g., if we had an episode indicating that *John loves Mary,* we could predicate that *It is nice that John loves Mary.* The relevant section of the graph would then be

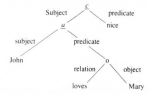

Further rules allow for construction of very complex memory structures but ensure that such structures will obey the rules for well-formedness. In fact, there is an exact correspondence between the idea of a well-formed graph and the notion of a well-formed string in mathematical linguistics.

Anderson and Bower's proposal is a broad one, and could not possibly be evaluated in detail here. We shall deal briefly with the manner in which they handle three key questions that must be addressed by any theory of data structures in LTM. These are the *encoding problem,* the *recall problem,* and the *relation between episodic and semantic memory.*

Anderson and Bower's grammatical rules specify the form structures must have when they enter memory. Rules are also needed to map from the input string to the appropriate graph structures. In their book, Anderson and Bower offer a simple grammar for a subset of English, but are clear that they do not regard it as a realistic model of psychological comprehension. Rather, they used it as an aid in writing a computer program that would make other tests of their hypotheses about LTM data structures. If we were to attempt a psychological model of language comprehension, in which the goal was to go from language to the Anderson and Bower data structures, we would probably take the general approach advocated by Schank. The output of Schank's comprehension rules is a data structure (which we have assigned to ITM) that, with only a few changes, could probably be made compatible with the Anderson and Bower structures. It remains for someone to go through the necessary details, to see if there are hidden problems. Similar sets of rules would have to be developed to explain our comprehension of stimuli other than speech. Such work has not yet been started in any serious way, although Anderson and Bower speculate that some work on computer analysis of visual scenes may be relevant.

A network model of LTM almost forces the theorist to look upon recall as a problem solving process. The memorizer is supposed to know not just what has been stated directly, but also what can be inferred from episodic memory. To be concrete, if the structure depicted in Fig. 16(b) is part of LTM, then a reasonable simulation program should be able to answer the question *"Where was the dog yesterday?"* One way to do this would be to analyze the questions to determine desired properties of the graph. A question answerer should know that (*a*) if there is any fact in memory that contains *dog* as a subject or object, *and* (*b*) if this fact occurs in a context with the time link *yesterday,* then (*c*) the *location* link of that context is the answer to the question. The view of recall as a process in which requirements are placed upon subgraphs, and subgraphs fitting the requirements are then searched for, is neither unique nor original with Anderson and Bower. (See, for example, Green's, 1963, discussion of the BASEBALL program for deductive information retrieval.)

Labeled graph theories of memory have a simple position on the distinction between episodic and semantic memory. They do not recognize any distinction. The argument against separate representations is that both semantic and episodic memory statements are propositions, distinguished only by their context restrictions and by the scope of the terms they contain. An episodic statement typically has a context in place

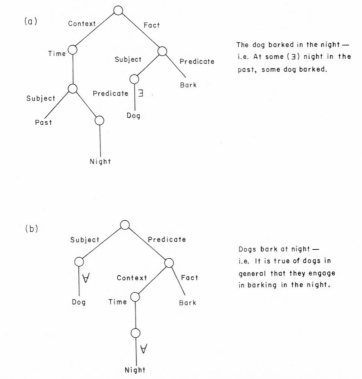

FIG. 17. Representation of episodic and semantic statements in the general manner used by Anderson and Bower.

and time and refers to specific objects. Figure 16, for instance, refers to the actions of a particular person and dog at a given point in space and time. A semantic statement is true in all contexts and may refer to classes of objects rather than to specific examples. Anderson and Bower propose to incorporate such statements into their network by failing to assert a context, and by labeling arcs with quantifiers ($\exists$ = "a particular object exists"; $\subset$ = "subset"; and $\forall$ = "all members of the class") to indicate the scope of reference. How this is done can be seen by contrasting the particular statement *A dog barked in the night,* which is diagrammed in Fig. 17, to the general statement *Dogs bark at night,* which is an assertion about all canines and all nights. Anderson and Bower are not clear about how quantifiers are assigned. Rumelhart, Lindsay, and Norman (1972), discussing the same problem, suggest that experience with a number of specific cases causes the more general quantifiers to be applied, in a sort of argument by generalization from specifics.

Labeled graphs are not themselves a theory of memory, since the idea is too broad. Any computer program intended to simulate a complete labeled graph model of all memory phenomena would contain so many interwoven, *ad hoc* assumptions that an experimental evaluation of the theory *in toto* would probably be impossible. (Consider how many such assumptions had to be introduced to handle the much simpler serial completion task!) In their book Anderson and Bower follow the familiar strategy of attempting to find simplifications of the theory which can be tested in isolation. A convincing case for their theory, or any other theory like it, will have to rest on an accumulation of findings from such experiments, since the "crucial experiment" probably does not exist. A second important factor in the acceptance of such models is simply the intuitive appeal they exert on psychologists. Such an appeal to aesthetics has been called an adequacy argument (Simon & Newell, 1971). The argument is that our cognitions are so complicated that, until very recently, we were the only beings who could do them. If a machine (computer program) can be constructed to mirror the performance of human thought, then, in the absence of evidence to the contrary, it is a presumptive model of cognition. This sort of reasoning is unlikely to appeal to the hard-headed empiricist, but it is widely accepted by cognitive psychologists, and there is no sense hiding the fact.

VII. CONCLUSIONS

Computer simulation is a method, not a theory of psychology. It is a method that forces us into a special mode of thought. In this chapter we have attempted to show what that mode of thought is, and how it colors our thinking about thinking. Others have attempted to do what we have done. Simon and Newell (1971), reviewing the fifteen years of work on cognition by themselves and their colleagues, came to four conclusions. By way of summarizing our own review, we shall present these conclusions and comment upon them.

1. *A few, and only a few, of the gross characteristics of the human information-processing system are invariant over task and problem solver.*

This is a discouraging statement for anyone who hopes to develop a general science of behavior. We would like to accept the assertion at one level, and reject it at another. Our reasons provide a good summary of our approach to computer simulation of complex thought.

Constancies between individuals and situations are certainly apparent at the system architecture level. The ideas of STM, ITM, LTM, and buffer memories are meant to apply to all people at all times. Similarly, we believe that the forms of internal representation of the external world are constant, in the sense that all people and all situations utilize only a few representations. There may be marked differences from individual to individual, and from situation to situation, in the choice of an internal representation for the task at hand. As we have seen, the choice of a particular internal representation will color all subsequent decisions about problem solving.

When we deal with programs and data structures we expect to find constancy at one level and change at another. The programming mechanisms described as psychological justification for a production system ought to remain the same, but the particular production system may vary widely for individuals and for tasks. The same principle holds true for the data structures in ITM and LTM. Presumably every data structure in the mind follows some grammar of formation, but within the constraints of this grammar different information can be stored in different ways. What we have said here is simply a computer oriented assertion that there is a universal grammar of thought that is held by everyone, but that within that grammar many specific thoughts can be formed.

2. *These characteristics are sufficient to determine that a task environment is represented as a problem space and that problem solving takes place in that problem space.*

Here Simon and Newell use ''problem space'' and ''task environment'' in a rather restricted sense. Imagine that an internal representation has been decided upon. We can think of a space of possible data structures representing the subject's knowledge about the problem at any one time. Problem solving can be thought of as a search through this space until a data structure defining a solution is uncovered. Productions are simply rules for changing structures, and a production system a set of rules partially specifying the order in which productions will be applied.

3. *The structure of the task environment determines the possible structures of the problem space.*

This statement calls our attention to the fact that the possible problem space is limited by our knowledge of the external world, and of the operations which are feasible in it, as well as being limited by the internal constraints of data structure grammars and system architecture bottlenecks.

4. *The structure of the problem space determines the possible programs that can be used for problem solving.*

If problem solving is a process for moving from one point to another in a defined space, then the problem solving programs must keep the data structures on which they operate within that space. There are also major constraints imposed by system architecture bottlenecks. The most serious of these is generally conceded to be in short-term memory. A problem solving program must arrange for STM never to be overloaded, lest vital information be lost. This requirement is vexing because STM serves not only as a way station for information being incorporated into the internal structures of ITM and LTM, it also serves as a bulletin board by which various subprocesses of the problem solving program communicate with each other. It is for this reason that the availability of efficient long-term codes is of such help in thought —by their use a great deal of relevant information may be packed into a single "symbol space" in STM.

A second, less well-established, bottleneck may have to do with the relatively long period of time required to alter data structures in LTM. Simon and Newell speculate that this process takes seconds or even tens of seconds. We would be inclined to place an even higher value on the "writing time" required by LTM. This is in marked contrast to the speed with which information can be assessed from either STM or LTM. This has been estimated to be on the order of fifty milliseconds.

The force of all these remarks can be summed up by offering another quote from the Simon and Newell (1971) review:

> When human beings are observed working on well structured problems that are difficult but not unsolvable for them, their behavior depends on certain broad characteristics of the underlying neurophysiological system that supports problem solving; but at the same time the behaviors conceal almost all of the details of that system . . . [p. 149].

Historically, computer simulation has been concerned with very complex tasks, such as chess or the solving of problems in mathematical logic. At this level of complexity, almost all behavior is controlled by the logic of the thinker's program, and not by the details of how individual productions are executed. There are, to be sure, limitations due to data structure and/or system architecture, but the program of a successful thinker has been designed to minimize these. By contrast, many of the paradigms of modern information-processing psychology, certainly most of those discussed in earlier chapters of this text, are designed to reveal system architecture, programming principles, and, to a lesser extent, data structures. Computer simulation provides us with a way to move, precisely, from the facts uncovered by the laboratory tasks to the complex behavior present in everyday cognition. A program may be a theory of how the laws and concepts developed in the laboratory apply to "real thought."

Traditionally, the attempt to apply laboratory derived psychological laws to explain complex thought have broken down on three grounds. The theories have been vague, it has not been clear that the proposed models are adequate to produce the behavior in question, let alone explain it, and there has been no way to test the predictions against actual behavior in a complex situation. Computer simulation is an excellent way to protect against the first two charges. The mere existence of a running computer program ensures that the model has been stated precisely. The fact that the program can solve certain problems attests to its adequacy. The third test, coordination with observable human behavior, is in no way easier to meet simply because one's model has been debugged on a computer. Whenever we can, we should seize the opportunity to coordinate program behavior with some observable human behavior.

Often there will be no such handy set of appropriate observations. In such cases the acceptability of a simulation will often rest on its intuitive and even aesthetic appeal to "knowledgable workers in the field." Ironically, the digital computer, a symbol of modern technology, has moved the science of experimental psychology a bit toward the acceptance of intuition.

REFERENCES

Abelson, R. The structure of belief systems. In R. Schank & K. Colby (Eds.), *Computer models of thought and language*. San Francisco; Freeman, 1973.

Abelson, R., & Reich, C. Implication modules. A method for extracting meaning from input sentences. *Proceeding of the 1st International Joint Conference on Artificial Intelligence*. Bedford, Mass. MITRE Corp., 1969.

Anderson, J. A., & Bower, G. H. *Human associative memory*. New York: Halsted Press, 1973.

Atkinson, R. C., & Shiffrin, R. M. Human memory: A proposed system and its control processes. In K. W. Spence & J. T. Spence (Eds.), *The psychology of learning and motivation*. Vol. 2. New York: Academic Press, 1968.

Atkinson, R. C., & Wescourt, K. Some remarks on a theory of memory. In S. Kornblum (Ed.), *Attention and performance V*. New York: Academic Press, 1974.

Barclay, J. R. The role of comprehension in remembering sentences. *Cognitive Psychology*, 1973, **4**, 229–254.

Baylor, G. W. Program and protocol analysis on a mental imagery task. *Proceedings of the 2nd International Joint Conference on Artificial Intelligence*, London: British Computer Society, 1971.

Bower, G. H. Organizational factors in memory. *Cognitive Psychology*, 1970, **1**, 18–46.

Bower, G. H., & Winzenz, D. Group structure, coding, and memory for digit series. *Journal of Experimental Psychology Monographs*, 1969, **80**(2), 1–17.

Bransford, J. D., & Franks, J. J. The abstraction of linguistic ideas. *Cognitive Psychology*, 1971, **2**, 331–350.

Broadbent, D. E. *Decision and stress*. New York: Academic Press, 1971.

Carrol, J., & Chang, J. J. Analysis of individual differences in multidimensional scaling via an *N* way generalization of Eckart-Young decomposition. *Psychometrika*, 1970, **35**, 283–319.

Chang, C. L. The unit proof and the input proof in theorem proving. *Journal of the Association for Computing Machinery*, 1970, **17**, 698–707.

Chase, W. G., & Simon, H. A. Perception in chess. *Cognitive Psychology*, 1973, **4**, 55–81.

Chomsky, N. Formal properties of grammars. In R. Luce, R. Bush & E. Galanter (Eds.), *Handbook of mathematical psychology*. Vol. 2. New York: Wiley, 1963.

Clark, H. H. & Chase, W. G. On the process of comparing sentences against pictures. *Cognitive Psychology*, 1972, **3**, 472–517.

Clarkson, G. A model of the trust investment process. In E. Feigenbaum & J. Feldman (Eds.) *Computers and thought*. New York: McGraw-Hill, 1963.

Colby, K. Simulations of belief systems. In R. Schank & K. Colby (Eds.), *Computer models of thought and language*. San Francisco: Freeman, 1973.

Collins, A., & Quillian, M. R. Retrieval time from semantic memory. *Journal of Verbal Learning and Verbal Behavior*, 1969, **8**, 240–247.

Collins, A., & Quillian, M. R. How to make a language user. In E. Tulving & W. Donaldson. *Organization of memory*. New York: Academic Press, 1972.

Craik, F., & Lockhart, R. Levels of processing: A framework for memory research. *Journal of Verbal Learning and Verbal Behavior*, 1972, **11**, 671–684.

Day, R. Individual differences in cognition. Paper presented at the meeting of the Psychonomic Society, St. Louis, November, 1973.

Ernst, G. W., & Newell, A. *GPS: A case study in generality and problem solving*. New York: Academic Press, 1969.

Feigenbaum, E. The simulation of verbal learning behavior. *Proceedings of the Western Joint Computer Conference,* 1961, **19**, 121–132.

Franks, J. J., & Bransford, J. D. The acquisition of abstract ideas. *Journal of Verbal Learning and Verbal Behavior,* 1972, **11**, 311–315.

Freedman, J., & Loftus, E. The retrieval of words from long-term memory. *Journal of Verbal Learning and Verbal Behavior,* 1971, **10**, 107–115.

Frijda, N. Simulation of human long-term memory. *Psychological Bulletin,* 1972, **77**, 1–31.

Gazzaniga, M. *The bisected brain.* New York: Appleton, 1970.

Gelernter, H. Realization of a geometry theorem proving machine. *Proceedings of the international conference on information processing.* Paris: UNESCO House, 1959.

Green, B. F. *Digital computers in research.* New York: McGraw-Hill, 1963.

Gries, D. *Compiler construction for digital computers.* New York: Wiley, 1971.

Hopcroft, J. E., & Ullman, J. D. *Formal languages and their relation to automata.* Reading, Mass.: Addison-Wesley, 1969.

Hunt, E. B. *Concept learning: An information processing problem.* New York: Wiley, 1962.

Hunt, E. B. Computer simulation: Artificial intelligence studies and their relation to psychology. *Annual Review of Psychology,* 1968, **19**, 135–168.

Hunt, E. B. What kind of computer is man? *Cognitive Psychology,* 1971, **2**, 57–98.

Hunt, E. B. The memory we must have. In R. Schank & K. Colby (Eds.), *Computer models of thought and language.* San Francisco: Freeman, 1973.

Hunt, E. B. *Artificial intelligence.* New York: Academic Press, 1974. (a)

Hunt, E. B. Quote the Raven? Nevermore! In L. Gregg (Ed.), *Knowledge and cognition.* Potomac, Md.: Lawrence Erlbaum Associates, 1974.(b)

Hunt, E. B., Frost, N., & Lunneborg, C. Individual differences in cognition: A new approach to intelligence. In G. H. Bower (Ed.), *The psychology of learning and motivation.* Vol. 7. New York: Academic Press, 1973.

Hunt, E. B., Marin, J., & Stone, P. *Experiments in induction.* New York: Academic Press, 1966.

Jensen, A. How much can we boost IQ and scholastic achievement? *Harvard Educational Review,* 1969, **39**, 1–123.

Kleinmuntz, B. The processing of clinical information by man and machine. In B. Kleinmuntz (Ed.), *Formal representation of human judgement.* New York: Wiley, 1968.

Knuth, D. E. *The art of computer programming.* Menlo Park: Addison-Wesley, 1969.

Kotovsky, K., & Simon, H. A. Empirical tests of a theory of human acquisition for sequential patterns. *Cognitive Psychology,* 1973, **4**, 399–424.

Lewis, J. L. Semantic processing of unattended messages using dichotic listening. *Journal of Experimental Psychology,* 1970, **85**, 225–228.

Lindsay, P., & Norman, D. A. *Human information processing.* New York: Academic Press, 1972.

Loftus, E. How to catch a zebra in semantic memory. Paper presented at the Minnesota Conference on Cognition, Knowledge and Adaptation, Minnesota, August, 1973.

Meyer, D. On the representation and retrieval of stored semantic information. *Cognitive Psychology,* 1970, **1**, 242–299.

Meyer, D. Verifying affirmative and negative assertions: The effect of negation. In S. Kornblum (Ed.), *Attention and performance IV.* New York: Academic Press, 1973.

Neisser, U. *Cognitive psychology.* New York: Appleton, 1967.

Neisser, U., & Weene, P. Hierarchies and concept attainment. *Journal of Experimental Psychology,* 1962, **64**, 640–645.

Newell, A., Shaw, J. C., & Simon, H. A. Elements of a theory of human problem solving. *Psychological Review,* 1958, **65**, 151–166.

Newell, A., Shaw, J. C., & Simon, H. A. Report on a general problem solving program for a computer. *Proceedings of the international conference on information processing.* Paris: UNESCO House, 1959.

Newell, A., Shaw, J. C., & Simon, H. A. Chess playing and the problem of complexity. In E. Feigenbaum & J. Feldman (Eds.), *Computers and thought*. New York: McGraw-Hill, 1963.

Newell, A., & Simon, H. A. Computer simulation of human thinking. *Science*, 1961, **134**, 2011–2017.

Newell, A. & Simon, H. A. *Human problem solving*. Englewood Cliffs, N.J.: Prentice-Hall, 1972.

Nilsson, N. *Problem solving methods in artificial intelligence*. New York: McGraw-Hill, 1971.

Paivio, A. *Imagery and verbal processes*. New York: Holt, Rinehart & Winston, 1971.

Posner, M. I. Abstraction and the process of recognition. In G. H. Bower & J. T. Spence (Eds.), *The psychology of learning and motivation*. Vol. 3. New York: Academic Press, 1969.

Posner, M. I., & Keele, S. Retention of abstract ideas. *Journal of Experimental Psychology*, 1970, **83**, 304–308.

Pylyshyn, Z. What the mind's eye tells the mind's brain: A critique of mental imagery. *Psychological Bulletin*, 1973, **80**, 1–24.

Quillian, M. R. Semantic memory. In M. Minsky (Ed.), *Semantic information processing*. Cambridge: MIT Press, 1968.

Quillian, M. R. The teachable language comprehender: A simulation program and a theory of language. *Communications of the Association for Computing Machinery*, 1969, **12**, 459–476.

Quinlan, J. R., & Hunt, E. B. A formal deductive problem solving system. *Journal of the Association for Computing Machinery*, 1968, **15**, 625–646.

Raven, J. *Advanced progressive matrices*. London: Lewis and Co., 1958.

Reed, S. K. Pattern recognition and categorization. *Cognitive Psychology*, 1972, **3**, 382–407.

Rips, L., Shoben, E., & Smith, E. Semantic distance and the verification of semantic relations. *Journal of Verbal Learning and Verbal Behavior*, 1973, **12**, 23–41.

Robinson, J. A. A machine oriented logic based on the resolution principle. *Journal of the Association for Computing Machilnery*, 1965, **12**, 23–41.

Rumelhart, D., & Abrahamson, A. A model for analogical reasoning. *Cognitive Psychology*, 1973, **5**, 1–28.

Rumelhart, D., Lindsay, P., & Norman, D. A. A process model of long-term memory. In E. Tulving & W. Donaldson (Eds.), *Organization of memory*. New York: Academic Press, 1972.

Schank, R. Conceptual dependency: A theory of natural language understanding. *Cognitive Psychology*, 1972, **3**, 552–631.

Schank, R. Identification of conceptualizations underlying natural language. In R. Schank & K. Colby. *Computer models of thought and language*. San Francisco: Freeman, 1973.

Schank, R., Goldman, N., Rieger, C. J. III, & Riesbeck, C. MARGIE: Memory analysis, response generation, and inference in English. *Proceedings of the 3rd International Joint Conference on Artificial Intelligence*, Stanford, California, 1973.

Shepard, R. N. The analysis of proximities: Multidimensional scaling with an unknown distance function. *Psychometrika*, 1962, **27**, 125–140.

Shepard, R. N. Recognition memory for words, sentences, and pictures. *Journal of Verbal Learning and Verbal Behavior*, 1967, **6**, 156–163.

Simon, H. A., *The sciences of the artificial*. Cambridge, Mass.: MIT Press, 1969.

Simon, H. A., Complexity and the representation of patterned sequences of symbols. *Psychological Review*, 1972, **79**, 369–382.

Simon, H. A., & Barenfeld, M. Information processing analysis of perceptual processes in problem solving. *Psychological Review*, 1969, **76**, 473–483.

Simon, H. A., & Feigenbaum, E. An information processing theory of some effects of similarity, familiarization, and meaningfulness in verbal learning. *Journal of Verbal Learning and Verbal Behavior*, 1964, **3**, 385–396.

Simon, H. A., & Gilmartin, K. A simulation of memory for chess positions. *Cognitive Psychology*, 1973, **5**, 29–46.

Simon, H. A., & Kotovsky, K. Human acquisition of concepts for serial patterns. *Psychological Review*, 1963, **70**, 534–546.

Simon, H. A., & Lea, G. Problem solving and rule induction: A unified view. (Complex information processing working paper 227). Psychology Department, Carnegie-Mellon University, 1972.

Simon, H. A., & Newell, A. Human problem solving: The state of the theory in 1970. *American Psychologist,* 1971, **26**, 145–159.

Trabasso, T., Rollins, H., & Shaughnessy, E. Storage and verification stages in processing concepts. *Cognitive Psychology,* 1971, **2**, 239–289.

Tulving, E. Episodic and semantic memory. In E. Tulving & W. Donaldson (Eds.), *Organization of memory.* New York: Academic Press, 1972.

Wason, P., & Johnson-Laird, P. *Psychology of reasoning.* Cambridge, Mass.: Harvard University Press, 1972.

Waterman, D. A., & Newell, A. Protocol analysis as a task for artificial intelligence. *Artificial intelligence.* Amsterdam: North Holland, 1971.

Wilks, Y. An artificial intelligence approach to machine translation. In R. Schank & K. Colby (Eds.), *Computer models of thought and language.* San Francisco: Freeman, 1973.

Wilks, Y. Understanding without proofs. *Proceedings of the 3rd International Joint Conference on Artificial Intelligence.* Stanford, Calif. 1973, 270–277.*(b)*

Williams, G. F. A model of memory in concept learning. *Cognitive Psychology,* 1971, **2**, 158–184.

Winograd, T. A procedural model of language understanding. In R. Schank & K. Colby (Eds.), *Computer models of thought and language.* San Francisco: Freeman, 1973.

Winograd, T. A program for understanding natural language. *Cognitive Psychology,* 1973, **3**, No. 1.

HUMAN INFORMATION PROCESSING:
TUTORIALS IN PERFORMANCE
AND COGNITION

INDEXES

AUTHOR INDEX

Numbers in italics refer to the pages on which the complete references are listed.

A

Abelson, R., 334, 335, *347*
Abrahamson, A., 333, *349*
Adams, J. A., 28, 31, 33, *36, 101, 127*
Aderman, D., 257, 264, *271*
Amundson, V. E., 116, *127*
Anastasio, E. J., 63, *81*
Anderson, J. A., 181, *183*, 285, 300, 349, *347*
Anderson, W. G., 237, *273*
Anisfeld, M., 257, *271*
Annett, J., 112, *127*
Anokhin, P. K., 30, 31, *36*
Armstrong, T. R., 31, *36*
Ashe, V. M., 115, *127*
Atkinson, J., 48, *81*, 98, *127*
Atkinson, R. C., 135, 138, 147, 167, 168, 169, *183*, 238, 240, *271*, 295, 296, *347*
Attneave, F., 189, 211, *226*
Audley, R. J., 75, *80*, 100, *127*
Austin, G. A., 189, *226*

B

Baddeley, A. D., 237, *272*
Bahrick, H. P., 35, *37*
Bairstow, P. J., 28, *38*
Bamber, H. K., 175, *183*
Banks, W. P., 258, *272*
Barclay, J. R., 299, *347*
Barenfeld, M., 278, 279, *349*
Baron, J., 248, 254, 256, 259, 261, 263, 265, *272*
Barro, G., 29, *39*
Barron, R. W., *273*
Bartlett, F. C., 27, *37*, 189, *226*
Baumal, R., 267, 268, 269, *275*
Baumeister, A. A., 109, *127*
Baylor, G. W., 293, *347*
Beggs, W. D. A., 24, 25, *37*

Bekker, J. A. M., 86, 109, *129*
Beller, H. K., 237, 243, *272*
Berlyne, D. E., 95, 96, *127*
Berman, A. J., 29, 30, *39*
Bernstein, I. H., 88, 115, 116, 126, *127*
Bernstein, N., 27, 30, 31, *37*
Berrian, R. W., 237, *273*
Bertelson, P., 90, 101, 111, *127*
Bevan, W., 48, 49, 57, *81*
Biederman, I., 88, *127*
Bilodeau, E. A., 1, *37*
Birdsall, T. G., 232, *275*
Birkhoff, G. D., 188, *226*
Bjork, R. A., 189, 222, *226*
Blecker, D., 48, 49, *81*, 248, *272*
Bledsoe, W. W., 234, *272*
Boies, S. J., 36, *38*, 116, 123, 124, *130*
Book, W. F., 34, *37*
Booth, T. L., 174, *183*
Borger, R., 117, *127*
Boring, E. G., 133, 158, *183*
Bowden, J., 24, 25, *37*
Bower, G. H., 209, *226*, 285, 300, 301, 340, *347*
Braine, M. D. S., 215, *226*
Bransford, J. D., 293, 294, *347, 348*
Brebner, J., 107, *127*
Briggs, G. E., 68, *82*
Briggs, P., 115, *127*
Broadbent, D. E., 1, *37*, 75, *80*, 90, 92, 101, 108, 109, 110, 119, 125, 126, *127*, 138, *183*, 251, 254, 269, *272, 273*, 282, 295, *347*
Broadbent, L., 87, *128*
Brown, D. R., 169, *185*
Brown, E. R., 194, 197, 198, 209, 210, *228*
Brown, L. T., 237, 238, *274*
Browning, I., 234, *272*
Bruner, J. S., 189, *226*, 232, 236, 238, *272, 273*
Bryan, W. L., 34, *37*
Buckley, W. F., 84, *127*
Buggie, S., 116, *130*
Burnham, D. W., 111, *130*

C

Carrol, J., 333, *347*
Cattell, J. M., 234, 247, 252, *272*
Chang, C. L., 288, *347*
Chang, H. T., 30, *37*
Chang, J. J., 333, *347*
Chase, W. G., 84, *130, 235, 272, 273, 279,
304, 307, 338, *347*
Chernikoff, R., 26, *37*
Chomsky, N., 189, 213, *226, 296, 347*
Christie, L. S., 138, *183*
Chu, P. K., 115, *127*
Clark, H. H., 304, 307, *347*
Clark, W. H., 191, *227*
Clarkson, G., 338, *347*
Clement, D. E., 193, *227*
Colby, K., 334, 335, *347*
Collins, A., 328, *347*
Connor, J., 243, *272*
Conrad, R., 258, *272*
Cooper, F. S., 260, *273*
Corcoran, D. W. J., 138, *183, 232, 272*
Craik, F., 301, *347*
Craik, K. J. W., 9, *37, 91, 128*
Cronnell, B., 249, *274*
Crossman, E. R. F. W., 13, 23, *37*

D

David, E. E., 29, *39*
Davis, R., 86, 88, *128*
Day, R. S., 120, *128, 300, 347*
Deese, J., 42, *81, 200, 227*
Delabarre, E. B., 113, *128*
Delattre, P., 260, *273*
Disch, K., 79, *81*
Ditzian, J. L., 88, 91, 94, 107, *128*
Donders, F. C., 179, *183*
Duffendack, J. C., 10, 11, 13, 14, 15, 29, *38*

E

Edwards, W., 76, *81*
Egeth, H., 48, 49, 57, *81, 119, 128, 160, 181,
183, 243, 248, 272*
Eichelman, W. H. 240, 248, *272*
Elithorn, A., 109, *129*
Elkind, J. I., 5, 6, *37*
Ells, J. G., 36, *37, 123, 128*
Epstein, W., 205, 207, *227*
Erickson, J. R., 216, *227*

Eriksen, B. A., 236, *272*
Eriksen, C. W., 45, 46, 47, *81, 138, 158, 183,
236, 237, 238, 240, 243, 244, 245, 246, *272*
Ernst, G. W., 286, 288, *347*
Estes, W. K., 134, 135, 147, 153, 158, 168,
169, *183, 184, 185, 194, 210, 211, 227, 238,
239, 240, 242, 243, 246, 270, *272, 275*
Evans, S. H., 63, *81, 211, 212, 216, 227*
Evarts, E. V., 26, *37*

F

Fearnley, S., 120, *131*
Fehrer, E., 86, *128*
Feigenbaum, E., 336, 337, *348, 349*
Fensch, L. K., 10, 11, 13, 14, 15, 29, *38*
Fisher, D. F., 64, 66, *81*
Fitts, P. M., 23, 24, *37, 64, 81, 122, 128*
Flowers, J. H., 65, *81*
Forster, J. D., 18, *39*
Franks, J. J., 293, 294, *347, 348*
Freedman, J., 330, *348*
Frijda, N., 334, *348*
Fritzen, J., 199, *227*
Frost, G., *37*
Frost, N., 300, 307, *348*

G

Galanter, E., 34, *38*
Gambino, B., 206, *228*
Gardner, E. D., 86, *128*
Gardner, G. T., 138, *184, 240, 241, 243, 244,
245, 246, 250, 270, *272, 274*
Garner, W. R., 45, 65, *81, 188, 189, 193, 195,
196, 202, 203, 204, 208, 211, 212, 214, 217,
220, 226, *227, 228, 236, 272*
Gazzaniga, M., 300, *348*
Gelernter, H., 286, 289, *348*
Gibbs, C. B., 18, *37*
Gibson, E. J., 248, 250, 256, 257, 259, 261,
263, 265, *272, 273*
Gilmartin, K., 279, 338, *349*
Gilmore, G., 48, *81*
Glanzer, M., 191, *227*
Gleitman, H., 246, *273*
Gold, C., 267, 268, *275*
Goldman, N., 297, *349*
Goodeve, P. J., 23, *37*
Goodnow, J. J., 189, *226*
Gottsdanker, R., 87, 89, 95, 107, *128, 131*
Gottwald, R. L., 195, 196, 203, 204, 217, 220,
227, 228

Gough, P. B., 215, 216, *227, 228*
Green, B. F., 343, *348*
Green, D. M., 120, *128,* 159, *184,* 192, 227
Greenwald, A. G., 30, *37,* 97, 118, 122, 123, *128*
Gregg, L. W., 209, 227
Gregory, M., 108, 109, 110, 119, *127,* 254, 272
Gries, D., 324, *348*
Gumbel, E. J., 163, *184*
Gyr, J. W., 30, *37*

H

Hake, H. W., 45, *81,* 236, 272
Hamilton, W., 137, *184*
Hammond, M., 248, 259, 261, 265, 272
Hansen, D., 260, *273*
Hart, S. G., 84, *128*
Harter, N., 34, *37*
Haviland, S. E., 56, *82,* 159, *184,* 248, 250, 251, 252, 259, 261, 262, 263, *274*
Hayes, W. H., 237, 238, *274*
Helson, H., 86, 113, *128*
Henneman, F., 9, *37*
Herman, L. M., 84, 86, 87, 88, 91, 92, 95, 96, 97, 100, 101, 106, 107, 109, *128,* 245, *273*
Hershenson, M., 265, *273*
Herzog, J. H., 22, *37*
Hick, W. E., 64, *81,* 87, 91, 92, *128, 129*
Hoffman, J. E., 236, 272
Holmgren, J. E., 135, 138, 147, 167, 168, 169, *183,* 238, 240, *271*
Hopcroft, J. E., 283, 296, *348*
Houk, J., 9, *37*
Howard, I. P., 120, *129*
Howarth, C. I., 24, 25, *37*
Howell, W. C., 64, *81*
Hubel, D. H., 234, 235, *273*
Huey, E. B., 252, *273*
Huff, E. M., 84, *128*
Hull, C. L., 97, *129*
Hunt, E. B., 287, 288, 292, 294, 296, 300, 303, 307, 334, 337, *348, 349*
Hunter, W. S., 137, *184*
Hylan, J. P., 137, *184*

I

Ingram, F., 260, *273*
Israel, A., 109, *128*

J

James, C. T., 265, *273*
James, W., 97, *129*
Jastrow, O., 84, *129*
Jensen, A., 292, *348*
Jex, H. R., 9, 15, 17, 20, *38*
Johnson, D. M., 189, 227
Johnson, G. C., 13, *37*
Johnson, N. F., 194, 199, 227
Johnson, W. A., 15, 17, 20, *38*
Johnson-Laird, P., 298, 309, *350*
Johnston, J. C., 255, 265, *273*
Jones, M. R., 188, 191, 192, 195, 200, 201, 206, 216, 227
Jonides, J., 48, *81,* 181, *183,* 243, 246, *272, 273*
Jordan, T. C., 26, *37*
Juola, J. F., 98, *127,* 135, 138, 147, 167, 168, 169, *183,* 238, 240, *271*

K

Kahneman, D., 93, 94, 116, 121, 125, *129,* 169, *184*
Kamlet, A. S., 88, *129*
Kantowitz, B. H., 84, 86, 87, 88, 91, 92, 95, 96, 100, 101, 104, 106, 109, 112, 113, 114, 119, 120, 121, 122, 124, 126, *128, 129,* 193, 215, *227,* 245, *273*
Kaplan, E. L., 269, *273*
Karlin, L., 99, 102, 103, 104, *129*
Karsh, R., 64, *81*
Kaufman, R. A., 200, 227
Kay, H., 86, *129*
Keele, S. W., 1, 23, 24, 27, 28, *37, 38,* 99, 100, 105, 122, *129,* 235, 245, *273,* 293, *349*
Keeney, T. J., 216, 227
Kellas, G. A., 109, *127*
Kelley, C. R., 21, *38*
Kerr, B., 84, 120, 123, *129*
Kerr, M., 109, 129
Kestenbaum, R., 99, 102, 103, 104, *129*
Klapp, S. T., 237, *273*
Klatzky, R. L., 56, *81*
Klein, R., 116, *130*
Kleinmuntz, B., 338, *348*
Klemmer, E. T., 111, *129*
Knight, J. L., 100, 104, 106, 112, 119, 120, 121, 122, 124, *129*
Knoll, R. L., 136, *184*
Knuth, D. E., 324, *348*

Kohlers, P. A., 269, *273*
Koster, W. G., 86, 101, 106, 109, *129*
Kotovsky, K., 196, 198, 199, 223, 224, 227, *228*, 313, 315, *348, 349*
Kreidler, D. L., 64, *81*
Krendel, E. S., 20, *38*
Kreuger, L. E., 248, 265, *273*
Kristofferson, A. B., 126, *129*

L

LaBerge, D., 125, *129*
Langolf, G. D., 23, 24, *38*
Lappin, J. S., 79, *81*
Lashley, K. S., 29, 30, *38*, 194, 202, 203, *227*
Laszlo, J. I., 28, 29, *38*
Lea, G., 313, *350*
Leeuwenberg, E. L. L., 218, *227*
Lemay, L. P., 6, 7, 8, 9, *38*
Leonard, J. A., 87, 125, *129*
Levin, A., 187, *227*
Levin, H., 269, *273*
Lewis, J. L., 301, *348*
Li, C. L., 30, *38*
Liberman, A. M., 260, *273*
Lindsay, P. H., 234, 235, *273*, 340, 344, *348, 349*
Lisker, L., *273*
Lockhart, R., 301, *347*
Loftus, E., 329, 330, 332, *348*
Logan, R. R., 113, *128*
Lordahl, D. S., 206, *228*
Lott, D., 249, *274*
Lowry, Y., 116, *127*
Luce, R. D., 97, *129*, 138, 159, *183*
Lunneborg, C., 300, 307, *348*

M

McCarthy, M. M., 258, *272*
McClelland, J. L., 255, 266, *273*
McKlveen, M. J., 125, 126, *130*
McLean, R. S., 209, *227*
McRuer, D. T., 9, 10, 20, *38, 39*
Magdeleno, R. E., 9, 15, 17, 20, *38*
Mandler, G., 267, 268, 269, *275*
Manning, L. C., 29, *38*
Marcus, N., 48, 49, 57, *81*
Marin, J., 337, *348*
Martin, J., 210, *227*
Massaro, D. W., 265, *273, 275*
Mattingly, I. G., 258, *273*
Mewhort, D. J. K., 237, 248, 259, *273*

Meyer, D., 308, 310, 311, *348*
Meyer, L. B., 188, *228*
Mezrich, J. J., 55, 266, *273*
Miller, G. A., 34, *38*, 189, 213, 214, 217, *226, 228*, 236, 238, *273*
Miller, J. G., 84, *129*
Miller, J. O., 56, *81*
Mingay, R., 109, *129*
Mintz, D. E., 113, *130*
Mitchell, R. F., 73, *81*, 88, *130*
Montague, W., 46, 47, *81*, 237, 238, *272*
Moore, G. P., 9, *38*
Moray, N., 93, 120, *130, 131*
Morton, J., 267, 268, 269, 271, *274*
Moy, M. C., 56, *82*, 159, *184*
Murdock, B. B., Jr., 205, *228*
Myers, J. L., 188, 195, *228*

N

Neisser, U., 1, *38*, 165, *184*, 232, 234, 235, 236, 238, 240, 245, 246, 247, 251, 257, 258, 262, *274*, 295, 337, *348*
Newbigging, P. L., 251, *274*
Newell, A., 277, 284, 286, 288, 289, 298, 302, 314, 318, 339, 344, 346, *347, 348, 349, 350*
Nickerson, R. S., 86, 89, 101, 111, 113, 115, *130*
Nilsson, N., 288, *349*
Noble, M., 18, *38*
Norman, D. A., 120, *130*, 234, 235, *273*, 340, 344, *348, 349*
Nottebohm, F., 34, *38*
Notterman, J. M., 22, *38*, 113, *130*

O

O'Connell, D. C., 206, *228*
O'Hara, J. R., 192, 195, 201, *227*
Ollman, R. T., 92, 110, *130*
Osser, H., 248, 256, 259, 261, 265, *272*

P

Pachella, R. G., 56, 64, 66, *81*, 239, *274*
Page, D. E., 22, *38*
Paivio, A., 285, *349*
Parzen, E., 152, *184*
Peacock, J. B., 101, 106, *129*
Pederson, N. N., 88, 126, *127*
Perrella, P., 29, *39*
Peterson, J. R., 24, *37*

Pew, R. W., 10, 11, 13, 14, 15, 16, 18, 28, 29, 34, 35, *38*, 59, *81*, 92, 96, *130*
Pick, A. D., 248, 256, 259, 261, 265, *272*
Pierce, J., 254, *274*
Pike, A. R., 100, *127*
Pillsbury, W. B., 249, *274*
Pollack, M. D., 46, 47, *81*, 237, *272*
Posner, M. I., 24, 27, 28, 36, *37*, *38*, 73, *81*, 88, 92, 116, 123, 124, 125, 126, *130*, 235, 237, 238, 240, 246, 258, *272*, *274*, 293, *349*
Postman, L., 236, 238, *273*
Poulton, E. C., 1, 7, 12, 13, 21, *38*, *39*
Preusser, D., 196, 217, *228*
Pribram, K. H., 34, *38*
Pylyshyn, Z., 286, *349*

Q

Quillian, M. R., 326, 327, 328, *347*, *349*
Quinlan, J. R., 287, 303, *349*

R

Raab, D., 86, *128*
Rabbitt, P. M. A., 79, *81*, 90, *130*
Radford, B. K., 24, *37*
Rashbass, C., 18, *39*
Raven, J., 292, *349*
Reber, A. S., 214, 216, *228*
Reed, A. Z., 113, *128*
Reed, S. K., 246, *274*, 293, *349*
Reich, C., 334, 335, *347*
Reicher, G. M., 238, 239, 248, 250, 251, 252, 254, 257, *274*
Remington, R. J., 84, 88, *130*
Restle, F., 194, 196, 197, 198, 200, 206, 209, 210, 218, 219, *228*
Reynolds, D., 95, 96, *130*
Rieger, C. J. III, 297, *349*
Riesbeck, C., 297, *349*
Rips, L., 333, *349*
Robinson, J. A., 334, *349*
Robinson, J. S., 237, 238, *274*
Rodgers, T. S., 260, *273*
Rollins, H., 305, *350*
Roos, R. N., 135, 167, 173, 176, 177, 178, 182, *185*
Rose, R., 115, *127*
Rouse, R. D., 232, *272*
Royer, F. L., 196, 217, *228*
Rupp, G. L., 10, *38*

Rumelhart, D. E., 141, 167, *184*, 240, 243, 244, 246, 250, 252, 253, 256, 257, 258, 262, 264, 265, 270, *274*, 333, 340, 344, *349*
Ryan, J., 209, 210, *228*

S

Sanders, A. F., 88, 117, 118, 119, 125, *130*
Sanders, M. S., 100, 126, *129*
Savin, H. B., 120, *130*
Schank, R., 297, 298, 339, *349*
Schmidt, R. A., 33, *39*
Schurman, D. L., 88, 115, 116, 126, *127*
Schvaneveldt, R. W., 84, 121, 122, *130*
Schwartz, B. J., 206, *228*
Segal, E. M., 88, *127*, 215, 227
Selfridge, O. G., 232, 245, 246, 262, *274*
Shaffer, L. H., 88, *130*
Shannon, C. E., 92, *131*, 211, *228*
Shaughnessy, E., 305, *350*
Shaw, J. C., 277, 284, 286, 339, *348*, *349*
Shelly, C., 35, *37*
Shepard, R. N., 301, 333, *349*
Shiffrin, R. M., 240, 243, 244, 245, 246, 250, *274*, 295, *347*
Shipstone, E. I., 189, *228*
Shoben, E., 333, *349*
Shuell, T. J., 191, *228*
Shulman, H. G., 118, 123, *128*
Shurcliff, A., 256, 257, 263, *273*
Sigler, M., 137, *184*
Simon, H. A., 189, 196, 197, 198, 199, 200, 215, 216, 217, 219, 220, 223, 224, 225, *227*, *228*, 277, 278, 279, 284, 286, 288, 289, 302, 313, 314, 315, 318, 337, 338, 339, 344, 346, *347*, *348*, *349*, *350*
Siple, P., 250, 252, 256, 257, 258, 264, 265, 270, *274*
Smith, D. E., 265, *273*
Smith, E. E., 56, *81*, 98, *131*, 248, 250, 251, 252, 257, 259, 260, 261, 262, 263, 264, 265, *272*, *274*, *275*, 333, *349*
Smith, F., 248, 249, 250, 252, 253, 255, 256, 258, 264, 265, 270, *274*
Smith, K. H., 189, 216, *228*
Smith, M. C., 86, 90, 92, 101, *131*
Smith, K. V., 29, *39*
Smith, P. G., 56, *82*, 159, *184*
Snyder, C. R. R., 125, 126, *130*
Spencer, T., 138, 158, *183*, 240, 243, 244, 245, 246, *272*
Sperling, G., 137, *184*, 236, 237, 238, 239, 240, 241, 243, 245, 258, *274*

Spoehr, K. T., 257, 260, 261, 262, 264, 265, 271, *274*, 275
Staniland, A. C., 209, 211, 214, *228*
Steger, J. A., 86, 113, *128*
Stelmach, G. E., 27, *39*
Sternberg, S., 48, 50, 51, 53, 54, 55, 56, 57, 58, 65, *81*, *82*, 135, 136, 137, 147, 157, 163, 165, 167, 168, 181, *184*, 238, 239, 240, 275
Stone, P., 337, *348*
Stubbs, C. L., 206, *228*
Summers, J., 116, *130*
Sumner, R. K., 225, *228*
Swanson, J. M., 68, *82*
Swensson, R. G., 64, 79, *82*
Swets, J. A., 192, *227*, 232, *275*

T

Tanner, W. P., 232, *275*
Taub, E., 29, 30, *39*
Taylor, D. A., 177, *184*
Taylor, D. H., 88, *128*
Taylor, F. V., 26, *37*
Taylor, H. A., 134, 135, 147, 158, 168, *184*, 238, *272*
Taylor, R. L., 240, *274*
Taylor, S. G., 169, *185*
Telford, C. W., 86, 101, *131*
Templeton, W. B., 120, *129*
Tenney, Y. J., 265, *273*
Theby, M. A., 206, *228*
Theios, J., 56, 61, 62, *82*, 159, *184*
Thomas, E. A. C., 138, *184*
Thompson, M. C., 265, *275*
Thurston, I., 248, 254, 256, 259, 261, 263, *272*
Tinbergen, N., 35, *39*
Todd, T. C., 191, 193, 195, 202, 211, 217, 218, 220, *228*
Tolkmitt, F. J., 91, *131*
Townsend, J. T., 135, 137, 138, 141, 142, 146, 148, 152, 164, 167, 169, 173, 176, 177, 178, 180, 182, *184*, *185*, 235, 243, *275*
Trabasso, T., 305, *350*
Traupmann, J., 56, *82*, 159, *184*
Treisman, A. M., 116, 117, 120, *131*, 138, *185*
Triggs, T. J., 84, 108, 109, 112, *131*
Trumbo, D., 18, *38*
Tulving, E., 267, 268, 269, *275*, 326, *350*

U

Ullman, J. D., 283, 296, *348*
Underwood, G., 120, *131*

V

Van Bergeijk, W. A., 29, *39*
VanGelder, P., 125, *129*
VanHoutte, N., 18, *39*
VanSant, C., 87, *128*
Venezky, R. L., 258, *275*
Vince, M. A., 24, *39*
Vitz, P. C., 191, 193, 195, 202, 211, 217, 218, 220, *228*
von Holst, E., 30, *39*
Vyas, S. M., 79, *81*

W

Walker, K. D., 205, *228*
Wall, S., 48, *81*, 181, *183*, 243, *272*
Wason, P., 298, 309, *350*
Waterman, D. A., 298, *350*
Way, T. C., 89, 95, *131*
Weaver, W., 211, *228*
Weene, P., 337, *348*
Weir, D. H., 10, *39*
Weiss, A. D., 86, *129*
Welford, A. T., 1, 23, *39*, 90, 91, 92, 94, 109, 117, *129*, *131*
Wescourt, K., 296, *347*
Wessel, D. L., 134, 153, *185*, 238, 239, *272*, *275*
Weyl, H., *228*
Wheeler, D. D., 236, 238, 250, 254, 257, 264, 265, 270, *275*
Wickelgren, W. A., 209, *229*
Wiesel, T. N., 234, 235, *273*
Wilks, Y., 299, *350*
Williams, G. F., 338, *350*
Winograd, T., 299, *350*
Winzenz, D., 209, *226*, 301, *347*
Wolford, G. L., 134, 153, 169, *184*, *185*, 239, *275*
Westcott, J. H., 6, 7, 8, 9, *38*, *39*
White, J. L., 33, *39*
Wilde, R. W., 6, *39*
Wilson, D. M., 34, *39*
Woodworth, R. S., 23, 24, *39*
Wrisberg, C. A., 33, *39*

Y

Yates, A. J., 29, *39*
Yellott, J. I., 64, 71, 72, 73, *82,* 125, *129,* 159, *185*

Yonas, A., 256, 257, 263, *273*
Young, L. R., 18, *39*

Z

Zaslow, M., 265, *273*

SUBJECT INDEX

A

Abelian group, 221
Accent, 196, 210
Accumulator Model of reaction time, 75–77
Accuracy task, 235
Acoustic-articulatory features, 233, 268
Acoustic code, 264
Additive Factor Method, 51–58
  and memory scanning, 55–57
  criticism of, 57–58
Alphabet, 188, 196, 218, 221, 225
Alternation, 190, 195, 226
Approximation-to-English (see also orthographic
    structure), 237, 248, 255, 256, 257, 265
Artificial language, 188, 216
Attention, 116–127, 241, 243, 245
Auditory pattern presentation, 203, 204, 205
Automation of a movement, 33–35

B

Backward recall, 202
Bandwidth
  defined, 5
  effect on tracking performance performance,
    5–6
Binary patterns, 195, 217, 225
Block Visualization Test, 293
Brown-Peterson Paradigm
  applied to memory for movements, 27

C

Channel capacity
  (see also limited capacity model), 35, 36
Commutativity, 221
Compensatory display
  defined, 5
  model of performance with, 6–9
  tracking performance with, 6, 10–11
Complement rule, 206, 219, 221–225

Complexity, 193, 195, 211, 216, 219
Comprehension, 269
Concept learning, 337
Concepts, 189, 203, 210
Confusability effects, 240, 243, 244, 254, 270
Cost-benefit analysis, 125
Constraint redundancy, 212, 217
Constraints, 187, 188, 212, 217
Context effects, 266, 267, 268, 269, 271
Contingent information processing, 88, 126
Controlled system, role in tracking performance,
  20–22
Converging operations, 236
Criterion value, 241
Critical features, 234, 235
Current control, 23

D

Data types, 281, 282, 285–294
Data structures, 325–344
Decision process, 233, 242, 244, 245, 249, 253,
  264, 270, 271
Detection task, 238, 239, 244
Deterministic vs probabilistic processing, 161,
  162
Dictionary, 329
Digit patterns, 201, 207, 219
Directed graph, 298
Discrimination redundancy, 212
Discrimination tree, 335–339
Distributed memory, 294–301
Doctrine of remote associations, 194
Dual coding, 286

E

Effector anticipation, 13, 21
Efferent copy, 30
Encoded groups theories, 195
EPAM, 336–339
Episodic memory, 326, 335–344

Equal-accuracy contours, 70
Error detection mechanism, 2, 5, 7, 15
Errors (see, variable error rates; also speed accuracy relations)
Expectancy, 101, 111, 189, 195, 196, 205, 211, 257, 264
Extraction stage, 233–236, 240–244, 247–251, 253
Eyeball, 259, 264, 270

F

Fast-guess model, 71–73
Fast-guess responses, 71
Feature analysis, 232–234, 243
Feature extraction capacity, 241–242, 245
Feature redundancy model, 252, 254–258, 264, 268, 270
Feedback
 elimination, 29
 levels of, 29–30
 manipulation of, 28–29
Figure-ground relations, 195, 196, 217
File structure, 284–285
Finite-state grammar, 213, 215, 225
Fitts' Law, 23, 121
Forced-choice procedure, 237, 239, 266
Fragment theory (see also sophisticated guessing model), 251
Free recall, 191, 200
Frequency, 254–255, 270

G

Gain, of a control system, 5
Goal tree, 291
Good pattern, 189, 220, 225, 226
GPS, 286–289
Grammar, 206, 214
Grapheme-phoneme translation, 258
Group relations, 221–226
Guessing, 237, 254

H

Handwritten English, 232
Hierarchical organization of motor control, 2, 18, 34–36
Hierarchical rule structure, 197, 209, 219, 224
Higher-order units, 247, 249–252, 254, 258, 260, 264, 267, 270, 271
Hybrid processing, 139, 141

I

Icon, 236–253
Identity rule, 221–225
Ideomotor, 97, 122–123
Images, 285, 286
Implicit vocalization, 237
Independent vs dependent processing and dependent vs independent processing, 134, 152ff, 163, 173
Information theory, 189, 211, 217, 220
Inhibitory association, 194
Initial impulse, 23
Inner loop control, 3
Instructions, 200
Interactive channels model, 243, 246, 270
Interchangeability, 203
Intercompletion time, def. 141, 143, 157, 164, 179 (exponential) footnote 4
Intermediate-term memory (ITM), 295, 297–300
Interpretation stage, 233–236, 241–244, 247, 249, 250, 255
Interstimulus interval, 85, 87, 89, 101, 124
Iso-accuracy contours, 67–68

L

Laws of pragnanz, 189, 196
Leaf nodes, 336
Lexical codes, 296
Limited capacity model, 90–92, 102, 105, 119, 121, 241, 243, 246, 270
Limited information assumption, 236
Limited processing time assumption, 236
Limited vs. unlimited capacity and unlimited vs. limited capacity, 135, 158ff, 169 footnote, 176
Linear model, 188
Linguistic machine, 296
Logogen, 99, 266, 268, 269, 271
Long-term memory (LTM), 300–301, 325–344

M

Macro-tradeoff speed vs. accuracy, 77–79
MAPP, 338–339
Mappings (equivalence), 144, 149, 154–155
Matching process, 233, 242, 243, 245, 249, 253, 258, 262, 264, 270
Mathematical learning theory, 188
Maximum uncertainty, 211, 212
Meaning, 187, 225
Means-end analysis, 287–288

Melody, 202
Memory feedback loop of compensatory tracking
    model, 8
Memory scanning, 50, 55–57
    and speed stress, 66–71
    correlation of errors & memory load, 69–70
Message, 211
Micro-tradeoff speed vs. accuracy, 77–79
Modality, 203, 204
Model, 139
Modern associationism, 193, 194, 202, 211
Morphological, 208
Motor command generator, 6
Motor memory, 26–27
Motor noise, 3–5
Motor physiology, 9
Motor program, 20, 33–35
Movements, simple positional
    models of performance of, 23–25
    relation of tracking, 25
    speed & accuracy of, 22–25
Multichannel tasks mappings (equivalence), 280
Multi-level motor control, 2–3, 12, 22, 30,
    33–36
Muscle mechanism, 6–7

N

Next rule, 218, 221–225

O

Operator difference table, 287
Order of completion, 139, 142–144, 169–171
Orthographic structure (see also Approximation-
    to-English), 248, 255, 258
Overload, 84

P

Pandemonium, 245, 262
Parameter comparator, 18–19, 33
Parallel models, standard, 161ff, 166–167
Parallel processing, 242, 246
Parallel vs. serial processing and serial vs. paral-
    lel processing, 135, 139ff, 169–177
Partial advance information, 87, 125–126
Partial report, 237, 240, 241, 243
Pattern judgments, 193, 195
Pattern model, 188
Pattern perception, 195, 220, 224
Pattern reconstruction, 199, 200, 209, 220

Perceptual anticipation, 7, 13
Perceptual-motor performance, 1, 36
    and information processing, 1
Perceptual parsing, 250, 258–262, 271
Perceptual readings, 232
Perceptual strategies, 247, 264–266, 271
Perceptual units, 234
Phonemes, 258, 262
Phonological code, 258, 261
Phonological rules, 249, 257, 262
Power spectrum
    defined, 4
    of motor noise, 4, 11
    of tracking with time delay, 10–11
Precognitive stage of learning, 20
Predictability, 189, 190, 254, 255, 259, 261
Prediction profile, 190
Presentation rate, 195, 203, 204
Preview display, 12–13
    model of performance with, 16–20
Primacy, 200, 202, 205, 207
Primitive function, 303
    cn, 331
    first, 331
    ident., 303
    name, 331
    next, 303, 315
    predecessor, 315
    same, 315
Probe RT, 123, 124
Problem-solving, 220, 224
Processing (actual) time (z), 139–141
Process limitation, 66
Production, 302
Production systems, 302–306, 309–310,
    315–322, 325, 331–332
Programming, 282–284
Pronounceability, 237
Propositions, 286–288, 294, 340
Proprioceptive input, role of, 21–22, 25–26
Psycholinguistics, 188
Psychological refractory period, 86
Pursuit display
    as means of introducing signal predictability,
        12–13
    defined, 5
    model of performance with, 16–20
    tracking performance with, 6, 13–16

R

Random signal (see tracking performance)
Random Walk Model, 75–77

Raspberry, 267
Rate of processing, 142, 144–146
Raven's Progressive Matrix Test, 292
Reaction time, 41–48
    and experimental logic, 45–58
    and performance accuracy, 58–71
    and word recognition, 235
    as dependent variable, 43
    definition of, 43–44, 58–61
    theoretical conception, 71–79
Reading, 231, 301
Reasoning, 334–335
Recency, 200, 202, 205, 207
Receptor anticipation, 13
Recognition, 192
Recognition procedure, 238, 239, 248
Reconstruction, 191
Redundancy, 211, 218, 251, 252
Reflection rule, 221–225
Regulator problem, as in servomechanism
    theory, 5
Rehearsal, 194, 209, 210
Repeat rule, 218
Report biases, 254
Resolution principle, 334
Response antagonism, 95, 96, 108
Response conflict, 95–97, 122
Response initiation, 100, 106
Response interdiction, 127
Response mode, 206
Response stage, 236
Response-stimulus interval, 109–110
Rhythm, 194, 199, 209, 210, 211
Root, 336
Rule-formulation theories, 196, 209, 210
Rules, 196–198, 202, 203, 217, 219
Runs, 190, 195, 196, 205–209, 217, 218

S

Same-different task, 237, 240, 243, 248
Schema instance, 28, 31
Schema memory, 27–28, 31
Scoring, 191
Search task, 235, 238, 240, 248, 265
Self-terminating vs. exhaustive processing and
    exhaustive vs. self-terminating proces-
    sing, 135, 147ff, 161, 175, 177, 181
Semantic features, 268–269
Semantic memory, 326–335
Sensory feature code, 295
Sequence, 188, 194, 200, 203, 210, 217

Serial anticipation, 205
Serial model, standard, def. 150–152, 160, 164
Serial pattern, 187–226
Serial position curve, 190, 202, 208
Serial processing, 242
Serial recall, 200–202
Series completion, 312–324
Servomechanism, 2, 12
    for intermittent correction, 9
    regulator problem, 5
Shape features, 249
Short-term character recognition, 50, 55–57
    (see also memory scanning)
Short-term memory (STM), 237, 240, 243, 245,
    258, 295, 296, 302–303, 324–325
Short-term predictor, of compensatory tracking
    model signal comparator, 7
    of compensatory tracking model, 7
    of voluntary movement model, 31
Signal predictability
    from preview, 13
    from pursuit display, 13
    from repetitive signals, 13
    model to account for, 16–20
Sine waves, tracking of
    performance, 14
    subjects' comments about, 15, 17
Single channel
    (see limited capacity model)
Single channel task, 280
Single-stimulation control condition, 88, 89
Sophisticated guessing model
    (see also fragement theory), 251, 264, 270
Spatial patterns, 189, 202, 205–207, 220
Spatio-temporal pattern, 203, 204
Speed-accuracy operating characteristics, 59
Speed-accuracy relations, 58–71
    and definition of reaction time, 58–61
    and discriminability, 65–66
    and double stimulation, 112–113, 119
    and experimental method, 64–65, 239
    and memory scanning, 66–71
    theoretical conceptions, 71–79
Speed-accuracy trade off (see speed-accuracy re-
    lations)
Spelling patterns, 250, 256–259, 264, 265, 271
Spelling-to-sound correspondence, 258
S-R compatability, 108, 117
S-R mappings, 107, 108
S-R notation, 283–284
Stage of processing, def. 142, 162
State limitation, 66
States, 287

Step inputs
  compensatory tracking response to, 8–9
Stimulus onset asynchrony, 87, 120
Strategies, 196, 214
String, 194, 208, 213, 214
Structure, 196–199, 206, 209, 211, 220
Subjective structure, 191
Subproblem generation, 289
Subprograms, 315, 324
Subtraction method, 46–51
  and memory scanning, 50–51
  criticism of, 47–51
Successive organization of perception, model of,
    15, 20
Syllables, 257, 258, 260
Symmetry, 188, 195, 196, 208, 221, 224–226
Synthetic features, 268
Synthesis, 269
System, def. 139
System architecture, 282, 294–301

T

Template matching, 234
Temporal patterns, 189, 202, 205, 207, 209, 220
Theory of signal detectability, 232
Threshold, 268
Time delay of a control system, 5
  in models of tracking performance, 9–11
Token node, 328
Total completion time (x), 152
Total report, 239–240, 266, 267
Tracking performance
  compensatory display, 6, 14
  continuous representation of, 9–10
  discrete representation of, 6–9
  pursuit display, 6, 14
  random signal, 5–6
  relation to simple movements, 25
  role of controlled system, 20–22
  role of signal predictability, 14–20
  sine wave inputs, 13–17
  with preview, 13

with repeated patterns, 16, 28
with time delay, 10–11
Transformational rules, 221
Translation process, 233, 249, 259, 260–264,
    267, 270–271
Tree structure, 197, 206, 219, 336
Type node, 328

U

Uncertainty, 211–214, 220
Unitization, 261
Unlimited capacity model, 244–247, 270

V

Variable-allocation-capacity model, 93–94,
    121–122
Variable error rates, 61–65
  and analysis of covariance, 63
  and double stimulation, 112–113, 119
  and energy integrator, 115
  and MANOVA, 63
  and memory scanning, 69–70
Variable types, 302
VCG model, 260, 262, 264, 271
Verification, 308–312
Visual pattern presentation, 203, 204, 205
Vocabulary, 188, 215, 225
Vocalic center group, 260

W

Well-formed graphs, 340
Word-letter effect, 257, 271
Word-nonword effect, 247, 248, 252–255, 262,
    271
Word shape, 249, 250

Y

Yes-no task, 238, 240, 243

Date Due